Oliver Goldsmith

Oliver Goldsmith

by
Ralph M. Wardle

Archon Books
1969

©1957 BY THE UNIVERSITY OF KANSAS PRESS
REPRINTED 1969 WITH PERMISSION
IN AN UNALTERED AND UNABRIDGED EDITION

SBN: 208 00755 5
LIBRARY OF CONGRESS CATALOG CARD NUMBER: 69-13631
PRINTED IN THE UNITED STATES OF AMERICA

TO

RUTH,

ALISON,

JEAN,

AND

NICHOLAS,

who thought it would never end.

Preface

This book is, curiously enough, the first attempt at a scholarly biography of Oliver Goldsmith published in the twentieth century. Although it presents no previously undiscovered Goldsmith manuscripts, it takes into account materials not available to or utilized by earlier biographers: notably the manuscript Memoir of Goldsmith now in the British Museum, the Boswell Papers, the prose Portrait of Goldsmith by Sir Joshua Reynolds, and the investigations of such Goldsmith specialists as Professors R. S. Crane and Arthur Friedman and the late R. W. Seitz.

My debts to my predecessors are manifold; to enumerate them would demand a bibliography of Goldsmith scholarship to date. Inevitably I have depended most on the pioneer work of Sir James Prior, author of the first full-scale biography, and Professor Katherine C. Balderston, editor of the *Collected Letters,* whose research has clarified the details of several obscure periods in Goldsmith's life. In quoting the letters I have retained Goldsmith's haphazard spelling, but have occasionally altered his punctuation to avoid confusion or ambiguity.

For aid in my own investigations I am grateful to Mrs. Charles F. Beckingham of London, Mrs. Donald F. Hyde of Somerville, New Jersey, Mr. J. B. McKeeman of the National Library of Scotland, Mr. D. Y. Neill of the Bodleian Library, Mr. David T. Piper of the National Portrait Gallery, the Reverend Canon W. Wynne Slack of Elphin, County Roscommon, Mr. H. A. C. Sturgess of the Honourable Society of the Middle Temple, Miss Helen Watson of the Assistant Registrar's Office at Trinity College, Dublin, and Professors Thomas W. Copeland, Arthur Friedman, Morris Golden, Frederick W. Hilles, and Frederick A. Pottle. All these people generously spared time to answer my queries and often to volunteer information or suggestions which shortened my task considerably. I am indebted also to Professors Clyde K. Hyder and Franklyn C. Nelick for their helpful criticism of the book in manuscript.

I wish also to thank the officers and staffs of the following libraries for their assistance: the Boston Public Library, the British Museum, the Harvard College Library, the Henry E. Huntington Library, the New York Public Library, the University of Omaha Library, the Library of the Royal Academy, and the Yale University Library. And I am obliged to the following for permission to reprint copyrighted materials: the University of Aberdeen Press and Professor Ralph S. Walker for quotations from his edition of *James Beattie's London Diary, 1773;* the Cambridge University Press and Professor Balderston for quotations from her edition of the *Collected Letters* of Goldsmith; the McGraw-Hill Book Company, Inc., for quotations from Professor Hilles' edition of *Portraits by Sir Joshua Reynolds* and Professor Pottle's edition of *Boswell's London Journal, 1762-1763;* and the Oxford University Press for quotations from Professor Chauncey B. Tinker's edition of the *Letters of James Boswell,* the Hill-Powell edition of Boswell's *Life of Johnson,* Professor Balderston's edition of *Thraliana,* and Professor James Clifford's *Hester Lynch Piozzi.*

But my warmest and humblest thanks are due to Mary Elizabeth Wardle, my willing and able copyist, critic, and proofreader. By rights this book is, like its dedicatees, at least half hers.

R. M. W.

The University of Omaha
April 4, 1957

Contents

Illustrations

Chapter I

Anomaly

"POOR Dr. Goldsmith! Lord bless us what an anomalous Character was his!" wrote Hester Thrale. And there were many who agreed with her. Some tried to find a word or phrase which would pin him down: Boswell called him *"un étourdi"*; Horace Walpole, "an inspired idiot";[1] and Tom Davies, "an inexplicable existence in creation." But most people merely shook their heads in disbelief—and told another story to illustrate the "absurdity" of this supposed man of genius.

Many such tales were current. People always enjoy dwelling on the failings of the great by way of consoling themselves for their own mediocrity. And Oliver Goldsmith lent himself admirably to their purposes. Even before his death the *Westminster Magazine* published a collection of "Humorous Anecdotes of Dr. Goldsmith," referring to him as the "Sancho Panza of English literature" and presenting evidence to confirm Garrick's later dictum that, although he "wrote like an angel," he "talked like poor Poll."

But how many of the stories of Goldsmith's absurdity are to be wholly credited? Was he really as much of a fool as people supposed? Consider, for example, the story which Colonel O'Moore, a friend of Edmund Burke, told. One afternoon, he claimed, while he and Burke were on their way to Sir Joshua Reynolds' house in Leicester Fields, they saw Goldsmith standing in front of a building and staring at a crowd of people who were shouting at some foreign women in a window above. The two men passed without attracting Goldsmith's attention and reached Sir Joshua's house before he did. When presently he arrived, Burke greeted him coolly and seemed reluctant to talk to him.

Goldsmith sensed his friend's attitude and asked what he had done to offend him. At first Burke seemed unwilling to reply, but at length he answered that he could not remain the friend of anyone guilty of such rudeness as Goldsmith had just displayed.

Goldsmith, aghast, begged for an explanation; whereupon Burke demanded: "Why, did you not exclaim, as you were looking

1

up at those women, what stupid beasts the crowd must be for staring with such admiration at those 'painted Jezebels!' while a man of your talents passed by unnoticed?"

"Surely, surely, my dear friend," Goldsmith cried, "I did not say so."

"Nay, if you had not said so, how should I have known it?"

"That's true," Goldsmith admitted; "I am very sorry—it was very foolish; I do recollect that something of the kind passed through my mind, but I did not think I had uttered it."[2]

This is an amusing story—but is it credible? Could Goldsmith have been so easily persuaded that he had spoken, only a few minutes before, words which had never passed his lips? Or if not, how can the story be explained?

If the story is true, it may well be that Goldsmith detected a twinkle in Burke's eye, recognized that his friend was indulging in a bit of humbug, and tacitly consented to go along with the joke for the sake of the fun which it would afford the company. One of Burke's biographers has already suggested that the joke was on Burke as well as on Goldsmith.[3]

But the story is probably not true at all; as Sir James Prior perceived, it sounds suspiciously like Colonel O'Moore's elaboration of an anecdote, reported by Boswell and Northcote, of Goldsmith's behavior on another occasion, when he was traveling in France with his friend Mrs. Horneck and her two pretty daughters. One day as they were standing at a window of their hotel watching a company of soldiers below, they discovered that they were themselves the center of attention. Thereupon Goldsmith, supposedly in a pique that the pretty Horneck girls should be accorded such notice, remarked airily that elsewhere he too had his admirers.

There are striking resemblances between the two stories: in both there are foreign women admired by a group of natives standing below them, and in both Goldsmith is irked that his own superior merits are being ignored. But in the account of the episode in France Goldsmith is at the window with the ladies, and he expresses his resentment to them. And one of those ladies, Mary Horneck Gwynne, later declared emphatically that the remark

2

was meant and received as a joke. "I am sure," she told Prior, "that on many occasions from the peculiar manner of his humour and assumed frown of countenance, that what was often uttered in jest was mistaken by those that did not know him for earnest."[4]

For that matter, there is abundant evidence that even his closest friends often misunderstood his attempts at humor. Take, for example, the occasion at the Club when, after having lost an argument, he mused: " 'Tis strange now . . . that I should be defeated so in this Argument; for I talked it all over this Morning by *myself* and had the better of you all to nothing."[5] Did Goldsmith expect this remark to be taken seriously? Or did he really mean it when he complained that Lord Camden once entertained him at dinner, but "took no more notice of me than if I had been an ordinary man"? Johnson accepted the remark at its face value and sprang to Goldsmith's defense, saying that Camden should indeed have "made up to such a man as Goldsmith."[6] But Goldsmith, though pleased at the implied compliment, was probably secretly amused.

Mr. Frederick Lewis Allen has divided mankind into two categories: goons and jiggers. "The goon," he explains, "is a person with a heavy touch as distinguished from a jigger, who has a light touch. While jiggers look on life with a genial eye, goons take a more stolid and literal view. . . . It would be misleading to say that goonishness consists of a lack of a sense of humor. I know many goons who have a perfectly good standardized sense of humor. They laugh as hard as anybody at a farce, and when an after-dinner story is told they shout mightily with the rest. What they lack is the playful mind."[7]

And there you have it: it was Goldsmith's misfortune that he was a jigger fallen among goons. Shakespeare, another eminent jigger, would have been similarly ill at ease if he had been dropped down into the middle of eighteenth century London literary society. And the literary lions would have been similarly puzzled by him, since he too was an anomalous man by their standards.

For they were ardent believers in decorum. They expected a distinguished man of letters to look and act like a distinguished man of letters and a clown to look and act like a clown. A dis-

3

tinguished man of letters who often acted like a clown—and always looked the part—was an anomaly indeed.

It was partly a matter of nationality. "In England," wrote the Irish Lady Morgan some years later, "conversation is a game of chess, the result of judgment, memory, and deliberation—with us it is a game of battledore, and our ideas like our shuttlecocks are thrown lightly one to the other, bounding and rebounding— played more for amusement than conquest, and leaving the players equally animated by the game, and careless of the results."[8] Goldsmith's conversational shuttlecocks, alas, often were not caught by his fellows—and frequently bounded back to blacken his eye.

Among other Irishmen he could be himself. Fortunately for him, there were dozens of them among his acquaintance during the years that he spent in London, and they must have been welcome company after an evening or two with his more sedate friends of the literati. But they were not, unfortunately, indefatigable writers like his literary friends, and we know very little about how Goldsmith behaved when he was among them.

However, one conversation between him and a congenial Irish friend survives, and it is worth repeating. It took place at Gosfield, country seat of Robert Nugent, Lord Clare, a Lord of the Treasury, the Vice-Treasurer of Ireland—a man of as much distinction in his own way as the literary gentlemen were in theirs. Yet there was a difference: Lord Clare was an Irishman—and a jigger. And he talked the kind of talk that Goldsmith relished.

The subject of the conversation was the actor Moffat, and Lord Clare said, quite seriously, that he admired the man's talents.

"But, my Lord," said Goldsmith, "you must allow he treads the stage very ill—he waddles."

"Waddles?" said his Lordship, "yes, he waddles like a goose— why you know we call him Goose Moffat."

"Well," Goldsmith continued, "and then, you know, when he endeavours to express strong passions, he bellows."

"Bellows? to be sure he does—bellows like a bull. Why, we call him Bull Moffat."

"Well, and then, my Lord, his voice breaks, and he croaks."

"Croaks? why the fellow croaks like a frog. We call him Frog Moffat." Then, after some hesitation: "But Moffat is a good actor."

"Why, yes," Goldsmith agreed, "barring the goose, and the bull, and the frog, and a few other things I could mention, and not wishing to speak ill of my neighbours, I *will* allow Moffat is a good actor."[9]

And then, no doubt, the two Irishmen, sober as owls thus far, exploded in roars of laughter. For this was their kind of fun—carefree, irrelevant, illogical, nonsensical; good Irish fun, in short. But what would Goldsmith's English literary friends have made of it?

On one occasion Goldsmith tried to divert Sam Johnson with a similar bit of nonsense—and, as might be expected, came a cropper. According to William Cooke, the two men were dining on rumps and kidneys at the King's Head Tavern in Holborn, and Johnson was moved to observe: "Sir, these rumps are pretty little things, but then a man must eat a great many of them before he fills his belly."

"Aye," said Goldsmith, "but how many of these would reach to the moon?"

"To the moon! aye, Goldy, I fear that exceeds your calculation."

"Not at all, Sir, I think I could tell."

"Pray then, Sir," said Johnson, interested in spite of himself, "let us hear."

"Why one if it was long enough."

Of course Johnson was not amused. After growling to himself for some time, he declared: "Well, Sir, I have deserved it; I should not have provoked so foolish an answer by so foolish a question."[10]

William Cooke, who tells this story, said of Goldsmith: "Sir, he was a fool. The right word never came to him. If you gave him back a bad shilling he'd say, 'Why, it's as good a shilling as ever was *born.*' You know he ought to have said *coined. Coined,* Sir, never entered his head. He was a fool, Sir." To which we might add: and William Cooke was a goon. Apparently it never entered his head that a man—especially an Irishman—might have preferred, for the joke's sake, to use a word which didn't make sense.

5

To be sure, Goldsmith was an *Anglo*-Irishman; yet as he himself said, "The natives [of Ireland] are particularly remarkable for the gaiety and levity of their dispositions: the English, transplanted there, in time lose their melancholy serious air, and become gay and thoughtless, more fond of pleasure, and less addicted to reasoning."[11] Or more likely, separated as they were from the austere influences of Puritanism which prevailed in England, they had retained the gaiety of their Elizabethan ancestors. For there was no Puritanical middle class in Ireland in the eighteenth century, and people like the Goldsmiths were a law unto themselves. Goldsmith and his father before him were not haunted by taboos; they were used to saying what popped into their heads, with no thought of how it might sound to others. In fact they were used to listeners who suffered from few taboos themselves and who encouraged irrational, even indecorous, talk. But such talk was bound to amaze—sometimes to offend—the eminently respectable people whom Goldsmith met in London literary circles.

Fortunately, however, one of his English friends came a good deal closer than the others to understanding Goldsmith's nature. That man was Sir Joshua Reynolds. He painted a portrait of Goldsmith which people found baffling: it looked so much like him and yet had such a surprising dignity about it! He began a character sketch—a prose portrait—of Goldsmith too, but he never finished or published it, and it has only recently been discovered, nearly two centuries after Goldsmith's death. It throws a good deal of light on the character of the anomalous man.

"Dr. Goldsmith's genius is universally acknowledged," wrote Sir Joshua. "All that we shall endeavour to do is to show what indeed is self-apparent, that such a genius could not be a fool or such a weak man as many people thought him." He adds: "The author was intimately acquainted with Dr. Goldsmith. They unbosomed their minds freely to each other, not only in regard to the characters of their friends, but what contributed to make men's company desired or avoided. It was agreed that it was not superior parts, or wisdom, or knowledge that made men beloved—that men do not go into company with a desire of receiving

6

instruction, but to be amused—that people naturally avoid that society where their minds are to be kept on the stretch."[12]

And so Goldsmith, eager to endear himself to his austere friends, tried to amuse them and, more often than not, baffled them. Once when he was at the theater with Lord Shelburne, he remarked offhandedly: "Pray, my Lord, . . . what can make People call your Lordship *Malagrida?* for by what ever I have heard Malagrida was a very *good sort of A Man.*" Johnson tried to explain this remark too: Goldsmith meant not to insult Shelburne, he claimed, but to defend the heretic Malagrida.[13] Again Goldsmith would have been nonplussed. But Reynolds caught the real intent of the remark, and in his "Portrait" he wrote: "What Goldsmith meant for humour was purposely repeated as serious," and he added the word "Malagrida" presumably to remind himself to include the Shelburne story in his final draft to illustrate his point. Apparently he regarded Goldsmith's remark not as a foolish mistake (as so many of his contemporaries did) or a "blunder in emphasis" (as Johnson did) but an intentional bit of humor which proved abortive.

Many of the stories told to illustrate Goldsmith's inordinate enviousness can likewise be interpreted as attempts to amuse his friends; in fact it was apropos of his alleged enviousness that Mrs. Gwynne remarked that "what was often uttered in jest was mistaken . . . for earnest." Consider the story, variously told by Davies, Murphy, and Boswell, of his visit to a performance of fantoccini. When one of his companions marveled at the dexterity with which a puppet handled a pike, Goldsmith supposedly became annoyed and cried out, "Why, that is nothing; I could do as well myself."[14] Surely, if he ever made the remark, he did not mean it to be taken seriously! Nor could he have been wholly in earnest when, according to Tom Davies, he asked other guests at a Royal Academy dinner to stop laughing at a humorous speaker lest they make him vain.[15] Or when he remarked, as Sir John Hawkins said, that he would tell a story if any of those present could understand it.[16] Or when he climbed on a chair to prove that he could deliver a speech as well as Burke;[17] or when he assured a group of friends that he could tell a story as well as

7

Garrick.[18] Or when, as Mrs. Thrale declares, he heard that a sentimental comedy by Hugh Kelly was enjoying a greater success
than one of his own plays, and consoled himself by gazing into a
mirror and murmuring audibly: "A handsomer Fellow than
Kelly however."[19] There is a pattern here which recurs in the
Horneck story and which Johnson mocked once when he was admiring the skill with which a coachman handled his horses:
"Were Goldsmith here now," he said, "he would tell us he could
do better."[20]

Because he was a sensitive man, Goldsmith must have awak-
ened to the realization, again and again, that his joke had miscar-
ried. But instead of admitting to failure, he pushed ahead and
succeeded only in making himself more absurd. When, for example, his friends demanded that he prove that he could speak
as well as Burke, he stammered out a sentence or two, then
became tongue-tied and was forced to give up, explaining feebly
that he was merely "out of luck" at the moment. When he attempted to prove that he could tell a story as well as Garrick, he
launched into a rather pointless tale of a cobbler and a baillie,
warning that "some people do laugh at this story and some do
not," and digressing to assure his listeners that the Goldsmiths
were people of substance who associated with only the finest folk
in their country. This time he may have been engaging in deliberate nonsense, or he may have intended to burlesque Garrick's
vanity and his propensity for monopolizing the attention of a
group. But it sounds as if, once again, he had made an absurd
claim in jest, realized its absurdity, and lapsed into even greater
absurdity because of his embarrassment.

For there can be no question about it: not all of Goldsmith's
absurdity was deliberate. Reynolds acknowledged that "to do
justice to the world, a man seldom acquires the character of absurd
without deserving it." And although many of the stories of
Goldsmith's alleged enviousness can be written off as deliberate
attempts to amuse, the very persistence of the pattern suggests
that he was plagued by a compulsion to measure himself against
other men. "It must be confessed," Reynolds wrote, "that whoever
excelled in any art or science, however different from his own,

was sure to be considered by him as a rival." Or as David Garrick put it: "Goldsmith never would allow a superior in any art, from writing poetry down to dancing a hornpipe."[21]

Yes, Goldsmith was, beyond any doubt, an envious man. His contemporaries' accusations of enviousness are not based wholly on dubious claims of momentary envy of the Horneck girls' beauty or the fantoccini's skill or Burke's oratorical powers or Garrick's reputation as a storyteller. For three men he felt a settled and lasting envy: Hugh Kelly, the Reverend James Beattie, and Samuel Johnson.[22] His jealousy of them is undeniable; in fact he made little attempt to conceal it. But if not pardonable, it was at least understandable; for, far from excelling "in any art or science, however different from his own," these men were his natural rivals—they had achieved a particular kind of recognition which he craved for himself.

Hugh Kelly was an Irishman like himself, a corset-maker turned sentimental dramatist, whose *False Delicacy* had won wide acclaim in the season when Goldsmith's *Good Natured Man* had enjoyed only a qualified success, and whose later play, *The School for Wives,* proved, in effect, that *She Stoops to Conquer* had not ousted sentimental comedy from popular favor. Although it is hard to believe that Goldsmith really found consolation in the thought that he was "a handsomer fellow than Kelly," he certainly envied him: Topham Beauclerk reported that the success of *The School for Wives* "almost killed Goldsmith with envy."[23]

As for James Beattie, he was another outlander, a Scot, whose *Essay on Truth* was extravagantly praised and won him a pension at the very moment when Goldsmith, embittered by debts and ill health, sorely needed one—and failed to receive it. Goldsmith made no secret of his resentment; as Boswell remarked, he was not necessarily more envious than other men, but he talked more about his enviousness than they did.[24] Why, he asked, should Beattie receive a pension for one book when he, who had written so many, went without? Johnson silenced him with the retort: "Ah Doctor, there go many Six pences to make one Guinea."[25]

The retort suggests one of the reasons for Goldsmith's envy of Johnson. It was based, again, on jealousy of the man's literary achievements; for Goldsmith indubitably felt a painful conviction that Johnson's reputation as a serious writer was more firmly grounded than his own. (Horace Walpole declared that Goldsmith envied Shakespeare,[26] and if so, it was for a similar reason: he was distressed by his inability to reach the heights achieved by Shakespeare.) Johnson aggravated Goldsmith's resentment by treating him, as he often treated his associates, now with playful derision, now with downright disdain. When Anthony Chamier asked Goldsmith whether, by the word "slow" in the first line of *The Traveller,* he meant "tardiness of locomotion" and Goldsmith replied that he did, Johnson broke in: "No, Sir; you do not"— and proceeded to tell him what he really meant.[27] To make matters worse, their friends made it perfectly clear that they re-garded Goldsmith as merely the pale shadow of Johnson. When the Reverend George Graham of Eton College dined with them and Goldsmith replied to a remark addressed to Johnson, Graham exclaimed: "No, 'tis not you I mean, Dr. *Minor;* 'tis Dr. Major, there."[28] Moreover, as time went on and Goldsmith's literary output far surpassed Johnson's, the Great Cham, who admitted that he was of an envious nature himself, seems to have envied Goldsmith.[29]

But why was Goldsmith not satisfied with his own considerable achievements? Why did he feel compelled always to compete with Kelly or Beattie or Johnson? Why did he insist, even in jest, that he could tell a story as well as Garrick, or deliver a speech as well as Burke, or handle a pike as well as a puppet could? Why should he "studiously copy the manner of Johnson," as Boswell claimed?[30] Why was it that, as Reynolds said, "for one week he took one for a model and for another week [another]?" Why was he not content to be himself? Why, but that he was tormented by a gnawing feeling of inadequacy? He was constitutionally incapable of attaining any lasting sense of satisfaction with his own nature or his native talents. He was the clown who agonizes because he cannot play Hamlet.

So much has been written about Goldsmith's chattering and his attempts to "shine" in conversation that it is easy to forget that he was essentially shy. The antiquarian John Croft observed that "he had a diffidence unnatural to his country about him."[31] And Goldsmith himself told a group, of whom Sir John Hawkins was one: "People are greatly mistaken in me: a notion goes about, that when I am silent I mean to be impudent; but I assure you, gentlemen, my silence arises from bashfulness."[32] Even more significant are his poignant words in the Introduction to *The Bee:* "There is not, perhaps, a more whimsically dismal figure in nature, than a man of real modesty, who assumes an air of impudence—who, while his heart beats with anxiety, studies ease, and affects good-humour."

How often did Goldsmith, eager to win approval from his fellows, "assume an air of impudence" and "affect good humour," then realize that he was merely confirming their belief that he was absurd and, in his embarrassment, fall into greater absurdity?

It was his misfortune that he suffered from a deep inner sense of dissatisfaction with himself. He was not content to be bashful; he felt that he must be the center of interest. Instead of passing his time merrily with his easy-going cronies in the London taverns, he associated with the literary lions. In their presence he was not satisfied to listen from a corner; as Reynolds said, he had a "horror . . . of being overlooked by the company." He elbowed his way to the middle of the room. Once there, "he had not that kind of prudence to take refuge in silence. He would speak on subjects [of] which he had not thought, and of which he was ignorant; . . . he wished to be the principal figure in every group." He strutted and grimaced, he flaunted his "unsuitably gawdy" clothes,[33] he tried to amuse, to be affable, to "shine." "He considered him as a friend indeed," Reynolds wrote, "who would ask him to tell a story or sing a song, either of which requests he was always very ready to comply with, and very often without being asked, and without any preparation, to the great amazement of the company."

Among simpler men he found other means of attracting the recognition which he needed. All his adult life he indulged in extravagant flourishes designed to dazzle: he gambled and squandered money, he was ridiculously generous. Yet on occasion he could inveigh against the evils of gambling or improvidence or unreasoning generosity. There was a strange lack of balance—of serenity and self-assurance—in the character of Oliver Goldsmith. Reynolds maintained that "Dr. Goldsmith's folly and absurdity proceeded . . . partly from want of early acquaintance with that life to which his reputation afterwards introduced him." And it is true, surely, that his troubles were complicated by the fact that he arrived in London an uninhibited Irishman with a thick brogue at a time when Irishmen were regarded as little better than savages.

But the roots of his trouble went a good deal deeper than Reynolds implied. First of all there was his appearance. His short, stocky body topped by a massive head, his pock-marked face with its protuberant forehead and upper lip made him "cut an ugly figure," as he had been reminded ever since childhood. No mirror could ever have convinced him that he was a handsome fellow. "The face you well know is ugly enough," he remarked wryly when he sent a miniature of himself to a cousin in Ireland.[34] And when someone suggested that a group of Johnson's and Garrick's friends present *The Beaux' Stratagem* at Lichfield in their honor, he remarked that he "should of all things like to try [his] hand" at playing the part of Scrub, the clown.[35]

In London literary circles his ugliness was a standing joke. When Mrs. Cholmondeley, Peg Woffington's sister, was called upon to toast the ugliest man she knew, she promptly named Goldsmith; whereupon a woman across the table rose, shook her hand, and declared that she hoped they might become better acquainted.—Johnson is supposed to have commented on the occasion: "Thus the Ancients, on the commencement of their Friendships, used to sacrifice a beast between them."[36]

Frances Reynolds, Sir Joshua's sister, maintained that Goldsmith's "aspect from head to foot impress'd every one at first sight with an idea of his being a low mechanic; particularly, I believe, a journeyman tailor." And she asserted that one day at her brother's house Goldsmith complained of being insulted by a stranger. " 'The fellow,' he said, 'took me for a tailor!' on which all the Party either laugh'd aloud or shew'd they suppress'd a laugh."[37]

The Reverend Percival Stockdale had a similar tale to tell. One day he and Tom Davies had been discussing Goldsmith at Davies' shop, and Stockdale had remarked that he "never saw a man who looked more like a taylor." Then Goldsmith himself entered, spent some time chatting with the two men, and, as he was leaving, asked if he could borrow a copy of Stockdale's newly published translation of Tasso's *Aminta*. Davies produced one, and Goldsmith declared: "Mr. Stockdale, I shall soon take measure of you."[38] Only with difficulty could Stockdale and Davies stifle their laughter. A distinguished man of letters who looked and acted like a tailor? "Anomalous" was the only word for him.

Other people, less genteel, were at no pains to conceal their mirth at Goldsmith's absurd appearance. One day when he was strolling along the Strand in London with a sword at his side, a passing bully pointed at him and roared: "Look at that fly with a long pin stuck through it!"[39] Nor was that the worst: shortly before his death a hostile journalist wrote a savage attack on him, citing his "monkey face" and "grotesque orang-outang figure."[40]

Yet his appearance alone was not enough to blight his life. No, Goldsmith's lack of self-confidence and his compulsion to compensate for it were the products of many disappointments, many frustrations. Moreover, there were many Oliver Goldsmiths—the child, the student, the philosophic wanderer, the apprentice, the man of letters—and to see how they blended to form the whole man, one must trace his life from the very beginning.

Chapter II
Young Man in a Maze
(1730?-1750)

IN the first place he was a Goldsmith—and the Goldsmiths were an odd lot. Early in the nineteenth century three members of the family living in different sections of Ireland told Sir James Prior "in nearly the same words": "The Goldsmiths were always a strange family; they rarely acted like other people; their hearts were always in the right place, but their heads seemed to be doing anything but what they ought." And Prior concluded from his own observation that "inattention to worldly matters, a certain eccentricity of character, and inability to get forward in life, seem to have characterized the Goldsmith race."[1]

The poet's father, the Reverend Charles Goldsmith, was a case in point. Of respectable Anglo-Irish stock, he was brought up at his father's house at Ballyoughter, near Elphin, in County Roscommon, and educated at the Diocesan School in Elphin and at Trinity College, Dublin. His father, Robert Goldsmith, "seems to have exercised no profession," but he had had the good fortune or good sense to marry Catherine Crofton, daughter of the Very Reverend Thomas Crofton, Dean of Elphin;[2] and since she "enjoyed a moderate fortune," Robert had been able to live the life of a country gentleman, care for a family of thirteen, and send at least two of his sons to Trinity College. The eldest son, John, left college without a degree and settled down at Ballyoughter; but Charles, as a younger son, was obliged to shift for himself. Accordingly, after receiving his degree, he took Holy Orders. It was a natural choice, and he might reasonably have expected to prosper in it: his grandfather and great-grandfather Goldsmith had both held livings in the Church of Ireland, and his grandfather Crofton and his father's cousin, Edward Goldsmith, had risen to be Deans of Elphin.[3] Besides, the life of a rector in eighteenth century Ireland was far from arduous, and Charles Goldsmith loved leisure.

14

But he advanced very slowly in his profession. He is said to have been curate in a Dublin parish for a time and to have served briefly in a parish named Dusham or Duneham. But by 1718, when he was twenty-eight years old, he had been granted no regular living. Yet on May 4 of that year he married Ann Jones, one of the five children of the Reverend Oliver Jones, Master of the Diocesan School at Elphin.[4] Doubtless he cheerfully assured his bride and himself that the Lord would provide.

And so He did, thanks to the good offices of Ann's family. Her uncle, the Reverend Mr. Green, Curate-in-charge of the parish of Kilkenny West, in County Westmeath, gave them the rental of a dilapidated farmhouse at Pallas, or Pallasmore, in the parish of Forgney, County Longford, and the young people settled there. By farming some nearby fields and assisting at the local church and at Kilkenny West, six miles away, Charles was able to support himself and his wife.

Soon, however, there were children to provide for. The first, Margaret, was born at Pallas on August 22, 1719, but died soon afterwards. A year and a half later, on January 13, 1721, Ann bore a second daughter, Catherine. Then came the first son, Henry, and a third daughter, Jane.[5] Charles Goldsmith's responsibilities were increasing steadily; yet his prospects were no better than ever. In 1729, when he was nearly forty years old and had been married eleven years, he was still dependent on the generosity of his wife's family.

At about this time, however, Ann's father died, and his widow determined to deed to her daughter the lease which he had held on a hundred-acre tract at Pallas—probably the land which Charles had been farming. To her dismay Mrs. Jones learned that the lease had expired with her husband's death. But she was a doughty soul, and, according to a family tradition, she gathered together a hundred golden guineas, rode the hundred miles from Elphin to Dublin on horseback behind her son, and tried to bribe the landlord to continue the lease. She was able, however, to retain only fifty acres of the property, and the Goldsmiths' hopes for relative prosperity were dashed.

15

Thus the year 1730 found the family little better off than before. And it was probably in this same year,[6] on November 10, that Ann gave birth to a second son, either at Pallas or at her mother's house, Ardnagowan, near Elphin.[7] The baby was named Oliver after her father.[8]

Luckily the Goldsmiths' fortunes soon changed for the better, for presently Ann's uncle, the Reverend Mr. Green, died or retired, and Charles succeeded him as Curate-in-charge of the parish of Kilkenny West. Suddenly he found himself with an income of nearly two hundred pounds a year—in addition to whatever profits he could realize on the fifty acres at Pallas. Of course he acted on his good fortune at once, and before long the Goldsmiths were settled in a roomy house[9] on a farm in the new parish, just outside the village of Lissoy (or Lishoy) on the highway between Athlone and Ballymahon. At long last the Lord had provided adequately for Charles Goldsmith.

Lissoy was an ideal place for a man born to live expansively. The house stood sixty yards from the high road, at the end of a double avenue of trees and close to Lough Ree. There were an orchard and a garden behind the house and seventy acres of farmland beyond, with cabins for the laborers who would do the chores and leave the master of the property free to minister to his little parish and to preside over his household in the genial manner of Dr. Primrose, the Vicar of Wakefield, or the complacent father of the Man in Black described in the twenty-seventh Letter of *The Citizen of the World:*

My father, the younger son of a good family, was possessed of a small living in the church. His education was above his fortune, and his generosity greater than his education. Poor as he was, he had his flatterers still poorer than himself; for every dinner he gave them, they returned an equivalent in praise; and this was all he wanted. The same ambition that actuates a monarch at the head of an army, influenced my father at the head of his table. He told the story of the ivy-tree, and that was laughed at; he repeated the jest of the two scholars and one pair of breeches, and the company laughed at that; but the story of Taffy in the sedan-chair, was sure to set the table in a roar. Thus his pleasure increased in proportion to the pleasure he gave; he loved all the world, and he fancied all the world loved him.

16

Charles Goldsmith has often been identified with the saintly Village Preacher in *The Deserted Village,* and certainly the two were alike in their geniality and generosity. But Charles was too much interested in the comforts of this world ever to achieve saintliness.

He was, however, a kindly, indulgent father, and he fostered a spirit of harmony and gaiety in his household. Hardship had not embittered him; instead it had made him all the more eager to enjoy the moderate prosperity which had been granted to him. Like the father of the Man in Black:

> As his fortune was but small, he lived up to the very extent of it; he had no intentions of leaving his children money, for that was dross. . . . We were told, that universal benevolence was what first cemented society; we were taught to consider all the wants of mankind as our own; to regard the 'human face divine' with affection and esteem; he wound us up to be mere machines of pity, and rendered us incapable of withstanding the slightest impulse made by real or fictitious distress: in a word, we were perfectly instructed in the art of giving away thousands, before we were taught the more necessary qualifications of getting a farthing.

In this relaxed atmosphere Oliver Goldsmith spent his first years. He was probably a solitary boy. As the son of an Anglican clergyman in Ireland he would hardly have been allowed to play with the wild Irish youngsters in the village; and although he was one of five brothers, Henry was seven or eight years his senior, and Maurice, eldest of the three boys born at Lissoy, was probably six years younger than he.[10] Yet Lissoy offered plenty of distractions for a growing boy, and Oliver seems to have made the most of them. Later in life, in his *History of Earth and Animated Nature,* he recalled chasing dragonflies, stealing birds' eggs from their nests, observing the honey-bags of bees, hunting young otters, and listening to the cries of wild birds: "Those who have walked in an evening by the sedgy sides of unfrequented rivers, must remember a variety of notes from the different water-fowl; the loud scream of the wild goose, the croaking of the mallard, the whining of the lap-wing, and the tremulous neighing of the jack-snipe. But of all those sounds there is none so dismally hollow as the booming of the bittern. . . . I remember in the place where I

17

was a boy, with what terror this bird's note affected the whole village." Although he had visited both the Scottish Highlands and the Swiss Alps in the meantime, he remembered the view from "a little mount" across the road from his father's house as "the most pleasing horizon in nature." And he cherished the memory of one Peggy Golden, evidently the Goldsmiths' dairy-maid, who sang old ballads like "Barbara Allen" and "Johnny Armstrong" in a voice which the Italian diva Columba Mattei could never hope to equal.[11] Such recollections and the nostalgic references scattered through *The Deserted Village* suggest that young Oliver was a sensitive boy who spent most of his time alone in the fields or at home with adults. His sister Catherine told Thomas Percy after his death that as a child he had been "serious & reserved but when in Spirrits none more agreeably so."

His formal education began early. Elizabeth Delap, a relative of the Goldsmiths, boasted in later years that she "first put a book into his hands"—apparently when he was only three years old. She could not say much for the results of her experiment; in fact she declared that he was one of the dullest pupils she had ever taught, and that she had doubted whether anything could ever be made of him. Yet she admitted that "he was docile, diffident, easily managed, and that his inaptitude for retaining his lessons might have arisen from the carelessness common to all children."[12]

Perhaps Mrs. Delap's methods were at fault; at least Oliver did better when he was sent to the village school three years later. His master, Thomas Byrne, was a veteran of the wars with Spain and a competent scholar who delighted in translating Virgil's *Eclogues* into Irish verse *ex tempore* and who relieved the drudgery of study by telling the youngsters fairy tales or lively stories of his adventures in battle. Young Oliver apparently responded more positively to this approach than to Mrs. Delap's, for soon he was trying his own hand at writing verse. His father and mother were overjoyed at this display of talent and encouraged him to continue. But, according to his sister Catherine, he was seldom satisfied with his poems and burned them almost as soon as he had written them.

Only one of these survives, but it is worth reporting for several reasons. Catherine Goldsmith Hodson recorded the poem and the incident which prompted it in the narrative of her brother's life which she sent to Bishop Percy, and it can best be repeated in her own skittish, ill-spelled words:

There was company at his fathers at that time he was turnd of seven. They were attended at tea by a little boy who was desired to hand the Kettle—but the handle being to hot the boy took up the skirt of his coate to put between him & it. But unfortunately the Ladys perceived some thing which made them Laugh immodarately, whether from the awkwardness of the turn or any thing that might be seen there I can't say, but the Doctor [i.e., Oliver] immeadietly perceived there·cause of Laughter & informd his father who promised him a reward of Gingerbread to write some thing on it, and as it was one of his earliest productions that can be recollected tho perhaps not fit for the Publick I shall insert it here

> Theseus did see as Poets say
> Dark Hell & its abysses
> But had not half so Sharp an Eye
> As our young Charming Misses
>
> For they c^d through boys breeches peep
> And view what ere he had there
> It seemd to Blush & they all Laughd
> Because the face was all Bare
>
> They laughed at that
> Which some times Else
> Might give them greatest pleasure
> How quickly the[y] c^d see the thing
> Which was their darling treasure.[13]

This is a curious story to emanate from a village rectory. Bishop Percy understandably omitted it from his Memoir of Goldsmith, but it tells a good deal. In the first place it reveals how uninhibited was the spirit which prevailed in the household at Lissoy. If Oliver Goldsmith later offended his staid friends in London, it was in part at least because he had been brought up among people who were anything but squeamish. Charles Goldsmith's suggestion was obviously indecorous, and so was his young son's poem. Neither Oliver nor his father stifled the impulse to violate the rules of decorum; both expected their friends to relish a joke

19

without bothering about whether it was in good taste. The taboos which prevailed in more conventional society meant nothing to the Goldsmiths or their friends.

Moreover, even if Mrs. Hodson dated the story a few years too early, it suggests that Oliver was displaying unusual precocity, for good or for bad. And he seems to have been attracting, thanks to his precocity, far too much attention from his elders. Later in life he was to write in *The Bee,* No. VI: "Every species of flattery should be carefully avoided; a boy who happens to say a sprightly thing, is generally applauded so much, that he continues a coxcomb all his life after. He is reputed a wit at fourteen, and becomes a blockhead at twenty. Nurses, footmen, and such, should therefore be driven away as much as possible. I was even going to add, that the mother herself should stifle her pleasure or her vanity, when little master happens to say a good or a smart thing."

While Oliver was still attending Byrne's school, his proud parents suffered a sudden blow: he contracted smallpox, and for a while they despaired of his life. Eventually he recovered, but his face was scarred with deep red pockmarks. "He really cut an ugly figure," Mrs. Hodson admitted. He had never been a handsome child: there was something ludicrous about his disproportioned head with its protruding forehead and upper lip and his receding chin. With the added scars he looked downright clownish; and of course he was soon made aware of the fact.

When he was able to return to school, his parents decided that he should have more advanced work than that offered by Thomas Byrne, and they sent him off to the Diocesan School at Elphin, now under the direction of the Reverend Michael Griffin. This was his first experience away from home; yet he was not thrust suddenly into alien surroundings, for he had relatives galore in the neighborhood of Elphin. He stayed in his uncle John's substantial house at Ballyoughter outside the town, and he was close to his grandmother Jones's place, Ardnagowan, the finest house in the county except for the Bishop's Palace. Eleven miles away, at Emlaghmore, was his aunt Jane, Charles Goldsmith's sister, and her husband, the Reverend Thomas Contarine, Prebend of Oran. And nearby was their daughter Jane Contarine Lawder, who lived with her husband at Kilmore. All these people were important and influential in the life of the region; Contarine[14] especially, as the friend and correspondent of the philosopher Berkeley and the antiquary Charles O'Conor of Belenagare, was one of the most highly respected clergymen in the diocese. Moreover, as great-grandson of a former Dean of Elphin, distantly related to another, and grandson of the former Master of the school which he was attending, Oliver might well have felt like a person of some consequence in his new environment. But his schoolmates were, of course, more amused at his grotesque appearance than impressed by his notable connections.

Yet he had one telling weapon—his wits—which he could use for protection; and he soon learned to rely on his wits. He distinguished himself in his school work, he wrote more verse—and he won the approval of his elders, if not his schoolmates. At times, when stung by the cruelty of others, he could be annoyingly brash. His sister Jane Goldsmith Johnson later reported that a relative who came to visit at Ballyoughter said to him, "Why, Noll, you are become a fright; when do you mean to get handsome again?" To which the boy retorted: "I mean to get better, Sir, when you do." And on another occasion, according to Mrs. Hodson, a young man who was playing the fiddle at a party at their uncle John's insisted that Oliver dance a hornpipe for the company. The boy refused until at last his uncle ordered him to comply. Then when he began to dance, the fiddler called out, "See Aesop!—How like Aesop he is!—The very man, by God!" But Oliver ignored the remarks and danced on until the fiddler was exhausted. Then he stopped short, turned on his taunter, and cried:

> The Herald proclaimed out then saying
> See Aesop dancing and his Monkey playing.

Mrs. Goldsmith was so impressed with her son's talents that she urged that he be sent to the university. But her husband refused at first to consider the suggestion; their eldest son Henry was about to enter Trinity College to prepare for Holy Orders, and Charles could not see his way clear to providing a university education for a second son. Oliver, he had decided, should be prepared for a career as a merchant.

21

But Ann continued to press her case, and soon she gained the support of other members of the family who thought highly of the boy's powers. Charles's brother-in-law, Thomas Contarine, joined in the plea; and, since he had no son of his own, he even volunteered to help pay Oliver's expenses at Trinity. So at last Charles yielded. And once the decision was made, he withdrew his son from the school at Elphin and sent him to another kept by the Reverend Mr. Campbell at Athlone, just five miles from Lissoy.

No record of Oliver's two-year stay at Campbell's school has survived. Charles Goldsmith evidently thought the instruction superior to that at the Diocesan School at Elphin, but the cirriculum at either—or at any school throughout the Kingdom—would have varied little. Secondary education in the eighteenth century was founded on the assumption that any educated gentleman should know Latin thoroughly, and that with such preparation he would have access to all the most important material available on any subject. Students preparing for the university were drilled in Latin rules, Latin paradigms, Latin translation—often at a sluggish pace which alert members of the class found disheartening. As for a precocious and imaginative boy like Noll Goldsmith, the reaction was inevitable: he rebelled.

The tedious curriculum was not the only cause of his rebellion. He had too long been mocked for his ludicrous appearance, had learned too well how to defend himself from mockers—had perhaps too often been punished by masters or schoolmates who found his brashness insufferable. It was as well for him that after he had been two years at Athlone the school was closed because Campbell was ailing.

Oliver was sent next to a school at Edgeworthstown, County Longford, under the direction of the Reverend Patrick Hughes, an old friend of his father's. And the change proved providential. He later told Bishop Percy that he had profited more from his years under Hughes (1741-1745) than from any of his other teachers. At Edgeworthstown he learned to find genuine pleasure in reading the Latin poets and historians, especially Ovid and Livy. He continued to write verse of his own too;[15] and when his brother

Henry chided him for the confused style of his letters, remarking that "if he had but little to say, he should endeavour to say it well," he applied himself to the task of improving his prose style.

Even more important: his personality underwent some salutary changes during his four years at Hughes' school. His new master was perceptive enough to diagnose the boy's difficulties and astute enough to cope with them. Seeing that Oliver was basically unsure of himself, he made a point of treating him as an intellectual equal. And the boy responded at once. Schoolmates later declared that in the course of his four years at Edgeworthstown the "short, thick, pale-faced pock-marked boy" who had been "awkward in manner, backward and diffident at first" gained "sufficient confidence to become a leader in boyish sports, particularly in the exercise of ball-playing, or fives, in which he displayed great activity." And although "in school he was considered indolent, though not destitute of talents; his disposition kind and generous, as far as school-boy matters were concerned; his temper sensitive, easily offended, though easily pleased," he was "always willing to join in such juvenile tricks and scenes of humor as were going forward." Removed for the first time from the protection of admiring relatives, he was learning how to get along with his fellows and to win their respect—not by displaying his precocity but by concealing it and acting like one of them. This was only another manifestation of that yearning for acceptance and approval which had underlain his earlier brashness and which was to remain with him as long as he lived.

On occasion, though, he could relapse into his old brashness. Take, for example, the story which Mrs. Hodson tells of his return to school after his last vacation at home before he finished his studies at Hughes' school. A friend, she claimed, had given him a guinea during his holidays, and he was determined to make the twenty-mile trip to Edgeworthstown as pleasant as he could. He spent the first day jogging along on his horse, stopping now and then to inspect a fine estate and managing to go only as far as the village of Ardagh by evening. There he hailed a passer-by (unfortunately one Cornelius Kelly, the local wag) and asked the way to the best house in the village. Kelly, seeing the opportunity for some fun, directed him to the home of a Mr. Featherstone, who did indeed have the best house in the place.

All unsuspecting, Noll rode up to Featherstone's door, called for the hostler, and gave him careful directions for the care of his horse. Then he stalked into the parlor, where the master of the house was sitting before the fire, and demanded a bottle of wine, to be followed by dinner, "comfortably good and in a hurry." A servant brought in the wine at once, and Noll generously shared it with his host, who seemed interested to know who his guest was—and to be properly impressed when he was told. Presently Mrs. Featherstone and her two daughters joined them, and supper was served—young Goldsmith meanwhile ordering up two more bottles and allowing the ladies to choose their favorite wines.

At last he went up to bed, specifying that he would have an early breakfast, which must include a hot cake, served in his room. And it was only after he was ready for the road on the following morning and called for his bill that he learned the embarrassing truth.[16]

The story is almost, but not quite, incredible. It sounds more like a scene from the first act of a comedy (as Goldsmith eventually made it) than an incident from real life. Yet a bumptious young man like Noll, with a guinea in his pocket to supply the self-confidence which he sorely needed, might conceivably have made such a blunder—though he would probably have sensed it before the evening was over. Oliver Goldsmith was to make many a blunder almost as absurd before his life ended—and often for the same basic reason.

A few weeks after the incident at Ardagh, Noll was pronounced ready for the university. For a while in 1743 it had looked as if his father might be able to pay all his expenses at Trinity when brother Henry, just appointed to a scholarship, had married suddenly and been obliged to leave the College and settle down at his family's old-farmhouse at Pallas as curate and teacher. But the money thus made available for Oliver's education was abruptly withdrawn the next year when his sister Catherine eloped with young Daniel Hodson, one of Henry's pupils and the son of a very substantial family who lived at St. John's, near Athlone.

Charles Goldsmith was outraged when he learned of his daughter's deceit; in his fury he prayed God that she might be forever barren. But when his anger cooled, he realized that young Hodson's parents had more cause to complain than he: they had entrusted their son to the care of Henry Goldsmith—and their trust had been violated. Somehow he must make amends. So Charles announced that he would settle four hundred pounds on the couple. Characteristically, he failed to consider that he had no such sum at his disposal.

The plan which he concocted for fulfilling his obligation was, as might be expected, foolhardy: he assigned to his new son-in-law the income from the farmland at Lissoy (worth about forty pounds a year) plus twelve pounds in tithes until such time as the four hundred pounds should be paid in full. And Oliver was told that he must enter Trinity College not as a pensioner, as his father and brother had been, but as a sizar—one who earned his tuition and board by waiting on the wealthier students, cleaning their boots, and carrying their books—and who was obliged to feed on the leavings from the Fellows' Tables.

Understandably the young man who had tried to cut so bold a figure at Ardagh rebelled at the thought of performing such menial duties, and he refused at first to apply for entrance to Trinity. However his uncle Contarine, who had himself been a sizar at the College, assured him that, since sizars were appointed by competitive examinations, the rank implied talent and should be regarded as an honor. Moreover, he added, he himself could never have attained his position in the Church or his enviable friendship with men like Bishop Berkeley if he had refused to be a sizar. So at last Noll consented, though reluctantly, to apply for admission to Trinity, and early in June, 1745, he set off on the eighty-mile trip to Dublin to take his examinations.

This was probably his first venture outside the small area bounded by Ballymahon, Elphin, and Edgeworthstown. But he would have found little that was not already familiar to him. There were the same undulating fields, the same trim gentlemen's estates, the same wretched cabins spilling forth ill-fed pigs and children; for although there were scattered sections of Ireland

25

which were comparatively prosperous, by far the greater part of the country suffered the direst poverty. Three years later, in an essay in *The Reformer,* Edmund Burke complained that the clothes of the peasants were "so ragged, that they rather publish than conceal the Wretchedness it was meant to hide." And he added:

Nay, it is no uncommon Sight to see half-a-dozen Children run quite naked out of a Cabin, scarcely distinguishable from a Dunghill. . . . Let anyone take a Survey of their cabins, and then say whether such a Residence be worthy anything that challenges the Title of a human Creature. You enter, or rather creep in, at a Door or Hurdles plaistered with Dirt, of which the Inhabitant is generally the Fabricator; withinside you see (if the Smoke will permit you) the Men, Women, Children, Dogs, and Swine lying promiscuously; for their Opulence is such that they cannot have a separate House for their Cattle, as it would take too much from the Garden, whose produce is their only Support. Their Furniture is much fitter to be lamented than described, such as a Pot, a Stool, a few wooden Vessels, and a broken Bottle: In this manner all the Peasantry, to a Man, live: And I appeal to anyone, who knows the Country, for the Justness of the Picture.

"I fancy," he observed presently, "many of our fine Gentlemen's Pageantry would be greatly tarnished, were their gilt coaches to be preceded and followed by the miserable Wretches, whose Labour supports them."[17]

Noll Goldsmith was probably not much troubled by such reflections as he made his way toward Dublin. He had seen similar conditions all his life and merely accepted them as a part of the general scheme of things. He had doubtless been assured since childhood that God had created some men to be rich and others to be poor, according to some quixotic plan of His own devising, and that He meant both rich and poor to accept their lot unquestioningly. The Goldsmiths were charitable people who never turned a beggar (and there were an estimated 35,000 of them roaming the highways of Ireland) away from their door; yet they never considered advocating any sweeping economic change. Rather, they rested content with their moderate circumstances, confident that God would in His own good time reward all men according to their desserts, and that meanwhile, as Mr. Pope had expressed it, "Whatever is, is right."

His arrival in Dublin surely thrilled him. The crowded, milling city of over a hundred thousand inhabitants was many times larger than any town which he had known. Its narrow, unpaved streets, choked with hackney coaches and sedan chairs, merchants and hawkers, peers and beggars, were confusing enough to take his breath away. Architecturally Dublin had little to recommend it; of the fine Palladian buildings which later beautified it, only the Parliament House had been completed in 1745. Like most eighteenth century cities it contained innumerable tall gabled houses with narrow windows, houses so huddled together that they kept the streets almost constantly in shadow. Sanitary conditions were dismally primitive; householders dumped their offal into the street, and the resultant stench was nauseating. After nightfall travel was perilous because there were few streetlights, and the inefficient volunteer watchmen provided little protection from footpads. And although travelers noted that the contrasts between rich and poor were less marked in Dublin than in the country, they were appalled by the numbers of beggars who infested all parts of the city. Especially revolting was the occasional display of an executed convict, stretched out headless on a bed of straw with a plate for contributions to pay for the poor creature's burial—and often a wailing widow and orphans alongside to heighten the pathos.

Yet Dublin had its charms too: life there was gay and hurried, one had the sense of being close to the heart of things, and there were infinite sources of entertainment. At first, however, Noll was obliged to forego those: he had still to pass his examinations for admission to Trinity. And he himself later declared that they were "a great deal stricter than . . . either at Oxford or Cambridge."[18]

On June 11 he presented himself for his examination—probably the same sort of exercise in translation from Latin and Greek as that given to Edmund Burke in the preceding year. Burke appeared before Dr. Pellesier, a Fellow of the College, who "brought out Francis' Horace, Dauphine's Virgil and Homer, with I don't know whose notes. He made me construe 'Scriberis Vario,' &c., 'Eheu fugaces Posthume,' &c., and in Virgil I began with the

103rd line of the sixth Aeneid, and in Homer with the 227th line of the third Iliad, and the 406th of the sixth." Then he was sent to Mr. Obbins, the Senior Lecturer, who examined him "very strictly . . . in the Odes, Sermons, and Epistles of Horace."[19] Such an ordeal could have been painful for Goldsmith, not yet fifteen years old and none too sure of himself, for his future depended on his showing in this one examination. But somehow he managed to satisfy the examiners, and was officially accepted as a student of "The College of the Holy and Undivided Trinity of Queen Elizabeth."

Soon he was settled in a garret room in Entry No. 35 of the College, probably with John Beatty, a former student at Edgeworthstown, who was admitted to Trinity on the same day. The room was, no doubt, a dismal place, for living quarters in the College were gloomy in the extreme, and students made no effort to brighten them. In *The Inventory of the Furniture of a Collegian's Chamber* a Trinity versifier described the typical dormitory room:

> Imprimis, there's a *Table* blotted;
> A tatter'd *Hanging* all besnotted;
> A *Bed* of Flocks, as one may rank it,
> Reduc'd to *Rug,* and half a *Blanket* . . .
> And *Chairs* a couple, (I forgot 'em)
> But each of them without a *Bottom.*[20]

The rooms were ill heated, ill lighted, and lacking in any sort of convenience. But discomfort was a general ailment among the students: Goldsmith's particular ailment was far more troublesome. Of the two or three hundred undergraduates at Trinity when he entered, only twenty-five or thirty were sizars; that is, he belonged to the lowest tenth of the group economically and socially. And he was never allowed to forget it: each class of student had its own uniform—from the noblemen, who wore wigs and fine gowns with gold and silver tassels, down to the sizars, who wore red caps and sleeveless gowns of coarse material, unadorned. Goldsmith always remembered the humiliation which he underwent as a sizar. In his *Enquiry into the Present State of Polite Learning,* published in 1759, he observed how grave a mistake it was that those who are "learning the *liberal* arts" should be "at the same time treated like slaves."[21] And when his brother Henry asked him whether he should plan to send his son to Trinity, presumably as a sizar, he replied: "If he has ambition, strong passions, and an exquisite sensibility of contempt, do not send him there, unless you have no other trade for him except your own."[22]

Yet Noll soon learned how to compensate for his difficulties, and his clownish appearance and his carefree ways won him friends. Among his closest associates were his former schoolmates John Beatty and Robert Bryanton, and he presently became acquainted with Edward and Charles Purdon, James Willington, Thomas Wilson, Michael Kearney, and Lauchlan Macleane— most of them pensioners and probably heedless young men like himself who took their studies lightly and did their utmost to make college life a lark. Somewhere he had acquired a German (that is, side-blown) flute, and thanks to a mellow voice he soon won a reputation as an impromptu entertainer. Edmund Burke and Thomas Barnard, later Goldsmith's friends in London, seem to have known him only slightly.[23] Like Samuel Johnson at Oxford, he was one of the habitual loungers at the College Gate when his duties as a sizar left him free, and more conscientious students regarded him with some disdain. One of them, William Jessop, wrote to Bishop Percy in 1785: "He was my college class fellow; but with regret I own that I knew him little, and was very seldom in his company. I had not sufficient penetration to discover in Admetus's herdsman the concealed Apollo. You never saw him until an intercourse with life must have, in some degree, planed down his ruggedness. But it is a fact that in his college days his aspect and manners were uncommonly against him."[24]

Had he been so disposed, Goldsmith could have gained at Trinity as solid an education as was available anywhere in the Kingdom; in fact Lord Chesterfield had declared in 1731 that the education offered there was "indisputably better" than that at the English universities. Under the imperious Dr. Richard Baldwin, Provost since 1717, the College had undergone many improvements. A fine Jacobean library had been completed in 1732, and the dingy old front was about to be replaced by a handsome 300-

foot façade. There was a new dining room too in 1745—but it proved to be so poorly constructed that it was torn down and replaced fourteen years later. Indeed students seem to have been skeptical of many of Baldwin's improvements. One wrote irreverently when the New Front was raised:

> Our Alma Mater, like a whore,
> Worn out with age and sin,
> Paints, and adorns herself the more,
> The more she rots within.[25]

Actually, though, Baldwin had brought about some sound academic improvements during his administration; notably he had insisted that the faculty perform the duties assigned to them. And for the times that was a startling innovation, since lecturers before then had rarely taken the trouble to appear at their scheduled lectures, even those announced as open to the public.

But Baldwin made no substantial changes in the curriculum; that was sacrosanct. Students merely continued the sort of close study of the classics which they had begun in the secondary schools. During his first year at Trinity Edmund Burke read Books VII-XII of the *Aeneid,* Epictetus's *Enchiridion,* the *Tabula* of Cebes, and the first nine chapters of Burgersdicius's *Logic.*[26] The first three, especially the *Aeneid,* might well have held Goldsmith's interest had they been properly presented; but even in college literary merits were ignored, and the classics were studied merely as exercises to develop the student's skill in translation.

The study of the classics was, however, relatively pleasant compared with the required work in Burgersdicius—"hideous Burgersdicius," Burke called him, and dismissed his system of logic as "blackguard stuff, a hoard of exploded nonsense, the scum of pedantry, and the refuse of the boghouse school of philosophy."[27] Nor was he alone in his attitude; for regularly once a year Trinity College students gathered in Molesworth's Fields and burned Burgersdicius in effigy. In 1770 Goldsmith wrote sympathetically of Thomas Parnell, another Trinity man: "His progress through the college course of study was probably marked with but little splendour; his imagination might have been too warm to relish the cold logic of Burgersdicius, or the dreary subtleties of Smig-lesius [another logician of the same school]."[28]

The result was that Noll Goldsmith was destined not to distinguish himself scholastically during his years at Trinity. His friend Kearney claimed that he once received a premium in the difficult January examinations, and Goldsmith himself boasted to Edmond Malone that he had been able to translate Horace's odes into English as well as anyone in the College. But in the kind of painstaking study demanded at Trinity Noll was never at home. A few years later he wrote to his brother-in-law Dan Hodson from Edinburgh that he was "read[ing] hard . . . a thing I never could do when the study was displeasing." He was subjected to a curriculum which offered no spark to the imagination, no challenge to a mind like his.

Nonetheless he was obliged to comply with the system in order to maintain his status as a student, and supervision was strict. Undergraduates were required to attend lectures faithfully and to be properly prepared. Goldsmith scanted his studies on occasion and was twice "cautioned" for poor preparation. Yet he "received the thanks of the house," as the expression was, two or three times for his diligence.[29] And he was obliged to do more than bluff. Each term began with an oral examination on the content of the previous term's work, and there were periodic declamations before the student body, as well as a weekly theme in Latin which each student was required to submit to his tutor. And Goldsmith's tutor was Dr. Theaker Wilder, the College martinet.

Charles Goldsmith had requested that Oliver be assigned to Wilder, the younger son of the family of Castle Wilder in County Longford. Knowing Wilder's reputation for scrupulous scholarship, Charles had supposed that he would bring out the best in Noll. But his choice proved to be unhappy; tutor and student were doomed never to be compatible. In the first place Wilder was a mathematician, and Noll's contempt for mathematics was ingrained. Moreover, Wilder was exacting: he expected his students to exert all their powers in their studies, and his pupil was disposed to do nothing of the kind. There was bound to be trouble—explosive trouble. For Wilder was an impulsive, irascible

31

man—so much so as to become a legendary figure in the history of the College. On one occasion he is supposed to have leaped into a speeding hackney coach and struck down the driver, who had accidentally flicked him with his whip in passing. On another, when he encountered a group of students dousing a troublesome bailiff under the College Pump, he allegedly cried, "Gentlemen, gentlemen, for the love of God, don't be so cruel as to nail his ears to the pump!"—whereupon the students immediately acted on the implied suggestion.[30] Years later Goldsmith "often declared that his tutor was the most depraved profligate and licentious being in human shape,"[31] and Thomas Wilson referred to his "savage brutality . . . better calculated to frighten than to allure."

Mrs. Hodson maintained that Wilder's harshness toward Goldsmith was dictated by his belief that the young man had genuine talents which he was failing to use. If so, he took the wrong approach. Instead of eliciting Noll's real powers by strengthening his self-confidence, as Patrick Hughes of Edgeworthstown had done, he tried to goad him into action by constant taunts and humiliation. Of course the method failed, and Goldsmith's brashness again came to the surface.

With a tedious curriculum, a bullying tutor, and always his harassing duties as sizar to plague him, Noll must have found life in Dublin disheartening and longed to abandon his studies, to escape from Burgersdicius and Wilder and his degrading position as lackey. And there were always avenues for at least temporary escape. Dublin offered manifold sources of amusement, and, according to Mrs. Hodson, he made the most of them whenever he received a remittance from home. It was all in keeping with his general pattern of behavior: everything at Trinity College seemed to conspire to make him painfully aware of his failure to measure up to the standards of others; but a few shillings in his pocket gave him a sense of confidence, and reckless spending made him feel as important as the next fellow. It was the story of the "inn" at Ardagh all over again.

If he had the price, he could saunter through the Rotunda Gardens and Assembly Rooms, listen to a concert at the music hall in Fishamble Street (where Handel's *Messiah* had first been sung in 1742), watch a bull-baiting at the Corn Market, join in the dancing at Donnybrook Fair, or see a play at one of the theaters. At the Smock Alley Theater in the season of 1745 alone he could have watched the great Garrick play Hamlet or Lear or Othello, or Mrs. Bellamy in the role of Cleopatra or Mrs. Millamant. Or, lacking the price of such amusements, he could always wander the busy streets to marvel at the passing show or venture outside the city to stroll in the fields. Before long he made friends in the town as well as in the College; in fact Prior reports a rumor that Goldsmith "formed an imprudent female attachment; which, but for the interposition of some of his friends, was likely to have terminated in marriage."

Every now and then, when the milder forms of diversion failed, there was a riot to relieve the tedium of studies. For example, on January 19, 1746, a young blade named Kelly drank too much, staggered to the theater in Smock Alley, climbed onto the stage, and rushed to the greenroom, where he "insulted some of the females there in the most gross and indecent manner." He was ousted at last, but a few nights later he returned with fifty henchmen, marched through the pit to the dressing room in search of Thomas Sheridan, the manager, and, when he failed to find him, slashed at chests and closets. For several nights thereafter they repeated the process, until finally Sheridan called the law to his defense.[32]

Early in 1747 Noll's activities were suddenly curtailed when news arrived from Lissoy that his father had died. Of course Charles Goldsmith had accumulated no wealth in the course of his leisurely life; like the father of the Man in Black he "left me— his blessing." Catherine Hodson's dowry was still not paid in full, and Mrs. Goldsmith was obliged to resign the Lissoy property to her daughter and son-in-law and move into a cottage in Ballymahon. She had now only the income from the farm at Pallas to support her, and she had her three younger sons still to raise. Obviously she could spare little or nothing for Oliver's expenses at the College.

33

He received occasional remittances from his uncle Contarine and other relatives, but often he must have been penniless. Thomas Wilson later recalled his "squalid poverty and its concomitants, idleness and despondence," and John Beatty remembered sharing his books with Goldsmith because Noll's had been pawned. Beatty recalled too how Theaker Wilder had seized the opportunity to mock Goldsmith on the occasion, comparing him to "the silly fellow in Horace—*Mutat quadrata rotundis.*" And many years later an idle shopper in a Dublin bookstall happened upon a tattered Greek Lexicon in which the distracted young man had written the words "I promise to pay, &c., &c., Oliver Goldsmith," showing where his thoughts had been when he should have been applying his mind to his studies.

Yet though grinding poverty may have tempered his brashness, it did not make him a miser. On the contrary it made him all the more eager to permit himself the luxury of a grand flourish when he had a few shillings to spend. Moreover, hardship drew him closer to suffering humanity; he knew the poor as he had never known them, knew from bitter experience how harsh their lot could be. He learned also how much a few pennies could mean to a human being in distress; he learned to share with others what little he had, to give even when he himself was in want. His cousin Edwin Mills said that one morning when he stopped at Noll's room at the College to take him to breakfast, Goldsmith called to him that he could not come to the door—that Mills must force it. When he did, he found his cousin trying to extricate himself from the mattress ticking. And presently he explained: the evening before he had met a wretched woman with five children who needed blankets more than he did. Of course he had given her his, and when the night grew chilly, he had ripped a hole in the ticking and crawled in among the feathers to keep himself warm.—A ludicrous story; yet who could condemn the unreasoning generosity which prompted the deed?

It was probably now, in his attempts to lay his hands on some ready cash, that Noll first resorted to gambling, the vice which plagued him as long as he lived. And he certainly turned to account his old skill at versifying. During his years at Trinity he had continued to write light verse and translations from time to time, and eventually he discovered that the owner of a shop at the Sign of the Reindeer on Mountrath Street would pay him five shillings apiece for ballads which he could dash off hastily about contemporary events. None of these survives; in fact Goldsmith would probably have disdained to acknowledge them. Yet he took enough interest in them to steal out in the evening to hear them sung in the streets—and to see for himself how well the public received them.

Meanwhile his resilient spirits sustained him, and his gregarious nature helped him to find means of escape from his misfortunes. Though often downcast, he could gain relief in joining the loungers at the College Gate when he had a moment to spare. Or he could bring together a few friends in his room and entertain them with his songs and his flute. His flute seems, indeed, to have served him as a sort of safety valve; he is said to have relieved his tension, when he was depressed, by blowing great squawks on the instrument.

On one occasion his yearning to be one of the crowd involved him in serious trouble. It began on May 21, 1747, when a bailiff violated the sanctuary of the College walls to arrest a student for debt. Such an infringement of collegians' rights was not to be borne, and the offending bailiff was taken captive and doused (according to the custom of the day) under the College Pump. Then matters went out of hand. In great good spirits the students, led by one "Gallows" Welch, but with Noll Goldsmith not the least of them, decided to engage in rioting. Others joined the mob, and presently someone suggested that they lay siege to the Black Dog (Newgate Prison) and release the student confined there. Unfortunately Constable Roe failed to go along with the fun: he ordered the guards to fire on the mob, and two men were killed. Then the riot ended—but the College authorities began an investigation at once to fix the blame on the ringleaders. When punishments were dealt out, four students were expelled from the College and four others were "publicly admonished." Among the latter was the luckless Noll.[33]

In the following month, having completed two years in residence at the College, he became eligible to apply for a scholarship. He was duly examined, but when the results of the examination were announced, he was granted only an "exhibition" on the Erasmus Smith Foundation. The award, apparently a sort of "honorable mention" given to those who had not qualified for scholarships, carried a premium of thirty shillings per term for the next academic year.

Obviously thirty shillings would not go very far toward paying the expenses of a term at the College; but it would do very well to provide a gala evening's entertainment for himself and his friends. So Noll invited them all, townsmen as well as students, women (in defiance of the College rules) as well as men, to gather at his room. They came and proceeded to disport themselves wholeheartedly. Joy was unconfined—so unconfined, in fact, that the hubbub soon reached the ears of Theaker Wilder. And before the merrymakers could be warned, he stormed into the room and scattered them one and all, except for the crestfallen host. Him he dressed down in unforgettable terms, giving him as a special memento a deafening box on the ear.

This was the last straw. Rather than face the final humiliation which almost certainly would have followed, Goldsmith sold his remaining books and whatever clothing he did not immediately need, and left the College, determined to make his fortune abroad.

For a few days he lingered in Dublin. Then when he had only a shilling to his name, he set off on foot, hoping to find passage on a ship outward bound.

He lived on his single shilling for three days; then he sold his waistcoat, then his shirts. When even that money was gone and his shoes were worn through, he went for twenty-four hours without a taste of food. At last, in desperation, he wandered into a wake, confident that he would find something to eat there. He was right: a poor girl offered him a handful of gray peas, and he gobbled them down, thinking them, as he later said, the most delicious morsels he had ever tasted.

By that time he knew that he had failed in his attempt to escape from his predicament. He sent word of his plight to his brother Henry at Pallas, and Henry came at once, bringing him some decent clothing and, no doubt, some rather astringent advice. At length Noll was persuaded that he should smother his pride, return to Trinity, apologize for his conduct, and settle down again to his studies. Together the brothers returned to Dublin, and Henry managed to convince Theaker Wilder that the prodigal had repented and would sin no more. So once again Noll was left to face the old exasperating existence. No escape seemed possible.

Now surely life was more harassing than ever. He was doubtless readmitted to the College only on trial, and he had to be circumspect every minute of the day. Moreover, he must submit to the jibes of Wilder, who could not resist the temptation to taunt the scapegrace. On one occasion, when discussing the center of gravity, Wilder is said to have asked, "Now, blockhead, where is your center of gravity?" and Goldsmith to have given an obscene retort which sent him to the foot of the class.[34]

Eventually he satisfied the residence requirements for his degree and left Dublin to stay at Emlaghmore, his uncle Contarine's house, while he prepared for his baccalaureate examination. There he could live cheaply and have access to his uncle's library while he read up on some of the subjects which he had slighted during his years at the College.

But although he had scanted the education in abstractions offered to him in the classroom, his years at Trinity had not been wasted. He had managed to gain a rather thorough, concrete education in the ways of the world. He had known the humiliation of serving those who thought themselves his betters, had borne insults and mockery, had seen the sufferings of the poor and shared them, had even been on the verge of starvation. And these experiences had brought him close to life at its lowest terms, had taught him to sympathize—to "feel with"—his fellow-beings and to understand them. Besides, he had learned, almost accidentally, that he had a certain knack for expressing himself which could, as a last resort, be turned to profit.

Unfortunately the faculty of Trinity College was interested solely in conventional academic achievements. And when in February, 1750, Noll headed east toward Dublin again to confront his inquisitors, he must have had misgivings. The examiners would almost certainly eye him with suspicion because of his irregular collegiate record. And who could tell what new embarrassments Wilder might have stored up for the occasion?

Yet he succeeded somehow in satisfying his examiners, and he emerged as a Bachelor of Arts. But he could have found little satisfaction in his success: he had learned to despise the degree itself and the system which it represented—and he must have been acutely aware that Trinity College thought no more highly of him than he did of it. Surely he and his examiners would have been dumbfounded could they have known that some day his statue would be raised outside the gates where he had so often loitered—or that the pane of glass on which he had idly scratched his name one day in his dismal room in Entry No. 35 would eventually be one of the treasured possessions of the College Library.

Back he went now to the country—to the family which had once taken such pride in him and prophesied so brilliant a career for him. Poor Noll had earned his degree at last—after five long years. Very well, then, let bygones be bygones; he must settle down now to serious work. His mother still had her three younger sons to raise, and she needed his help.

But Noll himself had other notions.

Chapter III
Philosophic Vagabond
(1750-1755)

THE Goldsmiths had no doubt as to what career Noll should pursue. There was not much choice in a subjugated country like Ireland for a man of his class, blessed only with a supposedly liberal education. Family tradition and influence dictated that he should take Holy Orders, and Thomas Contarine evidently hoped that he could arrange to have Noll succeed him in his living. Yet, however much he may have idealized such an existence later in life, Oliver Goldsmith had very little desire to settle down at the age of twenty as a country clergyman "passing rich on forty pounds a year." Like the Man in Black he hated, at that point in his existence, to think of wearing a long wig and a black coat all his life when he much preferred a short wig and a brown (or, more likely, crimson) coat.

No, Noll wanted a more spectacular career than his father's or his brother Henry's. Surely there were means whereby a young man like himself, educated in the ways of the world and endowed with a sense of humor, could win distinction. First of all he should travel, to gain a breadth of view which Trinity College had failed to supply. It was no accident that when he fled from the College after the disastrous party in his room, he had tried to find passage on a ship going abroad—anywhere abroad. Ireland offered too little scope for a young man who longed—who needed—to distinguish himself.

Unfortunately there was no one in Ireland or anywhere else who proposed to underwrite a Grand Tour of Europe. So he accepted the obvious course and settled down at his mother's cottage in Ballymahon or his uncle Contarine's house at Kilmore to read for Orders. And in due time he presented himself to Bishop Synge of Elphin for examination.[1]

But Bishop Synge was not impressed and declined, at least for the present, to approve the candidate. Why he was rejected no one knows. Mrs. Hodson said that the Bishop thought him too young, but intimated also that Synge may have had a candidate of his own for Contarine's living.[2] Others said that Goldsmith's record at Trinity stood against him; still others, that he shocked the Bishop by appearing for his examination in unseemly scarlet breeches. Whatever the reason, one must agree with Percy that Bishop Synge's decision was for the best. Surely the Lord never intended Noll Goldsmith to be a preacher.

Yet although he may have been relieved at his rejection, it was one more failure—one more blow to his self-confidence. He is said to have continued reading for Orders for a while; but he seems to have beguiled much of the time in visits to his brother-in-law Dan Hodson or his school friend Robert Bryanton or another acquaintance named Gannon, who kept two live seals. With his cronies he hunted, fished in the River Inny, tramped the fields, or played cards. At home he occasionally ran errands for his mother, and he may have taken French lessons from a local priest.[3] But he was the same incorrigible Noll who loved idleness and good company, and he frittered away much of his time playing the flute at the window of his mother's cottage,[4] taking lessons in sledge-throwing from the local blacksmith, or entertaining John Binley and Tom Allen and other loafers at George Conway's tavern across the road from the cottage.

Mrs. Goldsmith must often have wondered whatever would become of her son. He showed no promise of fulfilling the dreams which she had had for him when he was a boy. He was still writing light verse occasionally for the edification of his cousin Jane Lawder.[5] But where would that get him? He seemed no better than a wastrel; in fact he seemed a good deal worse than that if it is true, as local tradition has it, that he was caught robbing Lord Annaly's orchard with another ne'er-do-well named Jack Fitzsimmons, and was saved from prosecution and disgrace only because of his family's prominence.

At last Uncle Contarine stepped in. Perceiving that Noll was making little progress toward ordination, he managed to find him a post as tutor with a family named Flinn in County Roscommon. But although he supposedly remained with them for a year, nothing is known about his stay except that it ended abruptly when he resigned, claiming that he had been cheated in a card game. If the Flinns could afford to keep a tutor who was a graduate of Trinity College, they presumably represented the Irish gentry. But Noll was unimpressed; and he may have had them in mind when, soon afterward, he complained that "men of a thousand pound a year in Ireland spend their whole lives in runing after a hare, drinking to be drunk, and geting every Girl with Child, that will let them."[6]

He had, however, gained something by his stay with the Flinns: he had saved enough to buy a good horse and to put aside thirty pounds. And he determined to travel, as he had long yearned to do. So off he went in the direction of Cork.

Six weeks later he jogged back into Ballymahon on a pitiful nag which he had named Fiddleback because of its shape. His thirty pounds was gone, every penny of it. But whatever embarrassment he may have felt, he concealed; and, brash as ever, he had a tale to tell worth more than thirty pounds if one has a taste for the fanciful.

He had, he declared, ridden to Cork, sold his horse, and taken passage on a ship bound for America. But the winds were unfavorable, and so he passed the time in sight-seeing. A week went by, then two, and still the ship stood motionless. Then one day, when some new-found friends suggested a jaunt into the country, he gladly agreed.

Of course that was the day when at last the wind shifted and the ship set sail. But instead of hurrying home or trying to secure passage on another ship, he stayed on in Cork, letting his money gradually dwindle away. When he had only two guineas left, he bought Fiddleback and set off on the 120-mile trip to Ballymahon with only two half-crowns in his pocket.

Suddenly he recalled that a college friend named H—— had given him a standing invitation to spend a summer with him at his house eight miles from Cork; so he turned Fiddleback in that direction. On the way, however, he met a poor woman with eight children who sobbed out a sad story of her husband's being thrown in jail, leaving her with no means of support. Of course Noll was moved to give her one of his half-crowns. Then on he rode, confident that he would have an ample supply of money, once he reached his friend's house.

When he arrived there, he was set upon by "a large mastiff who had like to tear him to pieces." Then "an old Grim looking woman" came out, took his name, and announced his arrival to the master of the house, who rushed forth in his nightshirt, nightcap, and slippers to welcome him.

H—— explained that he was just recovering from a long illness and declared that he was overjoyed to have "the man he most loved on Earth" to keep him company. But when Goldsmith told him his recent adventures and added that he had but half a crown to his name, H—— seemed strangely uneasy. Dinnertime came and went with no sign of food. At last the old woman brought in two plates and a spoon and laid a table for them. On it she set a small bowl of sago, a little porringer of sour milk, and a piece of brown bread. Explaining that he was confined to such slops because of his illness, H—— pushed a spoonful of the mess into Goldsmith's mouth, and the guest was obliged to eat it or go hungry. At eight o'clock H——, repeating the adage about lying down with the lamb and rising with the lark, went off to bed, leaving Noll still hungry but with no choice but to follow.

The next morning, having had enough of this life, he announced that he must be off, and H—— urged him on his way, fearing, he claimed, that Goldsmith's family might be angry if he delayed longer. But when Noll asked for the loan of a guinea, H—— complained that his illness had left him almost penniless. He added, however, that he had a solution to the problem: Noll should sell his horse and borrow one of H——'s for the trip home. Goldsmith agreed, but asked to see the horse; whereupon H—— led him to his chamber, pulled an oak stick out from under the bed, and bade him ride away. Noll seized the stick and was eying his host thoughtfully when a knock at the outside door stopped him short.

The caller, Councillor F—— G——, chatted away politely for some little time while Goldsmith inwardly fumed. Presently he invited both H—— and his guest to join him for dinner at his house, and Goldsmith accepted, since he saw no likelihood of his being fed elsewhere. The three proceeded to the Councillor's house, where they were received by his two lovely daughters and spent a pleasant afternoon. When it was time to leave, the host urged Noll to stay on for a few days; whereupon Goldsmith declared that he would not "stir a step with the damᵈ paltroon" H——. Off went H—— with a sneer, Goldsmith told Councillor G—— how abominably he had been treated, the Councillor agreed that H—— was a scoundrel, and they both adjourned to the garden with the lovely daughters to bowl. After dark the girls played the harpsichord and sang while their father wept copiously, explaining that it was the first time they had enjoyed an evening of music since his dear wife's death.

The next day Noll announced that he must leave for home, but Councillor G—— would not hear of it. So for three days he lingered in that congenial company. And when at last he tore himself away, the old man offered him all the money in his purse, to say nothing of a horse and servant. Pride, however, prevented Goldsmith from accepting more than three half-guineas.

So ran the story. Of course the Goldsmiths' reactions were explosive. They were used, surely, to improvidence, and they enjoyed a joke as much as anyone; but this second return of the prodigal was too much to bear. His mother refused at first to have anything to do with him, and he had to stay with the Hodsons at Lissoy. But eventually she consented to see him and to hear his incredible tale. According to Mrs. Hodson, the poor woman, touched in spite of herself at the story, demanded at once whether Noll had written to thank the good Councillor G—— for his kindness. And when he admitted that he had not, "then says the Mother you are an ungratefull Savage a Monster," and all present joined her in deploring his ingratitude.[7]

But Noll was undismayed; he heard them out and then proceeded to assure them that the whole story was pure fiction, designed only to amuse them. Later, however, he told Mrs. Hodson that it was absolutely true. And so the Goldsmith family—and posterity—were left to decide for themselves which was the more extraordinary, Noll's flair for involving himself in amazing predicaments or his fertile imagination.

What next? There must have been painful family conferences, with long-suffering Mrs. Goldsmith worried and exasperated, the older brother and sisters and their spouses distinctly patronizing, young Charles and Maurice and Jack goggle-eyed with curiosity, and Oliver shamefaced but trying to brazen out his embarrassment. Of course no one stopped to think that he might capitalize on his extraordinary narrative powers.

At last someone suggested that he study law. It was a genteel profession, next in line to the clergy and teaching. Then Uncle Contarine, whose daughter had persuaded him to forgive Noll's escapade, handsomely offered to contribute fifty pounds so that he could cross over to London and study at the Temple. Apparently Goldsmith raised no objections; he never could resist a chance to travel. So once again there were preparations for his departure, then farewells. And then silence.

Weeks passed, and still no word from Oliver. What had happened this time? Had he been set on by highway robbers? Or lost at sea? Or had he merely neglected to write home? Then someone just back from Dublin reported seeing him there. The family investigated and found that he was indeed there—and penniless. So the prodigal was fetched home; and this time he had no beguiling tale to tell. He was, according to Mrs. Hodson, "a hart broken dejected being." The dismal truth was that he had met a Mr. S——, a friend from Roscommon, at a coffeehouse in Dublin, and that the two of them had gambled away every shilling of Uncle Contarine's fifty pounds.

Facing his venerable uncle with such a tale was humiliating; facing his distracted mother, mortifying. Contarine eventually forgave him again, but his mother never did. From this time forth they seem never to have communicated with each other. But although he might jest about her failure to write to him in later years[8] and may even have worn only half-mourning at her death, explaining that it was for a "distant relation,"[9] he must have suffered, as any decent man would, at the thought of how deeply he had hurt her.

44

Her bitterness is understandable, for she had been sorely tried all her married life. She had undergone the embarrassment of watching her father, her uncle, and her mother exerting themselves in her behalf while her irresponsible husband looked on unperturbed. When at last they settled at Lissoy, she enjoyed a relief from tension; still Charles's improvidence—especially his ridiculous behavior in the matter of Catherine's dowry—must have worried her. Then all too soon he died and left her with three small children to raise and only the income from her parents' lease on the Pallas farm as a means of support. Naturally she looked for aid to Oliver, who had been given a university education only at her insistence. But he had failed her miserably. And as time went on and she lost first the farm at Pallas and then her eyesight[10]— and still he did no more than send regrets that he could do nothing for her—her bitterness grew ever sharper.

Meanwhile Goldsmith was acutely aware of her disapproval, and though he tried to shrug it off with a jest, it pained him. He had enough of his mother in him to make him critical of his own behavior, and his longing for approval made him wince at the thought that he had failed dismally in the eyes of the one whose approval mattered most. Although his father is reflected in several of his fictional characters, there is, significantly, no trace of his mother in his writings. That subject was apparently too painful. But he could not forget it; it rankled—and further undermined his self-confidence.

His brother Henry took him in now at the old farmhouse at Pallas. He had come full circle—back to his first home. Although he had passed his twenty-first birthday, he was apparently little better able to take care of himself than when his mother bore him. He probably helped Henry in his school, perhaps hunted or fished or strolled across the fields to Ballymahon to join the lads at George Conway's. But he was a burden that his brother could ill afford to carry, and inevitably the two quarreled. Mrs. Hodson later refused to tell the cause of their disagreement, but it is not unreasonable to suppose that after "some months" Henry, kind as he was, let slip some word of criticism which made Oliver's raw feelings smart. He knew that he was a failure. But naturally he could not bear to be told.

Once again there were family conferences—this time, presumably, not at his mother's house or at Henry's, but at the Hodsons' or Uncle Contarine's. It was there, probably, that their distinguished cousin, the Very Reverend Isaac Goldsmith, son of the late Dean of Elphin and himself Dean of Cloyne, offered a suggestion: why not give the young man a medical education? One of the girls in the family seems to have remarked casually that Noll would make a good doctor—or words to that effect. The thought, negligible enough from a girl, took on real meaning when the Dean advanced it.

Then once again the family rallied around. There had never been any question about Noll's ability. If only they could make him apply himself! And since he seemed to take kindly to the notion of practicing medicine, they determined to send him to Edinburgh to study. Uncle Contarine promised ten pounds a year, and the Hodsons and Henry Goldsmith pledged fifteen pounds between them—on condition that he would report regularly on his progress. Then there were more preparations and more farewells, now grown a bit hackneyed—and sharpened this time, no doubt, by some rather pertinent advice.

At last, probably late in September, 1752, he set out. Because of the change from the Julian to the Gregorian calendar, this was the shortest month Ireland had ever known; but for Noll Goldsmith it was one of the most delightful. He was free at last from disapproving faces, he had a pocketful of money, and he could contemplate a promising future. His heart must have been high as he crossed the country, probably to Dublin again to embark for Glasgow. This time his ship evidently sailed on schedule; or if not, he managed to withstand the allurements of the city. And soon he was on shipboard crossing the Irish Sea and exulting, no doubt, in the thought that he had finally escaped from Ireland. This was, after all, his fourth attempt.

And now that he was on his own, who could tell how far he might wander? Eventually, of course, he would return—not as the incorrigible Noll, but as Doctor Goldsmith, resplendent in the velvet coat and sword which physicians affected in those days. Then at last his brothers and sisters—perhaps even his mother— would be proud of him. It would be a glorious day. But he was in no hurry to enjoy it. The world lay all before him. His day of triumph would come in its own good time, but meanwhile he had innumerable days of freedom to savor.

Presently he disembarked in Scotland and, after a short trip overland, reached Edinburgh. The city was less than half the size of Dublin and somewhat less than half as gay; yet he was eager to see its sights, and so he found lodgings, hired a caddy to deliver his luggage, and wandered out to look his fill.

He was probably not much taken with what he saw. Edinburgh in 1752 consisted of only the Old Town, with the Castle at one end, Holyrood at the other, and the Hie Gait between with its dozens of towering medieval buildings crowded together around narrow, malodorous closes. In the eighteenth century "medieval survivals" were regarded as little short of barbaric; and to one who had seen the elegant Palladian buildings that were now springing up in Dublin, Edinburgh would have appeared distressingly primitive. Goldsmith may have been attracted to the two castles because of their historical associations; he may have stopped to see the wretched buildings which housed the University of Edinburgh; he may have admired the view from Castle Rock toward Arthur's Seat and the Firth. But then, as later, he was probably not much impressed with the Scottish scene. "Hills and rocks intercept every prospect," he complained not long afterwards.[11] For him the broad green fields of Ireland had far more appeal.

But the sheer novelty of the city held his attention until well into the evening. Only when the long northern day ended did he think of returning to the house where he had taken lodgings.— But where was it? Suddenly he realized that he had failed to make a note of the address, and he had no notion which direction to take. For a while he wandered the streets, investigating one narrow entryway after another to see if it might be the one which led to the proper house, hidden away in a close. But he found not a clue.

47

Somewhere in that labyrinth a room was waiting for him, and in it all his possessions were safely deposited. But where was it?

Then, providentially, he happened on the very caddy who had delivered his luggage earlier in the day. And soon he was back in his room, and another Goldsmith blunder had passed into history. This time, fortunately, it was his secret and the caddy's; for once he did not have to put up with the meaningful glances of a disapproving family.

He soon moved from his first lodgings; he complained later that his landlady made the Sunday roast last all week, concluding with a broth made from the bones on Saturday. So he took a room in another house which catered to medical students and where he supposedly paid twenty-two pounds per year for room, board, and laundry. He assured his relatives that living was very dear in Edinburgh and that his lodgings were the cheapest in the city.[12] But he was probably misleading them—either because he was treating himself to more comfortable living than he cared to admit, or because he was concealing his extravagances by exaggerating the cost of necessities.[13] He was determined to get from life what his temperament demanded—even at the price of honesty.

Sometime in October he enrolled in the popular anatomy classes of the first Alexander Monro, the virtual founder of the Medical School at Edinburgh. Monro, who had studied in Paris and London and at Leyden under the great Boerhaave, had raised the school in its twenty-six years of existence to a position of prominence in its field, and by the 1750's his lectures were attracting more than 150 students each year. Unimpressive-looking but affable, he lectured extemporaneously in English (rather than the usual Latin), illustrating his points by dissections of both animals and human beings. "This man," Goldsmith wrote presently to his uncle, "has broght the science he Teaches to as much perfection as it is capable of and not content with barely Teaching anatomy he launches out into all the branches of Physick where all his remarks are new and usefull. Tis he I may venture to say that draws hither such a number of students from most parts of the world Even from Russia, he is not only a skilfull Physician but an able Orator and delivers things in their nature abstruse in so Easy a manner that the most unlearn'd may, must understand him."

In other respects Goldsmith was less enthusiastic. He would have been shocked by the University buildings, for they were, even for Edinburgh, extraordinarily dilapidated. In 1768 Principal Robertson observed that a stranger seeing them for the first time might well imagine that they were almshouses. "An area which, if entire, would have formed one spacious quadrangle, is broken into three paltry divisions," he wrote, "and encompassed partly with walls which threaten destruction to the passenger, and partly with a range of low houses, several of which are now become ruinous and not habitable."[14] When James Boswell was at the University a few years after Goldsmith's stay, students cherished a tradition that one of the bulging walls would some day fall on a very learned man.

As for the faculty, Goldsmith found it disappointing, except for Monro. Although he never registered as a regular student in the Medical School, he attended Andrew Plummer's lectures in chemistry, Charles Alston's in Materia Medica, John Rutherford's in the Practice of Medicine, and Robert Whytt's in the Institutes of Medicine. And his reaction to all of them was much the same. "Plumer Professor of chymistry," he assured his uncle, "understands his busines well but delivers himself so ill that He is but little regarded, Alston Professor of Materia medica speaks much but little to the purpose, the Professors of Theory and Practice say nothing but what we may find in the books laid before us and speak that in so droneing and heavy a manner that their hearers are not many degrees in a better state than their Patients."

Even so, Noll was enjoying his new life. Its freedom was delightful—freedom not only from his family but also from the University authorities. There was no Theaker Wilder here to scrutinize his every action; in fact the Medical School had little corporate existence. There was a physic garden of sorts, students had access to the Royal Infirmary, and there were six or seven professors lecturing regularly during the term. But there were no residence requirements, no supervision of students' conduct outside of class: a young man could attend the lectures as long as he liked and present himself for examination whenever he felt prepared to do so.

Of course Goldsmith was just the man to take advantage of freedom, though he took pains to assure his relatives that he was working hard. To Dan Hodson he wrote: "At night I am in my Lodging. I have hardly any other society but a Folio book, a skeleton, my cat, and my meagre landlady. . . . I read hard which is a thing I never could do when the study was displeasing." And to his uncle Contarine: "I am almost unknown to Every body Except some few who attend the Proffesors of Physick as I do. . . . I read a science the most Pleasing in nature so that my labours are but a relaxation and I may Truly say the only thing here that gives me Pleasure." It was just as well to let them believe that he was absorbed in plain living and high thinking.

But the truth was that he was the same Noll who loved to live well and who attracted friends wherever he went. He was elected to the Medical Society in January, 1753 (apparently without submitting the usual paper) and was soon known to the students as a first-rate teller of stories and singer of songs. Among his closest friends were Lauchlan Macleane, his old friend from Trinity, Joseph Fenn Sleigh, another Irishman, and William Farr, an Englishman. And soon he was extending his acquaintance beyond the circle of his fellow-students. All in all, he was having a gayer time than he cared to admit to the relatives who were paying his expenses.

He was certainly spending his money faster than he was receiving it. A few months after his arrival in Edinburgh he was complaining that he had been sent only four guineas of the fifteen promised by his brother and sister and was therefore drawing on them for ten more. By the following May he had drawn on Contarine for six pounds rather than the five he was entitled to—and he explained that, although he had drawn earlier than he should this time, "I absolutely will not Trouble you before the Time hereafter."

In this same letter he explained that he needed money badly just then because "I was obliged to buy Every thing since I came to Scotland Shirts not Even Excepted." And a glance at a tailor's bill which has survived reveals clearly one of the drains on his budget and suggests that he had been outfitting himself for somewhat livelier company than the skeleton, the cat, and the meager landlady who supposedly shared his lonely existence. On January 24, 1753, he bought two and a half yards of "rich Sky-Blew sattin" at twelve shillings per yard, one and a half yards of "white Allapeen" at two shillings per yard, and three-quarters of a yard of "fine Sky-Blew Shalloon" at one-and-nine per yard, not to mention four yards of "Blew Durant" and one and three-quarters yards of white fustian. On February 23 he was back again, and this time he bought two and a quarter yards of "fine Priest's Grey cloth" at ten-and-six per yard, two yards of black shalloon, a pair of fine black worsted hose, and one-eighth of a yard of "rich [Black] Genoa velvett." The total bill amounted to three pounds, fifteen shillings, nine and three-quarters pence, which was duly paid "by cash in full"—but not until the following November.[15]

Meanwhile he had finished his first term at Edinburgh and, eager as usual to see all the available sights, had treated himself to a tour of the Highlands. "I set out the first day on foot," he wrote to his uncle, "but an ill naturd corn I have got on my Toe has for the future prevented that cheap method of Travelling so the second day I hired a horse of about the size of a ram and he walkd away (Trot he could not) as pensive as his master. In 3 days we reachd the Highlands." He did not care much for what he saw. "Shall I tire you with a description of this unfruitfull country," he asked his friend Bryanton in a letter written after his return, "where I must lead you over their hills all brown with heath, or their valleys scarce able to feed a rabbet? Man alone seems to be the only creature who has arrived to the naturall size in this poor soil; every part of the country presents the same dismall landscape, no grove nor brook lend their musick to cheer the stranger, or make the inhabitants forget their poverty. . . ." And later, in his *Enquiry into the Present State of Polite Learning,* he lamented the plight of travelers when they stop at an inn in Scotland: "Vile entertainment is served up, complained of, and sent down; up

51

comes worse, and that also is changed; and every change makes our wretched cheer more unsavoury."[16]

None the less he was planning to remain in Edinburgh for another winter to hear Monro's lectures, and he had decided to cross over then to Leyden to hear Bernard-Siegfried Albinus's lectures in anatomy. He assured his uncle that he had "left behind in Ireland Every thing I think worth posessing, freinds that I love and a society that pleasd while it instructed . . . who but must regret his abscence from Kilmore that Ever knew it as I did, here as recluse as the Turkish Spy at Parris?" But his homesickness was not strong enough to prevent his making plans which would carry him even farther away.

Again one must beware of taking Goldsmith's remarks to his uncle Contarine at their face value. In his letter to Bryanton he complained, to be sure, about the desolateness of the country. But at the same time he revealed a good deal of interest in the Scots whom he had met:

. . . the Gentlemen here are much better bred than among us . . .; [they] have Generally high cheek bones, and are lean, and swarthy; fond of action; Danceing in particular: tho' now I have mention'd danceing, let me say something of their balls which are very frequent here; when a stranger enters the danceing-hall he sees one end of the room taken up by the Lady's, who sit dismally in a Groupe by themselves. On the other end stand their pensive partners, that are to be, but no more intercourse between the sexes than there is between two Countrys at war. The Ladies indeed may ogle, and the Gentlemen sigh, but an embargo is laid on any closer commerce; at length, to interrupt hostility's, the Lady directeress or intendant, or what you will, pitches on a Gentleman and Lady to walk a minuet, which they perform with a formality that approaches despondence. After five or six couple have thus walked the Gauntlett, all stand up to country dance's, each gentleman furnished with a partner from the afforesaid Lady directress, so they dance much, say nothing, and thus concludes our assembly. I told a scotch Gentleman that such a profound silence resembled the ancient procession of the Roman Matrons in honour of Ceres and the scotch Gentleman told me, (and faith I beleive he was right) that I was a very great pedant for my pains: now I am come to the Lady's and to shew that I love scotland and every thing that belongs to so charming a Country Il insist on it and will give him leave to break my head that deny's it, that the scotch lady's are ten thousand times finer and handsomer than the Irish. . . . I say it and will maintain it and as a convinceing proof of (I

52

am in a very great passion) of what I assert the scotch Ladies say it themselves, but to be less serious where will you find a language so prettily become a pretty mouth as the broad scotch and the women here speak it in it's highest purity, for instance teach one of the Young Lady's at home to pronounce the Whoar wull I gong with a becomeing wideness of mouth and I'll lay my life they'l wound every hearer. . . .

To be sure, he lapsed presently into a self-pitying strain:

But how ill my Bob does it become me to ridicule woman with whom I have scarce any correspondence. There are 'tis certain handsome women here and tis as certain they have handsome men to keep them company. An ugly and a poor man is society only for himself and such society the world lets me enjoy in great abundance. Fortune has given you circumstance's and Nature a person to look charming in the Eyes of the fair world nor do I envy my Dear Bob such blessings while I may sit down and laugh at the world, and at myself—the most ridiculous object in it. But you see I am grown downright splenetick, and perhaps the fitt may continue till I receive an answer to this.

Yet the impression persists that Goldsmith's life in Edinburgh was not as dismal as he chose to imply.

This is especially true of his second winter at the University. Since he was attending only Monro's lectures, he had plenty of free time; and there are hints that he had found, as usual, congenial company. He himself later recalled that on one occasion, when he was in expansive mood, he volunteered to draw lots with any one of a party of friends to see who should treat the entire group to theater tickets. And a friend reported that "his pocket [was] frequently drained, by his too often mixing in scenes of dissipation."[17] He could not resist the charms of good company, and he longed always to focus attention on himself by indulging in a dazzling flourish—often a costly one.

It was doubtless with a similar flourish that he called at his tailor's on November 23, 1753, paid his long-standing bill, and proceeded to run up another for even gayer finery: he bought some silver hat-lace, a length of silver chain, and a plate button, and had his hat laced and relined. Then he bought a fine small hat at fourteen shillings, three and a half yards of "best sfine high Clarett-colour'd Cloth" at nineteen shillings per yard, five and a half yards of "sfine best White shallⁿ." at two shillings per yard, and four yards of white fustian at sixteen pence per yard. And two weeks later he was back again to buy another pair of fine best black worsted hose—and perhaps other items. The rest of the account is lost.[18]

Not long afterward he remarked incidentally in a letter to his uncle: "I have spent more than a fortnight every second day at the Duke of Hamilton's, but it seems they like me more as a *jester* than as a companion; so I disdained so servile an employment; 't was unworthy my calling as a physician." And in another letter which survives only in a fragment: "I shew'd my Talent and acquird the name of the facetious Irish man. I have either dined or sup'd at his Graces this fortnight every second day. . . ."

Goldsmith was indeed extending his acquaintance! Somehow or other he had penetrated to the liveliest social circles that Edinburgh offered—so elevated that he could not resist telling his relatives about his social success even while he protested that he disdained it. His family would have heard of the Duke of Hamilton. In fact the saucy young Duchess was the former Betty Gunning of Castle Coote in County Roscommon. Although Goldsmith may have met them because of his own connections in Roscommon, nothing in his letters suggests that his family knew the Duchess personally. He had probably been admitted to her circle solely because of his reputation as an entertainer. But if he had established a reputation as a facetious Irishman, he was seeing more company than he was willing to admit to his relatives.

However, he had determined to accept no more favors from the Hamiltons. It was all very well to boast of intimacy with a duke, but pride forbade that he kowtow to a man whom he could not respect. "Poverty naturally begets dependence," says the Man in Black in the twenty-seventh Letter of *The Citizen of the World,*

and I was admitted as flatterer to a great man. At first, I was surprised that the situation of a flatterer at a great man's table could be thought disagreeable: there was no great trouble in listening attentively when his lordship spoke, and laughing when he looked round for applause. This even good manners might have obliged me to perform. I found, however, too soon, that his lordship was a greater dunce than myself; and from that very moment flattery was at an end. I now rather aimed at setting him right, than at receiving his absurdities with submission. To flatter those we do not know is an easy task; but to flatter our intimate acquaintances, all whose foibles are strongly in our eye, is drudgery insupportable. Every time I now opened my lips in praise, my falsehood went to my conscience: his lordship soon perceived me to be very unfit for service; I was therefore discharged; my patron at the same time being graciously pleased to observe, that he believed I was tolerably good-natured, and had not the least harm in me.

Probably with the same experience in mind Goldsmith wrote the only poem which survives from his stay in Edinburgh, "The Clown's Reply":

John Trott was desir'd by two witty peers
To tell them the reason why asses had ears;
"An't please you," quoth John, "I'm not given to letters,
Nor dare I pretend to know more than my betters;
Howe'er, from this time I shall ne'er see your graces—
As I hope to be sav'd!—without thinking on asses."

The letter in which he told Contarine of his friendship with the Hamiltons also announced that he had "seen all that this country can exhibit in the medical way" and that he was planning to leave Edinburgh on the following February 10. He planned now, however, to go to Paris for the spring and summer to hear the lectures of Ferrein, Petit, and Duhamel du Monceau, then proceed to Leyden at the beginning of the winter session. He was, consequently, in a valedictory frame of mind and was pleased to take inventory of his achievements to date and to report that all had worked out for the best:

The circle of science which I have run through, before I undertook the study of physic, is not only useful, but absolutely necessary to the making a skilful physician. Such sciences enlarge our understanding, and sharpen our sagacity; and what is a practitioner without both but an empiric, for never yet was a disorder found entirely the same in two patients. A quack, unable to distinguish the particularities in each disease, prescribes at a venture: if he finds such a disorder may be called by the general name of fever for instance, he has a set of remedies which he applies to cure it, nor does he desist till his medicines are run out, or his patient has lost his life. But the skilful physician distinguishes the symptoms, manures the sterility of nature, or prunes her luxuriance; nor does he depend so much on the efficacy of medicines as on their proper application.

But was he seriously taking inventory? Or was he merely trying to justify himself—especially his forthcoming jaunt to the Continent on his relatives' money? Of his plan to study at Leyden he added: " 't will be proper to go, though only to have it said that we have studied in so famous an university"—a rather expensive luxury, it would seem, for one in his position. Then came a significant remark: since he would be unable to draw on Contarine once he had reached the Continent, he was drawing now for twenty pounds, "the last sum that I hope I shall ever trouble you for."

This last draft was hardly within the terms of their original agreement, and Goldsmith surely realized the fact. There is, therefore, perhaps a touch of hypocrisy in his tender but rather rhetorical farewell to his uncle: "And now, dear Sir, let me here acknowledge the humility of the station in which you found me; let me tell how I was despised by most, and hateful to myself. Poverty, hopeless poverty, was my lot, and Melancholy was beginning to make me her own. When you—but I stop here to inquire how your health goes on? . . . I wish, my dear Sir, you would make me happy by another letter before I go abroad, for there I shall hardly hear from you."

Yet Goldsmith should not be written off, even temporarily, as a hopeless hypocrite. His hypocrisy—if hypocrisy it was—was only momentary. It was the desperate subterfuge of a young man who had been repeatedly frustrated—primarily by his own foolishness, to be sure, but nonetheless frustrated—in his attempts to gain from life what he most wanted: a chance to see the world. This was his opportunity. Ostensibly he was fitting himself to be a better physician; he may even have believed implicitly that that was his goal. Yet he was still writing verse occasionally, and his letters reveal how much joy he found in observing people and characterizing them. He yearned instinctively for a wider knowledge of men and their ways; what he had seen thus far only whetted his appetite. And events were in the long run to prove his yearning, even his hypocrisy, justified. For the medical education of Oliver Goldsmith was only a pretext, the sort of pretext which artists have used since the beginning of time to enable them to achieve their real goals.

Goldsmith told Contarine that he was taking "just 33 1. to France, with good store of clothes, shirts, &c., &c." He had managed astonishingly well on the twenty-five pounds per year allowed him by his relatives—assuming that he received all of it.[19] He had not only paid for his living (allegedly at twenty-two pounds per year) and tuition at Edinburgh, but had bought almost ten pounds' worth of clothing and taken a month's holiday in the Highlands. And how? Simple arithmetic will show that he must have had some other source of income. He might, of course, have found some sort of employment in Edinburgh; but if he had done anything of the sort, he would surely have told his relatives about it when he was trying to persuade them how carefully he was husbanding their funds. No, the thought of gainful employment probably never occurred to him. Rather, he borrowed, he ran up bills—and he probably gambled. Now and later his winnings at cards may have gone a long way toward supporting him.

Just as he was about to set out for France, he found himself in new difficulties. He had gone bond for a friend named Kennedy, who defaulted on his debts. Goldsmith was, of course, held responsible, and for a while it looked as though he might spend the months ahead languishing in jail rather than seeing the sights of Europe. However, his friends Macleane and Sleigh came to his rescue, and in good time he was off on his travels, although he must have sacrificed a share of the thirty-three pounds which he had laid aside for the trip.[20]

By the time he wrote his next letter to Contarine, he was settled in Leyden. And he had a strange tale to tell of his voyage from Scotland.

He had sailed, he declared, on the *St. Andrew,* a Scottish ship bound for Bordeaux. His choice of that vessel had been determined in part by the fact that six other young men had taken passage for the same voyage. They proved to be affable Scots, and when their ship put in at Newcastle-on-Tyne because of rough weather, he and his new friends went ashore to see the town. That evening,

while they were whiling away the time in a tavern, twelve grena-
diers and a sergeant burst in upon them, brandished their weapons,
and arrested them all in the King's name. Then Goldsmith learned
that his companions were in the service of the King of France and
had been in Scotland to enlist volunteers for the French army.

Although he protested that he was innocent of the charges
brought against the group, he remained in prison two weeks before friends in Edinburgh were able to secure his release. By that
time the *St. Andrew* had sailed away without him. Yet the fiasco
proved, he argued, to be a godsend. "Hear how providence inter-
posd in my Favour," he wrote to Contarine. "The ship . . . was
wreck'd at the mouth of the Graronne [*sic*] and every one of the
crew were drownd."

Noll had not lost his knack for getting himself involved in
comic opera situations—or, more probably, for imagining them.
This time he was doubtless trying to conceal from his uncle some
scrape or other,[21] or at least to account for his being in Leyden
rather than at Paris. When he was free to leave Newcastle, he
claimed, the only available ship had been bound for Rotterdam;
so he had taken passage on it. And soon he had sailed into the
harbor at Rotterdam and gazed down wonderingly into the broad,
fruitful expanse of land "embosom'd in the deep."

He was delighted with Holland from the outset. "Nothing
can Equall its beauty," he assured Contarine. "Wherever I turn
my Eye fine houses, elegant gardens, statues, grottoes, vistas
present themselves, but enter their Towns and you are charmd
beyond description. No, nothing can be more clean or beautifull."
And later, in *The Traveller,* he fondly recalled that "amphibious
world" with its

> slow canal, the yellow-blossom'd vale,
> The willow-tufted bank, the gliding sail,
> The crowded mart, the cultivated plain. . . .

The cleanliness and spaciousness were refreshing after his months
in dirty, crowded Edinburgh. Leyden, where he settled, was especially handsome. The broad streets, shaded by towering trees,
and the canals, with their handsome stone bridges, gave an im-

pression which all visitors admired. It was the sort of country that Goldsmith most liked—reminiscent of Ireland, and yet delightfully different!

By May 6 he was living at the house of a Madame de Allion and attending lectures at the University. Although again he did not register officially as a student,[22] he probably wore a sword (rather than the usual academic gown) like the regularly enrolled students, and frequented the Indian Cabinet and the gallery of the famous physic garden, which contained such oddities as a hippopotamus, a winged cat, and a mermaid's hand. He was listening to Albinus's lectures in anatomy in the octagonal anatomy hall with its urns and mummies and skeletons—that of the famous John of Leyden among others. But he was not much taken with what he heard there. "Physick is by no means Taught here so well as in Edinburgh . . .," he wrote to Contarine, "and the Professors [are] so very Lazy . . . that [British students] dont much care to come hither."[23] The one lecturer whom he approved of was the Professor of Botany, Jerome-David Gaub, or Gaubius, who had succeeded Boerhaave in 1729. In *Polite Learning* Goldsmith recorded a curious conversation with Gaubius, who wondered why English students now went to the University of Edinburgh rather than to Leyden—and concluded that as long as the professors at Edinburgh were poorly paid (and presumably, therefore, devoted to their work), Leyden could not hope to attract Englishmen.

Goldsmith missed the company of his countrymen in Leyden. He complained that there were only three or four British students in the entire university, and since he knew little or no Dutch, his social circle must have been small. What he saw of the Dutchmen themselves, however, made him not particularly eager to know them better. His impressions here were the reverse of what they had been in Scotland. "There," he wrote to his uncle, "you might see a well dresd Dutchess issuing from a dirty close and here a dirty Dutchman inhabiting a Palace. The Scotch may be compard to a Tulip planted in dung but I never see a dutch man in his own house, but I think of a magnificent Egyptian Temple dedicated to an ox." And with his unfailing ability to characterize, he wrote:

The modern dutch man is quite a different creature from him of former times, he in every thing imitates a French man but in his easy disingagd air which is the result of keeping polite company. The dutch man is vastly ceremonious and is perhaps exactly what a French man might have been in the reign of Lewis the 14th. Such are the better bred but the downright Hollander is one of the oddest figures in Nature. Upon a head of lank hair he wears a half cock'd Narrow leav'd hat lacd with black ribbon, no coat but seven waistcoats and nine pairs of breeches so that his hips reach almost up to his arm pits. This well cloathd vegetable is now fit to see company or make love but what a pleasing creature is the object of his apetite, why she wears a large friez cap with a deal of flanders lace and for every pair of breeches he carries she puts on two petticoats. Is it not surprising how things shoud ever come close enough to make it a match? When I spoke of love I was to be understood not in a—in short I was not to be understood at all. A Dutch Lady burns nothing about her Phlegmatick admirer but his Tobacco. You must know S^r every woman carries in her hand a Stove with coals in it which when she sits she snugs under her petticoats, and at this chimney Dozing Strephon lights his pipe. I take it that this continuall smoaking is what gives the man the ruddy healthfull complexion he generally wears by draining his superfluous moisture, while the woman depriv'd of this amusement overflows with such visciditys as teint the complexion and gives that paleness of visage which Low fenny grounds and moist air conspire to cause. A dutch woman and a Scotch will well bear an oposition. The one is pale & fat and the other lean and ruddy. The one walks as if she were stradling after a go cart and the other takes too Masculine a stride. . . .

Their pleasures here are very dull tho very various. You may smoak, you may doze: you may go to the Italian comedy, as good an amusement as either of the former. This entertainment always brings in Harlequin who is generally a Magician and in consequence of his Diabolicall art performs a thousand Tricks on the rest of the persons of the drama who are all fools. I have seen the pit in a roar of laughter at his humour when with his sword he Touches the glass another was drinking from. 'Twas not his face they laughd at for that was maskd. They must have seen something vastly queer in the wooden sword that neither I nor you S^r were you there cou'd see. In winter, when their cannalls are frozen, every house is forsaken and all People are on the ice. Sleds drawn by horses and skating are at that time the reigning amusements. They have boats here that slide on the ice and are driven by the winds. When they spread all their sails they go more than a mile and an half a minite. Their motion is so rapid that the Eye can scarce accompany them. Their ordinary manner of Travelling is very cheap and very convenient. They sail in coverd boats drawn by horses and in these you are sure to meet people of all nations. Here the Dutch slumber, the

French chatter and the English play cards. Any man who likes company may have them to his Taste. For my part I generally detachd myself from all society and was wholy Taken up in observing the face of the country. . . .[24]

He complained that "all nescsarys" were "extreamly Dear" and concluded his letter with the hope that he might be back in Ireland by the following March. But it is perfectly apparent that he was enjoying his stay,—that his sense of humor was tickled by the stolid Dutch. It was just as well, though, not to let one's financial sponsors think that this sojourn on the Continent was merely a lark.

Ellis, one of the British students at Leyden, said later that Goldsmith was, as might be expected, often short of money and that he replenished his supply by three means: teaching English,[25] borrowing, and gambling.[26] On one occasion, Ellis claimed, Goldsmith won a sizable sum, which he carried in triumph to Ellis's room the following morning. Ellis advised him to stop gambling immediately and to save his winnings to pay for completing his studies. Goldsmith agreed wholeheartedly with the plan—but gambled every penny of his profits away soon afterward and returned to Ellis for a loan.

Yet he set out in the late winter or early spring of 1755, not for Ireland, as he had suggested to Contarine that he would, but to Paris—ostensibly to complete his medical training with some lectures at the Sorbonne. But perhaps already he had another scheme in mind. Shortly before his arrival at Leyden the famous Danish author Ludvig Holberg died, and the literate public had' been reminded of his extraordinary travels through Europe as a young man. "Without money, recommendations, or friends," Goldsmith wrote later in *Polite Learning,* "he undertook to set out upon his travels, and make the tour of Europe on foot. A good voice, and a trifling skill in music, were the only finances he had to support an undertaking so extensive; so he travelled by day, and at night sung at the doors of peasants' houses to get himself a lodging." And the sequel? "He was honoured with nobility, and enriched by the bounty of the king; so that a life begun in contempt and penury ended in opulence and esteem."[27]

"A good voice and a trifling skill in music"? Goldsmith had both. For all his hardships he had apparently managed to keep his flute, which had gained friends for him in Ireland and Scotland and probably in Holland too—music knows no barriers of language. And he would certainly welcome the "opulence and esteem" which Holberg had eventually won. Moreover, though still a student of medicine, he was becoming more and more interested in the study of mankind. Consider the short shrift he gives his professors in his letters to Contarine as compared with his detailed accounts of the ordinary Scots and Dutchmen whom he saw. He had, surely, the ideal temperament for a philosophic vagabond.

And so he set out with one clean shirt and a small sum of money, borrowed from the accommodating Ellis. He would travel south to Paris. There he would hear some lectures, to be sure, but he would also have a chance to observe the life of a really large city—four or five times the size of Dublin—a city which was, beyond question, the very center of the civilized world. But before he left Leyden he came upon a nurseryman's shop where some especially fine tulip bulbs were for sale. And remembering his uncle Contarine's fondness for unusual flowers—and perhaps hoping to rid his conscience of any pangs caused by this latest junket—he ordered a package of the bulbs sent to his benefactor, spent his last shilling to pay the bill, and marched cheerfully forth toward Paris.

At first, travel along the Lowland countryside was pleasant and easy. He perhaps stopped at Louvain to hear a few lectures at the University there,[28] but soon he was pushing out across Flanders to Antwerp, gradually losing the sense of well-being that Holland had induced. "In Rotterdam," he wrote in *The Bee,* No. V, "you may go through eight or ten streets without finding a public-house. In Antwerp, almost every second house seems an alehouse. In the one city, all wears the appearance of happiness and warm affluence; in the other, the young fellows walk about the streets in shabby finery, their fathers sit at the door darning or knitting stockings, while their ports are filled with dunghills." Yet, philosophic vagabond that he was, he noticed that it was the mind of man, rather than his external circumstances, that determined his happiness. It was in Flanders that he saw a slave, described in another essay in *The Bee,* No. II, who was "maimed, deformed, and chained; obliged to toil from the appearance of day till nightfall, and condemned to this for life; yet, with all these circumstances of apparent wretchedness, he sung, would have danced but that he wanted a leg, and appeared the merriest, happiest man of all the garrison. What a practical philosopher was here! a happy constitution supplied philosophy, and though seemingly destitute of wisdom, he was really wise."

Goldsmith had long suspected that one could learn more from travel than from books or lectures. It was difficult, granted, to persuade one's family of the notion; a man might even have to deceive them a bit, to take advantage of their generosity, to seem to be studying human anatomy when he was actually studying human nature. But subterfuges had been used—successfully. And now that he was free to travel, now that he could observe the differences in men (and their essential similarity) and make comparisons, he was finding philosophic vagabondage well worth the discomfort of a few chilly nights in the open or an occasional slender meal. The education of Oliver Goldsmith was not yet complete, but it was progressing far more rapidly than when he had been at Trinity College agonizing over his Burgersdicius.

From Antwerp he went on to Brussels, famous then for its beauty and its cheap living, then to Maestricht, where he evidently stopped to admire the stone quarry "lighted up with torches." And soon he was in France, "gay, sprightly land of mirth and social ease," as he called it in *The Traveller.* His knowledge of the language was an asset here, and his clownish appearance must have won him friends. Soon he was crossing the fields toward Paris, then a walled city, doubtless holding his nose at the stench which issued from it constantly.

Despite its stench and its filth and countless other unpleasant features, Paris was bound to delight him: it was busy and gay in a manner which harmonized with his own animated disposition. Although the streets were so muddy that wayfarers were obliged to wear black clothing, there were amusements by day and night for all tastes and all pocketbooks: the Palais Royale, which contained the world's finest collection of paintings; the Jardins des Tuileries (open free to all but servants or members of the humblest classes), where ladies and gentlemen went to look and be looked at; and theaters, churches, libraries, promenades—all thronging with people from all over the civilized world. Among others there were Englishmen and Irishmen and Scots; and Goldsmith soon found a circle of convivial creatures like himself. He attended some lectures at the University; but, significantly enough, he did not record whether he heard Ferrein or Petit or Duhamel du Monceau, the professors whose reputations had supposedly attracted him to Paris; rather, he mentioned later only Professor G. F. Rouelle, the popular lecturer in chemistry whose lectures were so fashionable that society ladies and their voluminous skirts filled the hall and left no room for the students. "I have seen as bright a circle of beauty at the chemical lectures of Rouelle," he wrote in *Polite Learning,* "as gracing the court of Versailles"—though he certainly saw little of the court at Versailles. Like George Primrose in *The Vicar of Wakefield* he probably admired all the splendid mansions of the rich and the great—but from the outside only. He did, however, manage to attend the theater occasionally; at least he was later to describe the beauty of the actress Mademoiselle Clairon and the skill of a comedian playing in *The Miser* and *The Mock Doctor*.[29] And he did more than merely divert himself; he was still the philosophic vagabond, observing and reflecting on what he saw about him. In his walks through the environs of Paris he was struck by the abundance of wild game; it was, he believed, "a badge of the slavery of the people" that there should be so many fine birds at large while so many men went hungry. In *Animated Nature* he prophesied that some day these enslaved people would overthrow their oppressors.

Meanwhile how was he supporting himself? He could not have made his way around Paris singing for his supper, and there were far too many indigent Englishmen there to offer him much opportunity for giving English lessons. Probably he depended in large part on the gentlemanly dodges of borrowing and gambling. In 1757, in a letter to Dan Hodson, he remarked unashamedly that "at Present there is hardly a Kingdom in Europe in which I am not a debtor."[30] The hints on the techniques of genteel borrowing in the third issue of *The Bee* may well have been drawn in part from his own experience.

Eventually he is supposed to have joined a young Englishman setting out on his travels, and to have gone with him down to Strasbourg, across the Rhine, and, after a brief stay in Germany, on into Switzerland. He was still observing and reflecting—wondering at the clear speech of French parrots and deciding that it was not due to any peculiarity of the language but to the inordinate amount of time which their owners spent in training them; marveling at the clouds of ephemerae that gathered near sunset for three days during the summer along the Rhine and the Seine; admiring the Hainault scythe used in Germany and comparing it favorably with the English sickle; listening in at the Germans' "disputes at gradation"; viewing the falls of the Schaffhausen while they were frozen in columns; stopping off at Basle and Berne and Geneva.

Perhaps he had been traveling by coach all this time and lodging at inns. But if so, he evidently concluded that his earlier method of travel was preferable.[31] English travelers in the eighteenth century never ceased to complain about the hardships which they endured on the Continent: the inedible food, the uncomfortable beds, the vermin (much larger in France and Italy than the English variety, Goldsmith insisted in *Animated Nature*). At all events he seems to have parted from his English friend at Geneva and to have set off early in the summer of 1755 to explore the Alps by himself.

There he idled and allowed himself time to digest his impressions of the trip thus far. He was still alert to all about him and was apparently far better pleased with the Alps than most of his contemporaries, who shunned them except when obliged to make their way from France down into Italy. In *Animated Nature* he boasted that he had eaten "a very savoury dinner on the Alps" and described flushing woodcocks on Mount Jura and gazing timorously down into the "immeasurable gulf" of a chasm. He was astonished to see sheep actually following the sound of a shepherd's pipe. But more significantly, he was reflecting on what he had seen thus far on his trip and reducing his reflections to verse:

E'en now, where Alpine solitudes ascend,
I sit me down a pensive hour to spend;
And, plac'd on high above the storm's career,
Look downward where a hundred realms appear;
Lakes, forests, cities, plains extending wide,
The pomp of kings, the shepherd's humbler pride. . . .

No vernal blooms their torpid rocks array,
But winter ling'ring chills the lap of May;
No zephyr fondly sues the mountain's breast,
But meteors glare, and stormy glooms invest.

And he sent off his scribblings proudly to his "earliest friend," his brother Henry in Ireland, to whom the completed poem *The Traveller* would some day be dedicated.

From Switzerland he sauntered down to Piedmont and into Padua, where he remained for six months.[32] While there, he was reduced to new depths of penury, and in desperation wrote to Dan Hodson asking him to send the money to carry him back to Ireland.—Imagine the reception his letter received: Noll had somehow got himself down into Italy, and now he wanted his fare home! Nonetheless Hodson canvassed the family and sent him some money; but it never arrived.[33] Destitute as he was, he continued his travels through the northern part of the peninsula— he might never again have the chance to see this part of the world. He visited Venice, Verona, Florence, and perhaps Milan and Mantua; he viewed "Campania's plain forsaken" and was rebuffed when he begged a night's lodging from a "rude Carinthian boor"; and he marveled at the fact that man seemed to be "the only growth that dwindles" in this lush land.

Toward the end of 1755 he headed north again and traveled up across France toward the seacoast. He could not afford to linger, because war between France and England was imminent. Yet his senses were still awake to any novelty: he measured the depth of the "bed of black earth" over the Roman way in Burgundy; he studied the floating bee-houses in France and Piedmont and wondered why the English had never copied them; he mused at the sight of men knitting socks in provincial fields while their wives worked the fields; he investigated a method of making vinegar without fermentation; he paused to examine the crude shrines to the Virgin along the road and, if we are to believe his statement, unceremoniously lighted his pipe from the votive lamps beneath; and he was certainly jolted, as nearly all of Europe was, on November 1, when the unforgettable earthquake shook Lisbon to ruins.

Meanwhile he provided for himself as best he could: "leading the sportive choir With tuneless pipe"; stopping off at monasteries whenever he could find a fellow-Irishman in the community; debating in Latin for certain standing prizes available in Continental universities—or claiming the prize if no one accepted his challenge; and again probably borrowing from or gambling with the "Englishmen . . . leading a life of continued debauchery" whom a traveler could find "in all the great towns of Europe."[34] He was indeed a vagabond, following no prescribed plan, but seizing on whatever shift offered itself. And so he went, northward and westward, until at last he reached the coast. There he somehow managed to secure passage to England.

Thus at last the education of Oliver Goldsmith reached the end of its protracted major phase. The details of this part of it are obscure and will probably always remain so. He wrote a letter describing his travels to a Dr. Radcliff at Trinity College, but it was lost when the Doctor's house was burned. He also wrote letters to his brother Henry from Switzerland, to Dan Hodson from Padua, and to the Lawders from Leyden, Louvain, and Rouen; but they too have disappeared. There remain, then, only the scattered hints in his later works as a basis for reconstruction of his wanderyears.

But in truth the details are unimportant. Although it would be interesting to know what Oliver Goldsmith said or did on, say, June 5, 1754, or September 23, 1755, the loss of such information is not serious. What is important can be clearly inferred from his later writings: that on those days and every other day while he was traveling through Europe, he was observing, comparing, reflecting, reaching certain conclusions. He was older than the usual traveler on the Grand Tour and better able to digest what he saw; he was, moreover, moving more slowly, giving himself more of a chance to observe and reflect. "A man who is whirled through Europe in a post-chaise, and the pilgrim who walks the grand tour on foot," he declared in *Polite Learning,* "will form very different conclusions. *Haud inexpertus loquor.*"[35]

By the time he embarked at last for England he had formulated certain principles which would guide his actions and his thinking as long as he lived. Above all, his experience with men of all kinds had taught him a basic tolerance: tolerance for Catholics or Presbyterians, for Frenchmen or Scots, for Hanoverians or Jacobites, for Whigs or Tories, for monarchists or democrats, for women or children—yes, even for dogs or cats. He had seen enough of life, moreover, to know that, just as no man or no party is thoroughly good or thoroughly bad, so too there is no perfect government or religion—but that there are many which contain varying elements of goodness. Observation had convinced him, however, that the government and religion into which he had, happily, been born were as good as any—and better than most.

Thus he was presently able to show—in his thinking, if not in his actions—a measure of self-confidence which had been sorely lacking in the frustrated young man who had left Ireland for Edinburgh in 1752. He had needed a respite from the barbs of those relatives who—with perfect justice—had been angered by his failure to settle himself in life. He had needed freedom, a chance to organize his thoughts and set his sights. To be sure, the old scars were not fully healed; they would bleed again whenever he found himself the subject of mockery or scorn. But at least he had enjoyed a respite. And it had been worth all Uncle Contarine's money and his own discomfort.

George Primrose complained in *The Vicar of Wakefield* that he had gained very little from his travels, and in *Polite Learning* Goldsmith considered the relative merits of traveling and remaining at home as means of education and decided that, although a man could learn more of the world by travel, he could learn more of human nature at home—that travel gave a youth "easy address," helped him to shake off national prejudices, and taught him to accept the peculiarities of other nationalities without ridicule, but that the time consumed in travel might better be spent at home. And as he set out across the Channel and saw the coast of France receding behind him, he may well have been convinced that the only lesson he had gained from his travels was a purely negative one: that travel in itself does not make for happiness. He could boast of having seen innumerable sights—"lakes, forests, cities, plains," castles, cathedrals, libraries, museums—but they had added not a whit to his store of wisdom. As for the fund of odd bits of information which he had accumulated, they had no practical value; they would add nothing to his skill as a physician.

What he did not know was that across the Channel there was a growing interest in just such materials as he had stored up. Cosmopolitanism was in fashion in England, and readers were eager to learn more about the world beyond their own shores. And a man who had traveled widely, who had an eye for significant detail, and who could express himself entertainingly might hope to make a more brilliant and lasting name for himself than any physician, however skilled, could hope to achieve.

Chapter IV
Tinker? Tailor?
(1756-1759)

NOLL Goldsmith was a singularly unprepossessing figure as he stepped ashore in Dover on or about February 1, 1756. The Grand Tour of Europe, which was supposed to add the final polish to a young man of the world, had left him haggard and tattered. He looked more the clown than ever. And while his clownish appearance might endear him to Frenchmen and Italians, it and his broad Irish brogue were hardly calculated to win him friends among the English.

His wisest course would undoubtedly have been to make his way across the country and take the first ship home to Ireland. Surely it was not want of cash which prevented his doing so, for he had long since proved himself a master of the art of making his way in strange places without funds. No, there were more formidable barriers—mental barriers. His relatives had failed to reply to any of his letters from the Continent; they had even (or so he thought) ignored his frantic appeal for money when he was destitute in Italy. Apparently they had written him off as incorrigible; and he had no desire to confirm their estimate of him by returning to Ireland ragged and penniless. He knew from painful experience how humiliating that could be.

And so he lingered in England. He may have served briefly as an apothecary in a country town, and he seems to have been an usher in a school for boys.[1] But he bungled his chances of success there by applying for the position under a false name and, when he was asked for a reference, naming Dr. Radcliff, under whom he had studied at Trinity College. Then, too late, he realized that Radcliff could hardly recommend a man whose name he had never heard. So he dispatched a letter to him at once, admitting his duplicity and begging him to ignore the schoolmaster's letter.[2] And presently he was on his way—with few regrets. There seems to be at least a hint of autobiography in his remark, three years later, in *The Bee,* No. VI: "Every trick is played upon the usher; the oddity of his manners, his dress, or his language, is a fund of eternal ridicule; the master himself, now and then, cannot avoid joining in the laugh; and the poor wretch, eternally resenting this ill-usage, seems to live in a state of war with all the family."[3]

In good time he reached London, where his first reaction was probably not unlike that of Lien Chi Altangi, the philosophical traveler from China, who wrote in the second Letter of *The Citizen of the World:*

> Judge, then, how great is my disappointment on entering London, to see no signs of that opulence so much talked of abroad; wherever I turn, I am presented with a gloomy solemnity in the houses, the streets, and the inhabitants; . . . in the midst of their pavements a great lazy puddle moves muddily along; heavily-laden machines, with wheels of unwieldy thickness, crowd up every passage; so that a stranger, instead of finding time for observation, is often happy if he has time to escape being crushed to pieces. . . .
>
> From [the plainness of] their buildings, and from the dismal looks of the inhabitants, I am induced to conclude that the nation is actually poor; and that, like the Persians, they make a splendid figure every where but at home. The proverb of Xixofou is, that a man's riches may be seen in his eyes; if we judge of the English by this rule, there is not a poorer nation under the sun.

In certain sections of the new West End, conditions were better. But Goldsmith did not live in the West End; probably he lived, as he later phrased it, "among the beggars in Axe Lane." There life was hazardous, squalid, brutal.

To make matters worse, Londoners, like all Englishmen at the beginning of the year 1756, were feeling uncommonly depressed by the outbreak of the war with France (later to be known as the Seven Years' War). The treaty of Aix-la-Chapelle, greeted enthusiastically in 1748 by a people weary of strife, had proved deceptive. Now the fighting with the French, which had been so costly in America, was being extended to Europe and Asia. And who would bear the burden of the war? The common people, of course. And what did they care who enjoyed the balance of power in Europe or the control of Nova Scotia?

Certainly Noll Goldsmith did not care at this point. He had more immediate problems to solve. "You may Easily imagine what difficulties I had to encounter, left as I was without Friends, recommendations, money, or impudence [influence?]," he wrote later to Dan Hodson; "and that in a Country where my being born an Irishman was sufficient to keep me unemploy'd. Manny in such circumstances would have had recourse to the Friar's cord, or suicide's halter. But with all my follies I had principle to resist the one, and resolution to combat the other."[4] Eventually he was hired as an assistant in an apothecary's shop supposedly kept by a man named Jacob at the corner of Monument (or Bell) Yard on Fish Street Hill. It was a strange situation for a Bachelor of Arts with a remarkable record of foreign travel and study. But at least it was better than submitting to the exasperation of his relatives or the mockery of contemptuous pupils.

Presently he heard that Joseph Fenn Sleigh, who had helped him out of some of his scrapes in Edinburgh, was in London. So he dressed himself in his sorry best and went to call on his old friend. At first Sleigh did not recognize him; meager living had brought great changes in Goldsmith in the course of his two years on the Continent. But once he had identified himself, Sleigh made him welcome and set to work to find him a situation worthy of his training. It was probably now, if ever, that Goldsmith applied for and received his degree in medicine from Trinity College,[5] and soon he was established as a physician in Bankside, across the Thames in Southwark. But his troubles were not yet over: although he attracted plenty of patients, he received few fees. People who could afford to pay for medical care were not disposed to call in an unprepossessing Irishman with a thick brogue.

Goldsmith continued, however, to scrape along as best he could, trying always to maintain an appearance of prosperity that befitted his new dignity. He may have supplemented his income by working as a "corrector of the press" in the printing shop of Samuel Richardson in Salisbury Court—a job which he reportedly secured through a patient who worked in the shop.[6] There he is said to have met, among others, Edward Young, the aged author

72

of *Night Thoughts,* and to have urged Richardson, in vain, to publish a tragedy which Young had submitted to him.

Young was probably the "old poet" cited in Goldsmith's *Polite Learning,* who claimed that in bygone days, when noblemen patronized the arts enthusiastically, "a dinner with his lordship has procured him invitations for the whole week following—that an airing in his patron's chariot has supplied him with a citizen's coach on every future occasion."[7] But those days were past; authors in London in the 'fifties were, it seemed, forgotten men. They were dependent now on the booksellers, who were primarily interested in their own profit. Yet though writing might not provide a respectable income of itself, it could serve to supplement the slender living which Noll Goldsmith was making as a physician. In fact William Farr, another acquaintance from Edinburgh days, reported later that while he was in London in 1756 Goldsmith called on him "dressed in a rusty full-trimmed black suit, with his pockets full of papers" which proved to be the manuscript of part of a tragedy that Richardson was considering for publication.

"Nothing more apt to introduce us to the gates of the muses than Poverty," Goldsmith wrote in the following year to Dan Hodson. And as yet writing was, so far as he was concerned, only a means to the end of financial solvency. For that he was willing to undertake any project. One scheme he was considering, he told Farr, was a journey to the Holy Land to decipher the inscriptions on the so-called Written Mountains. To be sure, he knew no Arabic, but that deficiency could be quickly supplied. What attracted him was the princely sum of three hundred pounds a year which had been set aside for whoever undertook the task.

Meanwhile he continued his practice of medicine and exercised his "knack at hoping." If he could have pocketed his pride and returned to Ireland, he might have counted on developing a flourishing practice in any one of half a dozen towns where his family was known. But a threadbare existence in England was still preferable to prosperity in Ireland, and so he stayed on in London. Sir Joshua Reynolds said that Goldsmith called on his patients in a patched coat—and concealed the patch, throughout his consultation, by holding his hat over it. When his college

73

friend, John Beatty, visited him sometime before the end of 1756, he appeared in a green and gold suit and announced that he was practicing medicine and "doing very well." But Beatty could see for himself that Goldsmith's suit was old, the gold trimming tarnished, and his linen downright dirty. Poor Noll's ruse was not hard to penetrate.

Toward the end of the year he happened on another acquaintance, a young man named Milner, who had been a fellow-student at Edinburgh. His father, the Reverend John Milner, headmaster of a Presbyterian school for boys at Peckham, in Surrey, was ailing, and the son was looking for someone to take charge of the school for a few months. Why he supposed Goldsmith would be fitted for such a position is hard to imagine; perhaps he thought Noll's record of travel and foreign study would dazzle prospective patrons. At all events he offered him the position, and Goldsmith accepted it. Not that he wanted to teach school for the rest of his days; but he could not afford to turn down an offer which promised even a few months of steady income. Moreover, the Reverend Mr. Milner agreed to use his influence with a Mr. Jones, a Director of the East India Company, to secure Noll an appointment as a physician in the East Indian service.

So off he went to Peckham. And although he probably had misgivings about his job—since Milner's was a "classical" school which offered just the sort of curriculum that he deplored—he proved to be an unforgettable teacher. He entertained the boys with his tales and his flute; he joined in their sports, played tricks on them, and even treated them to sweets. Many years later when he met one of his "old boys," Samuel Bishop, on a London street and Bishop introduced his new wife, Goldsmith allegedly cried: "Come, my boy, I am delighted to see you; I must treat you to something; what shall it be? will you have some apples?" His salary was so taxed by his generosity to the students—and probably to any poor beggars in the neighborhood of Peckham—that he often had to ask for advances. And when Mrs. Milner suggested that she take care of his money as she did the boys', he replied genially, "In truth, Madam, there is equal need."

Yet much as they enjoyed his eccentricities, the students hardly respected him: they mocked his clumsiness in sports, took advantage of his lax discipline, and were, on occasion, impertinent. For example, once when he was discussing his love of music and referred to it as "a gentlemanlike acquirement," an insolent boy remarked, "Surely *you* do not consider yourself a gentleman." Goldsmith's temper flared, and he gave the boy a thrashing.[8] But he could not erase the insult or its implications: even among these callow adolescents he cut a ridiculous figure.

Characteristically, he seems to have found solace in the company of a servant named William, whom he made the butt of his jokes. On one occasion he molded a piece of Cheshire cheese into the shape of a candle and, giving William a real candle which resembled it, challenged him to see which of the two could eat his candle first. William watched dumbfounded while Goldsmith bit off piece after piece and swallowed them, with appropriate grimaces. When at last he had nearly finished, William popped the real candle into his mouth and bolted it down, only to learn how he had been duped. Another time Goldsmith forged a letter from William's sweetheart in Yorkshire and read it to the poor fellow, claiming that he had found it reprinted in a newspaper. Of course William was outraged—until Goldsmith admitted his deceit and advised him, as a friend, to forget the girl, since she had not troubled to write to him.[9]

On the whole his stay at Peckham seems to have been agreeable. He was secure for the present, and his future had never been brighter. He even took advantage of his favorable situation to report at last to his family. The letter has not survived, but it was probably pure boasting: he was acting headmaster of a school for young gentlemen, but would presently return to London to resume his medical practice—only temporarily, for soon he must set out for India and a comfortable appointment there. He was to learn that bragging of prosperity may yield annoying results.

When he finished his term at Milner's school, his Indian appointment was still not confirmed. But he had happened on another promising situation. At Milner's house he had met Ralph Griffiths, bookseller and proprietor of the *Monthly Review;* and

Griffiths had been shrewd enough to realize that a man of Gold-smith's experiences as student, traveler, and physician could be of considerable value on the staff of a critical journal like the *Monthly,* which undertook to review books on all subjects. Accordingly, he offered him a position as reviewer, paying him, in addition to his room and board, a salary of one hundred pounds a year. Of course Goldsmith accepted.

Soon he was installed in quarters above Griffiths' shop at the Sign of the Dunciad on Paternoster Row. He plunged into his work at once, writing steadily from nine until two every day in his eagerness to please his employer. In the *Monthly Review* for April, 1757, he was represented by only one brief review of a forgotten satire called *The Rival Politicians* and a translation of a French review of Mallet's *Remains of the Mythology and Poetry of the Celtes.*[10] But in May he reviewed four books, one of them a treatise in Latin on the plants of Piedmont, contributed a column of "literary news," and wrote twenty-three brief accounts of new books considered not important enough for fuller treatment.[11]

Of the three English books reviewed in detail, one was John Home's tragedy *Douglas;* another, by Goldsmith's former schoolmate Edmund Burke, was *A Philosophical Enquiry into the Origin of our Ideas of the Sublime and Beautiful.* Of the first he had little good to say: he declared that it had been overpraised by David Hume and others, and that it fell short of excellence not only in minor details but also in "poetic fire, elegance, or the heightenings of pathetic distress." Toward the second he was better disposed, and although he criticized Burke for "proceeding on principles not sufficiently established" and questioned some of his premises, he granted that the essay revealed sagacity, learning, even genius.[12]

But what is important is not what Goldsmith thought of the work of John Home or Edmund Burke, but the surprisingly self-assured tone in which he expressed himself. The young man who had seemed so unable to manage himself could manage his pen with surprising confidence; the clown who won disdain, even from schoolboys, could command respect when he hid his absurd person behind the printed page. He was, clearly, aware of his responsibilities as a literary critic and was approaching his new task conscientiously. Reviewing books had become more than a stopgap before he sailed off to India. "To direct our taste," he wrote, "and conduct the poet up to perfection, has ever been the true critic's province." Or again: "Poems, like buildings, have their point of view, and too near a situation gives but a partial conception of the whole." Here was no mischievous reviewer delighting, as did so many of his fellows, in his power to make or ruin reputations; he was a serious critic aware of his obligations to readers and writers alike. He who had been a vagabond little more than a year before, who had made rather ineffectual shifts to support himself as physician or teacher since then, seemed suddenly to have found his vocation.

But he soon lost his enthusiasm for his new occupation. The May issue of the *Monthly* contained the best work he ever did for the magazine. In June he wrote reviews of five historical books (including Smollett's *Complete History of England*) and nine notices of minor works. But in none of them was his criticism as pointed as in the May issue; and in the review of Smollett he seems unnecessarily captious, at least from hindsight: almost every fault he found in Smollett's work could be found as easily in his own later histories. By this time, no doubt, Goldsmith was reading and writing so rapidly that he had little time to digest his opinions.

Moreover, he was growing increasingly disgruntled. He later complained that both Griffiths and his wife supervised his work, that they sought quantity rather than quality, and that they presumed to revise his reviews without consulting him. Yet he remained with Griffiths for two more months, during which time he wrote only one review of any distinction. He depended more and more on summaries and excerpts, less and less on critical evaluation—partly no doubt because the books reviewed did not merit very serious consideration, but primarily because he had lost all sense of satisfaction in his task.

The one exception was his review of Thomas Gray's *Odes* in the August issue. Here he had a subject worthy of his best efforts. He had long dabbled in verse; now, apparently, he was giving serious thought to the art of poetry. He was concerned not only with technical details (such as the difficulty of writing odes in rhyme) but also with the content and purpose of poetry: "We cannot . . . without some regret behold those talents so capable of giving pleasure to all, exerted in efforts that, at best, can amuse only the few; we cannot behold this rising poet seeking fame among the learned, without hinting to him the same advice that Isocrates used to give to his scholars: *'study the people.'*" And presently: "Such a genius as Mr. Gray might give greater pleasure, and acquire a larger portion of fame, if, instead of being an imitator, he did justice to his talents, and ventured to be more an original." Goldsmith's emphasis on giving pleasure, on appealing to the people, on seeking originality, were not at all in the tradition of contemporary criticism. He was thinking for himself; and his concern with what literature should be and do points toward an inevitable inference: that he was tempted to experiment in noncritical writing himself.

He soon decided that reviewing—for Mr. and Mrs. Griffiths, at least—would never do; and in September he broke off his agreement with the publisher (by mutual consent) and moved to lodgings in the vicinity of Salisbury Square, near Fleet Street. There he was within easy reach of the Temple Exchange Coffeehouse, which he could use as headquarters for any bits of medical practice that came his way. But he was also near the booksellers; his break with Griffiths evidently did not mean that he had abandoned writing as a career—if only an auxiliary career. In fact he had contracted to translate Jean Marteilhe's *Mémoires d'un Protestant* for Griffiths and Dilly;[13] and he agreed to write for Robert and James Dodsley a survey of the state of literature in Great Britain and Europe, based on his observations during his travels.

Yet these odds and ends of medical practice and literary commissions gave him no fixed income,[14] and he was far from prosperous. Then suddenly his expenses were practically doubled by the arrival of his brother Charles from Ireland, expecting to be lodged and outfitted for whatever position Oliver could locate for him. The Hodsons had concluded from Noll's letter from Peckham that he was now affluent enough to think of repaying some of the favors done him in the past. Perhaps they even intimated that it was high time he considered discharging some of the debts which he had incurred while he was pursuing his leisurely education. And they sent word that his sister Jane was in difficulties and that his mother had lost the farm at Pallas.

Goldsmith was obviously on the defensive when he sat down on December 27, 1757, to explain himself to his sister and brother-in-law. His gratitude for their kindness to him in the past, he insisted, knew no bounds: "How much am I obliged to you . . . for such generosity (or why should not your virtues have the proper name) for such charity to me. . . . Sure I am born to ill fortune to be so much a debtor and so unable to repay! But to say no more of this; too many professions of gratitude are often considered as indirect petitions for future favours. . . ." Then, after telling of his plight when he first settled in London, he described his present situation:

. . . by a very little practice as a Physician and a very little reputation as an author I make a shift to live. Nothing more apt to introduce us to the gates of the muses than Poverty; but it were well if she only left us at the door; the mischief is, she sometimes chooses to give her company during the entertainment, and Want, instead of being gentleman-usher, often turns master of the Ceremonies. Thus upon hearing, I write, no doubt, you immagine, I starve, and the name of an Author naturally reminds you of a garret, in this particular I do not think proper to undeceive my Friends; but whether I eat or starve, live in a first floor or four pair of stairs [?] high, I still remember them with ardour, nay my very country comes in for a share of my affection.

But the thought of Ireland raised conflicting emotions:

Unaccountable fondness for country, this maladie du Pays, as the french call it. Unaccountable, that he should still have an affection for a place, who never received when in it above civil contempt, who never brought out of it, except his brogue and his blunders; surely my affection is equally ridiculous with the Scotchman's, who refused to be cured of the itch, because it made him unco' thoughtful of his wife and bonny Inverary. But not to be serious, let me ask myself what gives me a wish to see Ireland again? The country is a fine one perhaps? No!—There are good company in Ireland? No; the conversation there is generally made up of a smutty toast or a baudy song. The vivacity supported by some humble cousin, who has just folly enough to earn his—dinner.—Then perhaps ther's more wit and learning among the Irish? Oh Lord! No! there has been more money spent in the encouragement of the Podareen mare [a celebrated race horse] there in one season, than given in rewards to learned men since the times of Usher. All their productions in learning amount maybe to, perhaps a translation, or a few tracts in laborious divinity, and all their productions in wit, to just nothing at all. Why the plague then so fond of Ireland! Then all at once, because you, my dear friend, and a few more, who are exceptions to the general picture, have a residence there. This it is that gives me all the pangs I feel in seperation.

And presently he was assuring Hodson: "If next Summer I can contrive to be absent six weeks from London I shall spend three of them among my friends in Ireland. But first believe me my design is purely to visit, and neither to cut a figure nor levy con-·tributions, neither to excite envy or solicit charity; in fact my circumstances are adapted to neither. I am too poor to be gazed at and too rich to need the assistance of others." Thus, skillful manipulator of words that he was, he managed to convey the impression that he was devoted to his relatives, eager to see them and to serve them in any way, but unable to send them a penny. His practice as a writer was paying dividends of a sort.

How long his brother Charles remained in London is not clear, but eventually he returned to Ireland, learned cabinet-making, and emigrated to Jamaica. And early in 1758 Goldsmith himself left London, having been recalled to Peckham to take temporary charge again of Milner's school.

Toward the end of February, probably while he was still at Peckham, his translation of Marteilhe's book appeared with the title *The Memoirs of a Protestant, Condemned to the Galleys of France for his Religion: Written by Himself*. Like the original it was intended as propaganda against the cruelties allegedly practiced in the name of the Roman Catholic Church, and by way of intensifying its effect the publishers appended "An exact and authentic *List* of the *Protestants* who are now actually Slaves aboard the French Galleys upon Account of their Religion, taken in the year 1755." Of course Goldsmith had no particular quarrel with Roman Catholicism; in his preface he remarked that he hoped this work would teach Protestants to value their religion and the freedom which it gave them, but he was surely much more concerned about the twenty-pound fee which the translation would bring him. Yet, having accepted the commission, he evidently determined to execute it well. For all his ludicrous appearance and his carefree ways, he had a basic pride—the pride of an artist.

The material which he had to work with was far from stimulating: Marteilhe's account of his extraordinary adventures was pedestrian, often long-winded, and distinctly anticlimactic. But Goldsmith had shown in his personal letters a striking ability to create brisk narrative enlivened by telling details and expressed in a vigorous (if often careless) prose; and he now put his talents to good use.

His translation was never literal. Sometimes it was inaccurate; in the very first paragraph of the book he rendered "mil six cent quatre vingt quatre" as 1624. But otherwise he improved on the original in every respect. He broke down Marteilhe's tedious paragraphs and sentences, he lifted from the appendix a section describing life in the galleys and inserted it where it logically belonged, and he brightened Marteilhe's dull chronicle by supplying bits from his own imagination. The result is that Goldsmith's account of events is more vivid and moving to the reader than that of the man who actually experienced them. For he had a sense of the dramatic which Marteilhe utterly lacked; he wanted to make his reader see and feel the situations described, and he knew how to heighten—sometimes, it must be granted, inflate—his effects to that end. A single example will suffice to illustrate the point: for Marteilhe's "Pour lors je crus fermement qu'on m'avoit enterré avant ma mort, & que cet affreux Cachot seroit mon tombeau si j'y restois vingt quatre heures," Goldsmith writes: "What could I do? I resigned myself to Despair, and called on Death to deliver me from the merciless Persecution of my unfeeling Fellow-Creatures. I looked on myself as buried alive in this Dungeon, where the Light never penetrated; and found no Comfort there but in my Aspirations to the Father of Mercy."

If he had any doubts in his mind about his powers as a writer, this translation should have convinced him. It proved that he had the touch which would convert baser metal if not to pure gold at least to gleaming silver. Yet he felt so little pride in authorship that he had the translation published as the work of James Willington, a former fellow-student at Trinity College.[15]

By August Goldsmith was back in London, with his appointment to India at last assured: he was to serve as a civilian physician on the coast of Coromandel. But there was one difficulty: he must pay his own fare on the voyage out. Fortunately he had by him a possible source of income, the survey of the status of literature which he was preparing for Dodsley. And it occurred to him that he might realize a tidy profit if he handled the Irish sale of the book himself. To that end, he drew up proposals for the publication; and despite his aversion to letter-writing ("No turnspit gets up into his wheel with more reluctance, than I sit down to write," he once complained),[16] despite, too, his complaints about the lack of learning in Ireland in his last letter to the Hodsons, he managed, now that he had a pressing motive, to compose and dispatch six letters to Ireland, four of which survive.

To his cousin Edward Mills he wrote on August 7 an effusive expression of his admiration and affection, and only gradually revealed that he was asking a Dublin bookseller to send Mills a hundred proposals for the book and to accept any subscriptions that he might be able to raise among his acquaintance.

A week later he was writing to Robert Bryanton, first protesting his undiminished affection and his distress at his friend's failure to write to him, then slipping into playful banter about his literary pretensions:

Do you know whom you have offended? A man whose character may one of these days be mentioned with profound respect in a German comment or Dutch dictionary; whose name you will probably hear ushered in by a Doctissimus Doctissimorum, or heel-pieced with a long Latin termination. Think how Goldsmithius or Gubblegurchius, or some such sound, as rough as a nutmeg-grater, will become me? Think of that!—God's curse, Sir! who am I? I must own my ill-natured cotemporaries have not hitherto paid me those honours I have had such just reason to expect. I have not yet seen my face reflected in all the lively display of red and white paints on any sign-posts in the suburbs. Your handkerchief weavers seem as yet unacquainted with my merits or physiognomy, and the very snuff-box makers

appear to have forgot their respect. Tell them all from me, they are a set of
Gothic, barbarous, ignorant scoundrels. There will come a day, no doubt
it will—I beg you may live a couple of hundred years longer only to see the
day—when the Scaligers and Daciers will vindicate my character, give
learned editions of my labours, and bless the times with copious comments
on the text. You shall see how they will fish up the heavy scoundrels who
disregard me now, or will then offer to cavil at my productions. How will
they bewail the times that suffered so much genius to lie neglected. If ever
my works find their way to Tartary or China, I know the consequence.
Suppose one of your Chinese Owanowitzers instructing one of your Tar-
tarian Chianobacchi—you see I use Chinese names to show my own erudition, as I shall soon make our Chinese talk like an Englishman to show his.
This may be the subject of the lecture:

"Oliver Goldsmith flourished in the eighteenth and nineteenth centuries.
He lived to be an hundred and three years old, and in that age may justly
be styled the sun of literature and the Confucius of Europe. Many of his
earlier writings to the regret of the learned world, were anonymous, and
have probably been lost, because united with those of others. The first
avowed piece the world has of his is entitled an 'Essay on the Present State
of Taste and Literature in Europe,'—a work well worth its weight in
diamonds. In this he profoundly explains what learning is, and what learning is not. In this he proves that blockheads are not men of wit, and yet
that men of wit are actually blockheads."

But as I choose neither to tire my Chinese Philosopher, nor you, nor
myself, I must discontinue the oration, in order to give you a good pause
for admiration; and I find myself most violently disposed to admire too.
Let me, then, stop my fancy to take a view of my future self; and as the
boys say, light down to see myself on horseback. Well, now I am down,
where the d——l *is I?* Oh, Gods! Gods! here in a garret writing for bread,
and expecting to be dunned for a milk score! However, dear Bob, whether
in penury or affluence, serious or gay, I am ever wholly thine.

And he became so enamored of his chatter that he completely
forgot to mention the proposals for his book!

The following day he wrote to his cousin Jane Lawder, daughter of Thomas Contarine. At first he adopted a tone of injured
merit, then shifted to self-defense—and even allowed himself
some remarks which the Lawders might well regard as offensive:

Those who know me at all, know that I have always been actuated by
different principles from the rest of Mankind, and while none regarded the
interests of his friends more, no man on earth regarded his own less. I have
often affected bluntness to avoid the imputation of flattery, have frequently

seem'd to overlook those merits too obvious to escape notice, and pretended disregard to those instances of good nature and good sense which I could not fail tacitly to applaud; and all this lest I should be rank'd among the grinning tribe who say very true to all that is said, who fill a vacant chair at a tea table whose narrow souls never moved in a wider circle than the circumference of a guinea, and who had rather be reckoning the money in your pocket than the virtue in your breast; all this, I say, I have done and a thousand other very silly, though very disinterested things in my time, and for all which no soul cares a farthing about me. God's curse, Madam, is it to be wondered that he should once in his life forget you who has been all his life forgetting him self.

However it is probable you may one of those days see me turn'd into a perfect Hunks [i.e., a miser] and as dark and intricate as a mouse-hole. I have already given my Lanlady orders for an entire reform in the state of my finances; I declaim against hot suppers, drink less sugar in my tea, and cheek my grate with brick-bats. Instead of hanging my room with pictures I intend to adorn it with maxims of frugality, these will make pretty furniture enough and won't be a bit too expensive, for I shall draw them all out with my own hands and my lanlady's daughter shall frame them with the parings of my black waistcoat; Each maxim is to be inscrib'd on a sheet of clean paper and wrote with my best pen, of which the following will serve as a specimen. "Look Sharp. Mind the mean chance. Money is money now. If you have a thousand pound, you can put your hands by your sides and say you are worth a thousand pounds every day of the year. Take a farthing from an hundred pound and it will be an hundred pound no longer." Thus which way so ever I turn my eyes they are sure to meet one of those friendly Monitors, and as we are told of an Actor who hung his room round with looking glasses to correct the defects in his person, my appartment shall be furnished in a peculiar manner to correct the errors of my mind. . . .

Later he launched into a rhetorical tribute to his uncle Contarine, now grown senile: "He is no more that soul of fire as when once I knew him. Newton and Swift grew dimn with age as well as he. But what shall I say; his mind was too active an inhabitant not to disorder the feeble mansion of its abode, for the richest jewels soonest wear their settings. Yet who but the fool would lament his condition, he now forgets the calamities of life, perhaps indulgent heaven has given him a foretaste of that tranquillity here which he so well deserves hereafter." And finally: "But I must come to business, for business as one of my maxims tells me must be minded or lost." Then follows the request that Mr. Lawder will circulate his proposals.

Goldsmith's character does not always appear to its best advantage in these letters: his shifts from extravagant flattery to the business at hand, from joviality to grief, sometimes ring false and leave one questioning the man's sincerity. Yet the facility with which he shifts his tone from one paragraph to another manifests not only a superficial dishonesty but also a fundamental artistic ingenuity. Now and later Goldsmith was a virtuoso in the use of words: he could not resist displaying (if only to himself) his skill at manipulating his instrument. He was like an actor who so exults in his dramatic powers that he exercises them constantly in his everyday affairs. A modern reader may even suspect Goldsmith's sincerity when, in a letter to Dan Hodson written later in August, 1758, he insists that he is being entirely himself: "You can't expect regularity in a correspondence with one who is regular in nothing. Nay were I forc'd to love you by rule I dare venture to say I could never do it sincerely. Take me then with all my faults let me write when I please, for you see I say what I please and am only thinking aloud when writing to you."

In this letter he was more specific than he had been elsewhere about his plans for the future:

I suppose you have heard of my intention of going to the East Indies. The place of my destination is one of the factories on the coast of Coromandel and I go in quality of Physician and Surgeon for which the Company has sign'd my warrant which has already cost me ten pounds. I must also pay 50 Lb for my passage ten pound for Sea stores, and the other incidental expences of my equipment will amount to 60 or 70 Lb more. The Sallary is but triffling viz 100 Lb per ann. but the other advantages if a person be prudent are considerable. The practice of the place if I am rightly informed generally amounts to not less than one thousand pounds per ann. for which the appointed Physician has an exclusive privelege, this with the advantages resulting from trade with the high interest which money bears viz 20 per cent. are the inducements which persuade me to undergo the fatigues of sea the dangers of war and the still greater dangers of the climate, which induce me to leave a place where I am every day gaining friends and esteem and where I might enjoy all the conveniencies of life.

Here was a new attitude toward his literary career. Goldsmith was suddenly experiencing some qualms about the advisability of leaving London. "I am certainly wrong," he continued, not to be contented with what I already possess triffling as it is, for should I ask myself one serious question what is it I want? What can I answer? My desires are as capricious as the big bellied woman's who long'd for a piece of her husband's nose. I have no certainty it is true; but why can't I do as some men of more merit who have liv'd upon more precarious terms? Scaron us'd jestingly to call himself the Lord Marquis of Quenault which was the name of the bookseller who employ'd him, and why may not I assert my privelege and quality on the same pretensions? Yet upon deliberation, whatever airs I may give myself on this side of the water, my dignity I fancy would be evaporated before I reach'd the other. I know you have in Ireland a very indifferent Idea of a man who writes for bread, tho Swift and Steel did so in the earlier part of their lives. You Imagine, I suppose, that every author by profession lives in a garret, wears shabby cloaths, and converses with the meanest company; but I assure you such a character is entirely chimerical. Nor do I believe there is one single writer, who has abilities to translate a french Novel, that does not keep better company wear finer cloaths and live more genteely than many who pride themselves for nothing else in Ireland. I confess it again my Dear Dan that nothing but the wildest ambition could prevail on me to leave the enjoyment of that refined conversation which I sometimes am admitted to partake in for uncertain fortune and paltry shew. You can't conceive how I am sometimes divided, to leave all that is dear gives me pain, but when I consider that it is possible, I may acquire a genteel independance for life, when I think of that dignity which Philosophy claims to raise it above contempt and ridicule, when I thnk thus, I eagerly long to embrace every opportunity of separating myself from the vulgar, as much in my circumstances as I am in my sentiments already.

Evidently Goldsmith was widening his social circle. Men who had at first disdained him because of his odd appearance and manner had ended by accepting him as a friend. By this time he was doubtless well acquainted with Samuel Richardson and Edward Young, had formed a friendship with Dr. James Grainger, a graduate of the University of Edinburgh later famed as the author of *The Sugar Cane,* and was on friendly terms with the Reverend Andrew Kippis, the biographer, and the publishers Robert and James Dodsley. And soon he was introduced to Archibald Hamilton and Dr. Tobias Smollett, editors of the *Critical Review.* All these men were persons of talent and intellect, more distinguished, any of them, than the great majority of even Uncle Contarine's friends and correspondents. No one in Ireland could

SIR JOSHUA REYNOLDS' PORTRAIT OF GOLDSMITH

"Who wrote like an angel . . ."

(Reproduced, by permission, from the copy in the National Portrait Gallery)

Mr. Bunbury delint.   J. Bretherton fecit

Dr. GOLDSMITH.

WILLIAM HENRY BUNBURY'S SKETCH OF GOLDSMITH

"... but talked like poor Poll."

(Reproduced, by permission, from an engraving in the Theatre Collection of the Harvard
College Library)

boast of such a circle, and Goldsmith could not resist hinting, at least, his growing success in London. Nor could he help reflecting that he would have no such companions on the coast of Coromandel.

His letter to Hodson continued with a request for aid in distributing the proposals for his forthcoming book. Then, since he had some space left, he abandoned his attempts to dazzle his relatives and revealed that he was the same Noll, genial and irresponsible, whom they had known in the old days:

You see I never cease writing 'till a whole sheet of paper is wrote out, I beg you will immitate me in this particular and give your letters good measure. You can tell me, what visits you receive or pay, who has been married or debauch'd, since my absence what fine girls you have starting up and beating of the vetterans of my acquaintance from future conquest. I suppose before I return I shall find all the blooming virgins I once left in Westmeath shrivelled into a parcel of hags with seven children a piece tearing down their petticoats. Most of the Bucks and Bloods whom I left hunting and drinking and swearing and getting bastards I find are dead. Poor devils they kick'd the world before them. I wonder what the devil they kick now?

Yet though he begged for news of the Lawders, of his mother and his brother Charles and the Hodsons themselves, and though he offered to pay his brother Maurice's fare to London—perhaps later to India—and to secure him a position "if he would accustom himself to write and spell," he had apparently given up his plans for a trip to Ireland that summer. To be sure, he remarked, "I know not how my desire of seeing Ireland which has so long slept has again revived with so much ardour. So weak is my temper and so unsteady that I am frequently tempted, particularly when low spirited, to return home and leave my fortune tho' just now it is beginning to look kinder. But it shall not be. In five or six years I hope to indulge these transports." Yet the truth was that he had outgrown Ireland and the sort of society that he had known there. He had outgrown even the desire to return as a successful man and to savor his triumph. Moreover, as his letters reveal, he feared that his relatives would greet him coldly—that, in fact, they would not respond very enthusiastically to this latest appeal for assistance.

Eventually he realized that the Irish sale of his book was not going to yield any substantial profit. Then he had another happy thought: he could avoid the cost of the trip to Coromandel if he could secure an appointment as hospital-mate on a ship bound for India. He applied for such a position and was ordered to report for examination on December 21, 1758. But another obstacle loomed up: he had no suitable outfit to wear when he appeared before the examiners—and of course no funds to buy one. Yet he was resourceful if nothing else, and somehow he persuaded Ralph Griffiths to act as his security to a tailor. By way of repayment, he agreed to review four classical and antiquarian books for the December *Monthly Review*.

December 21 arrived, and Goldsmith appeared for examination in his new finery. Unfortunately, however, it failed to dazzle the examiners, and he was rejected. He was left then with a fine new suit of clothes, a tailor's bill, and no means of paying it. His solution to the problem was typical: he pawned his new coat, probably intending to use the proceeds to pay a part of his bill to the tailor. Then, as bad luck would have it, he met a Mrs. Martin, later his landlady,[17] whose husband had just been arrested for debt. And of course she carried away with her the money which Goldsmith had received for his coat.

In due time the tailor despaired of collecting his fee from Goldsmith and sent off a bill to Griffiths. Then trouble really boiled up. The publisher was outraged and dispatched a furious letter to Goldsmith, berating him for his irresponsible behavior and demanding that he return the books sent him for review. Goldsmith replied apologetically, but failed to produce the wanted books, although he assured Griffiths that they would be returned in good time. But Griffiths was not disposed to wait, and he replied that both he and the tailor would sue at once unless they received what was owed them.

All Goldsmith's skill as a master of words was now called to the fore. And he managed to outdo himself in an answer which blended abject apology, self-castigation, and injured pride:

Sir,
    I know of no misery but a gaol to which my own imprudencies and your letter seem to point. I have seen it inevitable this three or four weeks, and by heavens, request it as a favour . . . that may prevent somewhat more

fatal. I have been some years struggling with a wretched being, with all that contempt which indigence brings with it, with all those strong passions which make contempt insupportable. When then has a gaol that is formidable, I shall at least have the society of wretches, and such is to me true society. I tell you again and again I am now neither able nor willing to pay you a farthing, but I will be punctual to any appointment you or the taylor shall make; thus far at least I do not act the sharper, since unable to pay my debts one way I would willingly give some security another. No Sir, had I been a sharper, had I been possessed of less good nature and native generosity I might surely now have been in better circumstances. I am guilty I own of meanessess which poverty unavoidably brings with it, my reflections are filld with repentance for my imprudence but not with any remorse for being a villain, that may be a character you unjustly charge me with. Your books I can assure you are neither pawn'd nor sold, but in the custody of a friend from whom my necessities oblig'd me to borrow some money, whatever becomes of my person, you shall have them in a month. It is very possible both the reports you have heard and your suggestions may have brought you false information with respect to my character, it is very possible that the man whom you now regard with detestation may inwardly burn with grateful resentment, it is very possible that upon a second perusal of the letter I sent you, you may see the workings of a mind strongly agitated with gratitude and jealousy, if such circumstances should appear at least spare invective 'till my book with Mr. Dodsley shall be publish'd, and then perhaps you may see the bright side of a mind when my professions shall not appear the dictates of necessity but of choice. You seem to think Doctor Milner knew me not. Perhaps so; but he was a man I shall ever honour; but I have friendship only with the dead! I ask pardon for taking up so much time. Nor shall I add to it by any other professions than that I am Sir your Humble serv^t.

Oliver Goldsmith

P.S. I shall expect impatiently the result of your resolutions.

Apparently the letter accomplished its purpose; or perhaps Griffiths concluded that he would gain nothing by having Goldsmith clapped in prison. In any case the two effected a compromise: Goldsmith would discharge his debt by giving Griffiths the rights to a short life of Voltaire on which he was working. What became of the books which he had given his friend as security, no one knows.

In the midst of these complications, on or about January 13, 1759, Goldsmith wrote to his brother Henry. All the optimism of his August letter had now vanished: he was plunged into a deep depression. And although he did not mention his trouble with Griffiths, he was clearly discouraged about the Irish sale of his forthcoming book. Edward Mills and the Lawders had failed to acknowledge not only his letters but also subsequent letters which Henry had written them about the proposals. Noll had decided, therefore, to send over only 250 copies of the book—half the number which he had originally hoped to sell in Ireland. Meanwhile he was proceeding with his plans to set out for Coromandel. But he had little enthusiasm for the trip; he felt old and worn, lonely and sad:

I must confess it gives me some pain to think I am almost beginning the world at the age of thirty one. Tho' I never had a day's sickness since I saw you yet I am not that strong active man you once knew me. You scarce can conceive how much eight years of disappointment anguish and study have wore me down. If I remember right, you are seven or eight years older than me, and yet I dare venture to say that if a stranger saw us both he would pay me the honours of seniority. Immagine to yourself a pale melancholly visage with two great wrinkles between the eye brows, with an eye disgustingly severe and a big wig, and you may have a perfect picture of my present appearance. On the other hand I conceive you as grown fat sleek and healthy, passing many an happy day among your own children or those who knew you as a child. Since I knew what it was to be a man this is a pleasure I have not known. I have passd my days among a number of cool designing beings and have contracted all their suspicious manner, in my own behaviour. I should actually be as unfit for the society of my friends at home as I detest that which I am obliged to partake of here. I can now neither partake of the pleasure of a revel nor contribute to raise its jollity, I can neither laugh nor drink, have contracted an hesitating disagreeable manner of speaking, and a visage that looks illnature itself, in short I have thought myself into settled melancholly and an utter disgust of all that life brings with it. Whence this romantic turn that all our family are possessed with, whence this love for every place and every country but that in which we reside? For every occupation but our own, this desire of fortune and yet this eagerness to dissipate! I perceive my dear Sir, that I am at intervals for indulging this splenetic manner and following my own taste regardless of yours.

Then he paused to consider the fate of Henry's small son, who was slated to go to Trinity College. And, thinking of his own haphazard existence, he wrote:

The reasons you have given me for breeding up your son a scholar are judicious and convincing. I should however be glad to know for what particular profession he is design'd? If he be assiduous, and divested of strong passions, (for passions in youth always lead to pleasure) he may do very well in your college, for it must be ownd that the industrious poor have good encouragement there, perhaps better than in any other in Europe. But if he has ambition, strong passions, and an exquisite sensibility of contempt, do not send him there, unless you have no other trade for him except your own. It is impossible to conceive how much may be done by a proper education at home. A boy, for instance, who understands perfectly well Latin, French, Arithmetic and the principles of the civil law, and can write a fine hand, has an education that may qualify him for any undertaking. And these parts of learning should be carefully inculcated let him be designed for whatever calling he will. Above all things let him never touch a romance, or novel, those paint beauty in colours more charming than nature, and describe happiness that man never tastes. How delusive, how destructive therefore are those pictures of consummate bliss, they teach the youthful mind to sigh after beauty and happiness which never existed, to despise the little good which fortune has mixed in our cup, by expecting more than she ever gave. And in general take the word of a man who has seen the world, and studied human nature more by experience than precept, take my word for it I say that books teach us very little of the world. The greatest merit, and the most consummate virtue that ever grac'd humanity in a state of poverty would only serve to make the possessor ridiculous, they may distress but cannot relieve him.

That his bitter disillusionment sprang largely from his treatment by Griffiths is apparent in the curiously cynical bit of advice which follows and which he set down for the benefit of his nephew, then about three years old:

Avarice in the lower orders of mankind is true ambition, avarice is the only ladder the poor can use to preferment. Preach, then my dear Sir, to your son, not the excellence of human nature, nor the disrespect of riches, but endeavour to teach him thrift and oeconomy. Let his poor wandering uncles example be placd in his eyes. I had learn'd from books to love virtue, before I was taught from experience the necessity of being selfish. I had contracted the habits and notions of a Philosopher, while I was exposing myself to the insidious approaches of cunning; and often, by being even from my narrow finances charitable to excess, I forgot the rules of justice, and placd myself in the very situation of the wretch who thank'd my bounty. When I am in the remotest part of the world tell him this and perhaps he may improve by my example.

91

Presently he announced that he had canceled his plans for a trip to Ireland. He had heard that his mother was almost blind, and, he declared, "even tho' I had the utmost inclination to return home I could not. To behold her in distress without a capacity of relieving her from it, would be too much to add to my present splenetic habit." Yet he offered to pay his brother Maurice's fare to London and announced with some bravado that he was bringing out a life of Voltaire—"no more than a catchpenny— However I spent but four weeks on the whole performance for which I receiv'd twenty pound." Moreover, he subjoined a sample of the "heroi-comical poem" on which he was working. And he concluded with the surprising observation that "poetry is much an easier and more agreeable species of composition than prose, and could a man live by it, it were no unpleasant employment to be a Poet."

To tide himself over until his departure for India, he had begun work as a reviewer for the Tory *Critical Review,* sworn foe of the *Monthly* and its editor. The January, 1759, issue of the *Critical* contained his first contribution, a review of a new translation of Ovid's *Heroïdes.*[18] Goldsmith gave Barrett, the translator, short shrift for his conscientious, but tasteless, rendering of the original; he subjected the translation itself and Barrett's critical commentary to some rather sharp analysis; and at length he burst forth with a justification of his severity:

We have of late seen the republic of letters crowded with some who have no other pretensions to applause but industry, who have no other merit but that of reading many books, and making long quotations: these we have heard extolled by sympathetic dunces, and have seen them carry off the rewards of genius; while others, who should have been born in better days, felt all the wants of poverty, and the agonies of contempt. Who, then, that has a regard for the public, for the literary honours of our country, for the figure we shall one day make among posterity, that would not choose to see such humbled as are possessed only of talents that might have made good cobblers, had fortune turned them to trade? Should such prevail, the real interests of learning must be in a reciprocal proportion to the power they possess. Let it be then the character of our periodical endeavours, and hitherto we flatter ourselves it has ever been, not to permit an ostentation of learning [to] pass for merit, nor to give a pedant quarter upon the score of his industry alone, even though he took refuge behind Arabic, or powdered

92

his hair with hieroglyphics. Authors thus censured may accuse our judgment, or our reading, if they please, but our hearts will acquit us of envy or
ill-nature, since we reprove only with a desire to reform.

Goldsmith's crispness was doubtless prompted in part by the irritation which he had been suffering. His words show, nonetheless,
a growing sense of vocation: he was a man of letters with a responsibility to the community of letters. Perhaps he reflected wryly
that literature was in a parlous state when a writer like Barrett
was encouraged to publish, while one of genuine talents and
acumen was obliged to ship out to the coast of Coromandel to
make a living.

February came and went with no sign of the publication of the
Life of Voltaire, which in mid-January he had told his brother
was to appear "in a few days."[19] He was busy now preparing for
his departure for Coromandel and seeing his long-promised survey
of contemporary literature through the press. On Wednesday, the
21st, he spent the evening at his friend Dr. Grainger's, where he
was introduced to the Reverend Thomas Percy, Vicar of Easton-
Maudit and Rector of Whitby, in Northamptonshire. Percy had
arrived in London the day before with the manuscript of his
version of the Chinese novel *Hau Kiou Chooan,* but he was interested also in collecting ballads for his projected *Reliques of
Ancient English Poetry* and was pleased to learn that Goldsmith
had a good many old songs in his repertoire. Accordingly he
noted in his memorandum book: "Mr. Oliver Goldsmith at Mrs.
Martin's in Green Arbour Court, Little Old Bayley," for Goldsmith had settled now in a room in the household of the woman
whom he had befriended when he could little afford to do so.
The two men met again at the publisher Dodsley's on the evening
of February 26, and on Saturday, March 3, Percy stopped in at
Green Arbour Court.

He was rather surprised at what he found. The Court was
already much as Washington Irving described it in 1824: "a small
square, surrounded by tall and miserable houses, the very intestines
of which seemed turned inside out, to judge from the old garments
and frippery fluttering from every window."[20] The interior was
little better: Goldsmith's room was mean and dirty, and when he

offered his one chair to Percy, he himself was obliged to sit on the window-sill. He had been working on the manuscript or proofs of his survey of contemporary literature, but he pushed the papers aside, and soon the two men were engrossed in conversation. Then suddenly there was a knock at the door. A little girl stepped into the room, curtsied, and said, "My mamma sends her compliments, and begs the favour of you to lend her a chamber-pot full of coals." Yet Percy evidently felt that a conversation with Goldsmith was well worth the inconvenience or embarrassment which it entailed, for he returned for more on the following Tuesday.[21]

In March Goldsmith wrote for the *Critical* a review of John Langhorne's translation of Bion's elegy on the death of Adonis, published by Griffiths. He was lavish in his praise of both the original poem and Langhorne's translation, and to his critical remarks he appended some observations on the art of the elegy. They are sensible enough, but they are not original; for, as modern scholars have discovered, Goldsmith had translated them directly from the article "Elégie" in Volume V of the French *Encyclopédie*. He did not bother to acknowledge his debt.[22]

His favorable review of Langhorne's translation suggests that Goldsmith bore no grudge against either Griffiths or the *Monthly,* for which Langhorne wrote regularly. However, the *Critical* for February had contained a biting attack on the *Monthly* in a review of Grainger's *Letter to Smollett,*[23] and when Goldsmith's *Enquiry into the Present State of Polite Learning,* as it was finally called, appeared anonymously on April 2, the *Monthly* seized the opportunity to retaliate. Griffiths assigned the book to William Kenrick, soon to gain a reputation as one of the shrewdest and most disreputable hacks in London. And of course he made no attempt to criticize fairly. Goldsmith's passing allusion to "those Monthly Reviews and Magazines" as "dull and dronish" was enough to call down his wrath. "It requires a great deal of art and temper," Kenrick wrote,

for a man to write consistently against the dictates of his own heart. Thus, notwithstanding our Author talks so familiarly of *us,* the great, and affects to be thought to stand in the rank of Patrons, we cannot help thinking, that in more places than one he has betrayed, in himself, the man he so severely condemns for drawing his quill to take a purse. We are even so firmly convinced of this, that we dare put the question home to his conscience, whether he has never experienced the unhappy situation he so feelingly describes, in that of a Literary Understrapper. His remarking him as coming down from his garret to rummage the Bookseller's shop, for materials to work upon, and the knowledge he displays of his minutest labours, give great reason to suspect he may himself have had concerns in the *bad trade* of book-making. *Fronti nulla fides.* We have heard of many a Writer who, "patronized only by his Bookseller," has, nevertheless, affected the Gentleman in print, and talked full as cavalierly as our Author himself. We have even known one hardy enough, publicly to stigmatize men of the first rank in literature, for their immoralities, while conscious himself of labouring under the infamy of having, by the vilest and meanest actions, forfeited all pretensions to honour and honesty.[24]

Had Kenrick chosen to attack the style of the book, he might have done so with more justice; for it was painfully apparent that Goldsmith had given this work his best efforts—his self-conscious best. Instead of cultivating the naturalness and flow which he had achieved in his *Memoirs of a Protestant,* he tried to sound impressive—and often succeeded only in sounding as if he were trying to sound impressive. Perhaps he was indeed hoping that his book would be accepted as the product of a gentleman of taste rather than a penniless Irish hack.

The organization of the book is often faulty too; yet with all its defects, it has real merit. It is more than an enquiry into the state of polite learning; Goldsmith assumed that learning was in decline and sought to point out why: "To mark out, therefore, the corruptions that have found a way into the republic of letters, to attempt the rescuing of genius from the shackles of pedantry and criticism, to distinguish the decay naturally consequent on an age like ours, grown old in literature, from every erroneous innovation which admits a remedy, to take a view of those societies which profess the advancement of polite learning, and by a mutual opposition of their excellencies and defects, to attempt the improvement of each, is the design of this essay."[25] It was, in reality, the envoy of a man who would have liked to make a reputation as a writer, had despaired of doing so, and was abandoning the field with a plea for those who remained in it.

His survey of the state of polite learning, though "made on the spot," as he remarked, was superficial. Classical literature, he was convinced, had been stifled by the work of pedantic critics: "Men bred up among books, and seeing nature only by reflection, could do little, except hunt after perplexity and confusion. The public, therefore, with reason rejected learning, when thus rendered barren though voluminous; for we may be assured that the generality of mankind never lose a passion for letters, while they continue to be either amusing or useful."[26] Then, after a hasty survey of "The Obscure Ages," came an analysis of the state of modern Italian literature, which, Goldsmith claimed, had fallen into the hands of the affected *Virtuosi* and the pedantic *Philosophi;* then a quick look at the literature of Germany and the Netherlands, which had likewise been stultified by the efforts of hidebound critics: in fact, he observed, the German critics had succeeded so well in their efforts that much of contemporary German literature was written in Latin or French.

At last, after a few words about the learning of Spain, Sweden, and Denmark, he came to a consideration of France and England, where he reduced his pace and made his observations more penetrating. France in the reign of Louis XIV and England in the reign of Queen Anne had risen to glorious heights in literature, only to yield their glory into the withering hands of the critics in the following ages. Goldsmith insisted that it was idle to try to decide which of the two nations had enjoyed superiority in literature, but he made it fairly obvious that he preferred the English. Yet he was convinced that French literature had suffered less of a decline during the century, thanks in part to the native self-sufficiency of Frenchmen, who had been less swayed by the dictates of the critics.

He believed, therefore, that English letters would profit by adopting certain features of the French system: the French mode of granting patronage, for example, was superior to the English. In France, he maintained, an author received a little financial aid and a great deal of respect throughout his career, while in England he was accorded neither aid nor respect until he had fought his way to the heights, when he was often given a pension so generous that he need never exert his full powers again. The struggling English author was, therefore, dependent on mercenary book-sellers, who assigned him such dreary jobs and paid him so poorly that he was compelled to write more than he could possibly write well. Hence the contempt in England for the author who lived in a garret and wrote for bread, who sacrificed his standards and submerged his originality in a feverish effort to make a meager living. For him there was, at present, little hope. "But," he added, "there are still some men, whom fortune has blessed with affluence, to whom the muse pays her morning visit, not like a creditor but a friend: to this happy few, who have leisure to polish what they write, and liberty to choose their own subjects, I would direct my advice, which consists in a few words: *Write what you think, regardless of the critics.*"[27] Such men could, if they would, break the shackles clamped on by the critics; they could bring about the emancipation of literature. If only fortune had blessed Oliver Goldsmith with affluence!

In a way this was strange talk from a man who had in recent months been writing reviews for two critical journals. But it was consistent with what he had said in them; his definition of "the true critic's province" and his criticism of Gray's *Odes* in the *Monthly* and his objections to the pedant Barrett in the *Critical* had been directed to much the same ends. For William Kenrick was at bottom right: the author of *Polite Learning* was in truth one of those struggling authors for whom he was appealing. Beyond question he longed to do more than criticize others: he aspired to create—but he despaired of doing so under the prevailing conditions; and he was giving up the field to embark on a more lucrative, yet less truly rewarding, career on the coast of Coromandel.

Still he was doing so with some regrets, because he believed that the vocation of writer was, or should be, a noble one. The dedicated man of letters had, he was sure, much to offer his fellow-men: he was indeed their instructor—"a merciful substitute to the legislature," since "he acts not by punishing crimes but by preventing them." He was, however, prevented from fulfilling his mission by the mercenary bookseller, the unappreciative man

97

of means, the heedless public—but, most of all, by the pedantic critic who distracts writers from the interests of ordinary life, insists that they write by rule rather than from nature, encourages them to cultivate high-flown stylistic effects, cautions them against what is "low" or entertaining, discourages any sign of novelty or originality, in short, divorces them so completely from normal human interests that they can no longer command the attention of their fellow-men. Goldsmith abhorred the critic who judged English literature by Latin or Greek rules, or who sought knowledge in books rather than in life. Nature and Homer were not the same, Alexander Pope to the contrary notwithstanding. The Italians Metastasio and Maffei, who expressed themselves simply and naturally and who showed a wholesome interest in human emotions, seemed to Goldsmith to have a firm grasp of the true art of writing.

The book contains a wealth of incidental material: Goldsmith's recollections of past experiences, his opinions about the theater or contemporary education, his attitude toward Frenchmen—even hints of his religious beliefs. But, above all, it embodies his artistic credo, here stated most clearly. Never again was he to write a book not designed primarily to entertain; this once and this once only he dealt with his fundamental artistic principles—because, of course, he supposed that this would be his last opportunity to express them.

Goldsmith is too often, even today, considered an "inspired idiot," endowed with a gift for facile expression which enabled him to make even a survey of natural history, as Johnson said, as entertaining as a Persian tale. *Polite Learning* discloses, however, that he was a conscious artist, at odds with the spirit of his times, looking to life for inspiration rather than to books, impatient of rules established by misguided critics—an artist who wrote as he did on principle and whose theories anticipated in many details those of Wordsworth, Shelley, Lamb, Ruskin, and, in general spirit, the attitudes of the Romantic Revival with its stress on originality, interest in the common man, distrust of intellect, simpliciy of expression, and the dignity and freedom of the individual—especially the individual artist. One is constrained to say:

would he had written more such books! But Goldsmith would have scorned the suggestion. In *Polite Learning* he had announced his *credo*, he had stated (always incidentally to his central purpose) what he thought literature should be. And having stated clearly what he wanted to do, any sensible man would go ahead and do it.

Goldsmith must have been apprehensive when the book appeared: he had taken the critics to task—now what would they say of him? Kenrick's rancorous review proved his apprehensions justified; yet it could be discounted, since it was obviously prejudiced. And the review in the *Critical* for April made up for it. The author acknowledged that the survey of contemporary literature was in many ways superficial, but he cited Goldsmith's "lively turn of sentiment" and "brilliancy of expression," lauded the book as "a work of taste and merit," and hailed Goldsmith himself as an "ingenious author."

Encouraging words, these; and Goldsmith welcomed them. Here at last was the sort of recognition which he had sought for— had needed—all his life long. And the success of the book proved providential; for on March 22, just eleven days before it was published, the English public had received the startling news that Coromandel had been in French hands since April, 1758. To be sure, the English had just retaken it (hence the belated announcement), but fighting was continuing along the coast and threatened to do so for many months to come.[28] Thus Goldsmith's dream of prosperity in the wilderness was suddenly blasted. But he had already shown some hesitation about leaving London and the quest for literary fame, and he probably resigned himself quickly to the future which now seemed inevitable.

At first he merely continued to write occasional reviews for the *Critical*. His only contribution to the April issue was a review of a textbook of rhetoric, Ward's *System of Oratory*, which he dismissed as thorough but pedestrian. And instead of subjoining the usual excerpt of the book for the reader's edification, he announced that he would "fill up a page with a few observations of our own." To be sure, the "observations" echoed principles which he had expressed in *Polite Learning;* "these strong and vigorous emotions [which enliven oratory]," he declared, "can be no where taught, but they may be extinguished by rule." But they were not quite his, for once again he had had recourse to Volume V of the *Encyclopédie* and paraphrased, without acknowledgment, the articles "Elocution" and "Eloquence."[29]

In May he reviewed Arthur Murphy's play *The Orphan of China* for the *Critical,* and again came to the defense of originality and "feeling." He might well have mused, in passing, on the achievement of this other Irishman, born near Elphin only a few years before Goldsmith's own birth, who was now one of the most successful dramatists in London. Obviously some writers were prospering in England—and one of them was an Irishman!

During June and July Goldsmith continued his work for the *Critical,* but his reviews showed no striking independence of thought; in fact his discussion of a new edition of Massinger's plays in the July issue shows that he was still close enough to the critical spirit of his times to feel some disdain for Elizabethan drama. Shakespeare, he acknowledged, had added certain beauties to his dramas as if by chance; yet they were always subordinated to the "monsters and mummery" which his vulgar audience demanded. Massinger had no such redeeming graces; "he seldom rises to any pitch of sublimity, and yet it must be owned is never so incorrigibly absurd, as we often find his predecessor."

During the summer of 1759 Goldsmith must have had a good deal of time for diversion, and his new distinction as author of *Polite Learning* doubtless brought him opportunities to widen his circle of friends. At the town house of his editor, Tobias Smollett, there were frequent dinners for members of the staff of the *Critical;* and although Smollett spent three months of 1759 in King's Bench Prison for criticizing Admiral Knowles, his hospitality was not maimed by confinement, and he received his friends there. It may have been through Smollett that later in the year, after he had publicly praised *The Rambler,* Goldsmith was introduced to Samuel Johnson, the ungainly editor of the *Dictionary of the English Language.*

Not all Noll's friends were literary men. He still befriended— and doubtless shared his meager substance with—the poor people in Green Arbour Court. His landlady Mrs. Martin and her family were special favorites, and a relative of theirs later told Prior that Goldsmith had delighted in treating the Martin children to sweets or in playing the flute while they danced. Another favorite was a neighborhood watchmaker, whose quick wit made him stimulating company. Among such people Noll could unbend and submerge his worries about the future in the fun of the moment.

But presently his prospects brightened. His one contribution to the September issue of the *Critical,* a review of a new edition of Samuel Butler's prose works, was his last for several months. He had formed a new and promising connection—had been engaged by the publisher John Wilkie as editor and virtually sole contributor to a new weekly magazine, *The Bee,* announced as "a variety of Essays on the Amusements, Follies, and Vices in fashion: particularly the most recent Topics of Conversation: Remarks on Theatrical Exhibitions: Memoirs of Modern Literature, &c., &c." The first issue, which went on sale on Saturday, October 6, 1759, had as its epigraph the lines from Lucretius:

> Floriferis ut Apes in saltibus omnia libant,
> Omnia Nos itidem.

Obviously *The Bee* was ideally adapted to the talents of a literary dabbler like Oliver Goldsmith. With its appearance he advanced from the rank of reviewer to that of author.

The first issue was a *mélange:* there was an Introduction, in which the author assured his readers that he "intended to pursue no fixed method" but would follow "wherever pleasure presented"; there were two verse epitaphs, one "imitated from the Spanish," the other in Latin; there was a chatty essay on the English theater, comparing its actors unfavorably with those on the Continent; there was a sentimental tale, "Alcander and Septimius," announced as a translation from "a Byzantine Historian," but actually a retelling of Boccaccio's "Titus and Gisippus" in the *Decameron;* there were two translations: one of a letter from Voltaire describing his life in Switzerland, another (unacknowledged) of a passage from Justus Van Effen, presented as a letter from an Englishman traveling in Poland;[30] and there was "A

101

Short Account of the Late Mr. Maupertuis [the French Scientist],"
for which Goldsmith again had recourse to the *Encyclopédie*.
Throughout, the subject was humanity, the tone was humane, and
the style was essentially human. Goldsmith had only to be himself;
he could light like the bee wherever his fancy attracted him, and
his flair for interesting detail and lively expression made his
forages invariably interesting.

Yet composing a thirty-two-page magazine each week demanded the industry of a bee too. He might conceivably have
patched together the first issue from odds and ends which he had
written earlier; but as the weeks passed, he must have been
obliged to compose or translate a piece almost every day. The
second issue of the magazine contained a satirical essay on women's
dress, a letter from a traveler in Sweden (again an unacknowledged translation from Van Effen), a nostalgic piece entitled
"Happiness, in a Great Measure, Dependent on Constitution,"
another essay "On Our Theatres," and another translation of a
letter by Voltaire.

Although Goldsmith was known as "Dr. Goldsmith" now,[31]
he could hardly have had time for practicing medicine. In fact
Mrs. Martin's relative later told Prior that he had spent all day in
his room, and that on one occasion—probably when there was a
deadline to meet—a gentleman had called on him, locked the
door of the room, and stayed there until evening, when Goldsmith
emerged, ordered supper for two, and spent the rest of the evening cheerfully with his visitor.

To maintain his steady output, he was obliged to depend on his
past experience, on his reading, and on outright pilfering. In the
essay "Happiness . . . Dependent on Constitution," for example,
he recalled the simple joys of his childhood as contrasted with
the sophisticated pleasures of London; he described the happy
slave whom he had seen during his travels in Flanders, then
shifted to what he had read of the sprightly Cardinal de Retz, and
presently repeated an old jest, which he applied to one Dick
Wildgoose, "the happiest silly fellow I ever knew." In the essay
"On Our Theatres" he described Mademoiselle Clairon, the
French actress, as well as English actors and actresses whom he

102

GREEN ARBOUR COURT

Where Goldsmith lodged in 1759-60

(Reproduced from an engraving in the *European Magazine*)

GOLDSMITH'S ROOMS AT NO. 2 BRICK COURT, THE TEMPLE

(Reproduced, by permission, from the sketch by Hanslip Fletcher in Walter George Bell's *More about Unknown London,* published by John Lane The Bodley Head Limited)

had seen. The third number contained an essay "On the Use of Language," which referred to various "beggars of my acquaintance," whom he advised in the fine art of wheedling a loan; a jest from Pasquil, which he applied to "Bidderman, a Flemish folk hero," enlivened a tale in the fourth. In the same number there was the now famous "City Night Piece," describing a stroll through London after two o'clock in the morning, when he observed the "poor, houseless creatures" whom he longed to relieve. "Why," he asked, "was this heart of mine formed with so much sensibility! or why was not my fortune adapted to its impulse!" Even his lack of self-assurance, his penchant for self-castigation, cropped up in two essays: one "On Justice and Generosity," in *Bee* No. III, where with the aid of passages lifted from both Justus Van Effen and Volume V of the *Encyclopédie* he berates the man who makes a show of generosity when he has not paid his debts; another "Upon Political Frugality," in No. V, in which, again with the aid of the *Encyclopédie,* he deplored the lack of frugality among the English and even went so far as to say that "they who are generally called misers, are some of the very best members of society."

Obviously Goldsmith was not practicing what he had preached in his reviews about the virtues of originality; in fact scholars have discovered in *The Bee* alone more than a dozen unacknowledged borrowings from French sources, half of them from that useful fifth volume of the *Encyclopédie.*

How would he have justified such practice? He might, of course, have argued that since he was not signing his name to these essays, he was not actually claiming other men's work as his own. Or he might have maintained that by translating a Frenchman's work into English he was, in effect, merely borrowing ideas and making them his by expressing them in his own words. But probably he would not have bothered to defend himself. He regarded his contributions to *The Bee* as pure hackwork, not literature at all. Time was short, he had thirty-two pages to fill each week, and *The Bee* demanded a kind of writing that he had never before attempted. He had announced in his Introduction that he would "rove from flower to flower, with seeming inattention, but concealed choice," and he was exercising his prerogative of con-cealing some of his choices. He could hardly have foreseen that this work would be in print two centuries later—or that men would then take the trouble to track down his rovings.

Time was short indeed. For in addition to his work on *The Bee* he was probably contributing to the *Lady's Magazine*,[32] and he was certainly furnishing occasional pieces to *The Busy Body,* a periodical published three times weekly by Israel Pottinger and presumably edited by Edward Purdon, Goldsmith's old friend of Trinity College days. On October 13 he contributed a satirical letter describing the various kinds of clubs that were flourishing in London; on the 18th, "The Logicians Refuted," a humorous poem "in imitation of Dean Swift," which has often been reprinted as Swift's work; on the 20th, an essay describing a stroll through London during the public celebrations of the victories of the year 1759 and concluding with a plea for conciliation; and on the 22nd, a poem commemorating the capture of Quebec. A few weeks later, however, *The Busy Body* was merged with another peri-odical issued by a different publisher, and Goldsmith's connection with it ended.[33]

Meanwhile *The Bee* was not thriving. In the introductory essay to the fourth issue Goldsmith complained good-naturedly that his fame had "hardly travelled beyond the sound of Bow-bell," but consoled himself that "what my reputation wants in extent, is made up by its solidity." He was determined, however, not to pander to vulgar tastes in an effort to increase his circula-tion. In fact he seems rather to have done the opposite: his articles grew longer and more serious, and he printed fewer poems and tales. The change in spirit was apparent first in the essay "The Characteristics of Greatness" in the fourth issue; it emerged more clearly in the following week in "Upon Political Frugality," "Upon Unfortunate Merit," and "A Reverie," an evaluation of contemporary writers remarkable chiefly for its tribute to Samuel Johnson and his *Rambler*. The sixth issue contained only four items: a long and surprisingly thorough essay "On Education," in which Goldsmith announced that he would "dismiss all attempts to please, while I study only instruction"; a translation from Voltaire "On the Contradictions of the World"; and "Some Account of the Academies in Italy." The style was still informal, the development often included personal recollections or anecdotes— or borrowings from the *Encyclopédie*—but the purpose was more serious. Goldsmith had found one type of magazine unable to attract sufficient subscribers, and he was trying to evolve another type and attract other readers.

But this second type was not the type that came naturally to him, and soon he—or Wilkie—gave up the attempt: *Bee* No. VIII, which came out on Saturday, November 24, contained an adaptation of two essays from *The Humourist,* a popular magazine of fifty or sixty years earlier; "An Account of the Augustan Age of England," an excerpt from a series of essays, "The History of Our Own Language," published in the *Literary Magazine* in 1758;[34] and a brief discussion "Of the Opera in England." And that was the last of *The Bee.* Wilkie perhaps reprinted some copies of the exhausted first issue of the magazine and bound them up with his superfluous copies of the other seven.[35] But the resulting volume, published by Wilkie and Dodsley in mid-December, had only a limited sale.

The December *Critical Review* gave it a brief notice, observing that "although we will not compare [the author's] labours to the honied lucubrations of an Addison or a Johnson, we may safely aver, that they are greatly preferable to many modern funds of entertainment." But the January *Monthly Review* contained a much longer article by William Kenrick, who declared that most of the subjects treated in *The Bee* were "already sufficiently worn out" and its observations "frequently trite and common." "A Writer must, therefore, possess very extraordinary talents of spirit, humour, and variety of expression," he added, "to please, under such disadvantages." And he quoted long excerpts from the book to suggest that the author of *The Bee* had no such talents.

But Goldsmith could discount such criticism, considering its source. He had proved to himself and the booksellers that he had a rich store of literary materials and that he could turn out a lively, readable essay, tale, or poem at short notice. He still had his connection with the *Critical,* perhaps also with the *Lady's Magazine.*

105

And since new periodicals were appearing every week or two, the booksellers soon found other jobs for him. On December 29, 1759, Pottinger, who had published *The Busy Body,* brought out a new serial, the *Weekly Magazine; or, Gentleman and Lady's Polite Companion,* with Goldsmith as one of its principal contributors, perhaps its editor.

The Introduction to the new magazine, which may well have been by Goldsmith,[36] boasted that its staff included writers prepared to enlighten their readers on a wide variety of topics. "If, for example, the wind happens to . . . blow from the Hibernian shores, we intend to send out an author, properly prepared, to catch the inspiring gale, and work up our conundrums, carawitchits, rebusses, and artificial bulls."[37] Indeed the prevailing winds seemed to be from the west, for the first issue contained "A Description of the Manners and Customs of the Native Irish" and "Some original Memoirs of the late famous Bishop [Berkeley] of Cloyne." Of these the first sounds very much like Goldsmith's work, and the second was almost certainly his, since it contains an anecdote about Berkeley's student days at Trinity College reported by a schoolfellow "whose name was Contarine, and from whom I had the story." Goldsmith had apparently discovered that he could make copy even out of his recollections of Ireland.

More significant, however, is his article "Some Thoughts preliminary to a general Peace," later reprinted with an additional introductory paragraph and several minor revisions in the *Lady's Magazine* for October, 1761. In it Goldsmith expressed principles which were to underlie his political thinking for years to come. He was encouraged, he declared, to learn that George II and Frederick of Prussia had taken steps to assure peace in Europe, but he warned that England must not demand more favorable terms "than is consistent with the honour of our enemies to give, than is consistent with our own security to accept of." And presently he explained his rather puzzling second phrase: "Indemnification for what is past, and security for the future, are the essential objects in a treaty of pacification, but both these may be easily effected without any accession to our present dominions; and, instead of draining our natural country by peopling new acquisitions abroad, better it were could we abridge the enemy's power at home." In other words, nations need to learn to leave well enough alone; if stretched too far, a fabric may grow weak at the center.

In the same month Goldsmith contributed to J. Coote's *Royal Magazine* a philosophical tale entitled "Asem, the Man-Hater." It tells how Asem, oppressed by the evils of this world and about to seek escape in suicide, is led by the Genius of Conviction to a subterranean realm where men are free of all vice. There he discovers that the virtuous inhabitants are preyed upon by animals which they refuse to tyrannize over, that they can boast no achievements in the arts because they will not compete with each other, that they have no social ties because they suffer no fears, that they lack patriotism because. . . . In short Asem realizes that, with all its faults, the world is not so bad as he had supposed. He returns to it, prospers, and finds happiness. The wise man, like the wise nation, learns to let well enough alone.

And so had Oliver Goldsmith. Experience had convinced him that the doctrine of contented acceptance was the best guide to a satisfying life. Tinker? tailor? ploughboy? sailor? Doctor? . . . No, none of these. All his adult life he had been drifting toward a literary career. Why not swim with the current? He had fought for a chance to travel, only to conclude that travel could teach him little. He had studied to be a physician, only to find that he could not attract patients. He had wangled a position on the coast of Coromandel, only to find that his commission was worthless. Yet he had complained bitterly of the mercenary booksellers, only to find that they were to be his salvation. What could a sensible man do but accept the fate which seemed to be foreordained for him?

Surely there were worse fates. He was busy now, he had one reasonably successful book to his credit, and he was finding new outlets for his talents every month. Granted, he was still only a hack, living in a garret and writing for bread. Yet with good luck, determination, and proper guidance he might eventually find time to write for fame—and perhaps even achieve it.

Chapter V
Author by Profession
(1760-1762)

URING the first two or three weeks of January, 1760, Goldsmith continued to write for the *Critical Review* and the *Weekly Magazine*. For the *Critical* he reviewed Kedington's *Critical Observations upon the Iliad of Homer,* borrowing again from Volume V of the *Encyclopédie* to enforce his claim that servile worship or imitation of Homer is preposterous.[1] For the January 5 issue of the *Weekly* he wrote, presumably, two poems—a brief "Epitaph for Dr. Milner," his former employer, and a humorous sketch entitled "The Double Metamorphosis"— and three biographical essays: one a continuation of his Memoirs of Bishop Berkeley, another a brief but highly laudatory "Life of the Honourable Robert Boyle," and the third an amusing squib called "Serious Reflections on the life and Death of the late Mr. T—— C—— by the Ordinary of Newgate." This last was an ironic account of the escapades of the disreputable actor Theophilus Cibber, interrupted periodically with the refrain that all who knew him prophesied "that The—— would be hanged." As luck would have it, however, he was drowned. Hence the moral: "Let your actions be never so flagrant, you never can be hanged if born to die in a cold bath! ! !"

Goldsmith was at his best in this sort of nonsense. In the three months that he had been writing for magazines like *The Bee* and the *Weekly* he had turned out a surprising number of acceptable, sometimes thoughtful, essays, tales, and poems; but usually the effectiveness of his writing was in direct proportion to the amount of humor which it contained. And when he abandoned all pretensions to instruction and indulged his innate desire to entertain—as in the delightful "Elegy on that Glory of Her Sex, Mrs. Mary Blaize," in *Bee* No. IV—he had shown that he could outdo any writer in London.

As yet he had signed his name to none of his work, and the reading public probably knew him only as the author of *Polite Learning.* But the publishers were well aware of his talents; and when John Newbery decided that he wanted to spice the columns of his new daily, the *Public Ledger,* with essays in the manner popular since the days of Addison and Steele, he called on Goldsmith to provide the spice.

No one knows just how Goldsmith and Newbery first met. But whatever the circumstances, it was a happy meeting for Goldsmith. Newbery, whom Sam Johnson satirized affectionately as Jack Whirler in *The Idler,* had energy enough for half a dozen men—and benevolence enough for twenty. As a young man he had worked so assiduously in the offices of the *Reading Gazette and Oxford Mercury* that his employer, a man named Carnan, had willed him a half interest in the paper. In due time Newbery had married Carnan's widow—although she was six years older than he and the mother of three children—and in 1744 he had moved his family to London, where he could find more scope for his energies. By 1760 he was securely established in a shop at the sign of the Bible and Sun in St. Paul's Churchyard, where he ministered to Londoners' minds as a publisher of books and periodicals and to their bodies as a purveyor of patent medicines— among them, the famous Dr. James's Fever Powders, of which he was half-owner.

Yet success had not made him self-centered. He was an unusually generous stepfather and had advanced many a loan to needy authors—Sam Johnson among others.[2] To Goldsmith, who had complained so bitterly about mercenary booksellers, he was a godsend; for he eventually supplied the direction which the irresponsible Noll needed before he could achieve all that he was capable of. Later he hailed Newbery as "the honestest man in the nation"[3] and introduced him into *The Vicar of Wakefield* as the "philanthropic bookseller" who befriended Dr. Primrose when he was penniless. Today his interest in improving the quality of books for children is commemorated in the Newbery Award given annually for the most distinguished children's book published in the United States.

109

Newbery's *Public Ledger* first appeared on January 12, 1760. The issue of the 24th contained two letters, hidden away among the columns of news. The first, supposedly from "a resident of Amsterdam" to "Mr. ——, Merchant, in London," acknowledged receipt of two bills and introduced the bearer as "a native of Honan in China," a philosopher and an honest man, who understands English "though he is entirely a stranger to their manners and customs." The second, addressed to the merchant in Amsterdam by Lien Chi Altangi, obviously the new arrival, commented on "the gloomy solemnity in the houses, the streets, and the inhabitants" of London, which has convinced him that England is not opulent, as commonly supposed, but "actually poor." Goldsmith had decided that the best way he could spice the pages of the *Ledger* was to tell its readers how Englishmen looked to an outsider.

But he was not interested solely in satirizing the English. In the third letter, addressed to Fum Hoam, "First President of the Ceremonial Academy at Pekin," he mocked the absurd extremes to which English ladies and gentlemen went in their quest for beauty. But the mockery was double-edged: "I shall never forget the beauties of my native city. . . .," Lien observed. "How very broad their faces; how very short their noses; how very little their eyes; how very thin their lips! how very black their teeth!" Yet, if the English reader had digested the whole essay, his laughter at this line would have been tempered by Lien's earlier remark: "By long travelling, I am taught to laugh at folly alone, and to find nothing truly ridiculous but villainy and vice." And in truth these letters were not designed primarily to mock either English or Chinese manners: they were the considered observations of one who, like Oliver Goldsmith, had seen a good deal of the world, had achieved a tolerant attitude toward men of all nations, and was eager to sort out the good from the bad. In fact, in the fourth letter, published in the *Ledger* of January 31, Lien presented an astute analysis of English character, tracing its virtues and vices alike to a basic pride, occasionally mocking national weaknesses but more often revealing sincere admiration.

Although Goldsmith did not use the heading "Chinese Letters" until his fifth Letter appeared,[4] he was probably already on contract to supply two letters per week for the *Ledger*. It was an ideal arrangement for him. In the first place his salary, reputedly one hundred pounds per year,[5] supplied him with a basic income which would provide for his needs, yet relieve him from the intense pressures which he had been under while writing for *The Bee*. In the second place he was well equipped for the job, since he too was an outlander who was bound to regard the London scene with a certain detachment. Yet in 1760 an Irishman's reaction to English life would have interested no one, while it was fashionable to regard the Chinese as paragons of wisdom.

He had probably been introduced to the device of criticism by a foreign observer in Marana's *Turkish Spy*, which he mentioned in a letter to his uncle in May, 1753.[6] And his interest may have been whetted by the success of Horace Walpole's brief *Letter of Xo-Ho, a Chinese Philosopher at London, to his Friend Lien Chi at Pekin*, which one of his colleagues reviewed cursorily in the *Monthly Review* for May, 1757. Three months later, in the August issue of the *Monthly*, he himself had quoted Voltaire's words: "The success of [Montesquieu's] 'Persian Letters' arose from the delicacy of their satire. That satire which in the mouth of an Asiatic is poignant, would lose all its force when coming from an European."[7]

Although he took Montesquieu as the model for his series, Goldsmith was more indebted for specific materials to Lord Lyttelton's *Persian Letters* and, even more, to the less-known *Lettres Chinoises* of Jean Baptiste de Boyer, Marquis D'Argens, from which he sometimes lifted—or at best adapted—long passages.[8] He drew also on DuHalde's *General History of China*, which, along with Louis LeComte's *Memoirs and Observations . . . Made in a late Journey through the Empire of China*, he used, especially during the early months of the series, as a source-book for the sort of background information, anecdotes, maxims, or incidental references that would give the Letters verisimilitude.[9] For although he had earlier ridiculed the contemporary vogue for the Chinese,[10] he did not scruple to make capital of it now.

During the month of February he devoted all his efforts to the *Ledger* and the *British Magazine,* another new venture which Smollett had sponsored. In Letter No. VI Fum Hoam deplored his friend's enthusiasm for knowledge and his neglect of sensual satisfactions; then, by way of supplying more continuity and interest to the series, Goldsmith made him report that the Emperor of China had seized all the members of Lien's family except his son, whom Fum had managed to conceal and who was now determined to set out in search of his father. In the next Letter Lien quoted several passages, supposedly from Confucius,[11] to console himself for his misfortunes and, in addition, presented this justification for his wanderings: "A man who leaves home to mend himself and others is a philosopher; but he who goes from country to country, guided by the blind impulse of curiosity, is only a vagabond. From Zerdusht down to him of Tyanea, I honour all those great names who endeavour to unite the world by their travels: such men grew wiser as well as better, the farther they departed from home, and seemed like rivers, whose streams are not only increased, but refined, as they travel from their source." Goldsmith was learning that travel had distinct advantages for anyone who was to make a career of interpreting life.

On February 7 Lien returned to his discussion of the English passion for politics introduced in the fourth Letter, and presently turned his attention to gazettes, which he said revealed the dominant characteristics of whatever nation produces them. And, perhaps by way of relieving the seriousness of the last two papers, Goldsmith presented some sample news items burlesquing what he considered the typical gazette of each of several nations.

The Letter of February 9 continued the comic strain and again made Lien the butt of the jest. He has thought better, he assures Fum Hoam, of some of his first unfavorable impressions of the English; he has begun to find even the women tolerable and is touched by the affability of the strange women whom he meets on the streets after nightfall. One in particular has taken his watch in order to have it repaired free of charge, and he is preparing a formal speech of thanks to deliver to her when she returns it. Then, of course, in the next Letter, Lien realizes his error and launches into a discussion of sexual morality—most of which Goldsmith lifted from a similar passage about France in D'Argens' *Lettres Chinoises.*

The next Letter, published February 14, is Lien's description of the lands which he passed through on his trip from Pekin to Moscow. It too is taken almost word for word from D'Argens, and the letter of February 21, a discussion of English funerals and epitaphs, is largely Goldsmith's reworking of two other letters of D'Argens, plus two short excerpts from his well-thumbed fifth volume of the *Encyclopédie.*[12] He was back at his old tricks; for in his writing, as in his life, he often followed the line of least resistance.

And again, what can be said in his defense? Perhaps that he felt that he was not stealing when he translated another man's words into his own; perhaps that an unsigned work like the "Chinese Letters" need not be original, especially in the eighteenth century, when literary property was not as sacrosanct as it is today. But if one considers the results of some of Goldsmith's most patent thefts, the man is, in a sense, vindicated. His rather pedestrian essay on English burial practices, for example, led to the description of Westminster Abbey and the creation of the Man in Black, who, as Lien's mentor, heightened the satire of the Letters by his skeptical observations about English life as only a native could know it. Similarly, his description of Oriental civilizations in the tenth Letter suggested his defense of luxury in No. XI, a lively paper in which his philosophy of contented acceptance and his belief in literature as a source of pleasure are both implicit. This is, indeed, one of Goldsmith's most revealing Letters: it shows how deftly he could present an elementary essay in economics without sacrificing the genial tone of the series or the tolerant character of his Chinese sage. "In whatsoever light, therefore, we consider luxury," Lien declares, "whether as employing a number of hands, naturally too feeble for more laborious employment; as finding a variety of occupation for others who might be totally idle; or as furnishing out new inlets to happiness, without encroaching on mutual property; in whatever light we regard it, we shall have reason to stand up in its defence, and the sentiment of Confucius still remains unshaken, 'That we should enjoy as many of the luxuries of life as are consistent with our own safety, and the prosperity of others; and that he who finds out a new pleasure, is one of the most useful members of society.'" Goldsmith's creative powers were quickly germinated, and frequently a passage lifted from another writer provided the seed which flowered in an essay of unquestionable originality.

The final letter for February, published in the *Ledger* on the 28th, took a new course: Goldsmith now mocked the vogue for the Chinese which was partially responsible for the success of his series. Lien tells delightfully of a visit to a lady of quality who indulges a taste for useless *chinoiserie*—and who greets him with the words, "Bless me! can this be the gentleman that was born so far from home?"

"What next?" readers of the *Ledger* must have asked themselves. Of course it was to Goldsmith's advantage that they be kept wondering. Soon he had a regular following, and the editors acknowledged the importance of the Letters by giving them the leading position in every issue in which they appeared. One never knew what today's subject would be: Lien's experiences and reflections ranged from farce to philosophy. But they were never dull.

Meanwhile Goldsmith found time, during the month of February, to write two or three articles for Smollett's *British Magazine*.[13] One of these was the first installment of the well-known "Reverie at Boar's Head Tavern," another expression of the philosophy of contented acceptance. This time it is Dame Quickly who plays the philosophic vagabond—not through many lands but through many ages. "You will find mankind neither better nor worse now than formerly," she tells the sentimental Mr. Rigmarole as he mourns the departed glories of Falstaff's tavern.[14] And she is speaking for Oliver Goldsmith, who had, for the moment, found contentment himself. After years of indirection he had struck out a clear course: he had developed his powers of observing life and recording it entertainingly until they had become a source of pleasure for others and of profit for himself. No wonder he could play the optimist.

Still he must have suffered moments of depression. Although little is known of his personal life in these early months of 1760, beyond question his appearance and brogue won taunts as they did before and afterwards. Undoubtedly he made ridiculous blunders which threw his companions into gales of laughter. One anecdote of this period concerns a trick played on him by a bailiff who had a writ against him. Despairing of catching him in his rooms, he sent him a note asking him to come quickly to a coffee-house and signed as if by the steward of a nobleman who admired a poem by Goldsmith. Of course Goldsmith hastened to the coffeehouse—and was rescued by Archibald Hamilton, of the *Critical Review,* who happened along just in time to settle the debt. If the story is true, it suggests that Goldsmith was having his usual difficulty in keeping his expenses within his income. Probably the reasons were the same as always: gambling, inordinate generosity, and chronic improvidence. On the whole, though, he was better off than ever before. Life had been kind to him, and he reciprocated by writing kindly of life. In doing so he was acting on his conviction that a writer should brighten the lives of his fellows.

In the course of the next four months he continued to present his "Chinese Letters" regularly (ten in March, eight in April, ten in May, and eleven in June) and to make occasional contributions to other periodicals. Since no letters or anecdotes survive from these months, his essays are the only index to his thinking during this period, and they reveal that, now that he had settled down to a writer's career, his powers were rapidly developing. In order to give variety to the Letters, he approached new areas of thought and mastered them with surprising speed. And always the result of his reflections was, in effect, confirmation of his doctrine of contented acceptance.

In Letter No. XLIV he urged again acceptance of life as one finds it: "Every wish, therefore, which leads us to expect happiness somewhere else but where we are; every institution which teaches us that we should be better by being possessed of some-

115

thing new, which promises to lift us a step higher than we are, only lays a foundation for uneasiness, because it contracts debts which we cannot repay; it calls that a good, which, when we have found it, will in fact, add nothing to our happiness." The same attitude appears in the second and third installments of the "Reverie at Boar's-Head Tavern" in the *British Magazine* for March and April. Dame Quickly relates the scandalous history of the tavern and concludes by asking Mr. Rigmarole: "Have you, then, any cause to regret being born in the times you now live? or do you still believe that human nature continues to run on declining every age? If we observe the actions of the busy part of mankind, your ancestors will be found infinitely more gross, servile, and even dishonest than you. . . ." Moreover, in the first of a series of four letters called "A Comparative View of Nations," published in the June issue of the *Royal Magazine,* Goldsmith extolled Britain as "happiest of countries" and then pointed out that Providence always accommodates the wants of men to the climate and civilization in which they have been born. "I should esteem it my greatest happiness," he wrote, "could my travels conduce to [make Englishmen appreciate their blessings]; could they make one individual more happy in himself, or more useful to society; could I enlarge one mind, and make the man who now boasts his patriotism, a citizen of the world."

In less serious moments Lien continued his examination of English manners and institutions. He mocked the behavior of Englishmen at church (No. XLI) and in the theater (XXI), poured scorn on their quack doctors (XXIV) and degenerate aristocrats (XXXII), deplored their fondness for freak shows (XLV), and derided the disparity between rank and dress which prevailed in all ranks of society (LII). At the same time he did not hesitate to praise the English when he found "gleams of greatness" among them. In No. XXIII he cited their charity, especially their response to a subscription for the relief of French prisoners, and in No. XXXVIII he accorded extravagant praise to George II for his administration of justice—and lamented the injustice which prevailed in France under Louis XV.

Because the *Public Ledger* was a daily newspaper, Goldsmith inevitably approached political topics in his Letters, which must have served, in part at least, as a statement of editorial policy. And although the war with France was still in progress, he appealed always for peace—and contented acceptance. In No. XLII, a letter from Fum Hoam to Lien, he borrowed anecdotes from LeComte and DuHalde in order to contrast the peaceful history of China with that of the European nations, whose disastrous wars had gained them nothing. "Their princes," wrote Fum, "because they preferred ambition to justice, deserve the character of enemies to mankind." In No. XVII Lien considered the "frivolous motives" of the war with France and concluded that it had been brought about by the two nations' desire to possess Canada's furs, which obviously belonged to neither.[15] And the harmful effects of colonization, treated in passing here, are discussed more fully in No. XXV, where Lien gives an account of the kingdom of Lao. "When a trading nation begins to act the conqueror," he declares, "it is then perfectly undone"; for, as Goldsmith was later to write, "Where wealth accumulates . . . men decay." War, conquest, colonization, all are evidences of restlessness, of discontent, of failure to accept life as it is; and all are doomed to end in disaster.

Not all the Letters published in the months of March, April, May, and June were in so thoughtful a vein. Lien continued to offer his readers an infinite variety of subject matter: anything from a description of his garden in China to a tribute to Voltaire (whose death had been erroneously reported). Meanwhile narrative interest was sustained by the history of Lien's son, Hingpo, and his love for the beautiful Zelis; and the Man in Black emerged more clearly as a character, told his life story, and played a major part in several of the Letters. This device and the occasional insertion of a letter from Hingpo or Fum Hoam added variety to the series by introducing different points of view. Indeed Goldsmith sometimes abandoned the illusion which he had attempted to create and set down his thoughts without trying to sustain the fiction of their Chinese origin.

Every now and then the reader suspects that the Letters served as an outlet for Goldsmith's thinking about matters of a rather personal nature. Lien's remarks about marriage and women, in particular, may have special significance, considering that his creator was about to turn thirty and was in a secure enough position to think about taking a wife. In No. XVIII Lien tells a story from DuHalde[16] to demonstrate the folly of basing a marriage on romantic notions of love. In No. XIX (borrowed in part from D'Argens) he deplores the English convention of ridiculing the man whose wife has proved faithless, again urging a more sensible approach to marriage: "Marriage has been compared with a game of skill for life: it is generous in both parties thus to declare they are sharpers in the beginning. In England, I am told, both sides use every art to conceal their defects from each other before marriage, and the rest of their lives may be regarded as doing penance for their former dissimulation." In No. XXVIII he wonders at the number of old maids and bachelors in London and learns from the Man in Black (himself a bachelor) that it is not lack of opportunity that keeps women single, but "pride, avarice, coquetry, or affectation." And in No. XLVI Lien recounts a dream in which he sees several fashionable ladies observing their reflections in the magic looking-glass of Lao, "which reflects the mind as well as the body." The only one who escapes unscathed is a modest creature who proves to have been "deaf, dumb, and a fool from her cradle." And although Lien assures his correspondent that "dreams, you know, go always by contraries," a reader cannot help wondering how much of Goldsmith's attitude toward women is reflected in these Letters. He was not formed by nature to delight a London lady of the eighteenth century, and he may have resented their treatment of him.

Another subject bound to interest him, now that he had become an author by profession, was the state of literature in his time, and the Letters have a good deal to say on the topic. As might be expected, he often satirized what seemed to him the faults of writers of his generation; he could even afford now to raise a laugh at unsuccessful authors. But at the same time he was an author himself, and he took a proprietary and defensive attitude toward contemporary literature in general. In No. XL he who in his time had bewailed the decline of polite learning denied hotly that "the race of [English] poets is extinct." "Men of true discernment," he wrote, "can see several poets still among the English, some of whom equal, if not surpass, their predecessors. The ignorant term that alone poetry which is couched in a certain number of syllables in every line, where a vapid thought is drawn out into a number of verses of equal length, and perhaps pointed with rhymes at the end. But glowing sentiment, striking imagery, concise expression, natural description, and modulated periods, are fully sufficient entirely to fill up my idea of this art, and make way to every passion." He went on to declare that he could "see several poets in disguise" among the English, that "their Johnsons and Smolletts are truly poets; though for ought I know, they never made a single verse in their whole lives." On the other hand, "many of the writers of their modern odes, sonnets, trag-edies, or rebuses, it is true, deserve not the name, though they have done nothing but clink rhymes and measure syllables for years together."[17]

In another article, "A Dream: the Fountain of Fine Sense," in the *British Magazine* for May, Goldsmith borrowed again from D'Argens[18] to suggest several of the deterrents to contemporary literature. He described a mountain where hordes of people are indulging in reckless judgments on literature, a noble writer is complaining that his works are neglected while Pope's are read, and another nobleman is refusing to aid a young poet because "I never subscribe except for prints or drawings." Yet far above these, at the very summit of the mountain, stand a number of men who "unite gravity, sense, and humour." And among them are "John-son, Gray, and Mason, with some others of our own country, con-veying strong sense in the wildest sallies of poetical enthusiasm."

Goldsmith wrote some forty essays during the months of March, April, May, and June, 1760, and in them he showed that he was maturing as a writer: he tackled new areas of thinking, mastered them quickly, and adapted his views on them to his basic philosophy. And he must have enjoyed the process. He had a boundless curiosity about all aspects of life, and he could enter

119

with enthusiasm into his study of Chinese civilization in DuHalde or LeComte, of the effect of environment on man or animals in Buffon, of contemporary world affairs in his newspaper, or of contemporary literature in the reviews. Yet always, regardless of how grave his topic might be, he could wield words in such a way as to make his subject pleasing. He was the master of the graceful turn of phrase, the well (but never rigidly) balanced sentence or paragraph; and he knew the value of concreteness, no matter how abstract his subject might be. He knew how to turn an anecdote to account. For example, in the *Critical Review* for March, he found fault with two poems by an obscure writer named William Dunkin, one an epistle to Lord Chesterfield, the other an eclogue addressed to an unknown author named Lawson. Then, as if to compensate for the dullness of his review, he rounded it off with a delightful story of Brandelius and Mogusius, whose reputations as poets depended entirely on the poems which they had written in praise of each other.

Yes, Goldsmith must have been enjoying his work. As time passed, the "Chinese Letters" grew longer, although he seems to have been on a yearly contract. Soon he had, in addition to the satisfaction which rose from the success of the Letters in the *Public Ledger,* the flattering knowledge that they were being copied in other periodicals. Doubtless he fumed at such borrowing—though he was in no position to cry thief!—but at heart he knew it proved that he was making his mark.

Sometime in the middle of 1760 he celebrated his success by moving from his dingy quarters in Green Arbour Court to two rooms at 6 Wine Office Court, just off Fleet Street.[19] Newbery probably arranged the move, for Goldsmith's new landlady was a Mrs. Carnan, a relative of Mrs. Newbery by her first marriage. Goldsmith might well have hesitated to make the change, lest it work some hardship on Mrs. Martin, his landlady at Green Arbour Court. Tom Davies reported, however, that even after he moved away, Goldsmith "often supplied her with food from his table, and visited her frequently with the sole purpose to be kind to her."[20]

Across the court from Mrs. Carnan's house and a few doors down toward Fleet Street was the Cheshire Cheese Tavern, where Goldsmith could meet his friends. And he undoubtedly spent a good deal of time in such haunts. On one occasion he is said to have gone to Blackwall for a dinner of whitebait and, in the course of the evening, to have fallen into a discussion of Sterne's *Tristram Shandy,* of which he had a low opinion. Others present disagreed sharply with him, and eventually the discussion degenerated into a fist fight, which was jokingly reported in the press. And in the June 11 issue of Goldsmith's own paper, the *Public Ledger,* someone (perhaps his old foe, William Kenrick) told a story of his meeting three ladies while walking in the gardens of the White Conduit-House, inviting them to take tea with him, and finding that he lacked the money to pay the bill. To make matters worse, some friends happened along, discovered his predicament, and prolonged his embarrassment by claiming for some time that they could not lend him the money which he so desperately needed.

Goldsmith's "absurdities" were already becoming legendary. According to another anecdote of this period Jack Pilkington, son of the notorious Letitia, asked him for a loan of two guineas on the pretext that a friend in India had sent him two white mice which a great lady of the town (reports differ as to whether it was the Duchess of Marlborough, Manchester, or Portland) was eager to buy at a handsome figure. But of course he could not think of delivering them unless he had a proper cage for the mice and a proper suit of clothes for himself. When Goldsmith assured him that he had only half a guinea to his name, Pilkington suggested that he could easily raise the other guinea and a half by pawning his watch for a few hours until the sale had been completed. Needless to say, Goldsmith consented and Pilkington disappeared. This time he himself made copy of the incident; at least it is said to have inspired the tale of Prince Bonbenin and the white mouse in the "Chinese Letters."

As his acquaintance and his social activities widened, Goldsmith doubtless needed more than the hundred pounds a year which he was receiving from the *Ledger*. Accordingly, when the secretaryship of the Society for the Encouragement of Arts, Manufactures, and Commerce fell vacant in 1760, he applied for it.[21] Newbery, Grainger, and Johnson were all members of the society, and he probably felt that he could count on their support. But to strengthen his application he went to call on David Garrick, who was said to have a good deal of influence in the organization. Unfortunately Garrick recalled that Goldsmith had written disparagingly of his treatment of authors,[22] and he refused to aid him. So Goldsmith continue to depend wholly on the magazines for his livelihood.

The "Chinese Letters" appeared regularly through the summer and into the fall of 1760, with narrative interest supplied by news of the escape of Hingpo and his beloved Zelis, then the announcement that they had been separated. Meanwhile, Beau Tibbs was introduced, and Lien spent a hectic evening at Vauxhall with him and his wife, the Man in Black, and the latter's lady love, a pawnbroker's widow. There were other Letters of a humorous nature, but the prevailing tone of the Letters during this period was more serious. There were "moral essays": for example, No. XLVII, on the folly of trying to stifle emotion, No. LXVI (borrowed in part from Marivaux) on the difference between love and gratitude, and No. LXXVI (almost entirely from Marivaux) on the superiority of the graces to beauty. Lien sharply criticized the gluttony and stupidity of English clergymen (No. LVIII), the rivalries of the theaters (LXXIX), and of actors (LXXXV), and the restraints imposed on marriage by the legislation of Lord Hardwicke (LXXII).

Goldsmith seems to have had a growing awareness of his influence as a social critic. When London succumbed to a fear of mad dogs, Lien pointed out the folly of such hysteria (LXIX). When European governments hired Russian mercenaries, he warned that they were strengthening the Russians and offering them an opportunity for what today would be called infiltration (LXXXVII). When the English forgot their loss by the death of George II in their rejoicing at the accession of George III, Lien harangued them on their lack of decorum (XCVI). Meanwhile Goldsmith reiterated his belief in many of the ideas which he had presented in earlier Letters, especially the doctrine of contented acceptance: in No. LXV he borrowed again from Marivaux, this time the story of a sensible cobbler who stuck to his last and ignored a state procession; in No. XC he deplored the prevalence of suffering from the spleen; and in No. XCII he mocked the "philosophic misery" of those who fret themselves about unlikely happenings of cosmic importance.

Considered as a body, the forty-five papers which Goldsmith wrote during the last six months of 1760 reveal his breadth of interests and his skill as a professional journalist alive to the events of the day, willing to take a stand on them, and able to present his case convincingly. He continued to borrow occasional bits from earlier writers;[23] but in general the Letters were more original: they suggested less of the Chinese philosopher and more of the genial Irishman who had managed to make a living from his good nature. "I am an enemy to nothing in this good world but war," he wrote in No. LXXXV; "I hate fighting between rival states; I hate it between man and man; I hate fighting even between women!"

The result of his success was that he took more and more of a proprietary interest, even a professional pride, in his trade. For although he still bewailed the decline of polite learning in Europe (No. LXIII), he warmly defended contemporary English literature by means of a clever analogy in No. LXXV:

The volumes of antiquity, like medals, may very well serve to amuse the curious; but the works of the moderns, like the current coin of a kingdom, are much better for immediate use: the former are often prized above their intrinsic value, and kept with care; the latter seldom pass for more than they are worth, and are often subject to the merciless hands of sweating critics and clipping compilers: the works of antiquity were ever praised, those of the moderns read: the treasures of our ancestors have our esteem, and we boast the passion; those of contemporary genius engage our heart, although we blush to own it. The visits we pay the former resemble those we pay the great,—the ceremony is troublesome, and yet such as we would not choose to forego; our acquaintance with modern books is like sitting with a friend,—our pride is not flattered in the interview, but it gives more internal satisfaction.

123

Similarly, although he complained of the hardships of professional writers in No. LVII, he admitted in No. LXXXIV:

> A man of letters at present, whose works are valuable, is perfectly sensible of their value. Every polite member of the community, by buying what he writes, contributes to reward him. The ridicule, therefore, of living in a garret, might have been wit in the last age, but continues such no longer, because no longer true. A writer of real merit now may easily be rich, if his heart be set only on fortune; and for those who have no merit, it is but fit that such should remain in merited obscurity. He may now refuse an invitation to dinner, without fearing to incur his patron's displeasure, or to starve by remaining at home. He may now venture to appear in company with just such clothes as other men generally wear, and talk even to princes with all the conscious superiority of wisdom. Though he cannot boast of fortune here, he can bravely assert the dignity of independence.

And in No. XCIII he even defended "writing for bread": ". . . almost all the excellent productions in wit that have appeared here were purely the offspring of necessity; their Drydens, Butlers, Otways, and Farquhars, were all writers for bread. Believe me, my friend, hunger has a most amazing faculty of sharpening the genius; and he who, with a full belly, can think like a hero, after a course of fasting, shall rise to the sublimity of a demi-god."

During these same months Goldsmith continued his series "A Comparative View of Nations" for the *Royal Magazine* and contributed occasional articles to the *British Magazine*. But in the months of November and December his contributions to the periodicals fell off sharply: he wrote only six "Chinese Letters" for the *Ledger* in November and only three Letters for the *Ledger* and perhaps one article for the *British* in December. The reason for the falling off in his work was probably that he had been engaged to edit Wilkie's flourishing *Lady's Magazine*.[24] Apparently his new duties demanded a good deal of his time because, even for the *Lady's Magazine* itself, he wrote few new pieces and contented himself with reprinting essays which he had published earlier elsewhere.[25]

As for the "Chinese Letters," they appeared only intermittently after the turn of the year: six in January, three each month in February, March, April, and May, none in June, one in July, and two in August. As early as No. CIII in January Lien announced that he was planning to leave England soon, but it was not until No. CXXIII (August 14) that Goldsmith rounded out the series by having Lien describe the wedding dinner of Hingpo and Zelis (who turns out to be the Man in Black's niece!) in the presence of the Tibbses, the Man in Black, and the pawnbroker's widow, whose romance is shattered in the course of an argument over the proper method of carving a turkey. Lien concluded this final letter by announcing that he expected to set off soon on his travels to observe other countries, and the publisher added that the Letters would be brought out in two volumes, carefully revised, with some new Letters added and some dull ones omitted.

By this time the quality as well as the quantity of the Letters had declined. Goldsmith seemed to have much less to say than in the earlier Letters and to have written a Letter only when he had some specific criticism to offer. As a result they are often satirical, rarely philosophical; they lack the variety of the earlier papers in the series, and they reveal a good deal less of the author's thinking. The effect is distinctly anticlimactic. Indeed the only time he approaches the level of the most cogent of his earlier Letters is in his suggestion that Englishmen study the arts and sciences of foreign nations, especially those of Asia, in order to improve their own (No. CVIII). And in that he probably had a personal motive.[26]

On August 19, five days after the last Chinese Letter appeared, Goldsmith tried his hand at inaugurating a new series for the *Ledger*. It began with a letter, supposedly from a reader, urging that the paper include literary news in its columns and offering to furnish two letters on such topics each week. On the 22nd the *Ledger* contained a letter "Fashions in Learning," pointing out that there was in England a large reading public eager for instruction on specialized topics, for whom the popular essayist could do a real service. Then followed three letters treating such varied subjects as a "new invention for the discovery of latent disorders in the breast, by striking the thorax" (August 27), a new agricultural society in Switzerland (August 29), and a book describing a race of giants in South America (September 5). But on September 10, after complaining of the dearth of "literary news," Goldsmith returned to the sort of moral essay which he had pre-

125

viously included among the "Chinese Letters": a complaint against the extravagant preparations for the Coronation of George III. Then, after two more attempts in much the same vein, the series ended. Goldsmith seemed to have lost his enthusiasm for periodical-writing.

He continued, however, to serve as editor of the *Lady's Magazine*. Beginning with the issue of February, 1761, he published serially in it the "Memoirs of M. de Voltaire"—the Life of Voltaire which he had written two years earlier and which Griffiths had never published. Goldsmith himself had described it as "no more than a catchpenny," and it consists of little but a rapid summary of the events of Voltaire's life, drawn, undoubtedly, from materials already in print[27] and pieced out with occasional translations from his writings[28] or observations on the arduousness of the literary life. Still the work is not without merit. It abounds in entertaining anecdotes, it is narrated with Goldsmith's usual verve, and it holds the reader's attention so well that he is disappointed when it breaks off suddenly just after Voltaire's arrival at the court of Frederick the Great.

One point about the "Memoirs" deserves special notice. Midway in Goldsmith's account of young Voltaire's escapades he pauses to remark: "I am not insensible, that by recounting these trifling particulars of a great man's life, I may be accused of being myself a trifler; but such circumstances as these generally best mark a character. . . . Let this, then, be my excuse, if I mention anything that seems to be derogatory from Voltaire's character, which will be found composed of little vices and great virtues. Besides, it is not here intended either to compose a panegyric or to draw up an invective; truth only is my aim. . . ." Such an apology may seem superfluous to a twentieth century reader, but in 1761 the idea expressed was provocative. Ordinarily biographers presented only the praiseworthy public actions of a distinguished man—or, occasionally, the shocking details of the private life of a notorious sinner. To strike a balance, to present all the details and seek to penetrate to the truth, was a new notion. Samuel Johnson had expressed the principle in two essays, *Rambler,* No. LX, and *Idler,* No. LXXXIV, and he had practiced it in his *Life of Richard Savage;* but it had by no means been generally accepted. Naturally it appealed to Goldsmith, who had always been interested in studying the ways of human beings. Again he was aligning himself with the spirit of the future rather than with that of the past.

But the "Memoirs" proved nothing about his writing or his thinking in the year 1761; it had been written in 1759. Goldsmith had, indeed, accomplished very little in the course of the year. For the *Public Ledger* he had finished less than a third of the number of articles which he had produced in the previous year; for the *British Magazine,* one at most; and for the *Lady's Magazine,* little that was new. To be sure, he translated *Mémoires de Milady B.* by Charlotte-Marie-Anne Charbonnier de la Guesnerie, which Newbery published early in the year, and he began work on an oratorio, *Captivity,* and a history of the Seven Years' War.[29] But on the whole it was an unproductive year for him, and he did less and less as it advanced. By November or December he had probably given up his position as editor of the *Lady's Magazine;* yet he did not resume his work for other periodicals.

It was a strange time for him to abandon periodical-writing, for he was just beginning to attract critical attention. The *Court Magazine* for December singled him out, along with Johnson, Young, Gray, and a few others, from a list of fifty-six living authors and hailed him as a writer of "taste and understanding." And soon afterwards, in William Rider's *Historical and Critical Account of the Lives and Writings of the Living Authors of Great-Britain,* he was accorded one of the longest articles in the book. "Whilst he is surpassed by few of his Contemporaries with Regard to the Matter which his Writings contain," Rider remarked, "he is superior to most of them in Style, having happily found out the secret to unite Elevation with Ease, a Perfection in Language, which few Writers of our Nation have attained to, as most of those who aim at Sublimity swell their Expressions with Fustian and Bombast, whilst those who affect Ease, degenerate into Familiarity and Flatness."[30]

But then again perhaps such recognition had helped to alienate him from the magazines. After all, if he could succeed so well when he was writing for bread, what might he not achieve if he husbanded his talents and energies and directed them toward writing for posterity? He had been associating with men who had higher standards than he had been following, and they may well have set him to thinking about just what his aims were.

Back in May of 1761 Thomas Percy had come up to London again to arrange for publication of the ballads which he had been collecting and editing. On Friday, the 22nd, he recorded in his diary: "Sold Dodsley my Old Ballads," and on Monday, the 25th: "Tea wth Goldsmith." Then on Sunday, the 31st: "Ev^g at Goldsmiths with much Company."[31] Among that company was Samuel Johnson, whom Goldsmith had long admired but never before entertained.

When Percy called for Johnson at his rooms, he was surprised to find him looking uncommonly well turned out. When asked the reason, Johnson replied: "Why, sir, I hear that Goldsmith, who is a very great sloven, justifies his disregard of cleanliness and decency, by quoting my practice, and I am desirous this night to show him a better example."

Soon they were fast friends. And before long Goldsmith met Johnson's friend Joshua Reynolds. He must have taken special satisfaction in this second friendship, for Reynolds soon welcomed him at the parties which he gave in his splendid mansion in Leicester Fields. He was, too, a man of even more manifest distinction than Johnson in 1761; he was said to be enjoying an income of six thousand pounds per year and was well acquainted with the finest ladies and gentlemen in London.

Goldsmith surely delighted in these friends—in the pleasure of their stimulating company and in the distinction which they reflected on him. At the same time they made him more poignantly aware of his own limitations. They were acknowledged to be eminent in their fields; he was still only a poor hack.

In an effort to rise above that level, he concocted a new scheme. It was not entirely new: as long ago as June, 1759, in a review of Van Egmont and Heyman's *Travels* in the *Critical*, he had remarked that society would benefit considerably from an account of the travels of a man who went to the Orient in order to study

128

the "mechanic inventions" of Eastern nations, "even though all he should bring home was only the manner of dyeing red in the Turkish manner." And in an article in the *Public Ledger* later reprinted as No. CVIII of *The Citizen of the World* he had re-iterated the idea and sketched the sort of person who could best undertake the commission:

He should be a man of a philosophical turn; one apt to deduce conse-quences of general utility from particular occurrences; neither swollen with pride, nor hardened by prejudice; neither wedded to one particular system, nor instructed only in one particular science; neither wholly a botanist, nor quite an antiquarian; his mind should be tinctured with mis-cellaneous knowledge, and his manner humanized by an intercourse with men. He should be, in some measure, an enthusiast in the design; fond of travelling, from a rapid imagination and an innate love of change; fur-nished with a body capable of sustaining every fatigue, and a heart not easily terrified at danger.

Obviously he had a candidate in mind, and soon after Lord Bute came to power late in 1761 Goldsmith drew up a "memorial" de-scribing the advantages to be gained from a study of Oriental arts and sciences and asking for a subsidy to enable him to undertake the project. When Bennet Langton told Sam Johnson about the scheme later, Johnson observed flatly that Goldsmith was "the most unfit to go out upon such an inquiry," since he was "utterly ignorant of such arts as we already possess." He even maintained that Goldsmith would "bring home a grinding-barrow, which you see in every street in London, and think that he had furnished a wonderful improvement."[32] Lord Bute was apparently similarly unimpressed, for the memorial brought no response.

From Goldsmith's point of view the plan would have been ideal. He had not lost his yearning to travel, to resume the role of the philosophic vagabond who ventures forth not to measure mountains or buildings but to measure the minds of men and the achievements of nations. Again and again in his writings he had lauded the citizen of the world, and he longed to be one. To be sure, he had seen much of Europe; but so had many others. He wanted now to see Asia, to observe what few Englishmen had seen, and eventually to return with a report of his findings. He

129

was not necessarily abandoning the world of letters: rather, he was seeking new materials to report to the reading public.

But it was not to be. And soon he was contributing again to the magazines. In January, 1762, he wrote for the *British Magazine* a lively letter suggesting that the thinning ranks of the army be filled by women, recounting the exploits of some celebrated female warriors of past and present, and describing the pretty uniforms which the recruits might be given. Then in the January 20-22 issue of *Lloyd's Evening Post,* another of John Newbery's ventures, he published the first of a series of essays entitled "The Indigent Philosopher."[33]

The author of the essay announced himself to be one who "must write, or I cannot live," who "must, perhaps, for life, incur the reproach of venality." He continued, however:

I shall take no shame to myself for endeavouring to enforce morals or improve good humour. There is no shame in making truth wear the face of entertainment, or letting ridicule fly only at mental deformity; nor is there any shame in being paid for it. It is not every scholar who pretends to despise this prostitution of talents, whose works have sufficient beauty to allure our employer to propose terms of similar prostitution. It is not every Gentleman who can forego, like me, the common and vendible topicks of government abuse, on which I could descant perhaps with elegance, in order to select general follies; on which topick it is probable I may be generally disregarded. There is no merit, nor do I claim any in the benevolence of my present publication; but there is at least some in the selection of my subject: And shall I be ashamed of being paid a trifle for doing this, when Bishops are paid for scarce preaching on Sundays! Shall I be ashamed of doing this! This power, if I have any power, was the only patrimony I received from a poor father! And shall I be ashamed of this! *By Heavens I more glory in it, than if possessed of all the wealth that ever fortune threw on fools.*

Of course Goldsmith's words should not be taken with complete seriousness. Yet, even with proper discount for dramatic heightening, they have revealing overtones: Goldsmith seems to be on the defensive. He must write, he insists that he glories in his trade— yet he is aware of the general disdain for it, and, at bottom, he cannot help sharing this disdain.

In the papers which follow, there are other hints of this attitude. The third, in the *Post* for January 29-February 1, offers a rewriting of Smollett's resumé of contemporary literature in his *Continuation of the Complete History of England* with ironic allusions to the popular magazines, orators, and poets, concluding with a parody of Gray's "Bard." The fourth, in the issue of February 8-10, is a satiric treatment of popular magazines, accomplished by specimens from the supposititious *Infernal Magazine.* Goldsmith was out of sorts with periodical-writing: this article was, in effect, his farewell to the magazines. Except for one serious essay, "The Revolution in Low Life," in the *Post* for June 14-16, he made no further contributions to a popular periodical for nearly eleven years.

He continued, however, to accept hack jobs. For Newbery he may have revised the *History of Mecklenburgh* written by Mrs. Sarah Scott (sister of Elizabeth Montagu, Queen of the Bluestockings) and published on February 26, 1762.[34] And he certainly wrote the pamphlet *The Mystery Revealed,* a defense of Kent, the man accused of murder by the famous Cock Lane Ghost, which operated in the bedroom of an eleven-year-old girl. Newbery paid him only three guineas for this, but presently gave him ten pounds for his share in *The Art of Poetry on a New Plan,* published March 9.[35] And during the next few weeks he was kept busy on two projects: the first volume of a *Compendium of Biography* and the revision of his "Chinese Letters," both of which appeared anonymously on May 1.

The latter, in two volumes, contained an "Editor's Preface," the 119 Letters from the *Public Ledger,* the "City Night Piece" from *The Bee,* an essay from the *British Magazine,* and two papers (No. CXXI and CXXII) apparently never published before.[36] Goldsmith had changed the order of some of the original Letters in order to bring together those on related subjects, and had made extensive revisions in most of them. He took time to recast, to delete or expand—sometimes adding whole paragraphs— and to rephrase, striving to give the series a lasting literary quality. And he released the Letters under a new title which had long represented to him the acme of enlightened urbanity: *The Citizen of the World.*[37]

The book was well, if not enthusiastically, received. The *British Magazine* characterized it as "light, agreeable summer reading, partly original, partly borrowed." The May *Critical* observed: "Were we to examine these reflections of *our Citizen of the World* by the standard of originality, our pleasure would be greatly diminished; but let us view them with regard to utility, and we must confess their merit." The June *Monthly* praised "the excellent remarks upon men, manners, and things" in "these entertaining Letters," announced that they were said to be "the work of the lively and ingenious Writer of An Enquiry into the present State of Polite Learning in Europe," and expressed regret that their editors had "undesignedly offended" him in the past by an observation "entirely general in its intention."[38] Unfortunately, however, the book had only a limited sale; and although it was reissued before the end of the year, Newbery was advertising it as late as May, 1766, as the work of the author of *The Traveller,* apparently hoping thereby to dispose of his surplus stock. In time, interest in the volumes revived: there were Dublin editions in 1762 and 1769 and a third London edition in 1774, the year of Goldsmith's death. In France the book enjoyed much greater favor, and the translation by Poivre, published in 1763, went through seven editions in four years.

As time passed and tastes changed, *The Citizen of the World* gained readers in England. In the fifty years after Goldsmith's death it went through more than twenty editions, and today it is accepted as a minor classic, representing his best work in the essay. Although many of the contemporary references are meaningless without explanatory notes, and although modern readers might prefer to encounter more of the Tibbses and less discussion of the state of literature in 1760, the Letters are delightful. Taken as a unit, they have obvious faults in their lack of unifying structure or development and in the inconsistency of some of the opinions expressed, and they inevitably grow tiresome if one attempts to read the series from beginning to end. But for the reader who dips here and there, who does not bother about how much Goldsmith took from others or how accurately he used his sources, *The Citizen of the World* is rewarding. Goldsmith was free to approach any subject from mad dogs to marriage, and in doing so he revealed a good deal about London life and thought in the mid-eighteenth century. But he revealed more about himself: his opinions about politics or economics, his attitude toward his profession, his tolerance, his moderation, his good nature—and above all, his ability to comprehend the essentials of a given subject and to express his conclusions about it with a sure, but never heavy, hand.

The first volume of *A Compendium of Biography,* which also appeared on May 1, was a much less significant achievement. Newbery, who was always interested in disseminating miscellaneous knowledge widely and cheaply, intended to have the series run from antiquity down to the present, but the project was abandoned after seven volumes of Plutarch's "Lives" had appeared. The publisher evidently regarded the series as an experiment in periodical publication, because he advertised that the volumes would be sold "at the easy Price of Eighteen-Pence each" and would be issued on the first of the month "so that Gentlemen may have them with their Magazines."[39] Goldsmith's task was to prepare readable versions of from six to nine of the "Lives" for each volume; and although they were announced to be "abridged from the original Greek, with notes and reflections," he doubtless merely abridged—or if so minded, enlarged upon—an earlier translation. He was paid only about six guineas for each volume, and he evidently regarded the task as unworthy of his best efforts. The first volume began with a preface emphasizing the values to be derived from reading biography, but it and the biographies which followed showed little originality or enthusiasm. And the series evidently enjoyed very little success, since it seems never to have been reviewed or reissued.

Newbery published the second, third, and fourth volumes of the *Compendium* at brief intervals as they were completed and paid Goldsmith a total of twenty-three and a half guineas for them. But when Goldsmith wrote to acknowledge receipt of his fee for the third and fourth volumes, he complained: "As I have been out of order for some time past and am still not quite recovered the fifth volume of Plutarch's lives remains unfinish'd. I fear I shall not be able to do it, unless there be an actual necessity and that none else can be found. If therefore you would send it to Mr Collier I should esteem it a kindness, and will pay for whatever it may come to." And a few days later: "One Volume is done namely the fourth; When I said I should be glad if Mr Collier would do the fifth for me, I only demanded it as a favour, but if he cannot conveniently do it though I have kept my chamber these three weeks and am not yet quite recovered yet I will do it."[40] Probably Joseph Collier wrote most, if not all, of the fifth volume and perhaps also the sixth and seventh.

On July 7 Goldsmith received from Newbery two guineas "for the conclusion of the English history," probably a chapter or two supplied to bring up to date a new edition of a previously published text.[41] And before long he was abroad again, paying a visit to the "Cherokee kings" who were the sensation of London that summer. In *Animated Nature* he complained that they kept him waiting three hours while they applied their paint and feathers. His friend Samuel Derrick, Beau Nash's successor as Master of the Ceremonies at Bath, added that one of the chiefs embraced Goldsmith so warmly, in gratitude for a small gift, that Noll emerged with a streak of ochre on his cheek—and was promptly accused of wearing rouge.

Soon he left the city for a few weeks at Bath and Tunbridge. But he did not waste his time there. Through Derrick, probably, he was introduced to George Scott, executor of the estate of Beau Nash, who had died the year before, and Scott gave him access to Nash's surviving papers. Before long Goldsmith was at work on this new project, selecting the papers which seemed to be pertinent, studying the scene of Nash's triumphs, and gathering anecdotes from those who had known him. And on October 14, shortly after his return to the city, Newbery and a publisher named Frederick at Bath brought out anonymously *The Life of Richard Nash, Esq., Late Master of the Ceremonies at Bath, Extracted Principally from his Original Papers.*

This was in every way a more ambitious piece of work than the "Memoirs of M. de Voltaire": it was twice as long, it was based on original research,[42] and it was destined to remain for

many years the definitive treatment of its subject. And just as
Goldsmith had felt obliged to apologize for presenting Voltaire's
foibles, here he felt constrained to defend the very notion of a
biography of a trifler like Nash:

> I profess to write the history of a man placed in the middle ranks of life;
> of one, whose vices and virtues were open to the eye of the most undiscern-
> ing spectator; who was placed in public view without power to repress cen-
> sure or command adulation; who had too much merit not to become re-
> markable, yet too much folly to arrive at greatness. I attempt the character
> of one who was just such a man as probably you or I may be, but with this
> difference, that he never performed an action which the world did not know,
> or ever formed a wish which he did not take pains to divulge. In short, I
> have chosen to write the life of the noted Mr. Nash, as it will be the delinea-
> tion of a mind without disguise, of a man ever assiduous without industry,
> and pleasing to his superiors without any superiority of genius or under-
> standing.

Goldsmith tried in his Preface to justify his biography by maintaining that Nash had performed a genuine service to England
by refining the manners of society; yet he was forced to admit
that Nash was "a weak man, governing weaker subjects," or,
borrowing from Cicero, "the little king of a little people." He
declared that reading about Nash's life might save others from
similar follies—but this was only a concession to the spirit of the
times. So far as he was concerned, Nash was a human being—a
fallible human being much like himself in many respects—and,
like all human beings, interesting. He even went so far as to say
incidentally that "every man's own life would perhaps furnish
the most pleasing materials for history."

Echoing his remarks in the "Memoirs of Voltaire," he declared
that this book was "neither written with a spirit of satire nor
panegyric, and with scarce any other art than that of arranging
the materials in their natural order." But the book was not as
artless as he claimed. After tracing Nash's early life and his first
success at Bath, he relied on anecdotes so presented as to illustrate
Nash's kindness, vanity, wit, and final deterioration. And though
at times he sternly criticized his subject's frailties, the tone was
often apologetic, with considerable stress on Nash's generosity
and thoughtfulness. The "original papers" included added little

but an air of authenticity, which Goldsmith tried to strengthen by claiming to have known Nash personally. Actually these papers are in some ways a hindrance, because he exercised so little selection in his use of them that the final third of the book is overweight and anticlimactic. Nevertheless it is a successful biography: the reader feels, when he finishes it, that he *knows* Beau Nash, and, thanks to Goldsmith's easy style and his ability to report anecdotes vividly, that the process of becoming acquainted with him has been thoroughly pleasurable.

But as Professor Stauffer pointed out, the *Life of Nash* is more than a delightful book: it is important in the development of English biography.[43] Goldsmith's desire to present neither panegyric nor satire but truth, however dependent on Johnson, was a new theory of biography, and it was to prove a lasting one. In the "Memoirs of Voltaire" he had shown himself willing to act on that theory; here it animated his entire work. Moreover, his desire to reveal the whole man, piercing through the façade offered to the public and presenting all available details about him, anticipates the work of Johnson in his *Lives of the Poets* and of Boswell in his *Life of Johnson*. In short, Goldsmith's achievement in this one book qualifies him to be ranked as one of the pioneers of modern theories of biography.

The reviewers greeted it much as Goldsmith apparently feared they might. The October *Critical* remarked that "we cannot . . . but take pity on a writer of genius, thus tortured to give substance to inanity." The November *Monthly* disposed of it in two sentences, pronouncing it "a trivial subject, treated for the most part in a lively, ingenious, and entertaining manner." Yet the *Gentleman's Magazine* thought well enough of the book to summarize it in two articles in its October and November issues. And Goldsmith could always console himself with the reflection that the critics had praised his talents even while they were condemning his subject.

Moreover, except for two London editions and a third in Dublin, all in 1762, there was little demand for the book. Goldsmith had received at most twenty-eight guineas for his work on it,[44] which must have involved several weeks of research and writing, to say nothing of the expenses of his trip to Bath. He was certainly growing no richer as time passed. Prior, in a generous estimate, fixes his income for the year 1762 at less than 120 pounds,[45] a sum which was hardly adequate for a man of Goldsmith's tastes who had given at least one large party during the year, had been under the expense of an illness of several weeks, had enjoyed a vacation at Tunbridge and Bath, and presently was to run up a bill of fifteen pounds with his tailor, William Filby. In the course of the year he had progressed from writing articles to writing books; he was associating with more distinguished men and was attracting more attention from the critics. But he was far from prosperous: although he embarked on a new project as soon as he had completed the one in hand, he could not meet his expenses.

One project which reputedly attracted him at about this period was an edition of Pope's works. He wrote to the publisher Tonson, owner of the copyright, to suggest that he be commissioned to undertake such an edition; in reply he received a visit from one of Tonson's printers, who announced that the publisher was not interested. According to legend, Goldsmith was so infuriated at Tonson's ungracious manner of replying to his letter, and so outraged at the printer's insolence, that he tried to trounce him— and the two had to be separated.

Yet when he was asked to contribute to the *Poetical Calendar* which William Woty and the Reverend Francis Fawkes were preparing for publication, he refused, presumably because he had a low opinion of the other contributors to the volume. He borrowed several scientific books from Newbery on November 25 and may have started work on the *Survey of Experimental Philosophy* which was published after his death, but nothing came of it for the present. He was at work on a novel too—not the conventional sort of novel about a dashing hero and a languishing heroine, but one which had as its central characters a genial, vain, middle-aged clergyman reminiscent of his father and a sensible, benevolent nobleman of about his own age. It was an agreeable task because it enabled him to recreate the sort of life which he had known as a child—perhaps, also, to indulge in a bit of harm-

137

less introspection, seeing in the clergyman Oliver Goldsmith as he was and in the nobleman Oliver Goldsmith as he would have liked to be. But composing a novel demanded time and energy, and he could spare little of either to it.

Nevertheless he heedlessly involved himself in new expenses. Through Samuel Derrick he was introduced to the Robin Hood Debating Society, which met Monday evenings at the Robin Hood Tavern on Butcher Row. Then on November 17 he was elected to membership in the Society for the Encouragement of Arts, Manufactures, and Commerce, that society which he had hoped to serve as secretary just two years earlier. And although the historian of the Robin Hood reported that Goldsmith "comes but seldom" to meetings and Andrew Kippis said that he was overcome with confusion when he tried to address the Arts and Sciences, he had the satisfaction of being accepted into two organizations which Horace Walpole listed among the highlights of the city. Goldsmith's nature craved such recognition and could not resist it when it was offered.

Meanwhile he was seeing a good deal of Johnson and his distinguished friends. One evening when John Newbery's son Francis played Gnatho the Parasite in Terence's *Eunuchus* at the Merchant Taylors' School, Goldsmith sat in the Master's Box with a party which included the playwright George Colman, Johnson, and David Garrick.[46] After Johnson came back from a trip to Devonshire with Reynolds in September, 1762, he bought a copy of *The Life of Nash*. And when, not long thereafter, Goldsmith encountered a crisis, it was to Johnson that he turned.

Johnson told the story of this crisis many years later, and it was published, with variations, by Boswell, Mrs. Thrale, Sir John Hawkins, Richard Cumberland, and William Cooke.[47] The facts of the story seem to be that, inevitably, Goldsmith fell behind in his payments to his landlady, Mrs. Carnan, and that she finally called in the bailiffs to arrest him. In despair he sent to Johnson for aid, and Johnson sent him a guinea and hurried to Wine Office Court as soon as he was free to do so.

When he arrived, he found that Goldsmith had obtained a bottle of madeira for consolation in his distress, but had made no progress toward extricating himself from his difficulty. With characteristic good sense Johnson corked the bottle, told Goldsmith to calm himself, and asked whether he had any marketable manuscripts about him. When Goldsmith replied that he had an unpublished novel in his rooms, Johnson asked to see it, gave it a hasty examination, and carried it off to John Newbery's shop. Soon he was back again with sixty pounds in cash, enough to settle Goldsmith's debt and to give him sufficient assurance to berate his landlady for using him so badly. Thus ended the tragicomedy—and thus Newbery received the manuscript of *The Vicar of Wakefield*. On October 28 he sold a third share of it to Benjamin Collins of Salisbury, but it was not to be published until March of 1766.

Now Newbery, who had provided Goldsmith with most of his employment over the past three years, decided that he must step in and straighten out his writer's tangled affairs. First he arranged for Goldsmith to leave Mrs. Carnan's house and settle at Canonbury House in Islington, where he himself lived part of the time. Then he persuaded Goldsmith to entrust to him the direction of his finances. Publisher and author now agreed that Goldsmith would carry out whatever literary tasks were assigned him and that Newbery would hold all that Goldsmith earned, discharge his bills as they were presented, and give him pocket money whenever he needed it.

Sometime toward the end of the year 1762 he moved out to Islington and settled in his new quarters. But on Christmas Day he was back in London for dinner at Tom Davies' house on Russell Street in Covent Garden with the publisher Robert Dodsley and a mercurial young Scot named James Boswell, who had come up to London a few weeks before, hoping to wangle a commission in the Home Guards. The young man was in a turmoil: he was trying to launch himself simultaneously as a gentleman of fashion and a man of letters. He was in love with a young lady whom he called Louisa, but at the same time eager to lay siege to Sam Johnson. He had, in fact, gone to Davies' house in the hope of seeing Johnson there, but Johnson had left for Oxford for the holiday. Boswell contented himself with the thought that he was associating with literary men and proceeded to make the most of his company.

The conversation was animated; "It was," Boswell wrote later in his Journal, "quite a literary dinner." When they fell to discussing poetry, Goldsmith chose to be perverse. "The miscellaneous poetry of this age is nothing like that of the last," he declared; "it is very poor." And when he cited Dodsley's *Collection,* an anthology of contemporary verse, and Dodsley observed that it was "equal to those made by Dryden and Pope," Goldsmith countered: "To consider them, Sir, as villages, yours may be as good; but let us compare house with house, you can produce me no edifices equal to the *Ode on St. Cecilia's Day, Absalom and Achitophel,* or *The Rape of the Lock.*"

Presently Boswell ventured to ask, "And what do you think of Gray's odes? Are not they noble?"

"Ah, the rumbling thunder!" cried Goldsmith derisively. And he told how once, when a friend of his was praising Gray, he had improvised four lines vaguely resembling the opening of "The Bard" and had had the satisfaction of hearing his friend hail them enthusiastically.

"Well," said Boswell, "I admire Gray prodigiously. I have read his odes till I was almost mad."

But Goldsmith would not yield. "They are terribly obscure," he declared. "We must be historians and learned men before we can understand them."

"And why not?" asked Davies. "He is not writing to porters or carmen. He is writing to men of knowledge."

Goldsmith apparently decided that it was time to change the subject. "Have you seen [Isaac Bickerstaffe's comic opera] *Love in a Village?*" he asked. And when Boswell pronounced it "a good, pleasing thing," he was off again. "I am afraid we will have no good plays now," he remarked. "The taste of the audience is spoiled by the pantomime of Shakespeare."

"Nay," Davies objected, "but you will allow that Shakespeare has great merit?"

"No. I know Shakespeare very well."

140

Boswell, baffled at the man's brashness, tried another topic. "What," he asked, "do you think of Johnson?"

And now Goldsmith abandoned his high-handed approach. "He has exceeding great merit," he said. "His *Rambler* is a noble work."

When Boswell sat down to record the conversation in his Journal, he characterized Goldsmith as "a curious, odd, pedantic fellow with some genius," and, apropos of his remarks about Shakespeare, "a most impudent puppy."[48] And surely his words were well chosen; for Goldsmith was indeed curious and odd and impudent, and, given an impressionable young auditor, he doubtless affected to be pedantic. At the same time he was a man of "some genius." For the most part he had frittered his talents away in ephemeral articles, prefaces, revisions, translations, and hack jobs of one sort or other. Yet his *Citizen of the World,* his *Life of Nash,* and the unpublished novel which lay in John Newbery's office revealed that he had inner resources which he had scarcely touched. He had a varied store of experiences, a shrewd knowledge of human beings, and a lively sense of humor. Moreover, he had developed a fluid, polished prose style and narrative skill, and with direction he might turn them to account.

But he sorely needed direction; whatever success he had enjoyed had come to him almost accidentally, never as the result of any careful planning on his part. Although he was over thirty years old now, he was as wanting in discipline as when he had been sixteen. And his lack of discipline stemmed from that basic lack of self-confidence which still led him into such absurd displays as Boswell had witnessed. Self-confidence Goldsmith would never gain, and he would always astonish and antagonize people by his efforts to compensate for the want of it. But he had just received, thanks to the benevolence of John Newbery, that kind of directional force which he needed—which many an artist, before and since, has needed. It was, indeed, the beginning of a new era for Oliver Goldsmith. For with proper direction in his life, he stood a far better chance of achieving it in his writing.

Chapter VI
"One of the First Poets"
(1763-1765)

CANONBURY House was ideally located for a man who loved the country but could not forego the pleasures of the city. Goldsmith could spend the day studying, writing, or tramping the fields, and yet, after a sixpenny coach ride, be in London for an evening at the theater or supper with friends. The House itself was a curious hodgepodge of ancient buildings attached to a sixty-six-foot tower constructed originally in the fourteenth century but rebuilt in the seventeenth by William Bolton, the last Prior of St. Bartholomew's, Smithfield. It had been under lease to Francis Bacon from 1616 to 1625, and one room still had lodged in its wall a bullet said to have been aimed at Sir Walter Raleigh. John Newbery and his family used the paneled rooms on the second floor as their country home, and his stepdaughter, Anna Maria Carnan Smart, wife of the mad poet Christopher Smart, occupied another section of the buildings with her two daughters. Still another section was evidently leased to Mrs. Elizabeth Fleming,[1] who rented a room to Goldsmith and provided his board.

From his room high up in the buildings Goldsmith could look down on a "neat, trim garden" with "shapely holly, yew and bay" trees or out above the "stately elms" at the rear of the house to watch "the small white vessels smoothly glide" along the distant Thames. When he wanted companionship, he had only to walk down the road to the Crown Tavern or to hunt up one of the many writers or printers who lived in or near the Tower. Smart's little daughters, Mary and Elizabeth, were sometimes his companions too, for their playroom was on the floor where he lodged. Later in life Elizabeth recalled the questions and riddles which he had put to them—and her insistence that a pound of lead was heavier than a pound of feathers.[2]

It was a pleasant, relaxed sort of existence not unlike his life at Lissoy years ago. And he was as free as a child from financial worries. Now that Newbery had undertaken to act as his guardian, there would be no more fracases with landladies. Mrs. Fleming's accounts show that Newbery paid her fifty pounds a year in quarterly instalments, plus whatever extras she might have provided in the course of the three months. Goldsmith took full advantage of the arrangement: during one week in August, 1763, Mrs. Fleming supplied "one pint of mountain" and dinner for one guest on the 22nd, a bottle of port and tea for four gentlemen on the 24th, and dinner and tea for another on the 25th. Moreover, she not only bought sassafras, paper, and pens for her tenant, but also paid for his newspaper, his shoe cleaning, his laundry, and even his postage fees—and waited until the end of the quarter before being reimbursed by Newbery. Meanwhile Goldsmith drew on the publisher for books or cash or to settle his long-standing account with the tailor William Filby. It was a highly satisfactory arrangement from Goldsmith's point of view. From Newbery's it was somewhat less than that. By October 11 he had paid out 111 pounds, one shilling, and sixpence and had received in return literary work in the amount of sixty-three pounds. The balance was carried forward without interest charges.[3]

Why did Newbery assume such a responsibility? In part, of course, because he was a truly benevolent man, but perhaps also because he had confidence in Goldsmith's literary talents if not his financial acumen. He was convinced that Goldsmith was capable of accomplishing something of lasting value if he could be released from the constant pressures of writing for a living. Perhaps too he had seen a sample of the poem which Goldsmith was writing. So he assigned him enough in the way of hackwork to keep him at least partially solvent, and gambled on his turning his real talents to account.

Soon Goldsmith was given the most advantageous contract he had ever received. On March 31, 1763, he agreed to write for the publisher James Dodsley a two-volume *Chronological History of the Lives of Eminent Persons of Great Britain and Ireland* at three guineas per printed sheet, the completed work to be submitted within two years and not to exceed thirty-five sheets per volume. This was most reassuring; for the contract was worth a possible 210 guineas, far more than Goldsmith had been paid for any of his projects to date. Moreover, it required that his name be signed to the published work—apparently because that name was considered valuable to a publisher.

Meanwhile, on Thursday, February 3, he went up to Drury Lane to attend the opening of Mrs. Sheridan's comedy *The Discovery* and sat directly behind James Boswell and his Scottish friends George Dempster and the Honourable Andrew Erskine. Boswell, who was suffering from an attack of gonorrhea (contracted from the once-adored Louisa) and a guilty conscience, was delighted to see him and found that his conversation "revived in my mind the true ideas of London authors, which are to me something curious, and, as it were, mystical." It proved, however, to be a dull evening; "the play really acted heavily," Boswell wrote later, and he apparently enjoyed only the "many smart acrimonious things" which Goldsmith said about it. He was annoyed by the behavior of his two companions, who made him hold their places while they took their time about dinner. He told himself that he had been seeing too many Scots and too few Englishmen in London. "When I become an officer," he wrote in his Journal, "I shall . . . be more in the great world."[4] Yet in the weeks that followed he did not cultivate Goldsmith's acquaintance.

But on May 16 Boswell was introduced at last to "the great Mr. Samuel Johnson" at Tom Davies' shop, and after calling on him twice at his rooms in the Temple, he met him at Clifton's Chop House on Butcher Row on Saturday, June 25, and went with him to the Mitre Tavern on Fleet Street, where he told him his life history and asked his advice for the future. This was an excellent way to win Johnson's interest, and the two "sat till between one and two and finished a couple of bottles of port." In the course of the evening Goldsmith was mentioned, and Johnson said earnestly: "Dr. Goldsmith is one of the first men we have as an author at present, and a very worthy man too. He has been loose in his principles, but he is coming right."

That was enough. The next day, Sunday, Boswell, determined to beard another lion, walked out to Islington and called on the "very worthy man." Goldsmith served him tea and was "very chatty": he lamented "that the praise due to literary merit is already occupied by the first writers, who will keep it and get the better even of the superior merit which the moderns may possess. He said David Hume was one of those, who, seeing the first place occupied on the right side, rather than take a second, wants to have a first in what is wrong."[5] But when Boswell quizzed him about Johnson's friend Robert Levett, he silenced him with the words: "Sir, he is poor and honest, which is enough to Johnson."[6] He was not disposed to gossip with this inquisitive young Scot.

However, on the following Friday, July 1, he had supper with Boswell and Johnson at the Mitre. Before Johnson arrived, Goldsmith recited some verse which he had written, and Boswell "advised him to publish a volume." Goldsmith, doubtless aware that he was in the presence of a determined lion-hunter, remarked that Boswell "had a method of making people speak." When Boswell countered, "Sir, that is next best to speaking myself," Goldsmith added: "Nay, but you do both."

After Johnson's arrival Boswell "had curious ideas when I considered that I was sitting with London authors by profession" and was, he claimed, "very quiet and attentive." Yet he was obviously more interested in Johnson than in Goldsmith, and, as always when Goldsmith felt slighted, his brashness asserted itself. He "wanted too much to show away," Boswell noticed. "He tried to maintain that knowledge was not always desirable on its own account, as it was often attended with inconveniences. Johnson allowed that it might have disadvantages, but affirmed that knowledge *per se* was certainly an object which every man would wish to attain, although perhaps he might not choose to take the trouble necessary for attaining it."[7]

If Goldsmith sensed Boswell's disapproval, he had his revenge at the end of the evening, when he and Johnson went off to drink tea with Anna Williams, Johnson's blind friend and dependent, at her rooms on Bolt Court. In his Journal Boswell did not mention the incident, but it rankled; and years afterward, in his *Life of Johnson,* he wrote: "Dr. Goldsmith, being a privileged man, went with him this night, strutting away, and calling to me with an air of superiority, like that of an esoterick over an exoterick disciple of a sage of antiquity, 'I go to Miss Williams.' I confess, I then envied him this mighty privilege, of which he seemed so proud; but it was not long before I obtained the same mark of distinction."[8]

But Boswell's desire to associate with literary men was stronger than his envy, and he invited Goldsmith to dine with a party of friends at his lodgings on Downing Street, Westminster, on the following Wednesday, July 6. As luck would have it, however, he entertained William and Robert Temple in his rooms the previous evening, and they made so much noise that the landlord called in the watch and threatened to send them all to the roundhouse. Boswell determined to move out at once, and he was obliged to take his dinner guests to the Mitre. Johnson was among them, of course, and the others were Tom Davies, an Irish friend of his named Eccles, and the Reverend John Ogilvie, a Scottish poet who was eager to meet Johnson and whom Boswell was eager to show "upon what easy terms Johnson permitted me to live with him."

"Mr. Johnson was exceeding good company all this evening," Boswell reported in his Journal. Goldsmith was "in his usual style, too eager to be bright." Of his share in the evening's conversation Boswell recorded only that he "held a keen dispute with Johnson against that maxim in the British Constitution, 'The King can do no wrong'; affirming that what was morally false could not be politically true. And as the King might command and cause the doing of what was wrong, he certainly could do wrong." Johnson disagreed emphatically—knocked him down with the butt end of his pistol, as Goldsmith later phrased it. Goldsmith evidently subsided until the question of the merits of Scotland rose, and Ogilvie declared that there was very rich country around Edinburgh. This was an excellent opening, and Goldsmith leaped into it. "No, no," he said "with a sneering laugh"; "it is not rich country." But his remark was lost in Ogilvie's statement that Scotland had "a great many noble wild prospects"—which was the cue for Johnson's famous line: "I believe the noblest prospect a Scotsman ever sees is the road which leads him to England."[9]

As reported by Boswell, it was decidedly Johnson's evening. Obviously Boswell resented Goldsmith's intimacy with Johnson, and he may have given a prejudiced account of the conversation. On the other hand, Goldsmith doubtless resented the presence of this young pretender to Johnson's attention and "showed away" more than usual in an attempt to attract attention to himself. He seems not to have seen Boswell again in the course of the next month, and he probably had no regrets when Boswell left London for the Continent on August 5.

For the next two and a half years, during Boswell's absence, there was no eager scribe to record in detail the meetings of Johnson, Goldsmith, and their friends. But the two met regularly, for Goldsmith loved and admired Johnson and was flattered to be known as his friend. Dr. Maxwell, Reader at the Temple Chapel, listed Goldsmith among the number who gathered regularly at Johnson's rooms at noontime to chat while he lolled in bed and drank his tea.[10] And when in the following winter Reynolds suggested to Johnson that they form a literary club, Goldsmith was invited to be one of the nine charter members.

This honor implied the sort of recognition which he was always seeking. Election to the Club meant that he had been singled out by two men of unquestioned distinction and that he became the intimate friend of a group which included not only Johnson and Reynolds but six other men who had been born to or had achieved high position: the young aristocrats Bennet Langton and Topham Beauclerk, Edmund Burke, his father-in-law Dr. Nugent, Anthony Chamier, Secretary in the War Office, and Sir John Hawkins. The Club met regularly for supper every Monday evening at the Turk's Head on Gerrard Street in Soho, and members were required to attend at least two of every five meetings. The proceedings of the Club were kept secret, but the meetings were known to be long and the conversation animated.

Inevitably Goldsmith was accepted as the clown of the group. He had no objection to playing the part; in fact he fell naturally into it. But the result was that his fellow-members treated him

147

with playful condescension. As yet he had published nothing to command the respect of such men, and his frequent "absurdities" made them question his good sense. After Goldsmith's death, when Johnson, Reynolds, and Langton were discussing the merits of *The Traveller* one day at Reynolds' house, Sir Joshua ventured the opinion that they might have been prejudiced in its favor by "too great a partiality for him." Johnson, however, reminded him that "the partiality of his friends was all against him." "It was with difficulty," he declared, "we could give him a hearing."[11]

Yet condescension was better than solitude, and he was a faithful attendant at meetings of the group. At the same time he retained his other connections in London, and he must have been frequently away from his room at Canonbury House. In good weather he welcomed friends there; in August and September of 1763 Mrs. Fleming billed him six times for meals served to guests. But by December he had evidently decided that Islington was too far away from the center of things during the winter months, and he took temporary lodgings in the city, probably at Gray's Inn.[12] He retained his room at Mrs. Fleming's, however, and returned to it at the end of March.

Meanwhile there had been work to do. He had finished little or nothing of the *Chronological History* which he had engaged to write for Dodsley, but he had carried out several commissions for Newbery. When the publisher listed their accounts on October 11, 1763, he credited Goldsmith with the following:

Brookes' History 11/11/0
Preface to Universal History 3/ 3/0
Preface to Rhetoric 2/ 2/0
Preface to Chronicle 1/ 1/0
History of England ....21/ 0/0[13]
The Life of Christ 10/10/0
The Life of the Fathers 10/10/0
Critical and Monthly 3/ 3/0

Of these rather cryptic items all but the "Preface to Chronicle" have been identified. The first refers to the six-volume *System of Natural History* by R. Brookes, which Newbery published serially beginning August 1. Goldsmith seems to have revised the text and

148

to have written a general preface for the entire work and introductions for the separate volumes. The general preface contains a
critical history of zoological studies, an account written in the first
person of the merits of Brookes' work, and a description (probably
not by Goldsmith) of animals "newly come to my notice" and not
included in the text. Of the introductions, Goldsmith wrote probably four or five; but only the first, on quadrupeds, deserves special
notice. In it he had a favorite topic, and he wrote forcefully (with
some aid from William Derham's *Physico Theology*) about the
mysteries of the animal world, particularly the complexities of
adaptation and instinct. However, his enthusiasm left him in the
remaining introductions, and he drew more and more on Derham,
Abbé Pluche's *Spectacle de la Nature,* and his old stand-by, the
Encyclopédie, and less and less on his own talents.[14]

The last item on Newbery's list, "Critical and Monthly," undoubtedly refers, as Seitz suggested,[15] to the reviews of Brookes'
volumes which Goldsmith wrote for the *Critical Review* for
August and October and the *Monthly Review* for October. Neither
amounts to much more than a summary of the contents of the
early volumes of the *Natural History,* although in the *Critical*
Goldsmith praises the author's humor and his imagination. He
could afford to be generous, since he was evidently being paid
three guineas by Newbery in addition to whatever he received
from the editors of the two reviews.

The "Preface to Universal History" listed by Newbery was the
Introduction which Goldsmith wrote for *A General History of
the World, from the Creation to the Present Time* by William
Guthrie, John Gray, "and others eminent in this branch of literature." It was published by Newbery and several other publishers
serially in twelve volumes and an index, the first appearing on
April 2, 1764. This time Goldsmith's imagination was not sparked
by his subject matter, and he contented himself with pointing out
the values of history, particularly universal history,[16] and the
superiority of these·volumes to competitors in the field. Once
again he resorted to Volume V of the *Encyclopédie* to lighten his
labor.[17]

The "Preface to Rhetoric" was probably Goldsmith's contribution to a volume entitled *The Elements of Rhetoric and Poetry* brought out early in January, 1764, by James Dodsley, who collaborated with Newbery in occasional publications. No copy of the book seems to have survived. The "History of England" was Goldsmith's *History of England in a Series of Letters from a Nobleman to his Son at the University,* not published until the following June.

"The Life of Christ" and "The Life of the Fathers" were *An History of the Life of Our Lord and Saviour Jesus Christ, to which is added, The Life of the Blessed Virgin Mary* and *An History of the Lives, Actions, Travels, Sufferings, and Deaths of the most eminent Martyrs and Primitive Fathers of the Church, in the first four Centuries,* the second and fourth volumes of "The Young Christian's Library," advertised in Newbery's newspapers in December, 1764. As Seitz pointed out,[18] neither was a translation, as announced; the first was almost certainly an abridgment of Reading's *History of our Lord and Saviour Jesus Christ,—To which is prefix'd the Life of the Blessed Virgin Mary,* and the second was an abridgment of two works by William Cave, *Apostolici* and *Ecclesiastici. The Lives of the Fathers,* which contained forty brief biographical sketches, was a tiny volume intended for children. No copy of the *Life of Christ* is known to survive, but it was doubtless similar in format and intention. Like most of Goldsmith's other literary work during this period, these books added nothing to his stature as a writer.[19]

Meanwhile he was no better off financially than he had been before. The sixty-three pounds which Newbery credited to his account on October 11, 1763, fell short by nearly fifty pounds of the amount which Goldsmith had drawn. And on December 17 he borrowed an additional twenty-five guineas from the publisher. It was a comfort, surely, to know that Newbery would take care of all his needs. And he could always count on the 210 pounds that he would eventually receive from Dodsley for his *Chronological History.* Yet he seems to have counted on the income rather than writing the book. On March 10, 1764, he wrote from Gray's Inn to Dodsley asking him to "let me have ten guineas per bearer, for which I promise to account," and announcing that he would "call to see you on Wednesday next with copy &c."[20] But Dodsley had reason to be seriously concerned. Nearly a year had passed since they had drawn up their contract, Goldsmith had submitted no copy to date, and he was beginning to ask for advances.

He was certainly growing no richer under Newbery's guardianship, and he had done nothing thus far to strengthen his reputation as a writer. For even the two-volume *History of England in a Series of Letters from a Nobleman,* which appeared on June 26, 1764, was accepted by most readers as the work of a peer of the realm. Chesterfield, Orrery, and Lyttelton were all credited with authorship of the book, and as late as 1793 readers of the *Gentleman's Magazine* were arguing as to which of the three was the author.[21] Goldsmith himself must have been delighted at the success of his ruse, since it bore out in some measure his claim in *Citizen of the World,* No. LVII: "A nobleman has but to take a pen, ink, and paper, write away through three large volumes, and then sign his name to the title-page; though the whole might have been before more disgusting than his own rent-roll, yet signing his name and title gives value to the deed; title being alone equivalent to taste, imagination, and genius." For surely much of the popularity of the *History* was due to the fact that the literate public was pleased to have available a history of their country supposedly written by a judicious nobleman for the edification of his son at the university.

Although Goldsmith occasionally used the first person in his Letters, he made little attempt to individualize his noble lord. He seems to have had in mind a descendant of the urbane Sir William Temple,[22] and the writer gradually emerges as an enlightened, tolerant gentleman, reasonably devout and impartial, whose seasoned judgments on historical events would inspire confidence.[23]

In such a historian eighteenth century readers would be willing to excuse occasional carelessness or inaccuracies in the use of details, and that was to Goldsmith's advantage, since his method of composition was distinctly cavalier. William Cooke wrote that, while Goldsmith was working on the *History,* he spent his mornings reading "Hume, Rapin, and sometimes Kennet, as much as he designed for one letter, marking down the passages referred to on a sheet of paper, with remarks." Then he went riding or walking, came back for dinner and a convivial evening, "and when he went up to bed took up his books and papers with him, where he generally wrote the chapter, or the best part of it, before he went to rest."[24] Modern scholars have discovered that in the first fifty-one Letters he depended primarily on Rapin and Voltaire's *Essai sur les Moeurs,* usually drawing his facts from Rapin and his interpretations (even his prejudices) from Voltaire, but sometimes weaving phrases from each into sentences of his own.[25] He made no effort to conceal his borrowings; at times he named Rapin as his source, at others he referred to "a fine writer" or "a foreign writer." For neither Goldsmith nor his noble lord claimed to be a historian; theirs was a compilation, based on the fuller and more original research of other men.

After the fifty-first Letter Goldsmith abandoned the point of view of the noble lord and continued his history of the Georges in what "the editor" announced to be "a much inferior hand; for [these Letters] were drawn up by me." Probably he feared that the nobleman's point of view might prove a handicap when he tried to treat events or policies of recent years. Yet he made little change in the style of the Letters; there is no evidence of "a much inferior hand." He did, however, change his source books, relying now on Smollett's *Continuation of the History of England* and Burke's "History of the Present War" in the *Annual Register* for 1758-1761 and even quoting both on occasion to suggest his impartiality. Still he did not submerge his own opinions; in fact he sometimes did a very skillful job of converting Burke's facts to his own purposes.[26]

In the first Letter of the series Goldsmith made his noble lord tell his son Charles that, although history is the source of "true wisdom and real improvement," it is "useless . . . in the manner in which it is generally studied, where the memory is loaded with little more than dates, names, and events." "True wisdom," he adds, "consists in tracing effects to their causes. To understand history is to understand man, who is the subject. To study history

152

is to weigh the motives, the opinions, the passions of mankind, in order to avoid a similitude of errors in ourselves, or profit by the wisdom of their example." And later: "Not the history of kings, but of men, should be your principal concern."

In the Letters that followed he strove always to minimize the importance of battles and politics and to stress mercantile, social, and literary developments. At first, of course, he had few materials to work from, and he was obliged to depend on anecdotes to provide human interest. But as he progressed, he supplied an increasing amount of background material: he devoted, for example, one Letter to the Elizabethan Era, in addition to the three dealing with the events of Elizabeth's reign, and another to the literature of the Augustan Age. And as he approached his own period, he provided more and more detail: the reign of George II takes up thirteen Letters, which concern not only English history proper but England's position in world affairs. Moreover, though content at first to echo Voltaire's opinions in favor of Henry VII and James I or against Henry VIII and William III, he now presented his own ideas, many of which he had expressed earlier: the superiority of monarchical to republican forms of government, for example, or the dangers of overextending empire, or the decline of polite learning in England.

Reviewers treated the book rather coolly. "Who this Nobleman was, we are not informed," wrote Kenrick in the October *Monthly Review;* "nor, indeed, is it any great matter; as the reputation his Grace or his Lordship might justly acquire by this performance, would be no very distinguishing feather in the cap even of a Commoner"; and he dismissed the volumes with the remark that they seemed "well enough calculated for the use of schools." The author of the review in the *Critical* for August took much the same attitude, observed that the last letters did not seem inferior to the first, and implied that he doubted if a noble lord had any part in the production.

The public, however, was less critical, and the book went through twenty-five editions in the first sixty years after its publication. For some time thereafter it continued to appear in new editions, with more letters to bring the history up to date. Meanwhile, in 1786, it had been translated into French by Madame Brissot as *Lettres Philosophiques et Politiques sur l'Histoire de l'Angleterre,* with notes by her husband. And even today, when modern scholarship has unearthed so much material to vivify the writing of history, it offers a quick, lively summary of its subject.

On the same day that the *History* appeared, W. Nichol published Charles Wiseman's *Complete English Grammar* with a preface evidently written by Goldsmith at Newbery's request.[27] It was the sort of thing he had done before and could do very well: sixteen pages urging that English grammar be studied more carefully and explaining the methods and advantages of the present system. There are, however, two significant insertions: one a plea that students of English go on to study history, and the other a word of praise for the books published by John Newbery.

Meanwhile Goldsmith had another project still unfinished: the *Chronological History* which he had contracted to write for Dodsley. On August 8 he gave the publisher a receipt for thirty guineas for "writing and compiling a history of England";[28] but as Professor Seitz proved, this was not the *Chronological History.* Dodsley had evidently despaired of receiving the completed copy within the seven months remaining of the two years specified by their contract of March 31, 1763, and author and publisher had reached a compromise: instead of continuing work on the *Chronological History,* which would have demanded a good deal more in the way of research than Goldsmith was used to doing, he would make an abridgment of his *History of England in a Series of Letters from a Nobleman.*[29] Accordingly, he wrote *A Concise History of England,* so ingeniously paraphrasing the narrative portions of the first forty-eight Letters that his source was hardly recognizable. And Dodsley issued it with a reprint of a geography of England which he had published twenty years earlier, the two together bearing the title *The Geography and History of England Done in the Manner of Gordon's and Salmon's Geographical and Historical Grammars.* As for the finished sheets of the *Chronological History,* he apparently returned them to Goldsmith, who in turn sold them to the accommodating John Newbery for eight guineas on October 29.

As further evidence of good faith Dodsley paid Goldsmith ten guineas on October 31 for his manuscript of the oratorio *The Captivity,* which he had written earlier and which Dodsley and Newbery were to share. However, neither of the publishers saw fit to bring it out, and it remained in manuscript until the publication of the 1820 edition of Goldsmith's *Miscellaneous Works.*

The Captivity is not a great poem, but it has interest in the light of Goldsmith's later achievements. In dramatizing the story of the Israelites' captivity in Babylon and their release by Cyrus, he reveals no extraordinary power as poet or as dramatist—and it should be said in his defense that the text of an oratorio has distinctly limited possibilities for either. He does, however, show a surprising technical competence, considering that he had written no long serious poem hitherto. The poem is often reminiscent, carrying distinct echoes of Psalm CXXXVIII and recalling Dryden's and Gray's odes. Yet it discloses that Goldsmith was aware of verse and sound effects and could handle them effectively. It is, in short, the kind of verse that every poet must write by way of practice against the time when he has something to say. Fortunately Goldsmith now had something to say, and during the fall of 1764 he was reworking his thoughts into final form in *The Traveller.* Francis Newbery remarked in his Autobiography that Goldsmith often read him bits of the poem while he was living at Canonbury House.[30]

Sometime during the fall, probably at the end of September, Goldsmith left Islington and settled again at the Temple in London. At first he shared rooms with one of the butlers of the Temple, a man named Jeffs, in No. 2 Garden Court, above the Library of the Temple. He was not entirely satisfied with his quarters, and when Johnson called to inspect them, he apologized for them and assured his guest that he would soon be better situated. "Nay, Sir, never mind that," Johnson retorted. *"Nil te quaesiveris extra."*[31]

November was a busy month. Percy, now working on his proposed edition of *The Spectator,* was in town, and Goldsmith saw much of him. On Friday, the 16th, they had tea together in Goldsmith's rooms, and the following evening Percy took him out to supper. Then on Wednesday, the 21st, Johnson, Goldsmith, Percy, and the dramatist John Hoole dined at Tom Davies', and the next day Percy had dinner with Goldsmith and then spent the evening with him and Johnson at the home of a friend named Allen. On Monday, the 26th, the two men met again and spent the evening together, although it was Club night; and the next Wednesday they were at Hoole's with Johnson and a Mr. White. Then on Friday, the 30th, Percy called on both Johnson and Goldsmith at their lodgings in the Temple, evidently to bid them farewell, since he set off the next day for Northamptonshire.[32]

Occasional records like these of Percy's visit to London reveal what an active social life Goldsmith was leading. Yet not all his time was spent in social pursuits; he was busy now on the final draft of the poem which was to be his first serious bid for lasting literary fame. Percy states that he "wrote the lines in his first copy very wide, and would so fill up the intermediate space with re-iterated corrections, that scarcely a word of his first effusions was left unaltered."[33] Johnson had seen the poem in manuscript and had encouraged Goldsmith to complete it, even contributing nine lines to the conclusion.[34] John Newbery, too, must have seen it; in fact it was probably for the sake of this one poem in progress that he had chosen to underwrite Goldsmith's expenses for so many months.

But those who had not seen the poem still refused to take Goldsmith seriously. Sir John Hawkins declared that most members of the Club considered him a "mere literary drudge." They delighted to tell stories about his extraordinary behavior: Hawkins himself maintained that once when he had asked Goldsmith for some information for his *History of Music,* Goldsmith had taken down from a shelf the volume which contained the needed information, torn out six pages, and handed them to him.[35] There was no question about it: the partiality of Goldsmith's friends of the Club was, as Johnson said, "all against him."

But when, on December 19, Newbery published *The Traveller: a Prospect of Society,* they were forced to admit that the man had depths which they had never appreciated. He had begun the poem in 1755 while he was still a philosophic vagabond in Switzerland.

He had revised and expanded those lines in the course of many hours and over an extended period of time, and into them he had worked the results of years of thought. He had reflected on the theories which he wanted to express, had developed and polished them, had fitted them into an orderly sequence. And now at last he presented them to the public in enduring form as his first serious claim on the attention of posterity. It is significant that this poem was the first of his works to be published under his own name.

In the prefatory letter to the poem Goldsmith achieved one of his noblest gestures: instead of dedicating his work to a nobleman who might reward him with a pension, he addressed it to his brother Henry. It was the tribute of the prodigal to the stay-at-home. Goldsmith was sinking ever deeper into debt: he had begun the year owing Newbery nearly seventy-five pounds, and although Newbery had published several pieces by him in the course of the year, all had been paid for by October 11, 1763. His only discernible income during the year 1764 was the thirty guineas paid him by Dodsley on August 8, the eight guineas credited to his account on October 29 by Newbery for the discarded sheets of the *Chronological History,* ten guineas received from Dodsley on October 31 for his share of *The Captivity,* and perhaps another twelve guineas from Newbery for the Preface to Wiseman's *Grammar* and his share of *The Captivity*—a total of sixty guineas at most. Meanwhile he had spent probably six months at Canonbury House, where room and board alone cost him fifty pounds annually, and the rest of the year in London, where living was more expensive. Clearly his brother, living simply and much more cheaply in the country—"passing rich on forty pounds a year"—had chosen the wiser course. Goldsmith was wholly sincere when he wrote:

Dear Sir,—I am sensible that the friendship between us can acquire no new force from the ceremonies of a Dedication; and perhaps it demands an excuse thus to prefix your name to my attempts, which you decline giving with your own. But as a part of this poem was formerly written to you from Switzerland, the whole can now, with propriety, be only inscribed to you. It will also throw a light upon many parts of it, when the reader understands, that it is addressed to a man who, despising fame and fortune, has retired early to happiness and obscurity, with an income of forty pounds a-year.

I now perceive, my dear brother, the wisdom of your humble choice. You have entered upon a sacred office, where the harvest is great, and the labourers are but few; while you have left the field of ambition, where the labourers are many, and the harvest not worth carrying away. But of all kinds of ambition as things now are circumstanced perhaps that which pursues poetical fame is the wildest. What from the increased refinement of the times, from the diversity of judgments produced by opposing criticism, and from the more prevalent opinion influenced by party, the strongest and happiest efforts can expect to please but in a very narrow circle. Though the poet were as sure of his aim as the imperial archer of antiquity, who boasted that he never missed the heart, yet would many of his shafts now fly at random, for the heart too often is in the wrong place.

In the paragraphs that followed, Goldsmith expressed some views on poetry: that it was too often neglected for painting and music; that "the learned" had lately gone too far in their praise of "blank verse, and Pindaric odes, choruses, anapests, and iambics, alliterative care and happy negligence"; that verse written for political purposes degrades the name of poetry. Then: "What reception a poem may find, which has neither abuse, party, nor blank verse to support it, I cannot tell, nor am I solicitous to know. My aims are right. Without espousing the cause of any party, I have attempted to moderate the rage of all. I have endeavoured to show, that there may be equal happiness in states that are differently governed from our own; that every state has a particular principle of happiness, and that this principle in each state, and in our own in particular, may be carried to a mischievous excess."

Even before he begins to read the poem itself, the twentieth century reader is reminded, by this bald statement of the poet's purpose, how much modern notions of poetry have been affected by Romantic theory. This impression is strengthened by the first verse paragraph:

> Remote, unfriended, melancholy, slow,
> Or by the lazy Scheld, or wandering Po;
> Or onward, where the rude Carinthian boor
> Against the houseless stranger shuts the door;
> Or where Campania's plain forsaken lies,

A weary waste expanding to the skies:
Where'er I roam, whatever realms to see,
My heart untravell'd fondly turns to thee;
Still to my brother turns, with ceaseless pain,
And drags at each remove a lengthening chain.

The very literalness of the lines seems strangely unpoetic to the modern reader; the stereotyped language, the lack of vivid imagery, the use of statement rather than suggestion all leave him rather cold—the coldness being relieved only by the emotion expressed for the absent brother. As he reads on, he may be momentarily pleased by a graceful bit of description or touched by the poet's nostalgic emotions. But all too soon description and emotions are abandoned and reflection takes their place; the language becomes, if anything, more stereotyped, and the thought comes through too directly, too prosaically.

It is, however, unfair to judge the poem in terms of criticism which Goldsmith had never heard—to dismiss it as a series of generalized thoughts expressed in the idiom of a moribund literary convention. It is, in fact, in the best tradition of eighteenth century verse: it gives instruction while pleasing the senses. It abounds in ideas which Goldsmith had expressed elsewhere, but never so happily. Here are the nostalgic yearning for the simple life, the doctrine of contented acceptance, the compassion for human misery, the theory of man's adaptation to his environment, the belief in the balance of good and evil in earthly life, the dangers of aristocratic privilege set over against the benefits of luxury, the values of monarchical government, the debilitating effects of opulence and depopulation—all presented in clear progression from the point of view of an unprejudiced observer, a citizen of the world. If the thought seems hardly profound and the expression far from subtle, one must remember that Goldsmith believed that poetry should be addressed not to the happy few but to all men. It should be written for their pleasure too—and certainly he succeeded in making his poem pleasing; for although the imagery is seldom striking, the sound is always effective—set, usually, in a muted minor key, but capable of rising to heights of sternness and forcefulness when the subject demands them:

Where the bleak Swiss their stormy mansions tread,
And force a churlish soil for scanty bread.

"The sound is made an echo to the sense," and it is sound primarily that gives the poem its beauty. Goldsmith handles the heroic couplet not in the polished, epigrammatic manner of Pope or the stern, Latinate manner of Johnson, but in a smooth, flowing style which intensifies the serenity of the poem. It is significant, surely, that Goldsmith himself was a musician and, that he had little good to say of painting. In *The Traveller* he was a musician and a thinker, and as a concise, well-ordered, harmonious expression of "what oft was thought," the poem is a genuine achievement. At times it rises above the level of mere reflective verse and attains an emotional impact that is unforgettable. Crusty Sam Johnson was caught up by its power; when in 1773, during his travels in the Hebrides, he recited from memory the lines describing British character, they brought tears to his eyes.[36]

When the poem was published, it was immediately greeted with enthusiasm. Johnson, who reviewed it in the *Critical* for December, hailed it as "a production to which, since the death of Pope, it will not be easy to find any thing equal." John Langhorne, writing in the January *Monthly,* offered some carping criticism, but acknowledged that it was "one of those delightful poems that allure by the beauty of their scenery, a refined elegance of sentiment, and a correspondent happiness of expression." The *Gentleman's Magazine* for December was pleased to "congratulate our poetical readers on the appearance of a new poet so able to afford refined pleasure to true taste as the writer of the *Traveller.*" And the *London Chronicle* for December 18-20 declared that "it were injustice to this ingenious gentleman not to allow him a degree of poetical merit beyond what we have seen for several years." A second edition was published in March, 1765, a third in August, and six more within Goldsmith's lifetime,[37] most of them with careful revisions. For he considered this poem his masterpiece, and was happy to devote to it the pains which he had disdained to expend on lesser works.

Suddenly Goldsmith found himself a famous man. No longer could he complain, as he had done earlier: "Whenever I write any thing, the publick *make a point* to know nothing about it."[38] As Reynolds said, "His Traveller produced an eagerness unparalleled to see the author. He was sought after with greediness."[39] For a while it was rumored that Johnson had written the poem; and when Anthony Chamier asked Goldsmith the meaning of the word "slow" in the first line and Johnson corrected Goldsmith's interpretation, the rumor seemed to be confirmed.[40] Reynolds went so far as to ask Johnson whether he had written certain lines, but Johnson replied that he had written "not more than eighteen lines."[41] Chamier quizzed Goldsmith on the subject, and later reported: "Well, I do believe he wrote this poem himself: and, let me tell you, that is believing a great deal."[42] Inevitably, then, his friends began to regard him in a new light. Mrs. Cholmondeley, the woman who had toasted Goldsmith as the ugliest man she knew, declared, after hearing Johnson read *The Traveller:* "I never more shall think Dr. Goldsmith ugly."[43]

Of course, since recognition came so suddenly, Goldsmith could not take it gracefully. "He knew much was expected of him," Reynolds wrote. "He had not that kind of prudence to take refuge in silence . . .; he was impatient of being overlooked; he wished to be the principal figure in every group."[44] Joseph Warton, who met him soon after the publication of *The Traveller,* wrote a few months later: "Of all solemn coxcombs, Goldsmith is the first: yet sensible;—but affects to use Johnson's hard words in conversation."[45] And William Cooke reports that, when Hugh Kelly congratulated Goldsmith on his success and invited him to dinner, Goldsmith earnestly replied: "I would with pleasure accept your kind invitation, . . . but to tell you the truth, my dear boy, my 'Traveller' has found me a *home* in so many places, that I am engaged, I believe, three days—let me see—to-day I dine with Edmund Burke, to-morrow with Dr. Nugent, and the next day with Topham Beauclerc—but I'll tell you what *I'll do for you,* I'll dine with you on Saturday."[46]

Others found Goldsmith's manners less offensive; or perhaps he felt less obliged to assume unnatural airs when he was with them. One of the new friends whom he met at this time was Robert Nugent, later Lord Clare, himself an Irishman and a poet who could understand Goldsmith's nature and enjoy him for what he was. Soon Goldsmith was visiting Nugent's country place at Gosfield, in Essex, and meeting other men and women of high rank. It was Nugent who introduced him to the Earl of Northumberland, then slated to become Lord Lieutenant of Ireland. His Lordship had read *The Traveller,* thought highly of it, and invited Goldsmith to call on him, thinking that he might secure him some sort of preferment. But according to Sir John Hawkins, who said he was at Northumberland's house when the interview took place, Goldsmith merely told His Lordship that he had a brother in Ireland, "a clergyman, that stood in need of help." "As for myself," he explained to Hawkins afterwards, "I have no dependence on the promises of great men: I look to the booksellers for support; they are my best friends, and I am not inclined to forsake them for others."[47]

Back to the booksellers he went, for his success had by no means freed him from financial difficulties. The twenty guineas which Newbery had paid him for *The Traveller* would not go far toward liquidating his debt to the publisher or toward providing for the future. And since he observed that other publishers were capitalizing on his success by bringing out some of his earlier works, he decided to select what seemed to him the best of his essays and to publish them under his own name.

Essays by Mr. Goldsmith, which Newbery and Griffin issued on June 3, 1765,[48] was a collection of nine essays from *The Bee,* nine from *The Citizen of the World,* and eight from other sources, to which Goldsmith appended two humorous poems. In the accompanying preface he complained that although the essays subjoined had attracted little attention at their first appearance, "most of [them] have been regularly reprinted twice or thrice a-year, and conveyed to the public through the kennel of some engaging compilation." Then with characteristic candor: "As these entertainers of the public, as they call themselves, have partly lived upon me for some years, let me now try if I cannot live a little upon myself." And after apologizing for the triviality and triteness of the essays, he concluded: "Instead, therefore, of attempting to establish a credit amongst [the public], it will

162

perhaps be wiser to apply to some more distant correspondent; and as my drafts are in some danger of being protested at home, it may not be imprudent, upon this occasion, to draw my bills upon Posterity.—Mr. Posterity,—Sir,—Nine hundred and ninety-nine years after sight hereof, pay the bearer, or order, a thousand pounds worth of praise, free from all deductions whatsoever, it being a commodity that will then be very serviceable to him, and place it to the account of, &c."

But he did not have to wait so long for recognition. To be sure, Kenrick observed in the July issue of the *Monthly Review* that "the ingenious Author of the Traveller, will make no great addition, to the honour he acquired by that poem, from this publication." But the reviewer in the June *Critical* "most heartily recommend[ed] these essays to the favour of the public, and . . . ingenuously own[ed] that we now see in them many beauties that escaped our observation in their original form of publication," adding that such acknowledgment is "due to truth, justice, and the merit of an excellent writer." And the editor of *Lloyd's Evening Post* went so far as to say in the June 3-5 issue of his paper that the *Essays* proved that "one of the first poets in the English language [is] one of the first essayists too." The volume sold reasonably well: it went into a second edition, with two essays added, in the following year, was reissued eight times before the end of the century, and in 1788 was translated into French.

Yet such recognition made Goldsmith no richer, and when Reynolds and some other friends suggested that he turn his fame to account by setting himself up as a physician again, he decided to try out the scheme. He seems to have prepared for his new venture by calling on his tailor, William Filby, in June, 1765, and ordering a fine new outfit, including purple silk trousers, a scarlet roquelaure (a knee-length coat), a wig, and a cane. And in the excitement of his anticipated prosperity he left his rooms with the Butler Jeffs, took private lodgings at No. 3 King's Bench Walk in the Temple, and hired a manservant.

But the experiment failed. It was one thing to enjoy Goldsmith's poems and essays, but quite another to entrust your life to him when you were ailing. He was not formed to inspire confidence in matters of life and death, even when fortified by a cane and a manservant. He later claimed that he gave up the scheme because the dignity of his new position demanded that he stop frequenting some of his favorite haunts. "In truth," he declared, "one sacrifices something for the sake of good company, for here I am shut out of several places where I used to play the fool very agreeably."[49] But he probably had little practice to leave. A Mrs. Sidebotham, who consulted him on one occasion, received from him a prescription which her apothecary refused to fill. Goldsmith insisted that the prescription was quite as he intended it to be; the apothecary insisted that it was unsafe—and Mrs. Sidebotham declined to perform the experiment that would have proved which of the two was right. Instead she dismissed Goldsmith, leaving him to complain to Reynolds that he had learned a lesson and would prescribe no more for his friends. When the remark was repeated to Topham Beauclerk, he chided, "Whenever you undertake to kill, let it be only your enemies."

Meanwhile the Earl of Northumberland's interest in him stuck in Goldsmith's memory. Perhaps he had been foolhardy— even boorish—to refuse His Lordship's offer of aid. Percy's *Reliques of Ancient English Poetry* had just been published, and the Countess of Northumberland, to whom he had dedicated the volumes, had rewarded him by having him appointed tutor to her son and chaplain to the family. Perhaps Goldsmith too could win favor with the Northumberlands if they knew of his interest in ballads. It was worth trying. So he hunted up a ballad, "Edwin and Angelina," which he had written some months before, had a few copies printed privately with the words "for the amusement of the Countess of Northumberland" on the title-page, and sent one off to Her Ladyship.

The ballad, better known as "The Hermit," is a melodramatic tale of lovers reconciled after a long estrangement, expressed in language meant to be simple, but bearing more traces of the Augustan Era than of the Medieval. It was well thought of when it appeared, without the last two stanzas of the original version, in *The Vicar of Wakefield,* and Goldsmith himself told Joseph Cradock: "That poem . . . cannot be amended."[50] But it failed to inspire the Countess of Northumberland to any specific action in his behalf. After Goldsmith's death her husband told Percy that if he had known of Goldsmith's desire to travel to Asia, he would have secured him a pension from the Irish government. But Goldsmith had already rejected one offer of aid from him, and it probably never occurred to him to make another.

Apparently the booksellers were to be Goldsmith's only resort. Yet the booksellers had done very little for him in 1765; or rather, he had done very little for the booksellers. His only publication during the year, apart from the privately printed ballad, had been the *Essays* which he had collected and revised.[51] He was living on his reputation, enjoying the recognition which *The Traveller* had brought him and the fine friends whom he had met. How he was managing to support himself in the meantime is incomprehensible. He could and did rely in part on the hospitality of wealthy friends like Robert Nugent; perhaps a gift or loan from them helped along too—or a winning streak at cards. And there was always kindly John Newbery, who advanced him three guineas at an Arts and Sciences meeting one day and fifteen-and-six another time, when they met in a Fleet Street shop. Yet Newbery seems to have given up his guardianship of Goldsmith's financial affairs.

Obviously Noll needed a major project. Newbery had decided at last to bring out the novel which had lain in his shop since 1762, and Goldsmith was soon seeing it through the press. But he had little enthusiasm for the task; the novel hardly seemed worthy of him who had been hailed as "one of the first poets in the English language [and] one of the first essayists too."

What was a man to do—a man long on reputation and short on funds? There was always the theater, of course. Successful comedies paid well, and many of the best authors were writing them. The only difficulty was that sentimental comedies were the rage, and Goldsmith abhorred them.

But why not something different—a comedy in the old vein, designed to make men laugh? Surely it was worth trying.

Chapter VII
Novelist, Dramatist, Historian

(1766-1769)

IN February, 1766, James Boswell returned to London for a brief stay after his three years on the Continent. He paid duty calls on both Johnson and Goldsmith, and then, on Sunday, the 23rd, he met Goldsmith by chance at the Mitre Tavern. The two agreed to have supper together and sent word to Tom Davies to join them. Then they went to seek Johnson in his house on Johnson's Court, near Fleet Street, where he had moved from his lodgings in the Temple. But Johnson, who had been ailing, was "still bad" and felt unable to accept their invitation.

"Come then," said Goldsmith, "we will not go to the Mitre to-night, since we cannot have the big man with us."

Boswell reminded him, however, that they must return to the tavern to meet Davies. So Johnson called for a bottle of port for his friends, and they remained for a while to chat.

Goldsmith began the conversation. "I think, Mr. Johnson," he said, "you don't go near the theatres now. You give yourself no more concern about a new play, than if you had never had any thing to do with the stage."

"Why, Sir," Johnson retorted, "our tastes greatly alter. The lad does not care for the child's rattle, and the old man does not care for the young man's whore."

"Nay, Sir," Goldsmith protested; "but your Muse was not a whore."

"Sir, I do not think she was. But as we advance in the journey of life, we drop some of the things which have pleased us; whether it be that we are fatigued and don't choose to carry so many things any farther, or that we find other things which we like better."

"But, Sir," Boswell broke in, "why don't you give us something in some other way?"

"Ay, Sir," Goldsmith agreed, "we have a claim upon you."

But Johnson refused to be shaken. "A man is to have part of his life to himself," he insisted. And he went on to maintain that "the good I can do by my conversation bears the same proportion to the good I can do by my writings, that the practice of a physician, retired to a small town, does to his practice in a great city."

Boswell later wrote in his Journal that Goldsmith and he "could make nothing against him."

Presently, however, in the course of discussing his methods of writing verse, he admitted that he had not been entirely idle. "Doctor . . .," he addressed Goldsmith, "I made one line t'other day, but I made no more."

"Let us hear it," cried Goldsmith; "we'll put a bad one to it." But Johnson maintained that he had forgotten the line, and presently Goldsmith and Boswell left to meet Davies at the Mitre.

On the way Goldsmith asked whether Johnson's head was not failing.

Boswell acknowledged that Johnson seemed somewhat "more impatient of contradiction."

"Sir," Goldsmith declared, "no man is proof against continual adulation."

Presently they received word that Davies could not accept their invitation, and they went off to Goldsmith's lodgings in the Temple for a quiet supper.

Boswell was delighted with the rooms, and when they discussed "writing against authors from envy," he observed that Goldsmith's rooms, if anything, would rouse his envy.

They talked of this and that—of a remark about "Johnson and Goldsmith and those Blockheads" made by someone named Smith, of the difference between Frenchmen and Englishmen— but often the two were sparring. Goldsmith, perhaps irked at Boswell's accounts of his visits with Voltaire, Rousseau, Paoli, and various German princes, remarked that he had spent the summer "among the great," and, as Boswell later observed, "forsooth affected to talk lightly of this." But Boswell took comfort in the thought which he addressed to himself in his Journal: "You brought him down with Johnsonian principles and Johnsonian force."[1] And he went off presently to Scotland without making any further effort to see Goldsmith.

Goldsmith had some cause to be irritated these days. Here was Boswell back from a Grand Tour of Europe, all at his father's expense. Here was Johnson, comfortably settled for life on a pension of three hundred pounds from the King. And here was Goldsmith himself scraping along on the eleven guineas which he had borrowed from John Newbery on January 8.[2] And money was more important to him than ever before: he was associating with wealthy men, and his temperament demanded that he spend money as freely as they did. He could not economize; he must have fine clothes and splendidly furnished rooms in the Temple, and he could not resist the luxury of a grand flourish periodically. When Edward Lye canvassed members of the Club for subscriptions to his *Dictionarium Saxonico et Gothico-Latinum* soon afterward, Goldsmith put his name down for a copy, although he could scarcely have found it useful.[3] And when one Colonel Chevalier de Champigny turned up in London soliciting subscriptions for a proposed fifteen-volume history of England in French, Goldsmith managed to find the seven and a half guineas necessary to admit him to the list of subscribers, many of them of the royalty and nobility. But beyond the satisfaction of seeing himself publicly listed among the great, he gained nothing from his expenditure; for the Colonel Chevalier never published his volumes.

Meanwhile he was carrying out some routine commissions for Newbery: translating Formey's *Histoire Abrégée de la Philosophie* and probably continuing work on his *Survey of Experimental Philosophy*. At the same time he was seeing through the press the novel which Johnson had sold for him four years earlier and which he had finally put in publishable form.

On March 27 *The Vicar of Wakefield* was issued in two volumes, printed by Benjamin Collins of Salisbury and published by John Newbery's nephew Francis, who had evidently set up, on Paternoster Row, a branch of his uncle's business. Goldsmith's name did not appear on the title-page, but it was signed to the prefatory Advertisement, which read:

There are an hundred faults in this thing, and an hundred things might be said to prove them beauties. But it is needless. A book may be amusing with numerous errors, or it may be very dull without a single absurdity. The hero of this piece unites in himself the three greatest characters upon earth: he is a priest, an husbandman, and the father of a family. He is drawn as ready to teach, and ready to obey; as simple in affluence, and majestic in adversity. In this age of opulence and refinement, whom can such a character please? Such as are fond of high life, will turn with disdain from the simplicity of his country fire-side; such as mistake ribaldry for humour, will find no wit in his harmless conversation; and such as have been taught to deride religion, will laugh at one, whose chief stores of comfort are drawn from futurity.

Goldsmith seems to be out of sorts with his novel and with the public which he expects to ignore it. The latter attitude is doubtless a pose and recalls the conclusion of the Dedicatory Letter of *The Traveller;* the former is probably sincere and suggests that he disdained to point out the "beauties" which a casual reader might not perceive. He made few changes in later editions, and when a friend advised him to try to improve the novel, he replied that it was not worth the effort, since he would not be paid for his pains.

At first readers were inclined to agree. Johnson told Fanny Burney that *The Vicar* was "very faulty," that it contained no real life and little of nature, and that it was a "mere fanciful performance."[4] And although the book went through three editions in six months, they were small editions—so small that the publishers did not clear expenses until the fourth.[5] The reviewers seem to have been generally puzzled by the book. The *Monthly Review* for May began its criticism thus: "Through the whole course of our travels in the wild regions of romance, we never met with any thing more difficult to characterize, than the Vicar of Wakefield; a performance which contains beauties sufficient to entitle it to almost the highest applause, and defects enough to put the discerning reader out of all patience with the author capable of so strangely under-writing himself." The *Critical,* which usually reviewed Goldsmith's works in the month of their publication, postponed its review until the June issue and then approached the novel in a peculiarly evasive fashion. The reviewer mocked the Advertisement, asked why the author pub-

169

lished his book if he considered it so imperfect, but concluded that he must have had good reasons for doing so and that the demand for a second edition had justified them. Then he praised Goldsmith for his naïveté, observing that such simplicity is more difficult to achieve than the casual reader might suppose. And finally, after commending the characterization in the novel, he concluded: "But pray, Dr. Goldsmith, was it necessary to bring the concluding calamities so thick upon your old venerable friend; or in your impatience to get to the end of your task, was you rather not disposed to hurry the catastrophe?—Be this as it may, we cannot but wish you success, being of opinion, upon the whole, that your tale does no little honour to your head, and what is still better, that it does yet more to your heart."

In time, however, estimates of the novel became less equivocal. Burke had insisted from the outset that it was a genuine achievement and that its distinguishing merit was its pathos.[6] And as time passed and pathos became more fashionable, *The Vicar* came into its own. During the nineteenth century it averaged nearly two editions each year. And as Thackeray wrote in *The English Humourists*, it "found entry into every castle and every hamlet in Europe": it was translated into French seven times and into all the major European languages, as well as Hungarian, Bohemian, Rumanian, Hebrew, and Icelandic. In short, it became a classic. Writers of the Romantic Era outdid themselves in praise of the charming simplicity of the novel and its idyllic picture of human nature in the character of the Vicar. "We read [it] in youth and in age," wrote Sir Walter Scott; "we return to it again and again, and bless the memory of an author who contrives so well to reconcile us to human nature."[7] Goethe regarded it as the finest novel of his day, hailing the indescribable "effect which Goldsmith's 'Vicar' had upon [him] just at the critical moment of mental development."[8] And Dickens nicknamed his little brother "Moses" "in honour of the Vicar of Wakefield" and later adopted a corrupted form of the name, "Boz," as his pseudonym.[9]

Fanny Burney believed that the second half of the novel is superior to the first,[10] and most nineteenth century readers would probably have agreed with her. Confident that eventually virtue would triumph, they were content to wait patiently while calamity succeeded calamity in the Primrose family and the Vicar edified them with his sermons on submission to the will of God. But ingenious melodramatic plots have gone out of style—so too have pathos and conscious moralizing—and a modern reader is likely to prefer the first half of the book and to delight in its slow pace, its gentle humor, and especially the complex characterization of the Vicar. To Professor Baker the book is an "ironic idyll" deriving its effect from its comic overtones, which are almost completely lost in the second half.[11] And readers today are likely to agree that its charm rises from the subtle characterization of the Vicar— so virtuous and yet so fallible, so wise and yet so human, who complacently preaches what he fails to practice. Considering the book in retrospect, they may remember only minor incidents— Moses' purchase of the green spectacles, Mr. Burchell's cry "Fudge," the incongruous family portrait—and may agree with the reviewer who suspected that Goldsmith was merely hurrying events along in the later chapters in order to end his task.

But therein lies, in part, the greatness of the novel: it is capable of varying interpretations. It was something new and something old—a penetrating study of human character and a melodramatic romance. It can be read as idyllic or ironic, it can be regarded as representative of the sentimental novel or of the trend away from such fiction; it has meant many things to many readers, and future generations may regard it in varying or in wholly different lights. In effect it is an anomaly like its author and is therefore, in one respect, his most typical work. Like him it shows traces of genius and traces of absurdity; it has obvious weaknesses and yet irresistible charm. And anyone who would truly appreciate it should not try to criticize or analyze it, but should read and enjoy it as people have been doing ever since it was published. For despite its palpable faults, despite innumerable attempts to determine the sources of its plot, the prototype of the Vicar, or the locale of the action, it is an original and delightful novel which is likely to remain, in Professor Baker's words, "the best-read from that day to now, all the world over, of the books of the Fielding epoch."[12]

At the time, however, *The Vicar* added little to Goldsmith's reputation and nothing at all to his purse, since in 1762 he had sold the rights to it. He still had not found a major project to engage his powers.

He continued to be "very constant" at the Club. Johnson had been ill and "not over diligent" in attendance except when the group convened at his house.[13] Reynolds, however, appeared regularly at the meetings, and he and Goldsmith seem to have been seeing a good deal of each other, especially after midsummer of 1766, when Johnson went to Streatham for a long visit with his new friends, Mr. and Mrs. Henry Thrale.

For Goldsmith his friendship with Reynolds had many advantages. The artist was a more comfortable companion than Johnson—less the moralist and critic, more interested in frivolous pleasures, and far more likely to relish Goldsmith's absurdities. Moreover, he boasted a fine house in Leicester Fields and an elegant coach with carved gilt wheels and painted panels of the four seasons, which must have gratified Goldsmith's love for show. To ride through London in such an equipage, bowing to his friends along the way, or stopping to chat with the innumerable great ladies and gentlemen whom Reynolds knew well—and who had at least heard of Goldsmith—would have been balm to his frustrated ego. Gradually, through Reynolds, he was introduced to a new circle of acquaintance—notably to the Horneck family.

Mrs. Hannah Horneck, widow of Captain Kane Horneck of the Royal Engineers, was of Devonshire stock like Reynolds, had been known in her youth as the Plymouth Beauty, and was still a handsome woman. Her two daughters, Catherine and Mary, were pretty young girls of whom Goldsmith was genuinely fond and for whom he was soon writing playful verses, referring to Catherine as "Little Comedy" and to Mary as "the Jessamy [i.e., fashionable] Bride." Washington Irving magnified Goldsmith's fondness for Mary into a profound and unrequited love, but there is no evidence to support his supposition except a passage from a malicious attack in the newspapers.[14] In 1766 Mary was fourteen years old and Goldsmith thirty-six, and his affection for her would have been at least semi-paternal. He knew human beings

172

well enough to realize that to her he would have seemed like an old man. In fact, in *Citizen of the World,* No. LX, he had made Zelis refer to "a gentleman, a friend of my father, rather in the decline of life . . . about forty."

During the year 1766 Goldsmith's publications, apart from *The Vicar,* were practically negligible. In June Francis Newbery brought out his translation of Formey's *Histoire Abrégée de la Philosophie* as *A Concise History of Philosophy and Philosophers* and paid him twenty guineas for his work. It was a mere potboiler which appeared without his name and which added nothing to his literary standing. Sometimes it is incredibly careless: Goldsmith translates "depuis la mort de son Auteur [Aristotle] jusqu'au premier siècle de l'Ere Chrétienne" as "from the death of its author in the first century of the christian era." Yet, like almost everything else that Goldsmith wrote, the translation reveals his powers of smooth, facile expression. He did not hesitate to compress or expand Formey's sentences for the sake of clarity; he inserted relevant details from his own knowledge when he saw fit; and he translated the terse and often stilted language of the original into easy, conversational rhythms.

By this time he had begun work on his comedy; but to assure himself of some income in the meantime he discharged two minor hack jobs: a short English grammar for Newbery and an anthology of verse for the publisher Payne of Paternoster Row. The grammar, for which he received five guineas on December 28, seems never to have been published, but the anthology, *Poems for Young Ladies,* appeared anonymously in December, though dated 1767. It was an undistinguished piece of work inspired "in some measure," as Goldsmith stated in his Preface, by a remark in Dr. James Fordyce's *Sermons for Young Women* that poetry should play a part in female education. In this collection, Goldsmith declared, "Care has been taken to select, not only such pieces as innocence may read without a blush, but such as will even tend to strengthen that innocence." And he added the practical advice that the poems included would cost ten times as much if they were bought separately.

173

The anthology itself was divided into three sections: Devotional, Moral, and Entertaining; the selections, ranging from Homer to Goldsmith's own "Hermit," were chosen obviously with more attention to correctness of form and morality than to genius. The reviewers gave the book short shrift, the *Critical* for December observing that it could "by no means recommend the judgment of the author in his selection," and the *Monthly* for the following March approving of his choice but arguing that he could not in justice claim that the poems would strengthen innocence. The book went through two later editions, one in 1770 with Goldsmith's name on the title-page and another, with changes and additions, in 1785.[15]

During the early months of 1767 Goldsmith continued to see a good deal of Reynolds and his circle. In January,[16] when he was invited at the last minute to join a party at the home of Dr. George Baker, Reynolds' physician, he replied in a jocular strain with jesting allusions to the other guests, the Hornecks and the painter Angelica Kauffmann:

> Your mandate I got,
> You may all go to pot;

explaining that he had not shaved because of the cold weather; and scolding the "Devonshire crew"

> For sending so late
> To one of my state.[17]

In February he was at Reynolds' house the night that Johnson told an admiring group about his encounter with the King at Buckingham House. According to Boswell, who was not present, Goldsmith sat to one side on a sofa during the recital, pretending not to be interested in it. When someone asked him what ailed him, he replied that he was disturbed because Johnson had failed to supply the prologue which he had promised to write for his forthcoming comedy. But of course the company suspected that it was envy, rather than disappointment, that accounted for his lack of interest. At last, however, Goldsmith's better nature triumphed, and he blurted out: "Well, you acquitted yourself in this conversation better than I should have done; for I should have bowed and stammered through the whole of it."[18]

At about this time he joined the Wednesday Club, which met each week at the Globe Tavern on Fleet Street. There the humor was lively and broad; there he met quick-witted, irresponsible creatures like the comedian Tom King or Hugh Kelly, the ex-corsetmaker, now a popular dramatist. There too, according to his fellow-member William Ballantyne, he had as friends a great barrel of a man who loved to sing "Nottingham Ale" for the group and a wealthy pig-butcher who prided himself on his acquaintance with the distinguished author and delighted in addressing him as Noll. "Come, Noll," he would call as he raised his glass, "here's my service to you, old boy!" And when Goldsmith tried to discourage his familiarity by saying on one occasion, "Mr. B——, I have the honour of drinking your good health," the old fellow called back cheerily, "Thankee, thankee, Noll."[19]

On his way to one of the meetings of the Wednesday Club Goldsmith is said to have composed his mock epitaph for Edward Purdon, who died in April, 1767:

> Here lies poor Ned Purdon, from misery freed,
> Who long was a bookseller's hack;
> He led such a damnable life in this world,
> I don't think he'll wish to come back.

It was one of several bits of wry occasional verse which Goldsmith was turning out at this time. The reply to the invitation to Dr. Baker's party was another; so was "An Elegy on the Death of a Mad Dog," which Bill Primrose recites in *The Vicar*. Like the earlier "Elegy on Mrs. Blaize" these are trivial things, but deftly handled, and they doubtless helped to make Goldsmith a popular guest at all sorts of gatherings.

During the spring of 1767 he continued work on his play, but managed to find time also to compile another anthology, the two-volume *Beauties of English Poesy, Selected by Oliver Goldsmith,* which William Griffin published in April and for which Goldsmith was rumored to have received the handsome sum of two hundred pounds.[20] The brief Preface observes that, since there is "no collection of English poetry among us, of any estimation," these volumes will be of value to "such as either want leisure, skill, or fortune, to choose for themselves, . . . to our youth, particularly." Goldsmith claims no credit for his selection; "Every poem here is well known," he remarks, "and possessed, or the public has been long mistaken, of peculiar merit." In fact his major contribution to the anthology was preparing for each poem a perfunctory criticism of two or three sentences, "rather designed for boys than men."

The volumes were not well received. The *Monthly Review* for June declared emphatically that "from his preface, notes and introductions to these poems, one would almost be inclined to think [the editor] had never written before." And the reviewer, John Langhorne, added that no one who reads the introductions "can forbear crying out with the shepherd in Virgil, *Quid facient Domini, audent cum talia fures?*" The *Critical* for June was only slightly more favorable; the reviewer disagreed with Goldsmith's selections and with his introductory comments and was particularly offended at the inclusion of Prior's "Hans Carvel," an indelicate poem which, he felt, should never have been printed "in a selection of this kind." The public agreed with him; in fact Prior's poem "The Ladle" also was considered unsuitable for an anthology for young people, and as a result the book had only a limited sale and, except for a Dublin edition in 1771, was never reprinted.

Sometime during the spring of 1767 Goldsmith completed work on his comedy. He had intended to submit it for presentation at Covent Garden, but the affairs of the theater were so confused after the death of John Rich, one of the patentees, that he decided to risk offering it to Garrick for presentation at Drury Lane. Since Goldsmith hesitated to approach Garrick because of the actor's refusal to support him for the secretaryship of the Society of Arts and Sciences, Reynolds arranged for the two men to meet at his house, where Goldsmith gave Garrick the manuscript of the play.

Garrick carried it away with him, but took no immediate action. He seemed now to be planning to produce the play, now abandoning that plan. He told Johnson and Reynolds privately that he believed it would fail; yet he would give Goldsmith no definite decision. According to Tom Davies, Garrick wanted to be courted into accepting the play, and Goldsmith was unwilling to cater to his vanity.[21] He assured Reynolds haughtily that he could not put up with "such airs of superiority from one who was only a poor player." "No, no, don't say that," Reynolds retorted; "he is no *poor* player surely."[22]

The theatrical season advanced, and Goldsmith was as usual in need of money. On July 7 he borrowed ten pounds from John Newbery,[23] and a week later he received another ten pounds from him for compiling *The Present State of the British Empire,* which he evidently assembled hastily from several sources and which was published in the following year.[24]

Eventually Reynolds brought Goldsmith and Garrick together again in order to accomplish some sort of agreement. Garrick suggested changes in the play, but Goldsmith refused to accept them. Then Garrick offered to refer his suggestions to a third party for settlement. But whatever interest Goldsmith may have shown in this compromise ended when he learned that Garrick intended to name as arbitrator the Poet Laureate, William White-head, who sometimes served as reader at Drury Lane. Goldsmith was outraged. He had no intention of permitting his play to be judged by one of Whitehead's abilities.

It was probably now that he determined to take revenge on Garrick by attending a performance of Hall Hartson's tragedy *The Countess of Salisbury* in order to hiss it. However, he was so caught up by the play that he remained quiet until the fifth act. Then, recalling his intention, he rose from his seat, muttered "Brownrigg! Brownrigg! by God!" (alluding to the famous "ap-prenticide") and left the theater.[25]

By this time George Colman had assumed managership of the Covent Garden Theater; Goldsmith decided to offer his play to him. He submitted a copy, Colman read it and wrote back favorably, and Goldsmith replied on July 19 with obvious relief and gratitude:

> I am very much obliged to you, both for your kind partiality in my favour, and your tenderness in shortening the interval of my expectation. That the play is liable to many objections I well know, but I am happy that it is in hands the most capable in the world of removing them. If then Dear Sir, you will complete your favours by putting the piece into such a state as it may be acted, or of directing me how to do it, I shall ever retain a sense of your goodness to me. And indeed tho' most probably this be the last I shall ever write yet I can't help feeling a secret satisfaction that poets for the future are likely to have a protector who declines taking advantage of their dependent situation, and scorns that importance which may be acquir'd by triffling with their anxieties.

Clearly Goldsmith was not wholly above flattery; in fact he even directed some toward Garrick when he wrote to him on the following day:

> A few days ago Mr. Beard [Colman's predecessor at Covent Garden] renewd his claim to the piece which I had written for his stage, and had as a friend submitted to your perusal. As I found you had very great difficulties about that piece I complied with his desire, thinking it wrong to take up the attention of my friends with such petty concerns as mine or to load your good nature by a compliance rather with their requests than my merits: I am extremely sorry that you should think me warm at our last meeting, your judgement certainly ought to be free especially in a matter which must in some measure concern your own credit and interest. I assure you Sir I have no disposition to differ with you on this or any other account, but am with an high opinion of your abilities and with a very real esteem Sir
>
> Your most obedient humble serv^t
Oliver Goldsmith

Garrick was immediately mollified by Goldsmith's conciliating words, and he replied on the 25th from Lichfield, where he was visiting:

> I was at Birmingham when yr. letter came to this place, or I shd. have thank'd you for it immediately—I was indeed much hurt that yr. warmth at our last meeting mistook my sincere & friendly attention to yr. Play for the remains of a former misunderstanding wch. I had as much forgot as if it never had existed—What I said to you at my own house, I now repeat, that I felt more pain in giving my Sentiments than you possibly could in

receiving them. It has been the business & ambition of my Life to live upon the best terms with Men of Genius, & as I know that Dr. Goldsmith will have no reason to change his present friendly disposition toward me, so I shall be glad of any future opportunity to convince him how much

I am his obedt. Serv. & well wisher

D. Garrick.[26]

For the time being, at least, Goldsmith could enjoy a respite from his anxiety about his play.

He probably spent a part of the summer of 1767 in his room at Canonbury House, but his letter to Colman was dated from Garden Court in the Temple. Whether he had moved there from his rooms at King's Bench Court or was only visiting a friend is not clear. But he was presumably there when he read in the *St. James Chronicle* of July 18-21 a letter from "Detector" (perhaps his old foe William Kenrick) alleging that "The Hermit" was stolen from a poem by Thomas Percy, "A Friar of Orders Gray," published two years earlier in the *Reliques,* but was "as short of the merits of Mr. Percy's ballad as the insipidity of negus is to the genuine flavour of Champagne." Goldsmith felt obliged to reply to the charge. And while he had the attention of readers of the *Chronicle,* he disposed also of another writer who had accused him of having misrepresented in the press a recent translation of Blainville's *Travels:*

As there is nothing I dislike so much as newspaper controversy, particularly upon trifles, permit me to be as concise as possible in informing a correspondent of yours, that I recommended Blainville's travels because I thought the book was a good one; and I think so still. I said I was told by the bookseller that it was then first published; but in that it seems I was misinformed, and my reading was not extensive enough to set me right.

Another correspondent of yours accuses me of having taken a ballad I published sometime ago from one by the ingenious Mr. Percy. I do not think there is any great resemblance between the two pieces in question. If there be any, his ballad was taken from mine. I read it to Mr. Percy some years ago; and he, as we both considered these things as trifles at best, told me with his usual good-humour the next time I saw him, that he had taken my plan to form the fragments of Shakespeare into a ballad of his own. He then read me his little Cento, if I may so call it, and I highly approved it. Such petty anecdotes as these are scarcely worth printing; and were it not for the busy disposition of some of your correspondents, the public should never have known that he owes me the hint of his ballad, or that I am obliged to his friendship and learning for communications of a much more important nature.[27]

Fall came and went, and still Goldsmith's comedy was not presented at Covent Garden. Johnson, Reynolds, and Burke all thought highly of it: Johnson considered it the best English comedy since Vanbrugh and Cibber's *Provoked Husband*,[28] and Burke read it to several of his friends who gathered at his house to hear it on November 21.[29] It had been scheduled for performance in that same month, but had been postponed until the following January. Some said that Colman had agreed to withhold it until after Garrick had presented Hugh Kelly's *False Delicacy,* a sentimental comedy in the very vein that Goldsmith was hoping to displace.

In the meantime Goldsmith, who had borrowed from Newbery in July, had had no ostensible income since then. And when Newbery died on December 22, he may well have been pressed by executors of the estate for settlement of his debt. A report that he applied for the lectureship in Civil Law at Gresham College is hard to credit, since he was scarcely prepared to assume such a position. Yet desperation may well have prompted him to apply, and he could certainly have assured himself that he had, in his time, developed at short notice a working knowledge of other unfamiliar subjects. More credible is Basil Montagu's claim that Dr. James Scott called on Goldsmith at the Temple at about this time and offered him a handsome stipend if he would write in defense of Lord North's ministry, then under attack by John Wilkes and the mysterious Junius. Despite his shortage of cash, Goldsmith imperiously rejected the offer. In the Dedicatory Letter to *The Traveller* he had spoken his mind on the subject of writing for party, and he now dismissed Scott with the words: "I can earn as much as will supply my wants without writing for any party; the assistance therefore you offer is unnecessary to me."

By the turn of the year it began to look as if Goldsmith's play might be postponed until the next season, but it was finally scheduled for January 29. This was too late in the season for it to enjoy any extended run, but by now Goldsmith was doubtless eager to have done with it. Needing money as he did, he must have been in suspense to know whether the play would succeed; for although his friends thought highly of it, the professional men of the theater had shown themselves dubious.

January, 1768, was, therefore, an anxious month. He dined with a large group at Reynolds' house on the 4th, and a few days later entertained an Irishman named Roach and two others at dinner in his rooms. During the evening, before they went off to the theater, the group discussed literature, with Goldsmith praising Otway and Farquhar but damning Milton for all but his poetry. Then he picked up a newspaper and pointed to a note from Boswell enclosing the prologue which he had written for the opening of the Theatre Royal in Edinburgh. "And what do you think of our friend Boswell having the courage to venture upon poetry?" he asked. With mock gravity he read the opening lines of the poem:

> Scotland, for learning and for arms renown'd
> In ancient annals, is with lustre crown'd. . . .

"Ay, ay," he exclaimed, "Scotland is ever the burden of a Scotchman's song." And after more such comments: "Why, how simple the man must be to write such lines and call them poetry! And then to advertise them in the newspapers as his own by a formal letter to the printer! What were his friends about to let him expose himself?" And presently he added, probably with some satisfaction, that Johnson would be "either very angry or very witty with Boswell's verses."[30]

At last on the 29th of the month Goldsmith, probably resplendent in the "Tyrian bloom satin grain [coat?] and garter blue silk breeches" which his tailor had delivered a few days before, presented himself at Covent Garden for the ordeal of watching the first performance of *The Good Natured Man*. After months of waiting and with so much depending on this one performance, he must have been beside himself with apprehension. And his fears proved to be justified.

Johnson's grave prologue had a sobering effect on the audience, and the actor Powell's performance of Honeywood did little to cheer them. Shuter, however, playing Croaker, and Woodward, as Lofty, brightened things up, and all went reasonably well until the bailiffs' scene in Act III. By modern standards the scene is perfectly innocuous, but the first audience found it too "low." An ominous grumbling began as the scene proceeded, and when one of the bailiffs cried, "That's all my eye!" there were hisses from the gallery. The hecklers quieted down presently, however, and when Shuter read the "incendiary letter" in Act IV, he was cheered. But by that time Goldsmith was convinced that his play had failed. When the curtain fell, he went backstage to thank Shuter for his efforts, then left the theater to join members of the Club, who had agreed to gather at the Turk's Head for a party in Goldsmith's honor.

There he laughed and joked with his friends, sang a song about an old woman tossed in a blanket fourteen times as high as the moon, but ate not a mouthful. And when all except Johnson and him had left the tavern, he burst into tears and vowed that he would give up writing altogether. Two years later, when he and Johnson were Percy's guests at the Chaplains' Table at St. James's Palace, he told the whole story as an illustration of Virgil's line *"Premit altum Corde dolorem."* Johnson heard him through incredulously and at last observed: "So you did indeed Doctor . . .; but I thought till now it had been a secret, I am sure I would not have told it for the world."[31]

Goldsmith's distress proved, however, to have been unfounded. When the bailiffs' scene was deleted, the play continued for ten nights, a good average run, and it might have kept the stage longer if the season had not been so far advanced. The third, sixth, and ninth performances, which were the author's "benefits," yielded him approximately four hundred pounds, by far the largest sum he had ever received for any of his writings. Moreover, he was doubtless paid an additional fifty pounds by William Griffin, who published the play (including the controversial bailiffs' scene) on February 5. The printed version was more successful than the acted version; in fact it went through four editions in less than three weeks. And Johnson's gloomy prologue and Goldsmith's own sprightly epilogue enjoyed a success of their own: both were reprinted in the *Public Advertiser* for February 3 and in the *Gentleman's Magazine* for that month.

Twentieth century readers might expect the play to succeed better on the stage than when read, for it contains obvious flaws which would seem less noticeable in the theater. There are several striking characters: the lugubrious Croaker (borrowed, as Goldsmith admitted, from Suspirius in Johnson's *Rambler,* No. LIX),[32] his irrepressible wife, the fraud Lofty, the earthy bailiffs, and the good-natured Honeywood. But their distinguishing characteristics are sometimes neglected in the exigencies of the action. The play is at its best in its separate scenes, where action is slighted in order to achieve an effect—usually that of dramatic irony. The action itself, though ingenious, is often forced; exposition, dialogue, and soliloquies are frequently strained and unnatural; the reversal in Honeywood's character is sudden and unconvincing; and the final moralizing is heavy-handed. That is to say, the play in general reveals the strength and weaknesses of *The Vicar of Wakefield:* memorable characters and incidents, but often melodramatic action. The surprising thing is that Goldsmith's faults were not those expected of a novice in the theater: he had an instinctive feeling for what will be dramatically effective. Once again he had ventured into a new area of literature and had proved himself able to master its intricacies.

The Good Natured Man was, however, more than just an attempt to turn his literary skill to profit: he hoped also to undermine the popularity of the sentimental comedy which had dominated the theater in recent years. In his Preface to the published play he declared that he had been "strongly prepossessed in favour of the poets of the last age" and had sought to imitate their "nature and humour" and "to delineate character." Then, as a sort of half-apology for the bailiffs' scene, he added: "Those who know anything of composition, are sensible that, in pursuing humour, it will sometimes lead us into the recesses of the mean." But he pointed out that this scene, though "retrenched in the representation," had been restored in the printed version of the play. That is to say, he had yielded to popular taste in the theater, but he still hoped that "too much refinement will not banish humour and character from ours, as it has already done from the French theatre." He was convinced that the drama could be moral without sacrificing gaiety, and he proposed to prove it by returning to the example of that era of literature which he most admired. All this was, of course, consistent with theories which he had been preaching and practicing ever since he began writing reviews for Griffiths of the *Monthly*.

But the public was not yet ready for any sweeping reform in the theater. Hugh Kelly's *False Delicacy,* the sentimental comedy which opened at Drury Lane in the previous week, proved far more of a success than *The Good Natured Man*. The publishers sold ten thousand copies of Kelly's play in the first season and, in gratitude, honored him at a public breakfast at the Chapter Coffeehouse and presented him with a piece of silver worth twenty pounds. *False Delicacy* was better received by the critics too, for the bailiffs' scene in Goldsmith's comedy was considered too "low" to be acceptable. The *Gentleman's Magazine* for February praised the characterization and humor of the play, but observed that "the dramatic action . . . is a mere vehicle for them." Then the critic launched into an account of the "infinitely ridiculous" bailiffs' scene, which "depends upon the exhibition of manners, which the taste of the present age will scarce admit even in farce." The *Critical Review* for the same month offered similar praise of characterization and unfavorable criticism of "fable." As for the bailiffs' scene, "we neither wholly approve nor condemn it: . . . 'Humour (it is true) will sometimes lead us into the recesses of the mean;' but in pursuing humour into those recesses, the author, like Jove under Philemon's roof, should not wholly abandon the dignity of his own character." The February *Monthly Review* conceded only that the play was "an agreeable play to *read,*" since the scene of the bailiffs, "intolerable on the stage," proved not disgusting "in the perusal." The *London Chronicle* for January 28-30 "hoped the author will for the future wholly omit it," and the March *Scots Magazine* declared that the play had "much merit and many faults."

The success of *False Delicacy,* coupled with the fact that *The Good Natured Man* had been withheld until the former was presented, roused Goldsmith's envy and led to a break between him and Kelly, who had been his friend and fellow-member of the Wednesday Club. Naturally neither man approved of the other's play, and each is supposed to have made disparaging remarks which were duly reported to the other. When they met one day at Covent Garden Goldsmith is said to have broken down and congratulated Kelly on his success, and Kelly to have replied coolly: "I cannot thank you, because I cannot believe you."[33]

It was rumored that Goldsmith had planned to marry Kelly's wife's sister, but there is no confirming evidence. Indeed the whole question of Goldsmith's relationships with women is vague. Despite the report that he fell in love with a Dublin girl while he was an undergraduate at Trinity College, despite Washington Irving's suppositions about Goldsmith's affection for Mary Horneck, there is no proof that he ever took more than a passing interest in women. Before he achieved fame, he seems to have associated almost solely with men; afterwards, although he was often in mixed groups, he evidently never singled out any one woman for his attentions. Moreover, his attitude toward the sex in his Preface to the *Poems for Young Ladies* is generally condescending, and that in *The Citizen of the World* often seems hostile.

Psychologists might relate this hostility to his estrangement from his mother, but there is probably no need to probe so deep. Bachelorhood, especially among literary men, was commonplace in the Age of Reason; there were few social pressures toward marriage for a man of intellectual pursuits. To Goldsmith it would doubtless have seemed like a luxury which he could easily forego, financially pressed as he usually was. Furthermore, there was always the matter of his appearance. As early as 1753 he had written from Edinburgh to his friend Bryanton: "There are 'tis certain handsome women here and tis as certain they have handsome men to keep them company. An ugly and a poor man is society only for himself and such society the world lets me enjoy in great abundance."[34] He knew all too well that he was not formed to win favor from a woman, and his constitutional lack of self-assurance would militate against his wooing one—at least a lady.

Conceivably, like Charles Marlow in *She Stoops to Conquer,* Goldsmith may have been tongue-tied in the presence of ladies, but quite at ease with women beneath him socially—just as he was with children and humble people. He may even have been something of a rake in certain companies; at least Garrick wrote of him after his death:

> With the love of a wench, let his writings be chaste, . . .
> That the rake and the poet o'er all may prevail, . . .
> This scholar, rake, christian, dupe, gamester, and poet.[35]

And there is a puzzling remark in a portion of Boswell's *Journal of a Tour to the Hebrides* which he omitted from his published text: on Friday, October 22, 1773, after he had spent the previous evening drinking heavily, he wrote: "It humbled me to find that my holy resolutions at Icolmkill had been so ineffectual that the very day after having been there I had drank too much. I went to Mr. Johnson before he was up. He said first none of our Club would get drunk, but then, taking himself, he said Burke would get drunk and be ashamed of it; Goldsmith would get drunk and boast of it, if it had been with a little whore or so, who had allowed him to go in a coach with her."[36] But of course this evidence is too tenuous to admit of specific conclusions. If anything, it reveals more about Goldsmith's drinking habits than about his relations with women.

Certainly he was in a better position to consider marriage after the production of *The Good Natured Man* than he ever had been before. This was, in fact, the turning point in his career. Henceforth he was to receive larger fees for his work—and to spend his money more recklessly. But instead of marrying, he moved to new bachelor's quarters on the third floor of No. 2 Brick Court in the Temple, just above the rooms occupied by the lawyer William Blackstone. He had a large sitting room with handsomely carved paneling and three long windows overlooking Essex Court, a smaller room over Brick Court, and a windowless bedroom. He installed in his chambers a fine Wilton carpet, a sofa and chairs upholstered in blue morine, curtains of the same material, and tables and bookshelves.[37] And there he proceeded to enjoy his new prosperity. He was high enough in the building to be able to look out into the trees and watch the rooks nesting and to have quiet and solitude for his writings. Yet, as always, he craved companionship, and one of the other tenants in the building, a Mr. Children, recalled that Goldsmith had given many a gay party in his rooms.

One of his chief delights was to gather four or five congenial friends for breakfast in his chambers. He saw to it that there was enough food for him to distribute some to the poor women of the neighborhood; and when a well-to-do visitor protested that he himself could never have afforded such largesse, Goldsmith replied: "It is not wealth, my dear sir, but inclination. I have only to suppose that a few more friends than usual have been of our party, and then it amounts to the same thing."

After a leisurely breakfast the group would walk out to a country inn for dinner, and then return to the city in the evening for supper. He called such outings his "shoemaker's holidays," and to them he often invited the impecunious young Irishmen who gravitated to his door. One of his regular guests was an odd man known as Peter Barlow, who sometimes served as his amanuensis. Barlow always refused to pay more than a set sum for his dinner, regardless of how much it actually cost; yet Goldsmith paid the balance cheerfully and never failed to invite him again.

About the time that *The Good Natured Man* was presented, Tom Davies, prompted by the success of the *History of England in a Series of Letters to a Nobleman,* commissioned Goldsmith to write a history of Rome in two volumes for the handsome figure of 250 guineas. Having no other project under way, he went to work on it at once. Yet he continued to see a good deal of his friends, especially Reynolds, and on one occasion convulsed a party at Topham Beauclerk's by an ill-advised remark about his host's recent marriage to Lady Diana, divorced wife of Viscount Bolingbroke.[38] Eventually his social obligations became so pressing that, in order to maintain his writing schedule, he left his rooms at the Temple periodically and settled down in the country to devote himself to his work.

During the spring of 1768 he is supposed to have spent some time at Ilam, near Dove Dale, in Derbyshire, and he thought for a while of passing the summer at Percy's rectory at Easton Maudit in Northamptonshire. To Percy he wrote:

> I have been thinking of your Northamptonshire offer. I beg you'l send me an answer to the following Queries.
>
> 1. In the first place are there any prying troublesome neighbours?
> 2. Can I have a chamber to myself where I can buy coals, &c?
> 3. Will I not cumber the house and take up the room of others?
> 4. How long can you spare the appartment?
> 5. Is there a stage? The price. And can my books be carried down.
> 6. Can I have milk, meat, &c tea, in the place?
>
> And lastly will it be any way inconvenient to you or Mrs. Percy? And when will you want to be down yourselves?

But his plans changed when he and his friend Edward Bott, who occupied rooms across the hall from his in Brick Court, took a cottage eight miles from London, near the village of Edgeware and not far from Canons, the country estate of Lord Chandos. There he entertained Percy at dinner on May 7.[39] Usually, however, he kept to himself, enjoying the garden which surrounded his "Shoemaker's Paradise," as he called the house, studying and writing busily, or strolling out into the fields to jot down notes for later revision. Now and again he went up to the city to dine with friends and then drive back in the evening. According to a letter to Bott now lost, he and his friend sometimes had difficulty in making their way home after a festive evening. Once Bott struck a post by the roadside, but refused to admit that he had not been driving straight down the middle of the road.

The summer of 1768 must, however, have been clouded for Goldsmith, for in May of that year his brother Henry died. Although the two men had not met for many years, the bond between them was strong, and Goldsmith's grief must have been made more poignant by his realization that he had delayed his return to Ireland until it was too late to see the man whom he loved better than most other men, as he wrote presently in the

Dedication to *The Deserted Village*. On June 16 the tailor William Filby provided him with a suit of mourning, but his sorrow seems to have taken a more enduring form. For now, in moments spared from the *Roman History*, he began work on his second major poem, a tribute to the kind of life his brother had led.

In the fall he was back in London. He dined with Reynolds and Richard Burke, both just home from a trip to Paris, on October 24 and 25.[40] Yet he was unaccountably absent from the "Treat" which Reynolds gave for his friends—including Johnson, Burke, Dr. Nugent, and Percy—on April 27, 1769, to celebrate his elevation to knighthood after his appointment as President of the Royal Academy.[41]

He had, however, enjoyed an honor of his own earlier in the year. On Tuesday, February 14, he went with Johnson and Percy to Oxford, where they remained four days as guests of Robert Chambers, the Vinerian Professor of the Laws of England. And on the 17th Goldsmith was granted the degree of Bachelor of Medicine, without examination, as holder of the same degree from Trinity College.[42]

Meanwhile he had found time to write a first-rate epilogue for Charlotte Lennox's play *The Sister,* which lasted only one night, February 18, at Covent Garden. Strangely enough, someone who was unaware of his interest in the play asked him to join a party planning to hiss the performance because of the author's earlier attack on Shakespeare in her *Shakespeare Illustrated*. Of course Goldsmith refused, but some time afterward he mentioned the incident to Johnson. According to Boswell, who reported the story as told by Bennet Langton, Johnson was horrified at the suggestion and demanded of Goldsmith: "And did not you tell him that he was a rascal?" to which Goldsmith replied lamely: "No. . . . Perhaps he might not mean what he said."[43] Actually he was not averse to hissing a play on occasion, and in the same month, when he learned that John Home's *Fatal Discovery* was to be produced as the work of another man because the managers feared that Home's reputation would prejudice the public in advance, Goldsmith, according to Davies, tried to form a group to damn the play on the ground that "such fellows ought not to be encouraged."[44]

As time passed and Goldsmith's fame increased, his friends had more and more stories to tell of his "absurdities." William Cooke declared that once when he asked Goldsmith for a loan and Goldsmith replied that he had no cash at hand, Cooke suspected that he was lying to him. But when he returned to his rooms early the next morning, he found that Goldsmith had secured the needed money, wrapped it in a piece of paper, and left it under the door. When Cooke saw him the next day and pointed out that the money might easily have been stolen, Goldsmith replied, "In truth, my dear fellow, I did not think of that."

Someone else told of an incident at the Shilling Whist Club, which met regularly at the Devil Tavern: Goldsmith arrived at the club one evening, paid his coach fare, and then discovered too late that he had given the coachman a guinea instead of a shilling. At the next meeting of the club a man asked to see him, explained that he was the coachman, and insisted on returning the guinea. Touched, Goldsmith took up a collection from other members of the group in order to reward the man's honesty; but he learned later that the returned guinea was a counterfeit and that the coachman who had brought it was an impostor hired for the part by the members of the club.

Goldsmith was the butt of a good many practical jokes of this sort. Samuel Glover claimed that one day while the two were coming down Hampstead Hill after a jaunt in the country, Goldsmith noticed a family at tea in a cottage along the road and said that he would like to join them. "That can be immediately accomplished," said Glover; "allow me to introduce you." And he led Goldsmith into the house, greeted the family cordially, entered into an animated conversation with them, and only later revealed to Goldsmith that he had never seen them before. Another time, at supper at the Globe Tavern, some friends supposedly persuaded Goldsmith that the mutton chops set before him smelled bad and were unfit to eat. Then they arranged to have the waiter offer various reasons for not bringing other food, and Goldsmith was kept hungry until late in the evening.

How authentic these stories are, no one knows. Goldsmith's "absurdity" had become so legendary that men like Glover and "Conversation" Cooke, as he was called, might well be tempted to lend interest to a commonplace story—and distinction to themselves—by applying the story to him.

The booksellers, however, had a healthy respect for his talents and kept him well supplied with lucrative commissions. At the end of February he contracted with William Griffin to write "a new Natural History of Animals, &c." in eight volumes at one hundred guineas per volume. Then on June 13 he agreed to write for Davies within two years a history of England in four volumes at a total figure of five hundred pounds. The *Roman History* had been published on May 18 and had been so well received that Davies had concluded that any popular history signed with Goldsmith's name was sure to sell well. As for the author, he cheerfully accepted any offers made to him. He had struck a profitable lode in such popularizations, and he intended to mine it as long as it lasted.

The *Roman History* was much as one would expect it to be: a smooth, fast-moving survey of the subject. Goldsmith described the work frankly as a "compilation" in his Preface, and his method of composition was doubtless similar to that for the earlier *History of England in a Series of Letters of a Nobleman:* reading the recognized authorities and then digesting them more or less in his own words. This time, however, he confined himself almost entirely to straight narrative, with brief estimates of the characters of the principal figures, but few anecdotes and only occasional reflections on the moral lessons to be derived from Roman history. Some of these lessons echoed opinions which he had expressed earlier—especially the dangers of overexpansion, luxury, and commerce—but he resisted the temptation to belabor them and usually let the reader form his own conclusions. Moreover, he had little to say about the social background of the eras which he treated, and he referred to the great literary figures only incidentally. Throughout, however, the book is written with an assurance which inspires confidence. Although Goldsmith mentions such ancient authorities as Livy, Tacitus, or Plutarch only occasionally and rarely takes time to discuss conflicting reports of a given incident, he chooses his details so well and sometimes describes events so vividly, that the reader unconsciously feels that he is being instructed by one who knows his subject thoroughly, has investigated every aspect of it, and is presenting the facts objectively. This sense of security is doubtless unfounded, but the sensation is a comfortable one, and interest never flags.

The reactions of the reviewers were mixed. The *Critical* for June was wholly favorable. "This performance is seasonable, and well executed," it began. "Though the author in his preface modestly calls it, a compilation rather than a work, yet we hazard nothing in recommending it as an excellent and elegant digest of the Roman History." The September *Monthly,* however, found fault with Goldsmith's facts, his interpretations, and especially his syntax; and the reviewer, John Hawkesworth, concluded: "It is surely to be regretted, that the Author of the Traveller, one of the best poems that has appeared since those of Mr. Pope, should not apply wholly to works of imagination; for what can be more mortifying, than to see a good poet degenerate into a bad compiler of historical epitomes?" Yet the book went through fourteen editions before 1800; it was translated into French, German, Italian, and Greek; and, like others of Goldsmith's compilations, it continued to be in demand until the middle of the nineteenth century.

Since the book is so objectively written, it has little biographical interest. Yet one matter demands attention: the religious tone of certain passing remarks. Although Goldsmith had had a conventional religious training as a child and although his essays on popular preaching suggest that he must have attended church in later life, he has surprisingly little to say about religion in his published works. In his earlier writings he seldom offers more than an expression of confidence in Divine Providence, almost deistic in tone; and when Miss Milner of Peckham asked him what commentary on the Bible he would particularly recommend, he replied: "Common sense."[45] The *Roman History,* however, seems much more conventionally Christian: Jesus Christ is referred to as "our Saviour, Christ," Christianity is called "our holy religion," and Goldsmith writes of the reign of Tiberius: "Little more need be said of these times, but that, in the eighteenth year of this monarch's reign, Christ was crucified; as if the universal depravity of mankind, wanted no less a sacrifice than that of God himself, to reclaim them." Moreover, he remarks of the death of the Emperor Alexander that it proves "that neither virtue nor justice can guard us against the misfortunes of this life; and that good men are to expect their reward in a place of more equitable distribution."

Granted, this is no overwhelming proof of a change in Goldsmith's religious views. But it is a new kind of talk for Oliver Goldsmith. To be sure, the *Roman History* was designed for use in schools where anything short of orthodox belief might militate against its adoption; yet Goldsmith often rejects the interpretations of Christian historians, and in his Preface he states flatly that it would be unfair to judge pagan leaders by Christian standards. One suspects that Goldsmith's thinking about religion was becoming more conventional as he grew older. And the impression is borne out not only by other hints of orthodoxy in his later writings but by his remark to Boswell in 1773: "As I take my shoes from the shoemaker, and my coat from the taylor, so I take my religion from the priest."[46]

The summer of 1769 must have been a busy one for Goldsmith. As his fame increased, his responsibilities grew. He probably spent most of the summer at Edgeware again, for he had three major projects in hand. He seems not to have attended the Shakespearean Festival at Stratford on September 6—probably because he was no very ardent admirer either of Shakespeare or of Garrick, who had sponsored the affair. He was, therefore, denied the satisfaction of seeing Boswell making a spectacle of himself in Corsican costume by way of advertising his recently published *Account of Corsica.*

Boswell and Goldsmith did meet, however, on Thursday, September 21, at Davies' shop. It was their first reunion in three years, during which time Boswell had emerged as something of a literary man himself, and Goldsmith led off the conversation by remarking that he had heard Boswell highly spoken of at supper the night before and that George Colman had said his distinguishing characteristic was simplicity—"not in a sense of weakness," Boswell explained in his Journal, "but of being plain and un-affected."

Presently a man named Rose, headmaster of an academy at Chiswick, entered, and the group fell to discussing the work of the political writer Junius. Goldsmith compared it to a flower on a dunghill, maintaining that, because it appeared in a newspaper, it seemed good by contrast. Boswell, however, insisted that Junius' pen was keen—like a caustic, which corrodes sound matter as well as that which is corrupted.

After a while Rose brought up the subject of writing for profit and, perhaps thinking of Goldsmith's experience with *The Good Natured Man,* observed that writing for the stage was the easiest way to prosper in the literary world. But Goldsmith demurred; writing for Tom Davies was, he declared, more profitable. To prove his point he announced that he was being paid a thousand pounds for the natural history which he was writing. "That kind of writing is sure," he added; "whereas writing Plays is difficult, and their profits uncertain"; and he regaled his audience with an account of the unpleasant circumstances associated with dramatic authorship, on which he was certainly an authority.[47]

Goldsmith must have enjoyed Boswell's company that evening, for shortly afterwards he wrote to invite him to dinner at four o'clock on the following Tuesday to meet Reynolds, Colman, and some other friends.[48] It was probably a sumptuous affair, since that same day Goldsmith had received from William Griffin an advance of five hundred guineas on his proposed natural history. Unfortunately Boswell left only fragmentary notes of the conversation.

On Monday, October 16, Boswell entertained at dinner at his lodgings on Old Bond Street. His guests were Johnson, Reynolds, Garrick, Arthur Murphy, Isaac Bickerstaffe, Davies, and Goldsmith. One of the company was late in arriving, and Boswell suggested that dinner be served without him, saying, "Ought six people to be kept waiting for one?"

"Why yes," replied Johnson, "if the one will suffer more by your sitting down, than the six will do by waiting."

194

Meanwhile, Boswell records, Goldsmith "strutted about, bragging of his dress"; that very day his tailor had delivered to him "a half-dress suit of ratteen, lined with satin," "a pair of silk stocking breeches," and "a pair of bloom-colored ditto," and he was probably eager to make his friends aware of his new finery. Yet he was evidently in a playful mood and had apparently remarked that people were foolish to suppose that clothes could make a gentleman; for Garrick cried, "Come, come, talk no more of that. You are, perhaps, the worst—eh, eh!" And, ignoring Goldsmith's attempt to interrupt: "Nay, you will always *look* like a gentleman; but I am talking of being well or ill *drest.*"

"Well, let me tell you," said Goldsmith, "when my tailor brought home my bloom-colored coat, he said, 'Sir, I have a favour to beg of you. When any body asks you who made your clothes, be pleased to mention [William] Filby, at the Harrow, in Water-lane.'"

"Why, Sir," boomed Johnson, "that was because he knew the strange colour would attract crouds to gaze at it, and thus they might hear of him, and see how well he could make a coat even of so absurd a colour."

In his *Life of Johnson* Boswell does not record Goldsmith's reaction to this remark, but leaves the reader to assume that his ridiculous vanity was effectively deflated. But was it truly vanity that prompted Goldsmith's remark? Had his tailor made any such request? Or had he merely played the buffoon to amuse the company? If so, he had again, as so often, chosen the wrong company for his joke.

During the evening Goldsmith, perhaps crestfallen at the response to his remark, seems to have had little to say. Yet when Johnson declared that Dryden's poetry revealed a profundity that Pope's could never attain, he ventured to observe that Pope's character of Addison in "The Epistle to Dr. Arbuthnot" showed a deep knowledge of the human heart. And later, in a discussion of Lord Kames' *Elements of Criticism,* he said drily: "It is easier to write that book, than to read it."[49]

The spirits of the group must have been depressed that day, although Boswell fails to mention the fact. A few days earlier

195

when one of their associates, the hot-headed Italian Giuseppe Baretti, had been accosted by a street-walker whom he repulsed with a blow, he had been set upon by three ruffians. He drew a knife, stabbed two of them, then ran away in terror—and was arrested shortly afterward for the murder of one of the men.

Goldsmith and Baretti had never been friends. Tom Davies reports that Goldsmith "least of all mankind, approved Baretti's conversation; he considered him as an insolent, overbearing foreigner; as Baretti, in his turn, thought him an unpolished man, and an absurd companion."[50] Yet as soon as he heard of Baretti's trouble, he rushed to the magistrate's office to aid him. When the authorities refused to release Baretti on bail, Goldsmith rode with him to Newgate and offered to supply whatever money he needed for his support and defense.

On October 16, the day of Boswell's dinner, Baretti was let out on bail, and on the 20th Goldsmith appeared at the Old Bailey with Reynolds, Johnson, Burke, and Garrick to testify to the uprightness of Baretti's character. "I have had the honour of Mr. Baretti's company at my chambers in the Temple," he declared; "he is a most humain, benevolent, peaceable man. I have heard him speak with regard to these poor creatures in the street, and he has got some in the hospital, who have had bad distempers. I have known him three years. He is a man of as great humanity as any in the world."[51] Characteristically, he was appraising Baretti for his treatment of suffering humanity rather than his treatment of Oliver Goldsmith. And his testimony, along with that of the impressive array of other character witnesses, helped to secure Baretti's acquittal.

Indeed Goldsmith was by this time an influential figure in London. On November 13 Davies told James Granger that he had chosen Goldsmith as one of a select few who were to receive presentation copies of Granger's new *Biographical History of England*.[52] And in the following month he was nominated to the position of Professor of Ancient History and Johnson to the position of Professor of Ancient Poetry in the Royal Academy. Moreover, the achievements of both men were being recognized in a more lasting fashion: they were sitting for their portraits by their good friend Sir Joshua.

Goldsmith had arrived at last: he was acknowledged now to be a distinguished poet, essayist, novelist, dramatist, and historian. And he was more affluent than ever before. True, he was spending more money than he was making, and he had not yet been granted a pension. But commissions were coming in faster than he could possibly fulfill them, and his literary resources seemed inexhaustible.

He could, therefore, afford to be generous—not only to entertain his friends lavishly or to lend them money but to praise Joseph Baretti, to congratulate Hugh Kelly on the success of *False Delicacy,* to introduce Boswell to his friends, even to accept Johnson's occasional rebuffs. He could play to the hilt the part which came so naturally to him, the part of the good-natured man. The years of uncertainty and anxiety were, or should be, behind him now; and if he could learn to exercise only a moderate amount of caution, he might reasonably hope to enjoy prosperity and security as long as he lived.

Chapter VIII

"Man of Genius"
(1770-1772)

INEVITABLY news of Goldsmith's successes reached Ireland, and his relatives decided that he could well afford to repay some of the favors done him in the past. His brother Maurice, now living with the Lawders at Kilmore, wrote to ask him for assistance in finding a position in London and added that the Lawders were holding a small legacy which Thomas Contarine had left him at his death in 1758. And at almost the same time his sister Jane Johnson wrote that she was in sore straits and needed his aid.

Early in January, 1770, Goldsmith replied to Maurice. He began by assuring his relatives of his interest in their welfare:

> I should have answered your letter sooner, but in truth I am not very fond of thinking of the necessities of those I love when it is so very little in my power to help them. I am sorry to find you are still every way unprovided for, and what adds to my uneasiness is that I received a letter from My Sister Johnson by which I learn that she is pretty much in the same circumstances. As to myself I believe I might get both you and my poor brother in law something like that which you desire, but I am determined never to ask for little things or exhaust any little interest I may have untill I can serve you and him and myself more effectually. As yet no opportunity has offered, but I believe you are pretty well convinced that I will not be remiss when it arrives.

He could not resist a bit of bragging: "The King has been lately pleasd to make me Professor of ancient history in a Royal Accademy of Painting which he has just establishd." But he hastened to add that "there is no sallary anex'd" and that "honours to one in my situation are something like ruffles to a man that wants a shirt."

Of course Goldsmith could have helped Maurice. But he was not so disposed; and so he resorted to the kind of deception which he had used earlier with his family. Yet he had long been troubled at the Lawders' failure to write to him, and he hoped to conciliate them. Consequently he took the easy way out of two awkward situations and suggested that they use his legacy from Contarine to relieve Maurice and Jane:

I would by no means give any directions to my dear worthy relations at Kilmore how to dispose of money that is more properly speaking theirs than mine. All that I can say is that I entirely, and this letter will serve to witness give up any right or title to it, and I am sure they will dispose of it to the best advantage. To them I entirely leave it, whether they or you may think the whole necessary to fit you out, or whether our poor sister Johnson may not want the half I leave entirely to their and your discretion. The kindness of that good couple to our poor shattered family demands our sincerest gratitude, and. tho' they have almost forgot me yet If good things at last arrive I hope one day to return and encrease their good humour by adding to my own.

Then, by way of making the Lawders repent that they had treated him so coolly in the past, he added that he had "sent my cousin Jenny a miniature picture of myself, as I believe it is the most acceptable present I can offer. . . . The face you well know is ugly enough but it is finely painted." He promised also to send "some Metzotinto prints of myself, and some more of my friends here such as Burke, Johnson, Reynolds, and Coleman." And he concluded:

I believe I have written an hundred letters to different friends in your country and never received an answer from any of them. I dont know how to account for this or why they are unwilling to keep up for me those regards which I must ever retain for them. If then you have a mind to oblige me you will write often whether I answer you or not. Let me particularly have the news of our family and old acquaintances. For instance you may begin by telling me about the family where you reside how they spend their time and whether they ever make mention of me. Tell me about my mother. My Brother Hodson, and his son, my brother Harry's son and daughter, My Sister Johnson. The family of Bally Oughter what is become of them where they live and how they do. You talked of being my only Brother. I dont understand you. Where is Charles? A sheet of paper occasionally filld with news of this kind would make me very happy, and would keep you nearer my mind.[1]

If his family felt that he had neglected them, they could help remedy matters by paying more attention to him—especially if they expected to call on him for favors.

However, Maurice was not discouraged by the tone of his brother's letter. On February 24 James Lawder delivered to him the fifteen pounds to which Oliver had resigned his claims,[2] and presently he appeared in London at Goldsmith's rooms in the Temple.

He was not warmly received. "My brother Maurice was with me in London," Goldsmith wrote a few months later to Dan Hodson, "but it was not in my power to serve him effectually then; indeed in a letter I wrote him I desired him by no means to come up but he was probably fond of the journey." Evidently Goldsmith was not much impressed with his brother's talents, for he sent him back to Ireland with the advice that he give up his notions of trying to become a gentleman and find some useful trade, as their younger brother Charles had done.[3]

Yet although Goldsmith might deal rather highhandedly with his relatives, he was generous and hospitable as ever to others. Bright young Irishmen coming up to London for the first time were sure of a cordial welcome if they sought him out, and many did. Among his favorites were two young men destined to distinguish themselves later in life: Henry Grattan and Robert Day, who lived together in Essex Court in the Temple and frequented the Grecian Coffeehouse nearby, where they often met Goldsmith. "Occasionally he amused [his friends] with his flute or with whist," Day wrote in 1831, "neither of which he played well, particularly the latter, but in losing his money, he never lost his temper. In a run of bad luck and worse play, he would fling his cards upon the floor and exclaim, 'Bye-fore George, I ought for ever to renounce thee, fickle, faithless Fortune.' "[4]

In April, 1770, Goldsmith enjoyed another triumph when Reynolds' portrait of him was exhibited at the Royal Academy. Doubtless he found satisfaction in the attention that the portrait drew to him and comfort in the dignity with which it was executed. For Reynolds, who believed in blending realism and idealism in his painting, had managed to create a portrait that resembled Goldsmith closely and yet gave him a dignity that few people saw in him. Frances Reynolds remarked that "it was a very great likeness of the Doctor; but the most flattered picture she ever knew her brother to have painted."[5] It was, in fact, a touching tribute from a discerning artist to a friend who had been too often maligned. Reynolds divested him of his wig, concealed his gaudy clothes with a cape, and presented him as he was—a homely man, but a sensitive and thoughtful one. The artist felt justified in improving upon his original because he believed implicitly in decorum: when painting a distinguished man of letters who looked like a clown—or a tailor—one should minimize his clownlike or tailor-like characteristics and emphasize the features which reflected his inherent genius. And it was as a man of genius that Reynolds presented his friend. Yet he was not acting wholly on theory: his emotions were involved too. For he loved and respected Goldsmith, and he wanted his portrait to stand as a symbol of that love and respect.

The friendship of the two men was growing ever closer. They dined together frequently or spent the evening at such resorts as Vauxhall or Ranelagh. And soon Reynolds was aiding Goldsmith in some of his humanitarian projects. Reynolds' Engagement Book for 1771 lists "Goldsmith's girl," presumably as a possible model; and one of the artist's pupil-assistants at this time was Thomas Clarke, a young Irishman whom Goldsmith recommended to him—but who proved to be a "reckless dog" and was soon discharged.[6]

On May 26, the last day that the portrait of Goldsmith was on public exhibition at the Royal Academy, *The Deserted Village* was published by William Griffin in a handsome quarto volume[7] with a touching, yet restrained dedication to Reynolds: "Dear Sir,—I can have no expectations, in an address of this kind, either to add to your reputation, or to establish my own. You can gain nothing from my admiration, as I am ignorant of that art in which you are said to excel; and I may lose much by the severity of your judgment, as few have a juster taste in poetry than you. Setting interest, therefore, aside, to which I never paid much attention, I must be indulged at present in following my affections. The only dedication I ever made was to my brother, because I loved him better than most other men. He is since dead. Permit me to inscribe this Poem to you."

201

Then followed a defense of the thesis of the poem: "I know you will object (and indeed several of our best and wisest friends concur in the opinion,) that the depopulation it deplores is no where to be seen, and the disorders it laments are only to be found in the poet's own imagination. To this I can scarce make any other answer, than that I sincerely believe what I have written; that I have taken all possible pains, in my country excursions, for these four or five years past, to be certain of what I allege; and that all my views and enquiries have led me to believe those miseries real, which I attempt to display."

Moerover: "In regretting the depopulation of the country, I inveigh against the encrease of our luxuries; and here also I expect the shout of modern politicians against me. For twenty or thirty years past, it has been the fashion to consider luxury as one of the greatest national advantages; and all the wisdom of antiquity in that particular as erroneous. Still, however, I must remain a professed ancient on that head, and continue to think those luxuries prejudicial to states by which so many vices are introduced, and so many kingdoms have been undone."

Obviously Goldsmith was again seriously concerned with the thesis of his poem; like *The Traveller* it was a philosophical poem in which he had a serious argument to present to his contemporaries, and he did not intend to be shouted down by those who disagreed with his premises. He was convinced that the concentration of wealth in England was robbing the common people of their economic rights and causing wholesale emigration which resulted in personal tragedy and weakened the fiber of the nation. In the past he had defended luxury as one of the concomitants of civilization; now he believed that it had been carried too far and was causing actual hardship for the lower classes. Whether the trouble was due to the Enclosure Laws or to the development of country estates by the new plutocrats is relatively unimportant.[8] What matters is that Goldsmith believed that, unless depopulation was checked, the nation faced disaster. In good eighteenth century style he issued his warning in a poem rather than an essay.

Much of the poem is, therefore, direct—even hortatory—in expression. But Goldsmith had one distinct advantage in this poem: he was not trying to put forth half a dozen points of personal, economic, and political philosophy, as he had done in *The Traveller,* but simply to enforce a single idea. And since *The Deserted Village* was only eight lines shorter than the earlier poem, he was able to develop his point more fully. In doing so, he gave the poem most of its distinctive appeal to later readers. For much of this development is more personal and specific than anything in *The Traveller.* Goldsmith's emotions at recalling the village as it was—to which he "still had hopes . . . to return—and die at home at last"—waken an answering emotion in most readers. Goldsmith seems, too, more relaxed, less self-conscious; he reveals himself more fully, even allows his sense of humor play in the familiar lines about the Village Schoolmaster:

> . . . and still the wonder grew,
> That one small head could carry all he knew.

Moreover, Goldsmith's description of the life of the village[9]—especially the sketches of the preacher and the schoolmaster—create vivid pictures in the reader's mind and stir his imagination as it is never stirred in *The Traveller.*

Thus *The Deserted Village* succeeds on two levels that are scarcely touched in *The Traveller:* the appeal to the emotions and the appeal to the eye. It is more than a clear, harmonious expression of its thesis: it blends the characteristics of eighteenth century poetry with those of Romantic poetry, and in doing so it achieves virtual universality. Sophisticated readers today may find it ingenuous and sentimental, but the common reader from Goldsmith's time to the present has found it pleasing—and often moving. For as Professor Tinker has pointed out, every man has his Auburn, his haven from the hubbub of the world, and few can resist Goldsmith's evocation of it in *The Deserted Village.*[10]

Although Goldsmith probably had in mind the classical ideal of cultivated retirement—Horace's Sabine farm[11]—the great popular success of *The Deserted Village* sprang largely from the fact that its ideas were related to the Romantic primitivism which was already gaining ground. The poet's praise of rural life, his appreciation of nature, his humanitarianism, and his subjectivity all found sympathetic readers in his own time and, even more, in the generations which followed. Whether he wished to or not, Goldsmith virtually anticipated the Romantic Revival in all but his adherence to neo-classical diction. For, much as he admired simplicity of expression, he never subscribed to any such theory as Wordsworth advanced thirty years later: his farmers are still "labouring swains," and "No cheerful murmurs fluctuate in the gale." Yet he eschewed references to ancient myths or classical deities. His poem was addressed to all men, not the cultivated few, and he revised it carefully both before and after publication in order to heighten its clarity and simplicity. He wanted to speak to all kinds of readers, to stimulate their thoughts and to touch their hearts; and he succeeded. And although today the poem is perhaps more quoted than read, it has not lost its elemental appeal. Nor is it likely to do so.

It was an immediate success when it appeared. A second edition was published on June 7, a third a week later, a fourth on June 28, a fifth on August 16, and a sixth before the end of the year—and several of these editions were carefully revised, bearing witness to Goldsmith's continuing pride in the poem. It was translated into French by three different translators and eventually into German, Italian, Danish, Gaelic, Latin, Armenian, and Hindu; it inspired two imitations in English and one in French. And the critics were enthusiastic.

Johnson, who contributed the final four lines to the poem, preferred *The Traveller;* and most reviewers agreed with him in questioning the validity of Goldsmith's theories about depopulation and luxury.[12] But none of them denied the beauty and power of his verse. The *Critical* for June devoted eight pages to the poem, quoting generous passages and declaring that "in descriptive poetry Dr. Goldsmith has few superiors." The *Gentleman's Magazine* for the same month promised the reader "more pleasure than he has received from poetry since the days of Pope." And the June *Monthly Review* admitted that "as a picture of fancy [the poem] has great beauty; and if we shall occasionally remark that it is nothing more, we shall very little derogate from its merit." The reviewer, John Hawkesworth, added, apropos of Goldsmith's concluding envoy to poetry: "We hope that, for the honour of the Art, and the pleasures of the Public, Dr. Goldsmith will retract his farewell to poetry, and give us other opportunities of doing justice to his merit." Popular journals printed excerpts from the poem and communications in verse and prose from their readers—the *St. James Chronicle* alone contained seventeen—extolling Goldsmith's poetical powers and begging him to reconsider his avowed intention to write no more verse.

His position as a creative writer was now beyond question. He was generally recognized as second only to Johnson among contemporary men of letters—a position which he did not, of course, wholly relish. The two men were often coupled in satiric squibs in the newspapers, frequently to Goldsmith's disadvantage.[13] One writer described a supposed auction and characterized Johnson and Goldsmith as "the incomprehensible Holofernes and the impenetrable *Goodman Dull*." When Goldsmith complained about the article, Johnson, according to Mrs. Thrale, cried, "What Folly to be vexed thus about nothing.—What *harm* can it do a Man to call him Holofernes?" "It may do you no harm to be called *Holofernes*," Goldsmith supposedly countered, "but I don't like to be *Goodman Dull*."[14]

Although the poem assured Goldsmith's reputation, it failed to bring the pension for which he had been hoping, and he was obliged to rely for subsistence on advances from his publishers for work in progress.[15] Then he found himself assuming additional obligations when his nephew William Hodson arrived from Ireland seeking, like his uncles before him, to be settled in life.[16] This time Goldsmith did not send his visitor packing, as he had done before. William Hodson was a youth after his own heart: he had studied medicine at Trinity College, had been expelled for misbehavior, and had come to London determined to be an actor. He was obviously, unlike Maurice and Charles, a man of spirit—of the genuine Goldsmith stamp. "Sincerely I am charmed with his disposition," his uncle wrote to Dan Hodson, "and I am sure he feels all the good nature he expresses every moment for his friends at home."

Goldsmith would not hear of his becoming an actor; William was too much of a gentleman for that. "I dont know where he could have contracted so beggarly an affection, but I have turned him from it." And after employing him temporarily as an amanuensis, he outfitted him and arranged for him to study surgery under Dr. William Hunter, Professor of Anatomy in the Royal Academy. Then he wrote to Dan Hodson pledging twenty pounds a year for William's support and urging the young man's parents to lend their aid. Obviously Goldsmith could do a good deal by way of assistance for a needy relative when he was so minded.

Sometime in mid-June of 1770 Davies published an edition of the works of Thomas Parnell prefaced by a short life of the poet by Goldsmith. Parnell was a congenial subject for Goldsmith: he was interested in him as a fellow-Irishman whose writing he admired, and he had at his disposal a few anecdotes which he had gleaned from his father and his uncle Contarine, both of whom had been at Trinity College soon after the poet. But he referred to the biography as "this trifle"; and although Davies issued it a month later as a separate volume, Goldsmith did not attempt the sort of analysis that he had made in his *Life of Nash*. Instead he gave only a very brief summary of the events of Parnell's life, added an analysis of his character based partly on recollections of Charles Goldsmith and Thomas Contarine, reprinted a few letters from Pope and other contemporaries (as evidence of the respect in which Parnell was held), and then turned to general criticism of his writing and perfunctory remarks on the separate poems in Davies' new edition.

Goldsmith acknowledged aid from Parnell's nephew, Sir John Parnell, and from a Mr. and Mrs. Hayes, relatives of the poet, and George Steevens, the Shakespearean scholar; but he seems not to have consulted Parnell's daughter, who was still alive. He virtually admitted that his materials were meager, but actually they were sufficient for his purpose: to introduce the casual reader to Parnell's writing. Johnson agreed with him, and when he prepared his *Lives of the Poets,* he abridged Goldsmith's *Life of Parnell* instead of preparing a new one. Yet privately he told Boswell on March 31, 1772: "Goldsmith's Life of Parnell is poor;

not that it is poorly written, but that he had poor materials."[17] The reviewer in the *Critical* for July, 1770, agreed wholeheartedly, also finding fault with Goldsmith's complaints about contemporary poetry and his implied criticism of Gray's *Elegy*. "We are afraid," he remarked, "the doctor is growing intoxicated with fame, and insensible to all living eminence except his own." But one phrase in the article could have outweighed for Goldsmith all the adverse criticism: the reviewer referred to him as a "man of genius."

Goldsmith's "Epitaph on Dr. Parnell" was presumably written at about the same time as the *Life,* although it was not published until 1776. It was a conventional bit of lapidary verse, of the sort that neo-classical poets had been turning out for generations. Yet Goldsmith evidently cherished it, and one evening at Reynolds' house he asked Johnson to write an epitaph on Parnell at short notice, probably intending to display his own and suggest his superiority as an improviser. Johnson did as requested and read his poem to the group. It was much admired by all but Goldsmith, who said, "Ay, but this is in Latin,"[18] leaving the company puzzled by his reaction—dictated, no doubt, by Johnson's failure to play the game quite according to the rules which Goldsmith had in mind.

By the beginning of July, 1770, Goldsmith was ready for a holiday. He had plenty of work to keep him busy throughout the summer: he still had not fulfilled his contracts for a new history of England and a natural history. But he would perhaps be better able to settle down to those jobs after a few weeks' vacation. Besides, he loved traveling, he had not been abroad for fourteen years, and he had been invited to join Mrs. Horneck and her daughters on a jaunt to Paris. It sounded like an ideal vacation, and late in July he set out with the Hornecks for Dover, anticipating a gay holiday.

The trip proved disappointing. All the members of the party were "extremely sea-sick" crossing the Channel, and they had the uncomfortable suspicion, common to travelers, that they were being overcharged wherever they went. "We were glad to leave

Dover," Goldsmith wrote to Reynolds after they had reached Lisle,

because we hated to be imposed upon, so were in high spirits at coming to Calais where we were told that a little money would go a great way. Upon landing two little trunks, which was all we carried with us, we were surprised to see fourteen or fifteen fellows all running down to the ship to lay their hands upon them. Four got under each trunk, the rest surrounded and held the hasps, and in this manner our little baggage was conducted with a kind of funeral solemnity till it was safely lodged at the custom house. We were well enough pleased with the peoples civility till they came to be paid; every creature that had the happiness of but touching our trunks with their finger expected six-pence, and they had so pretty civil a manner of demanding it that there was no refusing them. When we had done with the porters, we had next, to speak with the custom house officers, who had their pretty civil way too. We were directed to the Hotel d'Angle-terre where a valet de place came to offer his service and spoke to me ten minutes before I once found out that he was speaking English. We had no occasion for his service so we gave him a little money because he spoke English and because he wanted it. I can't help mentioning another circum-stance. [Mary?] bought a new ribbon for my wig at Canterbury, and the barber at Calais broke it in order to gain six-pence by buying me a new one.

Goldsmith stopped at that point and never finished the letter; it was, he decided, too dull to send. But once arrived at Paris, he made another attempt on July 29, though with little more en-thusiasm:

The Ladies do not seem to be very fond of what we have yet seen. With regard to myself I find that travelling at twenty and at forty are very different things. I set out with all my confirmd habits about me and can find nothing on the continent so good as when I formerly left it. One of our chief amusements here is scolding at every thing we meet with and praising every thing and every person we left at home. You may judge therefore whether your name is not frequently bandied at table among us. To tell you the truth I never thought I could regret your absence so much as our various mortifications on the road have often taught me to do. I could tell you of disasters and adventures without number, of our lying in barns, and of my being half poisoned with a dish of green peas, of our quarrelling with postillions and being cheated by Landladies but I reserve all this for an happy hour which I expect to share with you upon my return. I have very little to tell you more but that we are at present all well and expect returning when we have staid out our month, which I did not care tho it were over this very day. I long to hear from you all, how you yourself do, how Johnson, Burke, Dyer, Chamier, Colman, and every one of the club do. I wish I could send you some amusement in this letter but I protest I am so stupefied by the air of this country (for I am sure it can never be natural) that I have not a word to say.

Yet despite his discomforts, his illness, and his homesickness, he was not entirely wasting his time. "I have been thinking of the plot of a comedy which shall be entituled a journey to Paris," he wrote, "in which a family shall be introduced with a full intention of going to France to save money"—with obvious results. He still had not lost his sense of humor, although it was not always appreciated. When he remarked at table that the meat was so tough that he had "spent less time with my knife than my pick tooth," nobody laughed. "I said this as a good thing . . .," he told Reynolds, "but it was not understood. I believe it to be a good thing." Another "good thing" was his remark, when the Horneck girls attracted more attention than he did, that elsewhere he too had his admirers. That remark was to have wide repercussions. As usual he enjoyed his greatest successes as a humorist when he was trying least—as, for instance, when he wagered that he could jump across a pool at Versailles and fell headlong into it.

He may have felt some personal disappointment in the trip, as Mary Horneck Gwynne later suggested, because he was not received with the acclaim which he expected in Paris. Perhaps, too, he was annoyed when a Mr. Hickey, a friend of the Hornecks, joined the party. But probably the main reason for his disappointment was that the trip was costing more than he could well afford. Living had proved to be higher than he had anticipated, and the Hornecks traveled in the finest style: in Paris they stopped at the Hôtel de Dannemark in the Faubourg Saint-Germain. He was spending as little as possible: he told Reynolds that "the whole of my own purchases here is one silk coat which I have put on and which makes me look like a fool." But he decided that he must abandon his plan to visit Devonshire with Reynolds in September; "for as soon as I arrive at Dover I intend to let the ladies go on, and I will take a country lodging for a couple of months somewhere near that place in order to do some business. I have so out run the constable that I must mortify a little to bring it up again."

The trip had proved a failure, so far as he was concerned, from start to finish; and he must have been glad to get home in late August or early September. Subsequently he told William Ridge that he would recommend Continental travel "to the rich if they are without the sense of *smelling,* and to the poor if they are without the sense of *feeling;* and to both if they can discharge from their minds all idea of what in England we term comfort."

He did not carry out his plan to settle in the country near Dover. Just before his departure from France—or perhaps after his arrival in England—he received a letter from Ireland telling him that his mother had died. He went, therefore, to London, and on September 7 was billed for a suit of mourning—or perhaps, in a final gesture of perverse rebellion, "half-mourning"—by his tailor, William Filby.[19]

On September 16 he visited Mr. and Mrs. Henry Thrale, probably to see Johnson, who had by this time become the almost permanent guest of the wealthy brewer and his volatile wife. Mrs. Thrale recorded the visit in such a manner as to suggest that it was her first meeting with Goldsmith, as it is her first mention of him in her journals. Unfortunately the entry survives only in fragmentary form:

. . . Delicacy on the other, but Johnson (for he was by) would not suffer it to go off so, and said the Dr. was only awed from fear of a reply, for continued he were Goldsmith to light upon a dumb man he would be wonderfully severe on him—this blow Murphy follow'd so closely, & struck the little Dr. so forcibly & so repeatedly that though I saw that day & have often seen Instances of his Malevolent disposition, made still more acrimonious from his unequall'd rage of shining in Conversation I could not avoid pitying him when I saw him so humbled under the lash of a man who though so far superior to him in Friendship Honour & every manly Virtue, in Person, Address, and every pleasing Quality, is not to be compar'd with him as a Writer, nor will be set in Competition with him by Posterity—Poor little Dr. how he does disgrace himself! and disgrace those Parts but for the possession of which even the Dog would be in haste to forsake his Company.[20]

Elsewhere she recorded that her daughter Queeney "read and persed" passages of *The Messiah* for Goldsmith on the same day, which was the day before the little girl's sixth birthday, and that "he wonder'd at her Skill."[21] But he was not to enjoy with the younger Thrales his usual success with children. According to their mother, they "hated" him—Queeney's reason being "because he is so disagreeable."[22] But she was an uncommonly haughty little creature, and she may have been annoyed, as her mother was, by Goldsmith's anomalous behavior. Hester Thrale was a determined lion-hunter who expected her lions to act the part. A lion who acted like a squirrel—sometimes like a monkey—baffled and disturbed her.

She complained especially about his curiosity. The first time he dined at her house, she wrote, he asked her husband how much his business yielded annually.[23] She said, too, that one day when he visited Johnson at her house while she was away from home, he was so consumed with curiosity to know what was in a large cedar chest that he begged Johnson to see if one of his keys would fit it.[24] Another time in her absence he wandered into her boudoir and "there did he examine every Box upon the Toylet, every Paper upon the Card Rack, every thing in short with an Impudence truly Irish."[25] She displayed at times a sort of maternal tolerance for his failings ("Poor little Dr."); but she probably disliked him. And since she was more interested in a telling anecdote than in scrupulous accuracy, her reports must be accepted with caution.

Soon after his return from France Goldsmith was obliged to settle down to serious writing. On September 15, the day before his visit with the Thrales, he signed a contract with Davies to abridge his *Roman History* into a single duodecimo volume. The publisher specified that Goldsmith's name was to be signed to the abridgment—evidence of the growth of his reputation. Davies wisely added that the fee of fifty guineas was to be paid "on . . . the delivery of the copy," although experience should have taught him that such a stipulation was futile. But the rival publisher Griffin had more cause to complain: it was now a year since he had advanced Goldsmith five hundred guineas for his proposed natural history, and the book was scarcely started.

211

Yet before settling down to fulfill any of his pending contracts, Goldsmith dashed off a short life of Bolingbroke, which Davies intended to use as an introduction to an edition of Bolingbroke's *Dissertation on Parties*. And slight as the task was—or as Goldsmith made it—Davies was obliged to put up with the usual delays. "Dr. Goldsmith is gone with Lord Clare [i.e., Robert Nugent] into the country," he wrote to James Granger on October 27; "and I am plagued to get the proofs from him of his Life of Lord Bolingbroke."[26]

The Life was published without the *Dissertation upon Parties* on December 19. It was obviously another potboiler, and Goldsmith wisely let it appear without his name. For this time he had no difficulty in finding the materials which he needed for his biography: they were available in the *Biographia Britannica,* and he helped himself liberally to what he found—so much so that Professor Friedman estimates that "fully four-fifths" of Goldsmith's *Life* was borrowed from the *Biographia*.[27] He added occasional interpretations of fact or a few facts of his own, most of them near the beginning of the biography; perhaps, as Friedman suggests, he began the work with some intention of producing an original piece of work, but, pressed for time, yielded to the temptation to rely almost wholly on the one source.

The result is a readable and fairly accurate biographical essay. It is more sympathetic than one might expect, considering contemporary opinions of Bolingbroke; in fact, in the light of the opening paragraphs, the reader suspects that Goldsmith was even more sympathetic than he cared to admit. But it is at best a "compilation," as Goldsmith would have said, and, like the *Life of Parnell,* it adds nothing to his achievement as a biographer. The *Monthly Review* for February, 1771, attacked it strenuously for its alleged errors of fact and "observation" and pointed out that it had evidently been "patched up, by the mere aid of amplification" from the account of Bolingbroke in the *Biographia Britannica.* The December *Critical Review* was more favorable, though far from enthusiastic: *"The Life of Bolingbroke* is evidently written by the author of *The Life of Parnell,"* the reviewer observed, "who has no reason to be ashamed of the performance." Davies thought well enough of it to reprint it three times in 1774 and 1775: as an introduction to an edition of Bolingbroke's *Works,* as one of the *Miscellaneous and Fugitive Pieces* published after Goldsmith's death, and as a preface to a new edition of the *Dissertation upon Parties.*

Goldsmith must have spent most of the winter of 1770-71 hard at work on his *History of England.* He dined with Percy, Johnson, Reynolds, and others at the Chaplains' Table at St. James's Palace on December 21 and puzzled them all by frankly telling about his tearful outburst after the first performance of *The Good Natured Man.* Then no more is heard of him until the following March 20, when Johnson remarked in a letter to Bennet Langton: "Goldsmith is at Bath, with Lord Clare."[28] He was back in London on April 15, however, writing to George Selwyn to ask him for some complimentary tickets to "the next Masquerade," and he was present at the first annual dinner of the Royal Academy on the 23rd.

It was a gala affair, and Goldsmith was singled out for marks of attention by several of the great men present. When the Earl of Lisburn complained that he wrote so little poetry, Goldsmith replied: "My Lord, by courting the Muses I shall starve; but by my other labours, I eat, drink, have good clothes, and enjoy the luxuries of life." Horace Walpole, who refused to be introduced to Johnson, consented to meet Goldsmith—although he later referred to him privately as "piddling Goldsmith" and declared that he had no desire to know "the silly Dr Goldsmith."[29] Goldsmith regaled him, Lord Hardwicke, and others with an account of the extraordinary ancient poems which had been discovered at Bristol. He was convinced that the manuscripts were genuine, although Johnson and Percy refused to take them seriously, and he showed such enthusiasm about the poems that Walpole was amused at his credulity. For Walpole had examined the poems two years before, had detected the hoax, and had rebuked the perpetrator of it, young Thomas Chatterton. His amusement died, however, when Goldsmith told him that the misguided young poet had killed himself in London during the previous August.

Lord Hardwicke was interested enough to want to investigate

the poems. The day after the dinner he wrote to Goldsmith suggesting that he stop off at Bristol on his next trip to Bath, and offering a rather elaborate procedure for testing their authenticity.[30] And now or later Goldsmith arranged with Dr. Francis Woodward of Bristol to be introduced to George Catcott, the pewterer who had sponsored Chatterton. Goldsmith was eager to buy the manuscripts, but he lacked the necessary cash—and Catcott would not accept a promissory note. Eventually Goldsmith was persuaded that the poems were Chatterton's own rather clumsy forgeries, but not before he had quarreled with his good friend Thomas Percy on the subject.

Shortly after the Royal Academy dinner Goldsmith left London unexpectedly. Lord Clare's son Colonel Nugent had fallen desperately ill in the city, and Goldsmith took him down to his father's house at Bath, where he died. Goldsmith remained with Lord Clare to comfort him in his bereavement and presently received a letter from his nephew William Hodson announcing that he had finished his surgical training and was hoping to find a post as surgeon's mate on a vessel bound for India. With it he enclosed a letter from his father, which explained his decision: Dan Hodson had informed his son that he would receive no further support from his parents and must make his own way thereafter. Goldsmith immediately exerted his influence and managed to have the young man appointed "full surgeon" on a ship sailing shortly for India.

When he returned to London, however, he discovered that his nephew was just about to leave for Ireland, having been summoned by his parents, who would not hear of his going to India. Goldsmith sat down to explain what he had done for William and to urge the Hodsons to be more reasonable. "It gave me great concern," he began, "to find that you were uneasy at your son's going abroad. I will beg leave to state my part in the affair and I hope you will not condemn me for what I have endeavoured to do for his benefit." Then he told how he had dissuaded William from becoming an actor, how he had set him to studying surgery, supplied him with forty-five pounds, and finally found him a profitable position as a surgeon. And now they were going to undo all in a stroke! If only they would realize that William was no longer a child! "He has laboured very hard since he left you," he wrote, "and is capable of living like a gentleman in any part of the world. He has answered his examinations as a Surgeon and has been found sufficiently qualified. I entreat therefore you will receive him as becomes him and you, and that you will endeavour to serve the young man effectually not by foolish fond caresses but by either advancing him in his business or settling him in life." Yet despite his momentary sharpness he concluded with the statement that he was "again just setting out for Bath, and I can honestly say I had much rather it had been for Ireland with my nephew, but that pleasure I hope to have before I die"; and he signed himself "Your most affectionate Brother."

Back he went then to Bath and Lord Clare. By this time he was completely at home with the Nugent family; John Gray, writing to Smollett on July 8, 1771, remarked that Goldsmith "now generally lives with his countryman, Lord Clare, who has lost his only son, Colonel Nugent."[31] He enjoyed strolling in the gardens or puttering about the Nugents' estate, Gosfield, where he planned an icehouse and a hothouse and had them built. He enjoyed, too, the easy joviality which prevailed in the Nugent household; one could be completely oneself with them, as he was that evening when he and Lord Clare discussed the dubious merits of the actor Moffatt. With the Irish Nugents he could relax, say whatever popped into his head, and be sure that it would not be greeted with amazement or scorn.

He could, as always, enjoy a joke on himself too, and the Nugents liked him for it. One day Mary, Lord Clare's daughter, tied his wig to a chair while he was napping, and when he awoke and stood up, the wig was pulled off his head. But he took the joke in good part, made use of it in his next comedy, and settled his debt to Mary Nugent by writing a riddle for her:

> The clothes we love best, and the half of an agent,
> Is the name of a Lady, to whom I'm obadient.[32]

Doubtless Goldsmith was as much amused as anyone when he wandered into the Duke of Northumberland's house at Bath absent-mindedly at breakfast time and sat chatting affably for some little while with the Duke and Duchess before he realized that he was not at Lord Clare's house next door. Or when he attempted to outlord His Lordship at an inn. But the same story told in London was not appreciated in quite the way that Goldsmith himself and the Nugents appreciated it. And when recorded by Mrs. Thrale, it served as further evidence of Goldsmith's "absurdity": "The Doctor told the following comical Story of his own odd Vanity—'I went with Lord Clare to an Inn, he called about him with an Air, and ordered one Dish after another, at last says he I thought *I* would call for something—that I might look important—Sir says the Landlady when my Lord has done Speaking I will listen to you: this says he did mortify me vilely.' "[33] Surely Goldsmith was not "mortified vilely" by the incident. If he had been, he never would have repeated the story.

Once, after he had returned to London, Lord Clare sent him a haunch of venison which occasioned the poem of that name. Acting on a hint from Boileau (who was in turn indebted to Horace) Goldsmith described in lively anapaests the dinner party that supposedly took place after a friend had carried the neck and breast away with him, promising that he would have a pasty made from them and served up to Johnson, Burke, and Goldsmith. Of course the dinner was a failure; Burke and Johnson could not come, and a Scotchman and a Jew substituted for them; the entrées were tripe and liver and bacon; and when it came time for the pasty to be brought to the table, the maid rushed in with the news that the baker,

> that negligent sloven,
> Had shut out the pasty on shutting his oven.

It is a trivial thing, obviously, but like many of Goldsmith's trifles, it has spontaneous charm. This was poetry intended for the Nugents rather than for the members of the Club—more representative of the man himself than some of his serious efforts.

Goldsmith spent a good part of the summer of 1771 busily writing at the cottage of a farmer named Selby on a hill just outside the village of Hyde, six miles from the city on the Edgeware Road. He was probably there on August 6, when his *History of England from the Earliest Times to the Death of George II* appeared in four volumes at a price of one guinea per set. The publishers Becket and DeHondt and Thomas Cadell had joined Davies in the venture, and they had brought out the history in handsome style, "adorned with the Heads of the Kings and Queens of England, neatly engraved."

But for all the elegance of the format, Goldsmith was under no illusions about the quality of his work. In his Preface he maintained that it was superior to previous abridgments of English history—but only because they were so poorly written. And he anticipated the criticism which his book was likely to receive: "It is impossible in the same work, at once, to attain contrary advantages. The compiler who is stinted in room, must often sacrifice interest to brevity; and on the other hand, while he endeavours to amuse, must frequently transgress the limits to which his plan should confine him. Thus all such as desire only amusement may be disgusted with his brevity, and such as seek for information may object to his displacing facts for empty description." His aim, he declared, had been to present "a plain unaffected narrative of facts, with just ornament enough to keep attention awake, and with reflection barely sufficient to set the reader upon thinking."

As for the originality of his materials, he observed rather cavalierly: "Were an epitome of history the field for displaying erudition, the author could shew that he has read many books which others have neglected, and that he also could advance many anecdotes which are at present very little known." He acknowledged, however, that his principal sources were Rapin, Carte, Smollett, and Hume, the last of whom he abridged only reluctantly, "as I scarce cut out a line that did not contain beauty." He might have added that he had made very good use also of his own *History of England in a Series of Letters from a Nobleman,* which he sometimes reproduced line for line.[34]

Considering Goldsmith's purpose, the new *History* was a genuine achievement. It was a lively, fast-moving narrative, tempered with occasional anecdotes in the early sections and with brief generalized estimates of the accomplishments of each monarch discussed; and although the paucity of dates is often confusing, the factual material is surprisingly accurate.[35] Moreover, Goldsmith presents his facts with such assurance—and without quibbling about conflicting evidence—that the *History* has the immediacy of an eyewitness account.

It lacks, however, the breadth that a modern reader expects in historical writing. Goldsmith presents little but the essential facts of political and military history; in fact he provides less social background than he did in his earlier history: he treats the great London fire and plague in a page and a half, and dismisses Elizabethan literature in two sentences. The result is that today the unrelieved narrative seems monotonous and too loaded with fact to be easily grasped. In its time, however, it was considered a singularly readable book. The *Critical Review* for February, 1772, declared that "we know not any work in which English history is so usefully, so elegantly, and agreeably epitomized." And the *Monthly* for December, 1771, while often critical of Goldsmith's treatment of his materials, praised the "dignity" and the "harmonious and flowing" qualities of his style. But what was more important (and, surely, manna to Oliver Goldsmith) was that both reviewers referred to the author of the *History* as a "man of genius."

On one score, however, the book encountered serious opposition. Goldsmith stated in his Preface that he sought to be impartial, but that his sympathy lay with monarchy rather than republicanism—"not from any empty notion of divine or hereditary right," but because "a king may easily be restrained from doing wrong, as he is but one man; but if a number of the great are permitted to divide all authority, who can punish them if they abuse it?" Yet it was naturally more difficult to be impartial in this book than in the *Roman History*. In treating the distant past Goldsmith could be objective enough, whether the subject was English history or Roman history. Thus, in the *History of England,* he declined to take one side or the other in reporting the conflict between Queen Elizabeth and Mary Queen of Scots; he declared that Charles I and Parliament were "equally culpable" in the events which precipitated the Commonwealth; and he even went so far as to point out that Oliver Cromwell was "a tender father" despite his faults. But when he reached the reign of George I, his "reflections" were more biased; and R. W. Seitz has shown that comparison of this *History* with the earlier *Letters of a Nobleman* reveals that Goldsmith was more of a conventional Tory partisan (though less an admirer of kings) in the later book.[36]

Seitz speculates that Goldsmith's change in attitude may have been motivated in part by his resentment of George III's failure to grant him a pension. It might also have been another reflection of the growing conservatism revealed in his treatment of religion in the *Roman History*. His expressed antagonism toward the Roman Catholic Church in general and the French nation and the Stuart family in particular by no means squares with the theories which he advanced in *The Citizen of the World;* indeed he sounds surprisingly patriotic when he hails the English people as "the most truly compassionate of all people" or the House of Commons as "the guardian of British liberty, and the admiration of mankind." Perhaps his recent disappointing trip to France had helped to convert the onetime citizen of the world to a more conventional and parochial kind of thinking.

Seitz's comparison of Goldsmith's two histories of England reveals also that he was less interested in reform—less of a "social philosopher"—in the later work. Contemporary readers even accused him of being "unfriendly to liberty,"[37] and their complaints were strong enough to prompt the publishers to issue an extended denial of the charge in the *Public Advertiser*. But Goldsmith himself refused to be alarmed. "I have been a good deal abused in the newspapers," he wrote to Bennet Langton, "for betraying the liberties of the people. God knows I had no thoughts for or against liberty in my head. My whole aim being to make up a book of a decent size that as Squire Richard [Burke?] says would do no harm to nobody. However they set me down as an arrant Tory and consequently no honest man. When you come to look at any part of it you'l say that I am a soure Whig." And as if to validate his last remark, Mary Nugent, who was seeing a good deal of him at this time, told her son in later years that Goldsmith was "a strong republican in principle, and would have been . . . a very dangerous writer if he had lived to the times of the French Revolution."[38]

But of course Goldsmith was neither a "soure Whig" nor a "strong republican," though he might have seemed so to a hidebound Tory. He was not an "arrant Tory" either; in short, he was not a party man, and he still believed in letting well enough alone. He may have been less interested in social reform than in his earlier history, but he retained his profound sympathy for the common man, as both *The Deserted Village* and (incongruously enough) his natural history reveal. He may have admired kings less, but he had no desire to displace them. As he pointed out in the Preface of his *History,* he favored monarchy because it seemed to him the safest form of government, the one least likely to evade the control of the governed. Presently, in conversation, he was to express his position succinctly and memorably in the words "I'm for Monarchy to keep us all equal."[39]

And in the long run his moderate position probably contributed to the success of his book. For though he himself did not live to the time of the French Revolution, his *History of England* did—and long outlasted it. In fifty years it went through twelve editions in its original four-volume form and twice as many in the one-volume abridgment that he made later. And even a hundred years after its publication it was still appearing in revised and expanded editions and selling widely to schools on both sides of the Atlantic. Few of Goldsmith's works have been more thoroughly read—actually read to shreds—than the *History of England.*

Shortly after the publication of the book Goldsmith left Farmer Selby's cottage on the Edgeware Road and returned to his rooms in the Temple. It was from there that he dated his letter of September 7 to Bennet Langton, who had written on the 4th to remind him of his promise to come down to Lincolnshire with Reynolds to visit Langton and his wife. Goldsmith explained that he had been in the country "quite alone trying to write a Comedy." *The Good Natured Man* had been revived during the previous spring, and its success had apparently inspired him to write another play. "It is now finished," he told Langton, "but when or how it will be acted, or whether it will be acted at all are questions I cannot resolve. I am therefore so much employd upon that that I am under a necessity of putting off my intended visit to Lincoln-shire for this season." Then, after reporting the news of their friends—Reynolds is just back from France, Beauclerk is studying chemistry and physics, Johnson is at the Thrales' after a visit to Derbyshire, Burke is busy farming—he added: "Every soul is visiting about and merry but myself. And that is hard too as I have been trying these three months to do something to make people laugh. There have I been strolling about the hedges study-ing jests with a most tragical countenance." And, in answer to a question in Langton's letter: "The natural History is about half finished and I will shortly finish the rest. God knows Im tired of this kind of finishing, which is but bungling work, and not so much my fault as the fault of my scurvy circumstances."

But he did not long repine. He dined with Reynolds that same evening, and he was soon plunged into the usual round of social affairs. When a Dr. Mackenzie wrote at about this time, asking him for an appointment, he replied that he was "engaged to dinner every day for this six or seven days."

He was regularly receiving marks of attention now—reminders of the position which he had attained. There was, for example, Langton's courteous invitation to visit him, subscribed "with great Respect and Regard." There was the engraving from Reynolds' painting "Resignation," inspired by a line in *The Deserted Village* and dedicated "to Dr. Goldsmith by his sincere friend and ad-mirer, Joshua Reynolds." There was the poem by Willis hailing Reynolds' "Resignation" and, incidentally, lauding the poet whose work had motivated the artist. And there was the spontaneous and sincere tribute of young James Northcote, Sir Joshua's pupil, who asked to be introduced to Goldsmith "because he is a notable man." Reynolds was much amused at the remark, and said that Goldsmith should thereafter be known as the notable man.[40] But Reynolds' laughter was never cruel; and besides, the truth of Northcote's phrase was undeniable: Goldsmith *was* a notable man. He must have been feeling unusually affluent too, because on December 10, 1771, he was able to spare twenty pounds for a payment on his long-standing debt to the estate of John Newbery.

At about the same time Joseph Cradock, a well-to-do amateur author whom Goldsmith had met at the actor Yates' house, asked him to write a prologue for his tragedy *Zobeide,* an adaptation of Voltaire's *Les Scythes* first performed at Covent Garden on December 10, 1771. Goldsmith turned out the desired prologue and sent it off to Cradock with apologies that he could not "take time to make it better." Actually, however, it was a clever piece, admirably adapted to the occasion and considerably above the level of most such verse. It was reprinted in the *Scots Magazine* for December, and the *Critical Review* for the same month cited it and Arthur Murphy's epilogue for *Zobeide* as "not excelled by many on the English stage."

In the following February Goldsmith received another request for an occasional poem, this one from the publisher William Woodfall. Augusta, Princess Dowager of Wales, had just died, and the enterprising Mrs. Cornelys, proprietress of the so-called Great Rooms in Soho, wanted to capitalize on the occasion by sponsoring a memorial concert for her fashionable clientele. She commissioned Woodfall to ask Goldsmith to write the words of an elegy, which would be set to music by a distinguished composer and performed by a group of prominent singers and actors. There were some rather rigid specifications: "It was wished by Mrs. Cornelys to have the Entertainment consist of two Parts," Woodfall wrote to Goldsmith,

both with a view of relieving the Performers and preserving the Auditors from Dulness from too great a length of solemnity. . . . The whole Matter is at present but an Idea; it is intended to perform *something* on the occasion of the Death of her late Royal Highness the P. Dowager; at present two speakers and three Voices with Chorus singers and a proper band are thought necessary; if it appears to Dr. G. that more or less may be proper for the occasion, and his opinion does not occasion an Expence inadequate to the ultimate view of Profit on the side of Mrs. Cornelys, it will be adopted. Secrecy as to the name of the Author shall be inviolably preserved.[41]

The major difficulty, however, was that the piece was to be ready for performance in less than two weeks.

Goldsmith agreed to supply the needed verse, provided his name should not be used, and he turned out his copy in less than three days. Then there were complications: Signor Mattio Vento, the Italian composer commissioned to furnish the music, felt that he could not do so without specific advice from the poet on the "Sense and Meaning" of the lines. So Woodfall was obliged to beg Goldsmith to meet with Vento, assuring him that the composer would not reveal his identity and, in turn, urging him not to let Vento know that the scheme had originated with Mrs. Cornelys and not with "some Persons of Consequence," as Vento had been led to believe.

Goldsmith promised to meet the composer on the following Sunday. Then, absent-mindedly, he arranged with Joseph Cradock to attend a rehearsal of the concert on Sunday so that Cradock, an accomplished musician, could criticize the performance. However, Goldsmith was able to postpone their meeting until the following day, and poet and composer met in secrecy and completed arrangements for the composition, which was performed in the Great Rooms on the following Thursday, February 20.

Although the poem was published and copies sold for a shilling on the evening of the performance, Goldsmith's name did not appear on them, and his authorship of the piece was not discovered until many years after his death. His reticence is understandable, for the *Threnodia Augustalis,* as the piece was called, was an adequate, but by no means distinguished bit of work—"a decent performance," as an anonymous critic wrote unenthusiastically in the *Monthly Review* for March—ground out to satisfy a demand. In the prefatory Advertisement to the poem Goldsmith explained that it had been "prepared for the composer in little more than two days: and may therefore rather be considered as an industrious effort of gratitude than of genius," and that it might "more properly be termed a compilation than a poem." The reader is not surprised, therefore, to find distinct echoes of Collins' poetry, sometimes passages copied almost line for line. Apparently Goldsmith felt that even a poem need not be strictly original if he withheld his name from it and presented it to the public as a compilation.

In March he was back at Farmer Selby's on the Edgeware Road working again on his natural history. He told his friends that he had sent down two post chaises full of books for his research, and added that "he believed the farmer's family thought him an odd character."[42]

He was not far wrong. Robert Selby, the farmer's son, later told Prior that Goldsmith would wander down from his upstairs room to the kitchen, stand rapt in thought before the fire, and then rush suddenly off to write down something that had occurred to him. At other times he strolled through the fields or stretched out in the shade to muse or read. At night he often read late in bed—and when he was not in the mood for reading, he kept his candle burning, eventually putting it out by shying a bedroom slipper at it—and, of course, spattering slipper and floor with grease.

Usually he had his meals carried up to his rooms, but when he had guests, he entertained them in the downstairs parlor. Reynolds and some other friends drove out for dinner on March 22, and Percy and his wife on the 31st.[43] On another occasion, Robert Selby recalled, a thunderstorm broke just as Goldsmith's guests were about to leave the farmhouse, and the poet organized an impromptu dance to entertain the younger members of the party until the weather cleared.

There were other anecdotes which the farmer's family never forgot. Once, for example, Goldsmith went to visit the writer Hugh Boyd, who lived nearby, and came home after dark in his stocking feet, explaining that his shoes had stuck in the mud. Another time he took the Selby children by carriage to a performance given by some strolling players in the neighboring town of Hendon. And he kept them all amused, coming, going, and at the play, by his jokes and chatter.

The young Selbys evidently did not share Queeney Thrale's opinion of Goldsmith; nor did most children. The Martin family at Green Arbour Court had found him delightful, and so had the Smart girls at Canonbury Tower. And George Colman the Younger, who as the son of the manager of Covent Garden had been entertained by some experts, said later that Goldsmith had been his favorite. The first time they met, when the boy was only five years old, Goldsmith had picked him up and dandled him on his knee—only to be greeted with a stinging slap on the face. Young George was locked into another room as punishment, and there he continued howling until Goldsmith stole in with a candle and succeeded in distracting him with a sleight-of-hand trick. Thereafter they were fast friends; and when he reached manhood Colman declared that he had preferred Goldsmith's company to Garrick's because, while Garrick played with a child to please himself, Goldsmith played to please the child.[44]

On Friday, April 10, 1772, Goldsmith left his retreat in the country to dine with General Oglethorpe, founder of the Georgia colony, at his house on Lower Grosvenor Street in London. The other guests were Johnson and Boswell, who had arrived from Edinburgh on March 21 and who "just sat and hugged" himself at his good fortune in being again in the company of the literary giants.

After they had discussed armorial bearings for a while, Boswell "started the question whether duelling was consistent with moral duty."

General Oglethorpe "fired at this," and cried, "Undoubtedly a man has a right to defend his honour."

Goldsmith now entered the conversation. Turning to Boswell, he said, "I ask you first, Sir, what would you do if you were affronted?" And when Boswell replied that he would be obliged to fight, Goldsmith countered: "Why then, that solves the question."

Of course it did nothing of the kind. And now Johnson advanced into the skirmish. "No, Sir," he began, "it does not solve the question. It does not follow that what a man would do is therefore right." And he launched into a rather lengthy monologue on the subject, concluding that "no doubt a man may lawfully fight a duel" if he receives an affront. So ended that phase of the conversation.

After they had listened to some reminiscences from Oglethorpe, someone raised the question of "how far people who disagree in any capital point can live in friendship together."

225

Johnson said that they could, but Goldsmith ventured to argue that they could not, since they lacked "the *idem velle atque idem nolle*—the same likings and the same aversions."

"Why, Sir," said Johnson, "you must shun the subject as to which you disagree." And he maintained that he could easily live with Burke. "I love his knowledge, his genius, his diffusion, and affluence of conversation; but I would not talk to him of the Rockingham party."

"But, Sir," Goldsmith objected, "when people live together who have something as to which they disagree, and which they want to shun, they will be in the situation mentioned in the story of Bluebeard: 'You may look into all the chambers but one.' But we should have the greatest inclination to look into that chamber, to talk of that subject."

Johnson was nettled. But he would not retreat. "Sir," he bellowed, "I am not saying that *you* could live in friendship with a man from whom you differ as to some point: I am only saying that *I* could do it."

Thus another topic was dismissed and Goldsmith overridden. He seems to have avoided expressing himself on any controversial subjects for the rest of the evening. He told the group about his quarters at Farmer Selby's; and when the subject of ghosts came up and Boswell "boldly avowed my belief" and Johnson declared that Edward Cave, "a man of sense," had assured him that he had seen a ghost, Goldsmith ventured to say that his brother Henry also claimed to have seen one. But all in all it could not have been a very comfortable evening for the "man of genius."[45]

Johnson and Boswell spent the next evening together, and sometime "between one and two" they joined Miss Williams for tea. Johnson brought up the subject of Goldsmith, remarking that he was "so much afraid of being unnoticed, that he often talks merely lest you should forget that he is in the company."

"Yes," said Boswell, "he stands forward."

"True, Sir," Johnson continued, "but if a man is to stand forward, he should wish to do it not in an aukward posture, not in rags."

226

Boswell was disposed to be tolerant. "I like very well," he said, "to hear honest Goldsmith talk away carelessly."

"Why yes, Sir," Johnson retorted; "but he should not like to hear himself."[46]

Three weeks after the dinner at General Oglethorpe's, on Thursday, April 30, Goldsmith was in London again, this time for a more relaxing evening. He and Joseph Cradock, both attired "in old English dresses," attended a masquerade at the splendid new Pantheon. It was a festive affair, quite to Goldsmith's taste, for he delighted in masquerades—had even been mocked in verse for his fondness for them.[47] This particular one was among the most elaborate ever undertaken: nearly two thousand guests thronged the fourteen elegant rooms of the Pantheon—duchesses and actresses without number in all sorts of lavish outfits, Sir Joshua Reynolds in domino, and the Horneck girls and their brother in similar French dancers' costumes. The party went on until dawn, when the masquers gobbled up for breakfast the remains of the food provided for supper, and then drove off in their coaches while humbler folk were starting the day's work.[48] Doubtless Goldsmith was among the last to leave.

The following Monday, May 4, Boswell and his friend William Julius Mickle borrowed General Oglethorpe's coach and drove out to the Selbys' farmhouse to call on Goldsmith. He was not at home, but they browsed about his room looking at his volumes of natural history and chuckling at his unorthodox method of taking notes: by scratching on the wall with a lead pencil descriptions of the grampus, the louse, the serpent, and other animals.[49]

Two days later, on Wednesday, the 6th, Goldsmith and Boswell met for dinner along with Burke, Beauclerk, and a number of others—but not Johnson. Accordingly Boswell recorded only scraps of the conversation in his Journal. They do not reflect particularly to his own credit. This time, it would seem, he was the one who was talking "merely lest you should forget that he is in the company."[50]

On Saturday, the 9th, while Boswell and Johnson were at the British Coffeehouse, Goldsmith's name came up again, and

Johnson revealed once more the sort of irritation which he had shown in the conversation in Miss Williams' company. "The misfortune of Goldsmith in conversation," he said, "is this: he goes on without knowing how he is to get off. His genius is great, but his knowledge is small. As they say of a generous man, it is a pity he is not rich, we may say of Goldsmith, it is a pity he is not knowing. He would not keep his knowledge to himself."[51]

In the past Johnson had been Goldsmith's staunchest defender and had seldom crossed swords with him in argument. What accounted for this new asperity in his attitude toward his friend? At this date it is impossible to determine; but it is at least possible that Goldsmith's successes of the last few months had irked the Great Cham. He could hardly help realizing that his edition of Shakespeare, fine as it was, could not stand up against Goldsmith's recent achievements as poet, dramatist, and historian. Furthermore, Johnson revered the aristocracy and delighted in his casual associations with men of noble birth, and he may have known that he was excluded from the fashionable parties where Goldsmith was welcome, and that Horace Walpole had refused to be introduced to him at the Royal Academy dinner, although he had met and conversed with Goldsmith. The pupil was threatening to outshine the master; and Johnson, after all, was human. Moreover, he admitted on occasion that he "had a tincture of envy in him,"[52] and he may well have felt an understandable resentment that his "little Goldy" should be receiving so much attention—even being hailed as a man of genius.

As yet Goldsmith showed no signs of relaxing his pace. He was working busily on his natural history, and on June 27 he received from William Griffin the final payment for it. He had turned out an unconscionable amount of work over the past two and a half years: he had written a play, two short biographies, several poems, a two-volume history of Rome, a four-volume history of England, and the better part of an eight-volume *History of the Earth and Animated Nature,* as the natural history was eventually called. Not all these books involved as much effort as he might profitably have devoted to them: one of the biographies, one of the poems, both the histories, and *Animated Nature* were in large part what he euphemistically called "compilations." But the very effort of assembling and digesting all the necessary materials and putting them, as he invariably did, into lively, readable form, was a mammoth task—and an exhausting one.

Inevitably his constitution broke down under the strain to which he had subjected it. On August 13, 1772, the *General Evening Post* reported that "Dr. Goldsmith has been dangerously ill of an inflammation in the bladder: he was cut on Sunday last by Mr. [Percivall] Pott, when an amazing discharge of purulent matter proceeded from the part."[53] He himself attributed his recovery, however, to Dr. James's Fever Powders, the patent medicine developed by Johnson's old schoolmate and marketed by the Newberys.

He was soon back at work, and early in December Davies and several other publishers issued the abridgment of the *Roman History*—a task which he might well have performed during his convalescence. For comparison of the abridgment with the original *History* reveals that Goldsmith merely went through a copy of the two-volume work, canceled out phrases, sentences, or paragraphs not absolutely essential to his narrative, and occasionally altered or supplied a word or phrase to make the new version coherent. Any author would have been glad to abridge one of his own works for fifty pounds; but not every author could have done the job so skillfully. It demanded a master of the art of "compilation"—and Goldsmith was that. From the publishers' standpoint, however, fifty pounds—a good half of it, no doubt, considered as payment for the use of his name—proved a very reasonable figure: the abridgment went through twenty-five editions in fifty years, was translated into French and Polish, and was still in use a hundred years after its first appearance.

By the time the book was published, Goldsmith was plunged again in his usual activities. He was at the Club on the evening of Monday, December 7, and two nights later he went with Percy and the architect William Chambers to see "the Italian Show of Birds &c in Cockspur Street"[54]—probably with an eye to gaining new information for his *Animated Nature*. Then on the 21st he received a letter from an obscure officer of the excise named

Thomas Paine, who asked his support for a petition to increase the salaries of excise officers—and added that he would soon call at Goldsmith's rooms. Of course there were countless other demands on his time—all the multifarious demands that fame brings to a man.

Yet he must have welcomed them and the active life which they necessitated. He even made quite gratuitous demands on himself for the sake of the satisfaction which they yielded him. One day he happened on a woebegone young Irishman of eighteen reading a volume of Boileau in the Temple Gardens. He struck up a conversation with the young man and learned that he was named McVeagh and that he had been stranded penniless in London when his elder brother died there while they were returning from their studies at a Jesuit seminary in France. Goldsmith invited him to his rooms, set him to work translating Buffon for the natural history, and tided him over until he could establish himself.

It was a satisfaction to be able to aid others thus, as he himself had been aided not so many years before. There were indeed many satisfactions in being a "notable man"—a "man of genius"— a man of means. For he was that too: his income for the years 1767-72 averaged four hundred pounds per year, a very respectable amount for a bachelor living in the Temple with no carriage and only one regular servant.

But it was not enough; he still could not make his income meet his expenses. He had wealth, but not prosperity—and certainly not security. He had been obliged to borrow again, and soon he complained that he had "a large sum of money to make up shortly."[55] He had a substantial budget of writing to do too, for he had received full payment for eight volumes of natural history which were still unfinished.

He had not lost his "knack at hoping." He could always hope for a pension; but that seemed no closer than ever, despite his growing fame. He could and did hope also for a substantial profit from the comedy which he had written. But that too seemed at a standstill. It was in George Colman's hands—had been for months—Colman, who had rescued *The Good Natured Man* when it seemed destined never to reach the stage. A successful comedy paid well; and those who had read this one—all but George Colman—were convinced that it would succeed. Yet it was apparently no nearer production than when Goldsmith had finished it fifteen months before.

Chapter IX
"Gooseberry Fool"
(1773-1774)

SHORTLY after the beginning of the New Year Goldsmith reached the end of his patience. For months he had been left wondering about the fate of his comedy; he was willing now to make almost any concession in order to have it staged. "I entreat you'l relieve me from that state of suspense in which I have been kept for a long time," he wrote to Colman. "Whatever objections you have made or shall make to my play I will endeavour to remove and not argue about them." There was one concession, however, which he refused to consider: "To bring in any new judges either of its merits or faults I can never submit to. Upon a former occasion when my other play was before Mr. Garrick he offered to bring me before Mr. Whitehead's tribunal but I refused the proposal with indignation: I hope I shall not experience as hard treatment from you as from him." He was perfectly candid about the reasons for his insistence: "I have as you know a large sum of money to make up shortly; by accepting my play I can readily satisfy my Creditor that way, at any rate I must look about to some certainty to be prepared." He concluded sharply: "For God sake take the play and let us make the best of it, and let me have the same measure at least which you have given as bad plays as mine."[1]

Colman returned the manuscript with marginal suggestions for revision, and it was probably now that Goldsmith asked Joseph Cradock to read and criticize the play. Cradock returned it with a joking epilogue and some suggestions for revision.[2] But he evidently intimated that acting on Colman's suggestions would only mar the play, since before long Goldsmith had submitted it to Garrick for possible production at Drury Lane.

Meanwhile he was writing away busily to earn the money which he needed to meet his current expenses. The publisher William Wilson of Dublin had asked him to prepare an edition of *The Spectator,* and he was probably working on it now.[3] And for the first time in more than ten years he had returned to his first means of support as a writer: the periodical press. The *Westminster Magazine,* which first appeared late in 1772, contained in its January, 1773, issue two articles by Goldsmith: "The History of a Poet's Garden" and "An Essay on the Theatre."

The first of these began with words which have a peculiar poignancy in the light of Goldsmith's state of mind at this time: "Of all men who form gay illusions of distant happiness, perhaps a poet is most sanguine." Then follows an account of a stroll through William Shenstone's garden at his estate, Leasowes, and a description of the ruin accomplished first by the poet's opening his garden to the public and then its undergoing "improvements" by later owners. And the moral? Shenstone should have let well enough alone. "You see, in the place before you," the Genius of the garden declares, "the paternal inheritance of a poet; and, to a man content with little, fully sufficient for his subsistence: but a strong imagination, and a long acquaintance with the rich are dangerous foes to contentment." It was the old doctrine of contented acceptance—plus its concomitant, the evils of wealth and luxury—which Goldsmith could preach, but never quite practice.

The second essay, often reprinted as "A Comparison between Sentimental and Laughing Comedy," was also significant: it is a defense of the sort of comedy which George Colman was so reluctant to produce. In characteristic eighteenth century fashion Goldsmith based much of his argument for "laughing comedy" on the ancients' insistence that comedy and tragedy should never be mingled in a single play. More convincing to a twentieth century reader, however, is his remark: "It is true, that amusement is a great object of the theatre, and it will be allowed that these sentimental pieces do often amuse us; but the question is, whether the true comedy would not amuse us more." At the present rate, Goldsmith speculated, humor will in time be driven entirely from the stage; eventually men may even lose the art of laughing. And there seems to be no good reason to expect a change; for the sentimental comedy is obviously easy to write. "Those abilities that can hammer out a novel," he declares, "are fully sufficient for the production of a sentimental comedy."

Yet at the very time that he was expressing his disdain for novels, he seems to have been hammering out one himself— perhaps a sentimental one. A man named Harris, who was an associate of the publisher Francis Newbery, told Prior that in the years 1771 and 1772 Newbery advanced Goldsmith between two and three hundred pounds on the promise of a novel, only to reject the final manuscript because the plot was too similar to that of *The Good Natured Man*.[4] Goldsmith read a part of the novel to a group of friends at Barton, the country house of Sir Charles Bunbury, whose brother William Henry had married Catherine Horneck. Otherwise nothing is known of it unless it was the anonymous *Triumph of Benevolence; or, the History of Francis Wills* sometimes attributed to him.[5] If so, he had whistled his principles entirely away and turned out a potboiler with all the faults of the sentimental drama that he so deplored.

For the February issue of the *Westminster Magazine* he wrote two articles: "The History of Cyrillo Padovano," an Italian monk who committed crimes in his sleep, and "A Register of Scotch Marriages," a warning against elopements, supposedly written by the landlady of an inn on the highroad to Scotland. Both were apparently dashed off for the ready cash that they would yield: the first began with a paragraph later incorporated into Goldsmith's natural history, and the second contained bits from the landlady's speech in Act V of *The Good Natured Man*. They were his last contributions to the *Westminster*. The March issue contained the article "Humorous Anecdotes of Dr. Goldsmith" that doubtless made him determine to break off his connection with the magazine.

By that time, however, he was in better spirits. Johnson and some other friends who thought highly of his comedy had exerted pressure on George Colman. No one knows how they proceeded, but eventually he was, as Johnson later phrased it, "prevailed on at last by much solicitation, nay, a kind of force" to accept the play for presentation at Covent Garden.[6]

234

But that created new complications, for Goldsmith had just submitted a copy of the play to Garrick. He had been wooing Garrick rather assiduously and was supporting him for election to the Club—and now, once again, he must ask him to return a play so that it could be produced at the rival theater.

The situation was delicate, and Goldsmith approached it cautiously. "I ask you many pardons for the trouble I gave you of yesterday," he wrote to Garrick. "Upon more mature deliberation and the advice of a sensible friend I begin to think it indelicate in me to throw upon you the odium of confirming Mr. Colman's sentence. I therefore request you will send my play by my servant back, for having been assured of having it acted at the other house, tho' I confess yours in every respect more to my wish, yet it would be folly in me to forego an advantage which lies in my power of appealing from Mr. Colman's opinion to the judgement of the town. I entreat, if not too late, you will keep the affair a secret for some time."

Garrick was undoubtedly quite willing to be rid of the play and to keep Goldsmith's secret. He had no assurance that the public would reverse Colman's verdict. By returning the play he would perhaps be spared the trouble of disputing its merits first with the author and then with adherents of the sentimental drama, one of whom, John Hoadly, complained in a letter to Garrick that "you seem now to give into Doctor Goldsmith's ridiculosity in opposition to all sentimentality."[7]

Presently, then, the play was in Colman's hands. But Goldsmith's troubles were not yet over. Colman, the author of sentimental comedies himself, had little enthusiasm for Goldsmith's "laughing comedy." On March 4 Johnson wrote to an American correspondent: "Dr. Goldsmith has a new comedy in rehearsal at Covent-Garden, to which the manager predicts ill success."[8] Unfortunately Colman's attitude proved contagious. The actor Smith rejected the part of Young Marlow because, he claimed, he did not have time to learn the lines; and Woodward, who was to play Tony Lumpkin, refused the part because Colman had told him that the play "dwindled and dwindled, and at last went out like the snuff of a candle." Substitutes were found, but some of Gold-

235

smith's friends were so disturbed by the changes that they advised him to postpone the play until the next season. He was determined, however, to proceed with it. "I should sooner that my play were damned by bad players," he said, "than merely saved by good acting."

Even his staunchest supporters agreed that his title, "The Mistakes of a Night," was ill chosen. Reynolds declared that he would damn the play if it were not given a new name, and Johnson told Tom Davies: "We are all in labour for a name to *Goldy's* play."[9] For a while it was called "The Old House a New Inn"; Reynolds favored "The Belle's Stratagem"; a few days before production Goldsmith decided on "The Novel; or, the Mistakes of a Night," using "novel" as a synonym for "fiction" or "invention." Only at the last minute he hit upon "She Stoops to Conquer," acting probably on a hint from one of the rejected epilogues.[10]

For even the epilogue was a source of trouble. Garrick provided a prologue in which "the Doctor" was announced to be ministering to the ailing Comic Muse, and Goldsmith asked Arthur Murphy to write an epilogue for him. However, as Goldsmith presently wrote in a letter to Joseph Cradock:

Murphy sent me rather the outline of an Epilogue than an Epilogue, which was to be sung by Mrs. Catley [scheduled to play the part of Miss Neville], and which she approved. Mrs. Bulkley [who was to play Kate Hardcastle] hearing this, insisted on throwing up her part, unless, according to the custom of the theatre, she were permitted to speak the Epilogue. In this embarrassment I thought of making a quarrelling Epilogue between Catley and her, debating who should speak the Epilogue, but then Mrs. Catley refused, after I had taken the trouble of drawing it out. I was then at a loss indeed; an Epilogue was to be made, and for none but Mrs. Bulkley. I made one, and Colman thought it too bad to be spoken; I was obliged therefore to try a fourth time, and I made a very mawkish thing, as you'll shortly see.[11]

It was not, in fact, until Sunday, March 14, that Goldsmith patched up a new epilogue based partly on his own last attempt and partly on Cradock's, and gave the play its name. And the first performance was to take place on Monday, the 15th—the Ides of March!

By this time he must have been almost beside himself with worry. When he told a friend the plot of his play and the friend

236

declared that it was too broad and farcical to succeed, Goldsmith thanked him for his candor and admitted that he felt his genius had deserted him.[12] And when he offered the copyright to Francis Newbery in settlement of the "large sum of money" which he had drawn for the rejected novel, he said honestly: "To tell you the truth, Frank, there are great doubts of its success." As for Colman, he was so sure that the play would fail that he refused to buy new costumes or settings for it.

Goldsmith's friends, fortunately, realized that he needed their support, and they continued to show genuine concern for his play. Percy and Beauclerk attended the rehearsal on Saturday, March 13, and Frances Reynolds went with a party of her friends to one of the morning rehearsals.[13] All who possibly could were determined to be present at the first performance and to lend what support the play might need.

At last the 15th arrived. During the day Goldsmith received a note from the bookseller Kearsley offering to send two or three of his employees to sit in the galleries if Goldsmith felt that they would be needed, and adding: "I go with a party of your Globe [Tavern] friends into the pitt."[14] Another group gathered for dinner with Goldsmith before the performance. It proved to be a rather cheerless occasion: all were in their soberest clothes because the Court was in mourning for the King of Sardinia, and they must have been apprehensive—and sympathetic with poor Gold-smith, who could not swallow a mouthful of his dinner.[15]

When the rest of the party went on to the theater, Goldsmith stole away, unequal to the ordeal of watching while the fate of his play was decided. According to William Cooke, a friend found him wandering in St. James's Park early in the evening and urged him to go to the theater so that he might be available if any last-minute changes needed to be made. He went then to Covent Garden and entered the theater in the middle of the last act, just as someone hissed the farcical scene in which Mrs. Hardcastle ends her long drive. "What's that?" he asked Colman, in alarm. "Psha! Doctor," said Colman, "don't be fearful of *squibs,* when we have been sitting almost these two hours upon a barrel of gunpowder."[16]

Actually, however, the play was a success. All Goldsmith's worries were in vain; his faith was vindicated. To Joseph Cradock he wrote: "The Play has met with a success much beyond your expectations or mine." But his triumph had been dearly bought, and he seemed hardly able to savor it. "I cannot help saying," he told Cradock, "that I am very sick of the stage; and though I believe I shall get three tolerable benefits, yet I shall upon the whole be a loser, even in a pecuniary light; my ease and comfort I certainly lost while it was in agitation."

The play was performed all twelve nights that the theater was available for the remainder of the season, it was presented at the Haymarket Theater during the summer, and it was revived at Covent Garden at Christmastime. And far from being "a loser . . . in a pecuniary light," Goldsmith gained from his three benefit performances (March 18, April 12 and 29) a profit of 502 pounds, eighteen shillings, and sixpence,[17] to say nothing of being relieved of his debt to John Newbery's son Francis, whose firm, Carnan and Newbery, published the play with minor revisions on March 26.[18]

It was well received in the press. The *Gentleman's Magazine* for April pronounced it "truly comic" and added that "the humour is irresistible; and pleases in the closet as well as in the theatre." The March *Critical Review* observed that what Johnson said of Shakespeare applied as well to Goldsmith, " 'whose excellence cannot be ascertained by the splendor of particular passages, but by the progress of his fable and the tenour of his dialogue' "; moreover, the reviewer maintained that "the utmost severity of criticism could detract but little from the uncommon merit of this performance." Readers were similarly enthusiastic: six thousand copies of the play were said to have been sold within a year of its publication, and the newspapers abounded in poetic tributes to the genius of Goldsmith and his victory over the sentimental comedy. Colman's disapproval of the play, by this time well known, was subjected to a good deal of ridicule. For example:

> Come, Coley, doff those mourning weeds,
> Nor thus with jokes be flamm'd;

Tho' Goldsmith's present play succeeds,
His next may still be damn'd.

As this has 'scaped without a fall,
To sink his next prepare;
New actors hire from Wapping Wall,
And dresses from Rag Fair.

For scenes let tatter'd blankets fly,
The prologue Kelly write;
Then swear again the piece must die
Before the author's night.

Should these tricks fail, the lucky elf,
To bring to lasting shame,
E'en write *the best you can yourself,*
And print it in *his name.*

Heartened by such declarations of faith in his talents, Goldsmith decided to follow them up with some remarks of his own in his preface to the published play—until he received a contrite letter from Colman, who had gone to Bath to escape the ridicule being poured on him. "Let me beseech you," the manager wrote,

to put me out of my pain one way or other. Either take me off the rack of the Newspapers, or give me the *Coup de Grace.* In a word, & without a figure, I beg if you think I was vile enough to *wish* ill to your play (whatever I thought of it) e'en say so in yr. preface to it—but if you acquit me of this in your own mind, absolve me in the face of the World. In the latter case, you owe me this justice, for you have occasioned me to be loaded with abuse, insomuch that had I been yr. most inveterate enemy, or had you been so to me, I cd. not have been treated otherwise. All this has been owing to a frankness and candour wch. I cd. never have exercised in so great a degree but to a friend. But enough of this; for I shall only repeat what I have said before, & what I have urged to you personally.

Goldsmith must have felt now that his revenge was complete. He evidently showed the letter to Johnson,[19] but in the Dedication to the play he contented himself with the remark: "The undertaking a comedy, not merely sentimental, was very dangerous; and Mr. Colman, who saw this piece in its various stages, always thought it so."

The play was dedicated to Johnson, who, for all his recent annoyance with Goldsmith, had proved himself a loyal friend.

Once again Goldsmith revealed his mastery of the happy phrase. "By inscribing this slight performance to you," he wrote, "I do not mean so much to compliment you as myself. It may do me some honour to inform the public, that I have lived many years in intimacy with you. It may serve the interests of mankind also to inform them, that the greatest wit may be found in a character, without impairing the most unaffected piety." And Johnson returned the compliment a few weeks later when he said in Goldsmith's presence: "I know of no comedy for many years that has so much exhilarated an audience, that has answered so much the great end of comedy—making an audience merry."[20]

Not everyone agreed with him. Horace Walpole admitted that it made the audience laugh, but he pronounced it "the lowest of all farces."[21] But Goldsmith would have been unperturbed by such criticism. When he asked Northcote his opinion of the play and Northcote replied that he would not presume to judge it, he asked, "Did it make you laugh?" And when Northcote replied that it did, he said, "Then that is all I require."[22]

And it has been making people laugh ever since. From the very first scene, when Mr. and Mrs. Hardcastle manage to keep the audience interested and amused while they provide the necessary exposition, the play is good fun. The dialogue is seldom witty, but it is lively and generally more natural than that of *The Good Natured Man*. Characterization too shows improvement: Mr. and Mrs. Hardcastle, their sprightly daughter, the changeable Marlow, and the irrepressible Tony Lumpkin are more entertaining, more consistent, and more convincing than the characters in the earlier play. But it is the plot, above all, that determines the effectiveness of the play—and the sustained dramatic irony that determines the effectiveness of the plot. Goldsmith had contrived (or perhaps sometimes borrowed) a series of ideal dramatic situations, and he developed them naturally without trying to improve the morals of his audience, as he did notably in the final speech of Honeywood in *The Good Natured Man*. Comparison of the two plays reveals that in the earlier one Goldsmith often compromised with sentimental comedy but that in *She Stoops to Conquer* he made a complete break. This play often borders on sheer farce; yet its appeal is irresistible, and it can still amuse audiences of all ages and all degrees of sophistication. It remains today one of the most frequently revived of all English dramas. It has even been translated into Esperanto.

Goldsmith's secondary purpose of combating the vogue of the sentimental comedy was not so easily accomplished. That he was seriously concerned with mocking its labored refinement is apparent in the second scene of the play, when Tony is praised by his alehouse companions "bekeays he never gives us nothing that's *low.*" In the *Monthly Review* for April the publisher William Woodfall, turned critic, deplored the improbability of Goldsmith's plot, defended what he called the "new" (that is, the sentimental) comedy, and regretted that the author of this play could not seem to divert the galleries without offending other members of the audience. And although theater-goers in general laughed at *She Stoops to Conquer,* they were just as willing to weep at Hugh Kelly's *School for Wives,* a mawkish play which enjoyed a tremendous success—much to Goldsmith's annoyance—before the year was out.

Thanks to his substantial profit from his play, Goldsmith was relieved from at least one source of annoyance. His debt to Francis Newbery was canceled, and he settled his account with the physician William Hawes[23] and paid his tailor, William Filby, fifty pounds on a bill which had been steadily mounting for the past eighteen months. He was able to play the good-natured man again, and he was in an expansive frame of mind when he wrote to his friend William Chambers, whose *Dissertation on Oriental Gardening* had been under attack: "Mr. Burke was advising me about four days ago to draw my pen in defence of your System, and sincerely I am much warm'd in the Cause. If I write it I will print my name to it boldly."[24]

But his respite was short-lived. On March 24 the *London Packet* contained an open letter addressed to him, which began:

The happy knack which you have learned of puffing your own compositions provokes me to come forth. You have not been the editor of newspapers and magazines, not to discover the trick of literary *humbug*. But the gauze is so thin, that the very foolish part of the world see through it, and discover the Doctor's monkey face and cloven foot. Your poetic vanity, is as unpardonable as your personal; would man believe it, and will woman bear it, to be told, that for hours, the *great* Goldsmith will stand surveying his grotesque orang-outang figure in a pier glass. Was but the lovely H——k as much enamoured, you would not sigh, my gentle swain, in vain.

Goldsmith was stung to the quick. The following afternoon he went with a friend named Captain Higgins to the shop of Thomas Evans, publisher of the *Packet,* and violently protested the allusion to Mary Horneck. Evans claimed that he knew nothing about the letter and leaned down to find a copy of the previous day's paper. Thereupon Goldsmith raised his cane and struck the publisher a blow across the back. Evans turned upon him, and the two fought, upsetting an oil lamp as they did so. At last the ubiquitous William Kenrick, who was generally believed to have written the offensive article, came in from another room and separated them. And soon Goldsmith, considerably battered and with his clothes splashed with oil, was sent home in a coach.

That same evening Garrick and Beauclerk stopped at his rooms to take him to the Turk's Head for the regular meeting of the Club. Beauclerk, "who had all the sportive talents of his ancestor Charles II and loved a little mischief, persuaded the poor Doctor to go all bruised as he was to the Club; to show the world how little he was affected by his late Rencounter."—So wrote Percy, who was present at the Club meeting, but who omitted the passage from his Memoir of Goldsmith "out of Tenderness."[25] The program for the evening was a reading of Chatterton's Rowley poems by Charlemont, and Goldsmith probably entered cheerfully into the discussion. But before the evening was over, he must have realized from Beauclerk's knowing smiles and Percy's pained glances that he had committed one more absurdity.

Of course the incident did not end there. The *Packet* for March 29 contained a detailed account of the scuffle, calculated to make Goldsmith's share in it especially contemptible, and a letter signed "Pasquin," which derided his play and his person, presented to the public for the first time the story of his alleged jealousy of the fantoccini, and accused him of having viciously attacked others in his newspaper articles. Meanwhile Evans threatened to sue for damages, and Goldsmith, who had no legitimate defense to offer, was obliged to settle for a donation of fifty pounds to a Welsh charity. But instead of dropping the matter there and hoping that the world would soon forget it, he dispatched a letter to the newspapers insisting that he was not, as charged, a newspaper scribbler, and raising the question of how far the freedom of the press should be permitted to go.

Naturally the whole affair created a stir. Boswell, reading in Edinburgh an account of Goldsmith's scuffle, assumed it was "an invention like Pope's stories of Curl[1]"; but when he arrived in London on April 2 he learned that it was perfectly true.

On Saturday, April 3, he called at Johnson's house late in the evening and, because Johnson was out, sat for a while with Miss Williams. He picked up a copy of the *London Chronicle* for April 1-3, found Goldsmith's letter in it, and read it aloud to her. It seemed to them both to be "so much in Dr. Johnson's manner" that they concluded he must have written it for Goldsmith. Accordingly, when Johnson came home, Boswell "asked him if Dr. Goldsmith had written it, with an air that made him see I suspected it was his." "Sir," said Johnson, "Dr. Goldsmith would no more have asked me to write such a thing as that for him than he would have asked me to feed him with a spoon, or to do any thing else that denoted his imbecility. I as much believe that he wrote it, as if I had seen him do it. Sir, had he shewn it to any one friend, he would not have been allowed to publish it. He has, indeed, done it very well; but it is a foolish thing well done. I suppose he has been so much elated with the success of his new comedy, that he has thought every thing that concerned him must be of importance to the publick."

"I fancy, Sir," said Boswell, "this is the first time that he has been engaged in such an adventure."

"Why, Sir, I believe it is the first time he has *beat,*" Johnson replied; "he may have *been beaten* before. This, Sir, is a new plume to him."[26]

Johnson was right, as usual; under the circumstances Goldsmith's letter was indeed a foolish thing well done. It gave his detractors all the more opportunity to deride him and only heightened his distress. The very next day he was to write a letter which revealed that he was suffering from disappointment and remorse. It was, oddly enough, a letter to Boswell, who he had every reason to suppose was in Edinburgh.

Before Boswell had set out for London he had read of the success of *She Stoops to Conquer,* had decided that Goldsmith was, after all, a man worth cultivating, and had composed a letter clearly designed to win Goldsmith's confidence. "I sincerely wish you joy," it began, "on the great success of your new comedy, *She Stoops to Conquer, or the Mistakes of a Night;* the English nation was just falling into a lethargy. Their blood was thickened and their minds *creamed and mantled like a standing pool;* and no wonder;—when their comedies, which should enliven them like sparkling Champagne, were become mere syrup of poppies, gentle, soporifick draughts." Then after more in the same style he announced that his wife had borne him a daughter on the evening that the play was first performed. "I am fond of the coincidence," he wrote. "My little daughter is a fine healthy lively child, and I flatter myself shall be blest with the cheerfullness of your Comick Muse. She has nothing of that wretched whining and crying which we see children so often have; nothing of the *comédie larmoyante.*" And he concluded: "I intend being in London this spring, and promise myself great satisfaction in sharing your social hours. In the mean time, I beg the favour of hearing from you. I am sure you have not a warmer friend or a steadier admirer. While you are in the full glow of theatrical splendour, while all the great and the gay in the British metropolis are literally hanging upon *your smiles,* let me see that you can *stoop to write* to me." In a postscript he added: "Pray write directly. Write as if in repartee."[27]

That was Monday, March 29. On Tuesday, the 30th, Boswell left for London. Why had he been so vague about his plans for his trip? Why had he so earnestly solicited a letter when he would be able, within a very few days, to see Goldsmith in person? Probably, as Professor Pottle has suggested, because he wanted to receive a letter from Goldsmith written at the height of his career.

Perhaps he even had some notion of "Boswellizing" Goldsmith, as Professor Tinker speculated.[28]

Goldsmith received the letter in due time and was undoubtedly gratified by Boswell's cordiality and his flattery. On Sunday, April 4, unaware that Boswell was already in London, he replied "as if in repartee," but with little indication of "the full glow of theatrical splendour." He began by thanking Boswell for his congratulations, but proceeded to assure him that a successful play was "great cry and little wool," that, in fact, this one had kept him "in hot water these three months." He added that "the stage earning is the dirtiest money that ever a poor poet put in his pocket" and that he fully intended to write no more plays. He brightened to congratulate Boswell on the birth of his daughter, who was sure to "become a CONQUEROR." And he promised to regale him, when next they met, with "long stories about my struggles and escapes"—cheerfully acknowledging that he is "the only *Poet militant*" in London and is likely to remain so until death. As for the fracas with Evans, he had, admittedly, behaved like a fool, though he doubted if anything would come of the proposed lawsuit. And he closed by urging Boswell to "come up to town and we shall laugh it off whether it goes for or against me."[29]

On Wednesday morning, April 7, Boswell stopped in at the Temple before Goldsmith was out of bed. When Goldsmith learned who his caller was, he roared, "Boswell!" Boswell ran to Goldsmith, and they had a "cordial embrace." Then, while Boswell sat on the side of the bed, the two men chatted about the success of *She Stoops to Conquer* and Goldsmith's trouble with Evans. Presently he showed Boswell a newspaper article intimating that Johnson was the father of the eldest Thrale boy, and the two agreed in deploring the scandal which, ludicrous as it was, might be believed by strangers.

After a while Goldsmith rose, and Boswell sat in the dining room while he dressed and ate breakfast. On a table he saw a letter from Francis Gentleman thanking Goldsmith for his generosity and enclosing a promissory note for fifteen pounds. Boswell reflected that Goldsmith was "the most generous-hearted" of men; "and now that he has a huge supply of gold by his Comedy all the needy draw upon him."[30]

Later in the day Boswell called on Topham Beauclerk at his house "on the terrace of the Adelphi," and Beauclerk told him how Goldsmith, mindful of his experience with Colman, had said recently in Johnson's company that someone ought to establish a theater for the presentation of new plays "in order to deliver authours from the supposed tyranny of managers." Johnson had disagreed; whereupon Goldsmith said: "Ay, ay, this may be nothing to you, who can now shelter yourself behind the corner of a pension."[31] This was baiting the lion indeed; yet Johnson did not strike back. Perhaps he felt that Goldsmith had been struck often enough lately. Their companions were prepared for his retaliation, but it never came.

In the course of the next few days Boswell found other occasions to discuss Goldsmith, probably in a sincere effort to reach a just estimate of his character. Boswell was an incurable collector of characters, and he liked to interpret and classify them. But Goldsmith's was a particularly elusive character: it did not lend itself to easy generalizations. Even Johnson seemed unable to make up his mind about the man. On Good Friday, April 9, Boswell told him that Goldsmith had said, "As I take my shoes from the shoemaker, and my coat from the taylor, so I take my religion from the priest," and Johnson said flatly: "He knows nothing; he has made up his mind about nothing."[32] Yet two days later, on Easter Sunday, when Boswell suggested that Goldsmith was one of Johnson's imitators, Johnson denied it. "But, Sir," said Boswell, "he is much indebted to you for his getting so high in the publick estimation." But Johnson refused to accept the implied compliment. "Why, Sir," he acknowledged, "he has, perhaps, got *sooner* to it by his intimacy with me."[33] As Goldsmith had told Boswell several years before, there was nothing of the bear about Johnson but his skin; and whatever resentment he may have felt toward Goldsmith had dissolved in his compassion for the man's recent hardships. He might still be annoyed by Goldsmith's thoughtless talk, but he could not forget or ignore the tribute which Goldsmith had paid him in the Dedication of *She Stoops to Conquer*.

The following day, Monday, April 12, Boswell had a chance to form an independent estimate of Goldsmith's abilities when he went to Covent Garden to see the new comedy. He "laughed most heartily and was highly pleased"—so much so that he left the theater before the farce began, so that he would not "put the taste of Goldsmith's fruit out of my mouth."[34]

He was, therefore, feeling well disposed toward Goldsmith on the next day when Johnson and Goldsmith called at his lodgings and took him to General Oglethorpe's house for dinner. He recalled that they had spent a "noble day" there in the previous year and feared that this one might prove disappointing by comparison. But it did not.[35]

Goldsmith brought up one of his favorite topics, the evil effects of luxury, and even maintained that the human race had grown smaller over the centuries because of luxury. Johnson disagreed emphatically, arguing that too few people felt the effects of luxury for it to have had so widespread an influence—and that although "the great increase of commerce and manufactures . . . hurts the bodies of people, . . . that is not luxury."

"Come," said Goldsmith, "you're just going to the same place by another road."

"Nay, Sir, I say that is not *luxury*. Let us take a walk from Charing-cross to Whitechapel, through, I suppose, the greatest series of shops in the world; what is there in any of these shops, (if you except gin-shops,) that can do any human being any harm?"

"Well, Sir," said Goldsmith, "I'll accept your challenge. The very next shop to Northumberland-house is a pickle-shop."

Johnson insisted that "there is no harm done to any body by the making of pickles, or the eating of pickles," and Boswell noted that Goldsmith "made but a bad figure with his pickles."[36] And there the matter ended, at least as far as Boswell was concerned. Goldsmith seems not to have convinced his companions that pickles were an artificial stimulant to appetite and might encourage gluttony, one of the worst evidences of luxury.[37]

At tea time Mrs. Oglethorpe and some other ladies joined the gentlemen, and the serious conversation was abandoned. Goldsmith entertained the group by singing Tony Lumpkin's song, "The Three Jolly Pigeons," and another one, "Ah, me! when shall I marry me?," which he had written for Kate Hardcastle, but discarded because Mrs. Bulkley could not sing. Now Goldsmith was at his best; he could relax and put all his efforts into entertaining his friends. There was no danger of his being misunderstood or misinterpreted. All the irritations of the past few weeks vanished—for the moment, at least.

Two days later, on Thursday, April 15, Boswell, Johnson, and Goldsmith dined at the home of General Paoli, the exiled Corsican patriot whom Boswell had met during his travels abroad. Also present was Vincenzio Martinelli, author of a history of England in Italian. In the course of the conversation Goldsmith urged Martinelli to write a supplement to his history, bringing it down to the present. But Johnson argued that Martinelli would only offend "almost all the living great" if he were to do so.

Goldsmith refused to be downed. "It may, perhaps, be necessary for a native to be more cautious," he declared; "but a foreigner who comes among us without prejudice, may be considered as holding the place of a Judge, and may speak his mind freely."

"Sir," said Johnson, "a foreigner, when he sends a work from the press, ought to be on his guard against catching the errour and mistaken enthusiasm of the people among whom he happens to be."

"Sir, he only wants to sell his history, and to tell truth," Goldsmith insisted; "one an honest, the other a laudable motive."

Johnson declared that both were laudable motives, but that he would advise a foreigner "to be at Calais before he publishes his history of the present age."

But Goldsmith would have none of his joking. "There are people who tell a hundred political lies every day, and are not hurt by it," he said. "Surely, then, one may tell truth with safety." And when Johnson pointed out that "a man had rather have a hundred lies told of him, than one truth which he does not wish should be told," Goldsmith protested: "For my part, I'd tell truth, and shame the devil."

"Yes, Sir; but the devil will be angry. I wish to shame the devil as much as you do, but I should choose to be out of the reach of his claws."

But still Goldsmith refused to jest. He had the last word, and it did him honor. "His claws can do you no harm," he said, "when you have the shield of truth."

Later, when someone speculated on whether the King would attend a performance of *She Stoops to Conquer,* Goldsmith said, "I wish he would," but added, with what seemed to Boswell "an affected indifference": "Not that it would do me the least good."

"Well then, Sir, let us say it would do *him* good," said Johnson, laughing. Then: "No, Sir, this affectation will not pass;—it is mighty idle. In such a state as ours, who would not wish to please the Chief Magistrate?"

"I *do* wish to please him," Goldsmith admitted. And he quoted Dryden's line, "And every poet is the monarch's friend," adding that it ought to be reversed.

"Nay," said Johnson, "there are finer lines in Dryden on this subject." And he quoted from *Absalom and Achitophel:*

> For colleges on bounteous Kings depend,
> And never rebel was to arts a friend.

General Paoli remarked that "successful rebels might" be friends to the arts, and Martinelli threw in the phrase "happy rebellions."

"We have no such phrase," said Goldsmith. And when Paoli asked, "But have you not the *thing?*" he replied: "Yes; all our *happy* revolutions. They have hurt our constitution, and will hurt it, till we mend it by another HAPPY REVOLUTION."

"I never before discovered that my friend Goldsmith had so much of the old prejudice in him," Boswell remarked after recording the conversation in his *Life of Johnson.* But of course it was new prejudice rather than old. As Goldsmith had intimated in his remark about Johnson's hiding behind the corner of a pension, and in his statement that it would do him no good if the

King attended his play, he was offended that he had received no pension. His *History of England* suggests that, while he was no admirer of the Stuarts, he was irked that George III had failed to recognize him. Moreover, Hastings' remark in Act II of *She Stoops to Conquer,* "We shall soon be landed in France, where even among slaves the laws of marriage are respected," was popularly interpreted as a slur at the King's opposition to the marriage of the Duke of Gloucester and Lady Waldegrave, and it had been greeted with cheers at the first performance, when the Duke was in the audience.

That the slur was deliberate became apparent this same evening at General Paoli's house. The General himself remarked of Goldsmith's play: *"Il a fait un compliment très gracieux à une certaine grande dame."*

Boswell, eager to have confirmation of the rumor, "expressed a doubt whether Goldsmith intended it," but Goldsmith only "smiled and hesitated." Paoli spared him further embarrassment by saying: *"Monsieur Goldsmith est comme la mer, qui jette des perles et beaucoup d'autres belles choses, sans s'en appercevoir."*

"Très bien dit, et très élégamment," said Goldsmith gratefully.[38]

It was perhaps on this same occasion that Goldsmith offended Martinelli and was offended in turn. According to Sir John Hawkins, who tells the story, Goldsmith later complained that Martinelli was a rude man; that once when Goldsmith remarked in his presence that "there were no good writers among the Italians," Martinelli said to the person next to him that Goldsmith was very ignorant.[39]

Goldsmith seems to have been speaking his mind more emphatically and fearlessly than ever before. George III was not the only object of his irritation; his challenging of Johnson's opinions and his refusing to respond to Johnson's jests were other manifestations of it, as was his ill-timed remark about Italian writers. And this irritability was caused not only by his failure to receive a pension but by ill health, overwork, the long series of frustrations before his comedy was produced, the humiliation of having his appearance and his character mocked in the public press—all these and a general failure to manage his career or his finances in such a manner as to yield him contentment. The man of genius had reached the summit of his achievements, only to find the rewards hardly worth the struggle of ascent.

On Wednesday, April 21, Boswell, Johnson, and Goldsmith were together again, this time for dinner at the Thrales' house. Goldsmith seems to have had little to say until the group fell to discussing the suicide of a Mr. Fitzherbert and, from that, moved on to suicide in general.

"Do you think, Sir," Boswell asked Johnson, "that all who commit suicide are mad?"

"Sir," replied Johnson, "they are often not universally disordered in their intellects, but one passion presses so upon them, that they yield to it, and commit suicide, as a passionate man will stab another." Then presently: "I have often thought, that after a man has taken the resolution to kill himself, it is not courage in him to do any thing, however desperate, because he has nothing to fear."

"I don't see that," Goldsmith interposed.

"Nay but, my dear Sir, why should you not see what every one else sees?"

"It is for fear of something that he has resolved to kill himself," said Goldsmith; "and will not that timid disposition restrain him?"[40]

But Johnson pushed on to his conclusion, and Goldsmith apparently had no more to say on the subject.

Yet he had been thinking about suicide—in the abstract, at least. Just four days earlier, on Saturday, April 17, he had gone with Percy and the Orientalist William Jones, a new member of the Club, to see the house where Thomas Chatterton had killed himself in 1768.[41] Here was another poet, another man of genius, who had managed his life badly. To him suicide had seemed the only remedy. How much could a man endure before life became intolerable?

At least the visit seems to have set him thinking about his own death. On the morning of April 21, the day of the Thrales' dinner party, he had breakfast with Thomas Percy, and it was probably

251

then that Percy agreed to serve as his biographer. On Wednesday, the 28th, a dismal, rainy day, he called at Percy's apartment in Northumberland House, dictated to him a note about his early life, and gave him a sheaf of manuscript materials which might prove useful to a biographer.

Meanwhile Boswell, unaware of Goldsmith's agreement with Percy, continued to seek the key to Goldsmith's enigmatic character. On Sunday, April 25, he visited him at the Temple and made notes in his Journal on their conversation.[42] On the following Tuesday he called on Johnson with Beauclerk and again seems to have brought the conversation around to the subject of Goldsmith. In his *Life of Johnson* Boswell thus records Johnson's remarks:

Goldsmith should not be for ever attempting to shine in conversation: he has not temper for it, he is so much mortified when he fails. Sir, a game of jokes is composed partly of skill, partly of chance. A man may be beat at times by one who has not the tenth part of his wit. Now Goldsmith's putting himself against another, is like a man laying a hundred to one who cannot spare the hundred. It is not worth a man's while. A man should not lay a hundred to one, unless he can easily spare it, though he has a hundred chances for him: he can get but a guinea, and he may lose a hundred. Goldsmith is in this state. When he contends, if he gets the better, it is a very little addition to a man of his literary reputation: if he does not get the better, he is miserably vexed.[43]

The text of the corresponding passage in Boswell's Journal differs significantly from this later version in certain respects. The first sentence reads: "He should not attempt as he does; for he has not the temper for it; he's so much hurt if he fails." The phrase "to shine in conversation" in the *Life* is apparently Boswell's own, and it does not accurately convey Johnson's meaning. Moreover, the word "mortified" in the same sentence and the word "vexed" in the final sentence are substitutes for "hurt" in the earlier version. Boswell was not necessarily trying to make Johnson's words seem less sympathetic; as a matter of fact, at this point in the *Life* he introduced the familiar story of Goldsmith's saying that Johnson would make little fishes in a fairy story talk like whales—as evidence of Goldsmith's frequent success "in his witty contests."[44] The fact remains, however, that his original version of Johnson's words suggests what is lacking in the record in the *Life:* that Johnson now understood Goldsmith's nature, realized that he was often "hurt," and sympathized with him.

After Boswell and Beauclerk had left Johnson's house, Boswell asked how a man as gifted as Goldsmith could talk and act so foolishly. "He wants the power of reason," Beauclerk replied. "He never knows when he's right."[45] His was, of course, the more common attitude toward Goldsmith.

On Thursday, April 29, the day after Goldsmith had given Percy the information for his biography, Boswell and Johnson, en route to General Oglethorpe's, were hailed by Reynolds and Goldsmith, who were riding aimlessly through Berkeley Square. They admitted that they were at a loss for entertainment, and Boswell commented ironically, "So you took us as guides." Johnson added: "I wondered, indeed, at their great civility."

Off they all rode then to General Oglethorpe's, where they found Langton and Henry Thrale. Eventually the conversation came around to the practice of eating dogs in Tahiti, and Goldsmith declared that the Chinese also ate dogs—in fact that dog-butchers were as common in China as cattle-butchers were in England. He added that a dog-butcher was always in danger of being attacked by dogs when he went out in the streets.

To this Johnson objected. "That is not owing to his killing dogs, Sir," he said; and he told of a butcher in Lichfield whom the Johnson family dog attacked regularly because of the "smell of carnage" on his person.

Goldsmith was unperturbed. "Yes," he said, "there is a general abhorrence in animals at the signs of massacre. If you put a tub full of blood into a stable, the horses are like to go mad."

"I doubt that," said Johnson.

"Nay, Sir," Goldsmith insisted, "it is a fact well authenticated."

Here Henry Thrale entered the conversation to observe wryly: "You had better prove it before you put it into your book on natural history. You may do it in my stable if you will."

But now Johnson rose to Goldsmith's defense. "Nay, Sir," he said to Thrale, "I would not have him prove it. If he is content to take his information from others, he may get through his book with little trouble, and without much endangering his reputation. But if he makes experiments for so comprehensive a book as his, there would be no end to them; his erroneous assertions would then fall upon himself; and he might be blamed for not having made experiments as to every particular."

Presently the character of David Mallet came up for discussion, and Goldsmith spoke slightingly of him. "Why, Sir," said Johnson, "Mallet had talents enough to keep his literary reputation alive as long as he himself lived; and that, let me tell you, is a good deal."

Goldsmith disagreed, but managed to do so in such a way as to pay Johnson a graceful compliment. "[Mallet's] literary reputation was dead long before his natural death," he declared. "I consider an authour's literary reputation to be alive only while his name will ensure a good price for his copy from the booksellers. I will get you . . . a hundred guineas for any thing whatever that you shall write, if you put your name to it."

Johnson returned the compliment by paying tribute to Goldsmith's achievement in *She Stoops to Conquer*. And although presently he took issue with Goldsmith's statement that Garrick was guilty of "mean and gross flattery" in inserting an extravagant compliment to the Queen in his revision of Beaumont and Fletcher's *The Chances,* he seems, on the whole, to have assumed a protective attitude toward Goldsmith, as if he were trying to spare his friend from being "hurt," as he had been too often in the past.[46]

The next day, Friday, April 30, was an important one in Boswell's life. Johnson had nominated him for membership in the Club, and the election was to take place that evening. Beauclerk entertained him at dinner, along with Johnson, Reynolds, Lord Charlemont, and some other members of the Club. And although Goldsmith was not present, he was the chief topic of conversation as Boswell later recalled it.

"It is amazing how little Goldsmith knows," Johnson began, apparently feeling free, in Goldsmith's absence, to express his candid opinion. "He seldom comes where he is not more ignorant than any one else."

Reynolds, always loyal to Goldsmith, protested: "Yet there is no man whose company is more liked."

"To be sure, Sir," said Johnson. "When people find a man of the most distinguished abilities as a writer, their inferiour while he is with them, it must be highly gratifying to them. What Goldsmith comically says of himself is very true,—he always gets the better when he argues alone; meaning, that he is master of a subject in his study, and can write well upon it; but when he comes into company, grows confused, and unable to talk." Here Johnson was penetrating to the heart of Goldsmith's trouble. But he stopped there and turned to Goldsmith's achievements as a writer, as if to counterbalance what he had just said about his ignorance. As usual, he was generous in his criticism: *The Traveller* was "a very fine performance"; so was *The Deserted Village,* "were it not sometimes too much the echo" of the earlier poem. And he concluded: "Whether, indeed, we take him as a poet,—as a comick writer,—or as an historian, he stands in the first class."

This seemed to Boswell to be going too far. "An historian!" he exclaimed. "My dear Sir, you surely will not rank his compilation of the Roman History with the works of other historians of this age?"

But Johnson stood by his statement. "Why," he demanded, "who are before him?"

Boswell did not hesitate. "Hume,—Robertson,—Lord Lyttelton," he cried.

"I have not read Hume," said Johnson; "but, doubtless, Goldsmith's History is better than the *verbiage* of Robertson, or the foppery of Dalrymple."

And although Boswell insisted that Robertson's "penetration" and "painting" made his work superior to Goldsmith's, Johnson would not hear of it. "Goldsmith tells you shortly all you want to know," he averred; "Robertson detains you a great deal too long. No man will read Robertson's cumbrous detail a second time; but Goldsmith's plain narrative will please again and again." Moreover: "Goldsmith's abridgement is better than that of Lucius Florus or Eutropius; and I will venture to say, that if you compare him with Vertot, in the same places of the Roman History, you will find that he excels Vertot. Sir, he has the art of compiling, and of saying every thing he has to say in a pleasing manner. He is now writing a Natural History and will make it as entertaining as a Persian Tale." And presently he was repeating for the company one of Goldsmith's most successful witticisms:

"I remember once being with Goldsmith in Westminster-abbey. While we surveyed the Poet's Corner, I said to him,

'Forsitan et nostrum nomen miscebitur istis.'

When we got to Temple-bar he stopped me, pointed to the heads [of executed rebels] upon it, and slily whispered me,

'Forsitan et nostrum nomen miscebitur ISTIS.'"

Soon it was time for the members of the Club to go on to the Turk's Head for their meeting, and Boswell was left to chat with Beauclerk's wife, Lady Diana, until news came that he had been duly elected. Then he hurried off to the meeting, where Johnson delivered a mock Charge to him and he joined with the others in ridiculing George Marriott's poem *The Jesuit,* which Goldsmith had brought to the Club. He had been inveigled into paying five shillings to hear Marriott read his poem at a public meeting, and he was evidently determined to get his money's worth by one means or other. Johnson declared that "bolder words and more timorous meaning, I think never were brought together."[47]

Goldsmith was in high spirits, Boswell noted in his Journal, and later in the evening he introduced the subject of equality. "Here's our monarchy man growing Republican," Burke said jestingly, adding that he should be called Oliver Cromwell rather than Oliver Goldsmith.

But Goldsmith was no republican, now or later, and he summed up his political stand in the effective sentence: "I'm for Monarchy to keep us all equal."[48]

On Friday, May 7, the next Club night, Boswell, Johnson, Goldsmith, and others dined at the home of the Dilly brothers, the booksellers. Although the conversation turned on the migration and nesting of birds, topics on which Goldsmith might have been supposed to be an authority because of his reading for his natural history, he offered only an occasional comment until Boswell brought up the subject of toleration and Johnson declared that "the only method by which religious truth can be established is by martyrdom."

"But how is a man to act, Sir?" Goldsmith asked. "Though firmly convinced of the truth of his doctrine, may he not think it wrong to expose himself to persecution? Has he a right to do so? Is it not, as it were, committing voluntary suicide?"

"Sir," said Johnson, "as to voluntary suicide, as you call it, there are twenty thousand men in an army who will go without scruple to be shot at, and mount a breach for five-pence a day."

"But have they a moral right to do this?" Goldsmith insisted.

"Nay, Sir, if you will not take the universal opinion of mankind, I have nothing to say. If mankind cannot defend their own way of thinking, I cannot defend it. Sir, if a man is in doubt whether it would be better for him to expose himself to martyrdom or not, he should not do it. He must be convinced that he has a delegation from heaven."

Goldsmith was adamant. "I would consider whether there is the greater chance of good or evil upon the whole," he said. "If I see a man who has fallen into a well, I would wish to help him out; but if there is a greater probability that he shall pull me in, than that I shall pull him out, I would not attempt it. So were I to go to Turkey, I might wish to convert the Grand Signor to the Christian faith; but when I considered that I should probably be put to death without effectuating my purpose in any degree, I should keep myself quiet."

Johnson was obviously nettled by Goldsmith's insistence, and he launched into a defense of his own position which concluded by his repeating that, to submit to martyrdom, "a man must be persuaded that he has a particular delegation from heaven."

"How is this to be known?" Goldsmith asked. "Our first reformers, who were burnt for not believing bread and wine to be CHRIST——"

But before he could finish his sentence, Johnson broke in. "Sir, they were not burnt for not believing bread and wine to be CHRIST, but for insulting those who did believe it."

At the moment Goldsmith seems to have abandoned hope of making his point, and Boswell and a Dissenting clergyman named Mayo continued the argument with Johnson. Gradually Goldsmith grew restless, and after a while he picked up his hat and, according to Boswell, "sat like a man at a gaming table still going to take a throw if possible." Boswell imputed his restlessness to "a wish to get in and *shine,*" but he may have had to stop at Covent Garden before going to the Club. It was the night of Lee Lewes' benefit of *She Stoops to Conquer,* and Goldsmith had prepared a special epilogue for him.[49]

At one point in the conversation Goldsmith attempted to speak, but his words were lost in another salvo from Johnson, who was sitting at the opposite end of the table. Exasperated, he threw his hat on the floor, scowled at Johnson, and muttered, *"Take it!"* Then when another member of the group, the Reverend Mr. Toplady, the hymn-writer, tried to make a remark and Johnson seemed about to interrupt him, Goldsmith said icily: "Sir, . . . the gentleman has heard you patiently for an hour; pray allow us now to hear him."

"Sir," said Johnson, "I was not interrupting the gentleman. I was only giving him a signal of my attention." And as a final thrust he added: "Sir, you are impertinent."

That silenced Goldsmith. After a while he left the house, and in due time Boswell, Langton, and Johnson set out in a coach for the Club meeting. As they rode along, Boswell observed that it was a pity that Goldsmith kept trying to shine, and Langton said that he was unlike Addison, who remarked that he "had but nine-pence ready money," though he "could draw for a thousand pounds."

"No," said Boswell, "Goldsmith has a great deal of gold in his drawers at the Temple, but he will always be taking out his purse."

Johnson added that it was often an empty purse.

But when they reached the Turk's Head and found Goldsmith "silently brooding over Johnson's reprimand," Johnson said quietly, "I'll make Goldsmith forgive me"—and then called: "Dr. Goldsmith,—something passed to-day where you and I dined; I ask your pardon."

"It must be much from you, Sir, that I take ill," Goldsmith responded immediately. And soon his depression vanished, and he and Langton were joking about a hilarious escapade which they had shared.[50]

It was now almost time for Boswell to return to Edinburgh, and he had undoubtedly concluded, during his six weeks in London, that Goldsmith was indeed an anomaly. Of one thing he was certain: that beneath Goldsmith's unquestionable affection for Johnson lay a gnawing envy, and in the *Life of Johnson,* after reporting the conversation at the Dilly brothers' dinner and the Club meeting afterward, he inserted two anecdotes to illustrate that envy. The first concerned a remark which Goldsmith made when Boswell quoted Johnson as if he were an indisputable authority on matters of literature: "Sir, you are for making a monarchy of what should be a republick." The second told of Goldsmith's annoyance when a foreigner interrupted him in the middle of a spirited monologue with the words: "Stay, stay,—Toctor Shonson is going to say something." To these he added a third as evidence of Goldsmith's self-importance: when Tom Davies reported that Johnson had told him, "We are all in labour for a name to *Goldy's* play," Goldsmith said irritably, according to Boswell: "I have often desired him not to call me *Goldy.*"

Yet much as Boswell might be puzzled or annoyed by Goldsmith on occasion, he enjoyed his company, as did others who found him similarly puzzling; and on May 9, before he set off for Scotland, he stopped in at the Temple to bid him good-bye.

Goldsmith was in a captious mood. When he learned that Johnson was planning to tour Scotland with Boswell, he observed sourly that Boswell would find him "a dead weight" to carry and that he would "never be able to lug him along through the Highlands and Hebrides." Then when Boswell praised Johnson's abilities, he asked: "Is he like Burke, who winds into a subject like a serpent?" Boswell replied, "Johnson is the Hercules who strangled serpents in his cradle."

But Boswell was disposed to be tolerant, and in the *Life of Johnson* he remarked at this point that "Goldsmith had not more [envy] than other people have, but only talked of it freely."

259

On other subjects Goldsmith chatted affably enough. Boswell told him about "the mode of our law practice," and Goldsmith promised to write for him "a paper in some cause." Then, at Boswell's request, Goldsmith wrote down the words of the song "Ah me, when shall I marry me?" which he had sung at General Oglethorpe's house four weeks before. At last Boswell went on his way, not realizing "it was a last farewell."[51] He wrote a letter to Goldsmith on June 1, but it has been lost, and Goldsmith seems not to have answered it.[52]

It was high time now for Goldsmith to settle down to some serious work. Since the presentation of *She Stoops to Conquer* he had had little time for concentrated—or profitable—writing. To be sure, he had adapted Sir Charles Sedley's translation of Brueys and Palaprat's *Le Grondeur,* but this job was trifling: he had dashed it off hurriedly and presented it to the actor Quick in gratitude for his contribution, as Tony Lumpkin, to the success of *She Stoops to Conquer*. He compressed the three acts of the original into one, reduced the number of characters, discarded the subplot, and sharpened the dramatic action, converting Sedley's rather tedious comedy of manners into an entertaining farce. It was presented at Covent Garden with *King Lear* and an interlude by Samuel Foote on Saturday, May 8; but although it was well received, it was never repeated.[53]

Goldsmith still had several commissions unfinished. There was always the natural history, on which he had labored so long; but by this time it must have been near completion. There was the second edition of the *History of England* too, as well as the abridgment of it, which he had long since agreed to make. His major project at this time, however, was the *Grecian History*. By June 22 he had completed the first volume and received payment of 250 pounds for the whole work. But this was another "compilation," hardly rewarding enough to satisfy the demands of his creative energies. In fact he seems to have given only half his mind to the task: when Edward Gibbon happened into his rooms one day while he was writing, and Goldsmith asked him "the name of the Indian king who gave Alexander so much trouble," Gibbon supposedly replied, "Montezuma"; and Goldsmith would have written it into his text if Gibbon had not stopped him.

One curious feature about the *Grecian History* is perhaps significant. Although the work is, like Goldsmith's other histories, a rapid survey of the subject, concerned almost entirely with military and political history, he devotes sixteen pages to an account of the trial and death of Socrates. Incidentally he remarks: "In this long interval, death had sufficient opportunities to present itself before his eyes in all its terrors, and to put his constancy to the proof, not only by the severe rigour of a dungeon, and the irons upon his legs, but by the continual prospect and cruel expectation of an event of which nature is always abhorrent. In this sad condition he did not cease to enjoy that profound tranquillity of mind which his friends always admired in him. He entertained them with the same temper he had always expressed; and Crito observes, that the evening before his death, he slept as peaceably as at any other time." And later:

Socrates passed the rest of the day with his friends, and discoursed with them with his usual cheerfulness and tranquillity. The subject of conversation was the most important, and adapted to the present conjuncture; that is to say, the immortality of the soul. What gave occasion to this discourse was, a question introduced in a manner by chance, Whether a true philosopher ought not to desire, and take pains to die? This proposition taken too literally, implied an opinion, that a philosopher might kill himself. Socrates shews that nothing is more unjust than this notion; and that man appertaining to God, who formed and placed him with his own hand in the post he possesses, cannot abandon it without his permission, nor depart from life without his order. What is it then that can induce a philosopher to entertain this love for death? It can be only the hope of that happiness which he expects in another life; and that hope can be founded only upon the opinion of the soul's immortality.

These are strange words to appear in a volume of history—especially a history so compressed that all Greek literature is treated in less than four pages. What prompted Goldsmith to linger so over the death of Socrates and to wrestle with the problems of death and suicide? Was he again anticipating his own death and preparing himself to face it with equanimity?

He was still interested enough in the immediate future to want a major project in which he could become absorbed. Accordingly, he conceived a plan for an elaborate Dictionary of Arts and Sciences, which he would edit and to which his distinguished friends would contribute. Johnson agreed to furnish a paper on ethics, Burke was to abridge his *Sublime and Beautiful* and to write an essay on Berkeley's philosophy, Reynolds was to discuss painting, and Garrick, acting. Garrick also persuaded Dr. Charles Burney, father of Fanny, to prepare an essay on music.[54] All seemed to be progressing splendidly, and Goldsmith drew up a Prospectus of the new work, which he had printed and distributed. Apparently he developed a good deal of enthusiasm for this new project. Joseph Cradock says that he showed him an essay intended as an introduction to the Dictionary, and said: "Here are some of the best of my prose writings."[55]

But he still did not settle down to concentrated work. Instead of going to the Selbys' farmhouse for the summer of 1773, he remained in London, doubtless seeking distraction from the worries which harassed him when he was alone. On May 23 he dined at Sion, the Duke of Northumberland's estate, with Percy, Beauclerk, Burke, Horace Walpole, and several others.[56] Then soon afterward he met the Reverend James Beattie, the Scottish poet and philosopher, who was visiting in London with his wife and who was honored at several parties given by Goldsmith's friends.

On Wednesday, June 9, Reynolds entertained the Beatties, Goldsmith, Garrick, Beauclerk, and others for dinner at his house in Leicester Fields, and Goldsmith stayed on for supper with the Beatties, the Bunburys, and Mary Horneck. Goldsmith was "very entertaining and merry" and urged Beattie to call on him at the Temple. Before the party broke up, Sir Joshua invited most of the company to dine with him on the following Monday at his new villa on Richmond Hill.[57]

On Friday, the 11th, Goldsmith had tea with the Beatties at Reynolds' house and then went on to the Club meeting with Sir Joshua. Then on the following Monday Frances Reynolds called for Mr. and Mrs. Beattie at noon in Sir Joshua's coach and drove them down to Richmond, where Goldsmith, the Bunburys, Mary

Horneck and her mother, and the three Burkes had already gathered. It was a clear, windy day, and the company had "much chearful conversation" and enjoyed the "charming walks and prospect." After dark they set out for London in two coaches. It was "rainy and dark" now, and one of the coachmen was drunk; consequently they "met wt. more than one adventure" on the way, but finally reached London at about eleven o'clock. All in all, though, it had been a delightful outing.

However, during the course of the day Frances Reynolds drew Beattie aside and gave him "some particulars of Goldsmith." "He, it seems, not only is, but even acknowledges himself to be, envious of all contemporary authors whose works are successful," Beattie noted in his Diary,

and has several times spoken wt. some peevishness of the attention that has been shown to me in England. "Why should he have a pension?" (he said one day in a company where I happened to be mentioned)—"For writing the minstrel? Then surely I have a better claim." One of the company told him, that my claim was founded on the Essay on Truth, a work of public utility, and which had been attended wt. danger or at least no small inconvenience to the Author. Here Foote the player interposed: "I have read (said he) the Minstrel and think it an excellent poem; but the Author of the Essay on Truth is peculiarly entitled to publick encouragement for writing one of the best and most ingenious books which have appeared this age."

On Thursday, July 1, Mrs. Beattie "being indisposed . . . took a vomit," but her husband dined with Reynolds and again saw Goldsmith, who, having heard that Beattie had been presented to the King the day before, "was very curious to know the particulars." But Beattie, feeling an understandable antagonism after what he had heard from Miss Reynolds, "did not give him full satisfaction." Later Sir Joshua told Beattie that Goldsmith was "hurt not a little" that Beattie was receiving so much more attention than he himself had ever enjoyed.

As the summer advanced, Goldsmith still seemed unable to settle down to steady work. His projected Dictionary of Arts and Sciences came to naught because, according to Tom Davies, the booksellers hesitated to entrust so expensive a project to "a man with whose indolence of temper and method of procrastination they had long been acquainted."[58] He was suffering frequent attacks of strangury and was growing more and more irritable—"irascible as a hornet." He quarreled with his old friend Tom Davies, he quarreled with his servants—who are said to have annoyed him deliberately because they knew that presently he would outdo himself in kindness to make up for his momentary anger. Meanwhile he made foolish efforts to repair his wounded pride. "I am as a lion baited with curs," he told his young protégé McVeagh. And when in company, he tried again to shine—and failed dismally. On July 5 Beauclerk wrote to Lord Charlemont that he had been to the Club only once recently and had been "entertained by Goldsmith's absurdities."[59]

To make matters worse, James Beattie was receiving further recognition. On Friday, July 9, he and Reynolds were awarded honorary degrees at Oxford on the occasion of Lord North's installation as Chancellor of the University, and each was cited in a special encomium and given a rousing ovation by the audience. Goldsmith's envy abated momentarily when the newspapers reported that both he and Beattie were to be granted pensions; and when they met accidentally on July 20, he congratulated Beattie on his honorary degree and told him about the rumors. But as time passed there was less talk of Goldsmith's pension, while Beattie's seemed to be assured. Then again Goldsmith's envy flared up—and was ill concealed. "Every body rejoices that [Beattie] will get his pension," wrote Hester Thrale to Johnson; "every one loves him but Goldsmith, who says he cannot bear the sight of so much applause as we all bestow on him. Did he not tell us so himself, who could believe he was so amazingly ill-natured?"[60]

The more vehemently Goldsmith expressed his envy, the more he alienated the friends whom he so much needed just now. At the Thrales' house one day he said in Johnson's presence, "They talk of Beattie for an Author; and what has Beattie done compared to me; who have written so many Volumes?" This was too much for even Johnson to accept, and he replied, "Ah Doctor, there go many Six pences to make one Guinea." "There is no disputing with Johnson," Goldsmith declared resignedly, "for if his Pistol misses Fire, he'll knock you down with the Butt end."[61]

But the cruelest cut came when Goldsmith learned that Reynolds, who had been copying his portrait of Goldsmith for the Thrales' "Streatham Gallery," had begun work on an allegorical painting of Beattie in which the philosopher was represented as standing confidently with his *Essay on Truth* under one arm while the Angel of Truth, beside him, triumphs over various evil spirits, one of whom closely resembles Voltaire. From his friend Sir Joshua, this was more than Goldsmith could bear silently, and he lashed out bitterly. According to Northcote (whose memory had doubtless refined the original) his words were:

"It very ill becomes a man of your eminence and character, Sir Joshua, to condescend to be a mean flatterer, or to wish to degrade so high a genius as Voltaire before so mean a writer as Dr. Beattie; for Dr. Beattie and his book together will, in the space of ten years, not be known ever to have been in existence, but your allegorical picture, and the fame of Voltaire will live for ever to your disgrace as a flatterer."[62]

Nonetheless Reynolds and Goldsmith continued to be close friends. On August 4 they were at Vauxhall with Garrick and George Fitzmaurice, and on the 7th Edward Gibbon told a friend that he had attended "a few parties with new acquaintances who are chained to London (among whom I reckon Goldsmith and Sir Joshua Reynolds)."[63] On the 13th Goldsmith was at Streatham for dinner with the Thrales and a large group which included Dr. and Mrs. Beattie. But it must have been in some ways a lonely month. Johnson left on his tour of the Hebrides on August 6, and Sir Joshua set out soon afterward on a trip to Devonshire.

Shortly before Johnson left London he dined at Reynolds' house in the company of a Mr. Eliot who made some disparaging remarks about Goldsmith. Again Johnson rose to his friend's defense. "Is there a man, Sir, now," he demanded, "who can pen an essay with such ease and elegance as Goldsmith?"[64] It was a shame that Goldsmith could not have heard the words. He needed defenders as never before.

He seems often to have been on Johnson's and Boswell's minds as they traveled together through the Highlands and on to the Hebrides, and his name occurred frequently in their conversation.

Sometimes Johnson's remarks about him were merely incidental, as when on August 14 at Boswell's house he said, apropos of the will which Langton had recently made, that it would be ridiculous for Goldsmith to make a will, because he had nothing to leave. Or when, on September 24 at Talisker on the Isle of Skye, he remarked that Percy could tell an anecdote better than Goldsmith.[65]

At other times, reminded somehow of Goldsmith's weaknesses, Johnson was outspokenly critical. When Boswell remarked on October 2 at Armadale that Goldsmith "spoke at all ventures," Johnson agreed. "Rather than not speak," he said, "[Goldsmith] will talk of what he knows himself to be ignorant." If he were with two founders, "he would fall a talking on the method of making cannon, though both of them would soon see that he did not know what metal a cannon is made of." And on October 22, at Moy on Loch Buy, Johnson made the puzzling remark already quoted: "Goldsmith would get drunk and boast of it, if it had been with a little whore or so who had allowed him to go in a coach with her."[66]

Yet on the whole Johnson was disposed to defend Goldsmith when he could, and Boswell seems to have been similarly tolerant. On August 25, after their visit to St. Andrews, they sketched an imaginary university faculty made up of members of the Club, and both agreed that Goldsmith should occupy the chair of poetry and ancient history. On October 1 at Ostaig Boswell said that Goldsmith was "the better for attacks," and Johnson concurred. And on August 31, when Boswell observed at Anoch in Glenmorison that "Goldsmith has acquired more fame than all the officers [of the] last war, who were not Generals," Johnson said, "Why, sir, you will find ten thousand fit to do what they did, before you find one who does what Goldsmith has done. You must consider, that a thing is valued according to its rarity." Boswell, who was evidently beginning to understand Goldsmith's basic trouble, commented in his *Tour to the Hebrides:* "I wish our friend Goldsmith had heard this."[67]

When Johnson returned to London, he found Goldsmith no better off, financially or mentally, than when he had left. Yet the poor man insisted on keeping up an appearance of gaiety and prosperity, and he gave lavish parties which he called his "Little Cornelys," alluding to the extravagant entertainments staged by Mrs. Cornelys in her Great Rooms in Soho. A Mr. and Mrs. Seguin, an Irish merchant and his wife, later recalled his jolly gatherings, at which they were introduced to many of his distinguished friends. Sometimes he entertained especially for the Seguin children, for two of whom he had stood as godfather, and then he strove unflaggingly to keep all merry—singing his favorite songs, dancing, playing games, or clowning. Once when he was dancing a minuet with their mother, he cut such an odd figure that she and the children could not keep from bursting into laughter, in which he joined heartily. He would play blindman's buff or forfeits with the young Seguins, pretend to cheat them at cards, put on his wig backwards—anything that might please them. And always there was an elaborate supper served up for the guests, although Goldsmith's health permitted him to take only a cup of boiled milk.

One night at a dinner in Goldsmith's rooms Johnson and Reynolds were so disturbed at the extravagance of the menu which Goldsmith had planned that, according to Andrew Kippis, they refused to eat any of the second large course set before them. The other guests followed suit, and the food was carried away from the table untouched. Goldsmith could ill afford such expenditures, and something must be done to bring the man to his senses.

Yet he refused to be warned; he would stop at no sort of folly provided it kept his mind from his troubles. On Saturday, December 11, he dined at the Beauclerks' with the Garricks, Lord and Lady Edgcumbe, and Horace Walpole, who wrote afterward to Lady Ossory:

I . . . was most thoroughly tired, as I knew I should be, I who hate the playing off a butt. Goldsmith is a fool, the more wearing for having some sense. It was the night of a new comedy, called *The School for Wives,* which was exceedingly applauded, and which Charles Fox says is execrable. Garrick has at least the chief hand in it. I never saw anybody in a greater fidget, nor more vain when he returned, for he went to the play-house at half an hour after five, and we sat waiting for him till ten, when he was to act a speech in *Cato* with Goldsmith! that is, the latter sat on t'other's lap, covered with a cloak, and while Goldsmith spoke, Garrick's arms that embraced him made foolish actions. How could one laugh when one had expected this for four hours?[68]

What Walpole did not realize was that Goldsmith was distressed by the success of Kelly's play. This was one more blow to his wounded pride, and he countered by pretending to ignore it and giving himself up to nonsensical distractions.

But he could not spend all his time at parties. When they ended he had to face grim reality. He still had no major project in hand; he still had no pension. His only achievements in recent weeks had been a "Poetical Exordium" which Mrs. Yates recited at the opening of the opera season on November 20, and perhaps a paragraph in praise of James Townsend, who was running against John Wilkes for the office of Lord Mayor of London.[69] If the latter was his, he had evidently, in desperation, abandoned his cherished principle against writing for a political party.

Meanwhile Kelly's *School for Wives* continued to attract capacity audiences and enthusiastic praise. Charles Fox might pronounce it "execrable," Beauclerk might consider it "good for nothing," and Lord Charlemont might declare that he never read "worse stuff." The fact remained that Londoners had shown by their support of the play that *She Stoops to Conquer* had by no means driven sentimental comedy from the stage. Once again Hugh Kelly was triumphing over Oliver Goldsmith. As Beauclerk wrote to Lord Charlemont, "It . . . has almost killed Goldsmith with envy."[70]

Garrick, who was sharing the success of *The School for Wives,* seems now to have realized Goldsmith's plight and to have been eager to aid him. He even offered to revive *The Good Natured Man* at Drury Lane for Goldsmith's benefit, and Goldsmith wrote to him hopefully on Christmas Eve: "Your saying you would play my 'Good-natured Man' makes me wish it. . . . I will give you a new character in my comedy and knock out Lofty which does not do, and will make such other alterations as you direct." This to the man whose earlier suggestions for revision of the play he had so sternly rejected!

In the same letter Goldsmith reveals that Garrick had recently lent him forty pounds. "The money you advanced me upon Newbery's note I have the mortification to find is not yet paid," he wrote, "but he says he will in two or three days. What I mean by this letter is to lend me sixty pound for which I will give you Newbery's note, so that the whole of my debt will be an hundred for which you shall have Newbery's note as a security. This may be paid either from my alteration if my benefit should come to so much, but at any rate I shall take care you shall not be a loser."

Garrick sent the sixty pounds off immediately. Then Goldsmith, his spirits suddenly buoyed up by temporary prosperity, wrote back on Christmas Day: "I thank you! I wish I could do something to serve you. I shall have a comedy for you in a season or two at farthest that I believe will be worth your acceptance, for I fancy I will make it a fine thing. You shall have the refusal. . . . Im sorry you are ill. I will draw upon you in one month after date for sixty pound, and your acceptance will be ready money part of which I want to go down to Barton with. May God preserve my honest little man for he has my heart." Garrick endorsed the letter "Goldsmith's Parlaver" and tucked it away among his papers.

As for Goldsmith, he dashed off a reply to the rhyming letter which Catherine Bunbury had sent him inviting him to spend New Year's at Barton.[71] He began with a mock-serious complaint in prose about the "sarcasms" and "soloecisms" in Catherine's letter, then shifted to anapaests to describe an imaginary game of Loo in which he had, as Catherine suggested, taken the ladies' advice, only to come to grief. Then came an account of the trial at which the ladies are accused of pilfering from "Yon solemn fac'd odd looking man." And finally: "I chalenge you all to answer this. I tell you you cannot. It cuts deep. But now for the rest of the letter, and next—but I want room—so I believe I shall battle the rest out at Barton some day next week. I dont value you all." And soon he was on his way to Barton, where he could forget his worries again and enjoy the congenial company of his friends.

Mary Horneck Gwynne later told Prior that Goldsmith seemed completely carefree at Barton. "Come now and let us play the fool a little," he would cry, and he would give himself over wholly to the kind of nonsense which he always loved: singing his favorite songs, romping with the children, roaring about his luck at cards, or teasing the ladies about their timid bidding.

Because of his good nature he was subjected to the sort of practical jokes which eighteenth century ladies and gentlemen relished. Once, for example, one of the party deliberately soiled the black silk coat which he wore with ruffles to breakfast—and no sooner had he had it cleaned than it was unaccountably spattered with paint. Another time someone mussed his wig, and he asked Bunbury's valet to arrange it; it was returned in such repair that the guests had to smother their laughter whenever he wore it. On another occasion, Mrs. Gwynne remembered, he and Lord Harrington argued about the depth of a certain pond, and Goldsmith declared that it was not so deep that he would hesitate to retrieve anything valuable at the bottom. Immediately His Lordship tossed a guinea into the water, and Goldsmith reached for it and, of course, lost his balance.[72] He was undaunted, however, and soon emerged with the guinea, declaring that he knew plenty of ways of using this or any other guinea that Harrington had to spare.

Goldsmith did not mind making a fool of himself if people laughed at him rather than scorned him. At Barton he could be himself again, as he had been at Lord Clare's, as he could always be with simple people or children. As Reynolds said, he "did not seem to care whether [the laugh] was with him or at him" as long as his companions kept laughing.[73]

In one respect, however, visiting such fine houses was undoubtedly bad for him. Although Mrs. Gwynne insisted that the stakes at cards were always low at Barton, it may be significant that he felt that he must have sixty pounds before going there. To be sure, he told Garrick that he intended to use only part of that sum for the trip. But Joseph Cradock claimed that "the greatest real fault of Dr. Goldsmith was, that if he had thirty pounds in his pocket he would go into certain companies in the country, and in hopes of doubling the sum, would generally return to town without any part of it."[74] Perhaps after the ladies had retired and

270

the gentlemen took over at the card table, the stakes at Barton were raised.

At about this same time Goldsmith enjoyed another holiday—a stay of two or three weeks at Windsor with a friend named Purefoy. From there he wrote to Cradock and Percy telling them he had been notified that a part of the proof of his natural history had been delivered to his rooms at the Temple, and asking them to stop in and read it for him. The two men met at his apartment and found that the section to be read concerned birds. "Do you know anything about birds?" Percy asked. "Not an atom," said Cradock; "do you?" "No," Percy acknowledged, "I scarce know a goose from a swan." But they set to work and soon dispatched the job.[75]

Eventually Goldsmith returned to London and was obliged to confront reality again. He still had not found a major project. On February 20, 1774, he wrote to the publisher Nourse, who had bought from Griffin the rights to the natural history, thanking him for an overpayment and asking if Griffin could now buy back a partial share in the book. "As I have thoughts of extending the work into the *vegetable* and *fossil* kingdoms," he added, "you shall share with him in any such engagement as may happen to ensue."

By this time the *History of Earth and Animated Nature* had been advertised for immediate publication. But Goldsmith's *Grecian History,* the second edition of *The History of England,* and his abridgment of the book were still pending. He had perhaps begun work on a translation of Scarron's *Roman Comique,* and Dodsley had given him five guineas for a revision of his old *Enquiry into Polite Learning.* But he seemed unable to undertake anything new or original, and he must often have asked himself if his powers had deserted him.

In an attempt to aid him, Joseph Cradock suggested that he publish by subscription an annotated edition of *The Traveller* and *The Deserted Village,* thinking that it would at least enable his friends to assist him without seeming to offer him charity. But Goldsmith showed no enthusiasm for the proposal: he merely gave Cradock his own copies of the poems, saying, "Pray do what

271

you please with them." And when Cradock returned the poems with suggestions for revision, Goldsmith accepted them without argument. He seemed to have lost all interest in his work. Yet he showed a spark of his old pride when he said, "As to my 'Hermit,' that poem, Cradock, cannot be amended."[76]

On February 12 Beauclerk wrote to Lord Charlemont that Goldsmith had no time for the Club now because he had "got into such a round of pleasures."[77] Yet he attended the meeting on March 4 and unsuccessfully nominated Edward Gibbon for membership, although Charles Fox, George Steevens, Sir Charles Bunbury, and Dr. George Fordyce were all elected.[78]

But his round of pleasures offered only momentary distraction. His health was no better, and when Joseph Cradock invited him to dine with him and his wife, Goldsmith said, "I will; but on one condition—that you will not ask me to eat any thing." Cradock reluctantly accepted the condition, and Goldsmith took only some wine and biscuits. Later "the Doctor appeared more cheerful . . . and in the course of the evening he endeavoured to talk . . ., as usual, but all was force."[79]

Deprived of almost all his other pleasures, Goldsmith consoled himself now by indulging in extravagant expenditures for clothing. George Steevens wrote to Garrick on March 6: "If the *bon ton* should prove a contagious disorder among us, it will be curious to trace its progress. I have already seen it breaking out in Dr. G. under the form of many a waistcoat."[80] And Goldsmith's tailor's bills reveal that, in the face of all his debts, he had spent no less than fifty pounds for new clothing in the course of the year 1773.

He found some comfort, too, in a new group which met from time to time for dinner at the St. James's Coffeehouse or the British, and which was composed in part of members of the Club—Burke, Garrick, Reynolds—but also of others like Samuel Foote, Richard Cumberland, and Caleb Whitefoord, who would hardly have qualified for membership in that august body. Dr. Johnson was noticeably absent, and the whole tone of the gathering was informal. They did not meet regularly, they had no planned program, and the conversation was often frivolous. It was a group ideally adapted to Goldsmith's tastes, and it provided at last the impetus for a piece of work into which he could pour all his best energies.

At one of the meetings Goldsmith suggested that he and Garrick try their skill as writers of epigrams by preparing epitaphs for each other—"grave epigrams," as Burke promptly defined them.[81] Immediately Garrick replied that his entry was already finished, and he recited to the group:

> Here lies poet Goldsmith, for shortness call'd Noll,
> Who wrote like an angel, but talked like poor Poll.

Of course the lines were greeted with an uproar, and Goldsmith, taken aback, was obliged to concede defeat.

Yet he did not forget the challenge which Garrick had presented; in fact it seems to have appealed to his imagination, and he determined to retaliate. Soon he was at work on a whole series of epitaphs of all the members of the club—now biting, now tender, but always witty. He was in a valedictory mood, and he spoke with candor; yet as he warmed to his task he must have found it comforting—even stimulating—since it proved that his old powers had not decayed. He was even able to raise a laugh at himself again: when he listed the appropriate dishes brought to the dinner described at the beginning of the poem, he put down "Magnanimous Goldsmith" for "a gooseberry fool."

Eventually he decided to move down to Farmer Selby's where he could have more leisure for writing. He who was used to spending months revising and polishing his longer poems seemed determined to turn this one out in short order.

He worked rapidly. No longer was he coercing his talents into an alien pattern. His instinctive understanding of his fellows, his faculty for choosing the telling detail, his knack for the deft phrase—all lent themselves admirably to the job which he had undertaken. He was writing again—writing with the old verve— and knew that he was succeeding. William Cooke said that Goldsmith offered to show Burke a copy of the poem in its unfinished state, but insisted that Burke must not reveal its contents. On cross-examination, however, he admitted that he had already given a copy to Mrs. Cholmondeley. And it soon appeared that he had made several copies for friends—who in turn had copied off the poem for others.[82] He could not keep secret his exhilaration at the return of his powers.

He talked now of giving up his rooms in the Temple altogether and settling permanently at the Selbys', and is said to have sold the lease on his rooms. He had been born to rural life, and it was in the country that he belonged. He had idealized it from afar often enough; now he would retire to it. There his expenses would be lower; his health would improve; he would be tempted by fewer distractions; his literary powers would revive and flourish.

But it was too late. Before he had finished his poem, he suffered another severe kidney attack; and toward the end of March he returned to the city, where he could be within easy reach of a physician. He assured Mrs. Selby that he would return soon. "I . . . mean to remain as long as you will permit me," he said; "the retirement of your place is agreeable to me."

Back in town he found relief from his kidney trouble, but he continued to run a fever. He was expected at the Club on Friday, March 25, to congratulate the newly elected members. But he failed to appear. He was seriously ill again, and in an attempt to cure himself he took two ounces of ipecacuanha wine as an emetic.

At eleven o'clock that evening he called William Hawes, who examined him and found his pulse only moderately accelerated.[83] He complained of a violent headache, said that he had taken an emetic, and insisted that he now wanted to take a Dr. James's Fever Powder to reduce his fever. Hawes objected to his doing so after taking the emetic and recommended, instead, a mild opiate.

At first Goldsmith seemed willing to accept the physician's advice, but then suddenly he demanded again that he be given a Fever Powder. Under protest Hawes returned to his office and sent him some powders. Meanwhile, however, he had received Goldsmith's grudging permission to call in Dr. George Fordyce, one of the new members of the Club. Fordyce had returned home from the Club meeting by the time Hawes' servant reached his house, and he went directly to Goldsmith's rooms and confirmed Hawes' decision that it would be unwise for him to take the powders.

But Goldsmith had had medical experience himself, and he believed that the powders had benefited him in the past. Accordingly, he took one of the powders which Hawes had sent—then, as if in defiance, one or two more.

In the morning when Hawes called, Goldsmith seemed to be dozing; so he left without disturbing him. Later in the day, however, he suffered severe fits of vomiting and diarrhea. "Damn that Hawes!" he said to his servants, "I ordered him to send me James's powder and he has sent me some other." He had some powders fetched from the shop of Francis Newbery, son of John and now proprietor of Dr. James's Fever Powders, and he continued to take them. But the vomiting and diarrhea went on, and that evening when Hawes called he was "extremely reduced." He seemed too exhausted to talk; yet he apologized for not following Hawes' recommendations.

Fordyce also called on Saturday evening, and was so concerned at Goldsmith's condition that he went to Hawes' house and urged him to summon Johnson's friend Dr. Turton for consultation if he did not notice a marked improvement on the following morning.

Saturday night Goldsmith's diarrhea and vomiting continued. Sunday morning he seemed "absolutely sunk with weakness." And when Hawes suggested calling in Dr. Turton, he consented.

Hawes now resigned the case. Goldsmith had evidently developed a strong antipathy toward him, for he asked his servants to pay Hawes' bill, and he sent for an apothecary named Maxwell to attend him. Meanwhile Dr. Turton and Dr. Fordyce saw him twice every day and conferred on his condition. But there was little they could do. As Joseph Cradock said later, "All was inwardly disturbed."[84]

During the course of the following week he rallied at times, but when Percy visited him on Sunday, April 3, Goldsmith was barely able to recognize him.[85]

At one point Dr. Turton, puzzled that his pulse rate was so much faster than his fever warranted, asked, "Is your mind at ease?"

"No, it is not," Goldsmith replied.[86]

They were his last recorded words. Shortly after three o'clock on the morning of Monday, the 4th, he was seized with violent convulsions. And an hour and a half later, he died.

Chapter X
"A Very Great Man"

IN his "Portrait of Goldsmith" Sir Joshua Reynolds remarked that the very people who had ridiculed Goldsmith when his back was turned were eager to meet him the next day.[1] And when his friends learned that they would see him no more, they were disconsolate. Reynolds himself is said to have been unable to paint for the rest of the day, and Burke to have burst into tears. Boswell wrote to Garrick from Edinburgh: "I have not been so much affected with any event that has happened of a long time. I wish you would give me who are at a distance, . . . some particulars with regard to his last appearances."[2] And when he visited London in the following year and dined again at General Oglethorpe's, he remarked in his Journal that the company had been treated to a good dinner with Sicilian wine—"But I missed poor Goldsmith."[3]

Meanwhile, on June 24, 1774, he had complained in a letter to Johnson: "You have said nothing to me about poor Goldsmith."[4] On July 4 Johnson replied: "Of poor dear Dr. Goldsmith there is little to be told, more than the papers have made publick. He died of a fever, made, I am afraid, more violent by uneasiness of mind. His debts began to be heavy, and all his resources were exhausted. Sir Joshua is of opinion that he owed not less than two thousand pounds. Was ever poet so trusted before?"[5]

On the following day he wrote to Langton in much the same terms: "He died of a fever, exasperated, as I believe, by the fear of distress. He had raised money and squandered it, by every artifice of acquisition, and folly of expence." He enclosed a Greek tetrastich which he had composed in Goldsmith's honor. But more moving was his spontaneous remark: "Let not his frailties be remembered; he was a very great man."[6] Of all the tributes to Goldsmith, none was more apposite.

Not all his acquaintances were so charitable. Horace Walpole, so staunch a supporter of Dr. James's Fever Powders that he vowed he would take them if his house was afire, wrote to William

Mason on April 7: "The republic of Parnassus has lost a member; Dr Goldsmith is dead of a purple fever, and I think might have been saved if he had continued James's powder, which had had much effect, but his physician interposed. . . . The poor soul had sometimes parts though never common sense."[7] And William Kenrick paid his last respects in four bitter lines:

> By his own art who justly died,
> A blundering, artless suicide;
> Share, earth-worms share, since now he's dead,
> His megrim, maggot-ridden head.[8]

But there were many others, less articulate, for whom Goldsmith's death was a keen personal loss—humble people who crowded the stairs to his rooms in the Temple to say their farewells—people like the Misses Gunn, two milliners who had earnestly told Joseph Cradock: "Oh, sir, sooner persuade him to let us work for him, gratis, than suffer him to apply to any other; we are sure that he will pay us if he can."[9] Goldsmith was mourned by dozens of people who had known and cherished the warmth of his friendship. The *Universal Magazine* for April contained an essay "On Friendship," imputed to him and presumably conveyed to the editors by his estranged friend Hugh Kelly.[10] "Friendship," it read, "is like a debt of honour; the moment it is talked of it loses its real name, and assumes the more ungrateful form of obligation. From hence we find, that those who regularly undertake to cultivate friendship, find ingratitude generally repays their endeavours." Goldsmith had never needed to cultivate friendship: his infectious good nature had attracted to him innumerable friends among young and old, rich and poor, wise and simple.

In the absence of his relatives his friends were obliged now to take charge of affairs. Reynolds and William Hawes took the initiative and at first planned a large public funeral with a list of distinguished pallbearers and burial in the Abbey. But they found his finances in so grave a state that they decided to spend what money was available for a monument to his memory. Accordingly, at 5:00 P.M. on Saturday, April 9, he was buried privately in the Temple Burying Ground;[11] and two years later the monument was erected in the Abbey. It had been executed by the sculptor Nollekens and bore an epitaph by Johnson which contained the fitting words: *"Nullum fere scribendi genus non tetigit, nullum quod tetigit non ornavit."*[12]

Because the funeral was private, no member of the Club attended. Only a few friends were present: Robert and John Day, Reynolds' nephew the Reverend Mr. Palmer, William Hawes, a man named Etherington, and Hugh Kelly, who is said to have shed tears of remorse over the grave. Shortly before the burial took place, Mary Horneck asked that the coffin be opened so that she could have a lock of Goldsmith's hair as a memento.

He left no will. His brother Maurice, as next of kin, arrived presently from Ireland, but he soon learned that his trip had been in vain; and early in June he left London, none the richer for his trouble. Edward Bott, Goldsmith's neighbor in the Temple, who had shared his "Shoemaker's Paradise" at Edgeware, was the principal creditor and was given such papers as survived. The furniture of his rooms and his substantial library were catalogued and sold at auction on July 11.[13]

Contemporary publications took account of Goldsmith's death. There were conventional obituaries as well as ecstatic poetic tributes, many of them published in book form and duly reviewed in the critical journals: *A Monody on the Death of Dr. Oliver Goldsmith, The Tears of Genius on the Death of Dr. Goldsmith, The Druid's Monument,* and the like. And there were, in two popular magazines, collections of anecdotes illustrating his enigmatic character. The *Westminster Magazine,* which had published "Humorous Anecdotes of Dr. Goldsmith" a year before, printed a second installment in the month of his death. In the following month the *Universal Magazine* contained, in addition to the essay "On Friendship," a collection of anecdotes by Samuel Glover, reprinted in the *Annual Register* for 1774. Meanwhile, in July, the publisher Swan brought out a *Life of Dr Goldsmith* by Glover, who had obviously worked it up from these anecdotes and who compensated for his lack of factual information by supplying generous excerpts from Goldsmith's works.

279

Because there had been a good deal of discussion of the circumstances surrounding Goldsmith's death, William Hawes prepared *An Account of the Late Dr. Goldsmith's Illness, So Far as Relates to the Exhibition of Dr. James's Powders: together with Remarks on the Use and Abuse of Powerful Medicines in the Beginning of Acute Disease,* describing in detail his handling of the case and maintaining that, although James's Fever Powders had on occasion done much good, they should not be taken without the advice of a physician. The packets of Fever Powders, he added, varied considerably in weight and must, therefore, vary in strength.

Francis Newbery, proprietor of the company which prepared the powders, could hardly ignore this challenge; and he promptly printed in the newspapers a denial of Hawes' claims, including with it statements from Goldsmith's servants, John Eyles and Mary Ginger, and his nurse, Sarah Smith, intimating that the powders given to Goldsmith were not genuine Dr. James's Fever Powders. Hawes countered with a "third" edition of his pamphlet, denying Newbery's charges and appending statements to validate his original claims and to defend his own character. Nor was that the end of the affair: two years after Goldsmith's death Hawes was still battling with the manufacturers of the Fever Powders.[14]

In the meantime Goldsmith's posthumous works had been appearing; for although he had little in the way of property, he left a good deal of copy, finished or unfinished. First to be published was *Retaliation,* the poem which had been inspired by Garrick's mock epitaph. It was incomplete (Goldsmith had stopped work on it in the middle of his epitaph for Reynolds), and it was evidently rushed through the press, being published by Kearsley on April 19, just fifteen days after Goldsmith's death.

It begins with an account of an imaginary dinner, to which each member of the club at St. James's Coffeehouse brings an appropriate course: Burke, "tongue, with a garnish of brains"; Garrick, a salad ("for in him we see / Oil, vinegar, sugar, and saltness agree"); Reynolds, lamb; and "Magnanimous Goldsmith, a gooseberry fool." Afterward, replete with food and wine, the poet muses:

> let me sit while I'm able,
> Till all my companions sink under the table;
> Then, with chaos and blunders encircling my head,
> Let me ponder, and tell what I think of the dead.

The most interesting of the epitaphs today are those which concern the most famous members of the club, barring Goldsmith himself: Burke, Garrick, and Reynolds. By good fortune they are, with the exception of the unfinished epitaph for Reynolds, the best in the poem—for the obvious reason that Goldsmith knew these men better than the others. The epitaph for Burke is mordant—probably because Goldsmith knew that Burke would not resent a touch of bitterness if it were well done—and the line "And to party gave up what was meant for mankind" has caused Burke's biographers a good deal of concern, though it should not if one takes into account Goldsmith's long-standing conviction that a literary man should eschew politics. The epitaph for Garrick is especially successful: Garrick, thanks perhaps to his recent loan of a hundred pounds, is "an abridgment of all that was pleasant in man"; yet "the man had his failings, a dupe to his art":

> On the stage he was natural, simple, affecting;
> 'Twas only that when he was off he was acting.

The poem abounds in such lines, which express tersely a whole facet of the subject's personality. Goldsmith's insight into human character and his profound sympathy are both called into play here, and by means of them he manages to make some trenchant bits of analysis which are presented so that they will not give offense: for each thrust of the rapier there is a compensating pat on the back. And the poem represents Goldsmith at his best as a versifier: he gives his anapaestic couplets a compressed, Pope-like sharpness and achieves striking antithetic effects by balancing line against line or half-line against half-line. Even the epitaphs for forgotten men like the attorney Hickey are still good reading:

> Here Hickey reclines, a most blunt pleasant creature,
> And slander itself must allow him good nature;
> He cherish'd his friend, and he relish'd a bumper;
> Yet one fault he had, and that one was a thumper.

Perhaps you may ask if the man was a miser?
I answer, No, no, for he always was wiser.
Too courteous, perhaps, or obligingly flat?
His very worst foe can't accuse him of that.
Perhaps he confided in men as they go,
And so was too foolishly honest? Ah, no!
Then what was his failing? come tell it, and burn ye:
He was, could he help it?—a special attorney!

The poem was eagerly read when it appeared: it went through four editions in two months and four more in the next three years. Moreover, it stimulated other writers: Garrick wrote two replies, Richard Cumberland another, and Dean Thomas Barnard a third. Caleb Whitefoord, a member of the club who had not been mentioned in the poem, seems to have prepared an epitaph for himself and passed it off as Goldsmith's work. Someone else wrote one for Johnson, and Hester Thrale wrote a whole series of similar sketches for the friends whose portraits hung in her "Streatham Gallery."[15] In short, Goldsmith's poem established a vogue of ironic lapidary verse; but none of the imitations reached the level of the original *Retaliation*.

On June 15, 1774, Goldsmith's *Grecian History* was brought out by several publishers acting, apparently, under the direction of William Griffin, with whom Goldsmith had contracted for the task. It was another compilation, similar in almost every respect to those which had preceded it, although it contained more anecdotal material and treated in considerable detail the structure of the Greek city-states. Because Goldsmith did not live to write a preface for the book, he did not acknowledge his sources except for occasional passing references to Plutarch, Thucydides, or Arrian. However, the review of the book in the *Critical* for November remarked that it followed the work of the historian Stanyan rather too closely. But potential buyers were not deterred by this matter, and, like Goldsmith's other histories, it became a minor classic in its time. It went through twenty editions in fifty years and was still being issued in new and expanded editions in the 1850's. Meanwhile someone had brought out an abridged edition of the book, and it had been translated into French, German, Italian, Spanish, and (a genuine accolade!) Greek.

On July 1 Goldsmith's most substantial literary legacy, the long-promised natural history, was published by Nourse in eight volumes as *An History of the Earth and Animated Nature*. In his Preface the author announced that his book was something entirely new in the modern languages. Pliny and other ancients had anticipated him, he admitted; in fact he had originally intended to translate Pliny, but when Buffon's *Histoire Naturelle* was published, he realized that "the best imitation of the ancients was to write from our own feelings and to imitate nature." He added that he was seeking to combine what seemed to him the two functions of natural history: "First, that of discovering, ascertaining, and naming all the various productions of nature. Secondly, that of describing the properties, manners, and relations, which they bear to us, and to each other." And later: "But my chief ambition is to drag up the obscure and gloomy learning of the cell to open inspection; to strip it from its garb of austerity, and to shew the beauties of that form, which only the industrious and the inquisitive have been hitherto permitted to approach." In other words, Goldsmith wanted to share with others his curiosity about nature and his interest in it. "The mere uninformed spectator," he said, "passes on in gloomy solitude, but the naturalist, in every plant, in every insect, and every pebble, finds something to entertain his curiosity, and to excite his speculation."

He acknowledged that he was indebted to Buffon for most of his material about quadrupeds. But he pointed out that he had "added, retrenched, and altered" what he found and had developed a system from "the great and obvious distinctions that [Nature] herself seems to have made"—that is, he had organized his discussion of quadrupeds under such headings as "animals of the cat kind," "animals of the sheep kind," and the like. Moreover, when he went on to treat animals other than quadrupeds, he had no guide. "As I would affect neither modesty nor confidence," he wrote in his Preface, "it will be sufficient to say, that my reading upon this part of the subject has been very extensive; and that I have taxed my scanty circumstances in procuring books, which are on this subject, of all others, the most expensive."

As usual, though, his reading was not as extensive as he would have his readers believe. Miss Winifred Lynskey has proved that he drew liberally on secondary sources: he referred glibly to the work of such eminent naturalists as Brisson, Réaumur, and Swammerdam, but he relied for his information on popularizers of science like Willughby, Pluche, Derham, and Brookes (for whose *System of Natural History* he had written the prefaces back in 1763).[16] Yet as Miss Lynskey observes, Goldsmith could, when necessary, digest admirably a difficult technical work, as when he summarized Abraham Trembley's definitive two-volume study of the polypus in a single chapter.

And although he depended on other writers for his basic facts, his development was his own. He had an intense curiosity about nature as well as man, and his medical studies and his travels had enabled him to gratify it and to gather a store of observations which now proved useful. He had managed to see a surprising number of oddities: an ocelot, a genetto, East Indian oysters two feet across, albino Negroes, a horse that ate oysters, a raven that could sing the Black Joke, a parrot that could recite the Ninth Commandment, and a host of others. He could not afford to surround himself with animals, as Buffon had done, but he obviously went out of his way to visit the zoo at the Tower of London, the Queen's Menagerie at Buckingham Gate, and whatever exhibitions of strange creatures might be held in London. He had read widely in travel books too, and he had the inquisitiveness to seek out people whose information or experience could supplement his own: he had questioned painters about human physiognomy, had asked the carpenter of Commodore Byron's famous voyage about a race of giants which he had reportedly seen; he had talked to dwarfs at fairs, to a lip-reader, to the lion-keeper at the Tower; and when Reynolds' little niece, later Mrs. Gwatkin, told him that she had heard that her brother and sister had dropped water on her pet goldfinch from a great height and that it had died of fright and turned black, he urged her to get the particulars of the accident so that he could refer to it in his book.[17] The scraps of information which he gathered from such investigations gave his book a distinct immediacy and made it very definitely his own.

284

To be sure, errors crept in. Some of his theories—that of racial differentiation, for example—were due to the misconceptions of his era; but others were the result of his own carelessness or ignorance. Johnson is said to have remarked, when told that Goldsmith was writing a natural history: "Goldsmith, Sir, will give us a very fine book upon the subject; but if he can distinguish a cow from a horse, that, I believe, may be the extent of his knowledge of natural history."[18] And as if to prove the point, Goldsmith solemnly stated in his book that cows lose their horns at the end of three years and then grow new and permanent ones.[19] Yet Johnson himself had said at General Oglethorpe's house that it would be impossible for Goldsmith to verify all the details he presented, and Burke observed, in his review of the book in the *Annual Register* for 1774, that it would be received "with partiality and indulgence."

And rightly so; for with all its flaws, the book contained an astonishing amount of information presented in a remarkably readable fashion. Johnson had prophesied that it would be as entertaining as a Persian tale, and so it was. Goldsmith stated in his Preface that he would not attempt to imitate "the warmth of [Buffon's] style" or "the brilliancy of his imagination"; but he did not need to apologize for his own presentation. By rearranging Buffon's material and discussing related animals, beginning with the most commonly known of the species, he achieved not only a clearer organization but also a coherence and smoothness lacking in Buffon. And always he did his best to make his reader's task as agreeable as possible: he announced from time to time that he would omit certain details in order to avoid tediousness (or when he felt that he must include a good deal of detail, he apologized for doing so); he deliberately inserted an anecdote now and again "to enliven a heavy chapter"; he worked in humorous comments if he thought they would brighten his text; and he included a surprising number of references to nonscientific literature—Aristophanes, Cicero, Montaigne, Shakespeare, Milton, Pope, Fielding, among others—in order to enrich his descriptions. Yet such devices never interfere with the clarity of his presentation; rather, they enhance it.

Moreover, because of his frequent use of the first person, his accounts of his own experiences, and his allusions to his tastes and opinions,[20] his personality gradually emerges and wins the reader's interest and sympathy. It is a patient, kindly teacher who is speaking—a well-read, well-traveled bachelor (for he reveals that fact too), a lover of nature (especially of birds and dogs; for worms and caterpillars he had a distinct aversion) with a whole-hearted enthusiasm for his subject and a sincere desire to make the reader share that enthusiasm. He is a profoundly sympathetic person too—sympathetic not only with his reader but with mankind and animals—especially the poor and oppressed among men and the hunted among animals.[21] Moreover, he is a devout Christian, with a strong conviction that Providence has ordained all for the best,[22] and that men—especially Englishmen, who are singularly blessed—should accept their lot contentedly.

Toward the end of the book there is a noticeable falling-off of Goldsmith's interest and, consequently, of the reader's. The style seems more hurried, descriptions are brief and businesslike, and comparison with Goldsmith's sources reveals that he is following them more closely.[23] The reason for the change is obvious: as his health failed and his worries increased, he had little energy and enthusiasm to spare to his task. And he was probably conscious of the change, for he told Joseph Cradock: "I never took more pains than in the first volume of my 'Natural History'; surely that was good, and I was handsomely repaid for the whole."[24] Nourse, the publisher, must have been handsomely repaid too, for the book was a striking success despite its cost of two pounds, eight shillings, per set. Eventually it went through twenty-two editions, some corrected and expanded, the last appearing in 1876.

On July 2, the day after *Animated Nature* was published, Kearsley issued Goldsmith's abridgment of his *History of England;* on the 28th Dodsley published the revised edition of *Polite Learning.* This was the last of his literary legacies for the time being, but in 1775 Griffin brought out a translation of Scarron's *Roman Comique* which was announced as Goldsmith's work, "a few sheets excepted," although actually he seems to have revised seven chapters of an earlier translation and then copied almost verbatim the rest of the translation, as far as he went.[25] None of these three volumes adds to his achievement as a writer, but both the *History of England Abridged* and the early chapters of the translation reveal once again his extraordinary powers of selection and expression. In the abridgment he chooses the essential passages judiciously and fuses them by means of effective bits of transition; in the *Comic Romance* he excises Scarron's less successful attempts at humor, yet develops the suspense and keeps his translation always sprightly and colloquial. Goldsmith's unerring artistic sense colored even the most workaday jobs.

Meanwhile interest in his earlier works had not waned. In 1774 Davies published his biographies of Parnell and Bolingbroke in a volume of *Miscellaneous and Fugitive Pieces,* and in 1775 Griffin brought out two collections of his writing: *Select Poems* and *Miscellaneous Works.* Then in 1776 Kearsley published "The Haunch of Venison," the poetical epistle to Lord Clare which had never before been printed, and Carnan and Newbery issued *A Survey of Experimental Philosophy,* which, from hints in the prefatory Advertisement and from the unevenness of tone throughout, seems to have been the "Natural Philosophy" for which John Newbery had paid Goldsmith sixty-three pounds back in 1766. It had probably lain half-printed in the publishers' shop for some years, and they seem to have released it with misgivings: shortly after Goldsmith's death it was announced for publication on May 1, 1774, but it was delayed for two years.

It was, of course, another compilation, by far the least successful that Goldsmith ever wrote. The book is strangely inconsistent: at bottom a systematic exposition of the principles of physics, it varies from simple presentation of facts, clarified by homely illustrations or elementary experiments, to more complicated discussions, with frequent references to the foremost authorities; yet occasionally the reader encounters a lively passage written in brisk style and heightened by humor and anecdotes in the manner of *Animated Nature.* The explanation for the shifts of tone is, undoubtedly, that the book was "compiled" from many sources, written over a long period of time, and never completely revised.[26]

In 1777 a group of Dublin booksellers combined to issue a volume of *Poems and Plays by Oliver Goldsmith* with a prefatory biography by Edmond Malone based on Glover's earlier work. Then in 1780 the firm of Newbery and Johnson issued another *Poems and Plays,* and several London publishers brought out a two-volume *Poetical and Dramatic Works,* both with Malone's short biography as preface. But still nothing had been heard of the "official" biography which Thomas Percy had promised to write. As early as March 28, 1775, he had shown Boswell the materials which he had gathered for his task,[27] but five years had passed without a hint that the biography itself or the edition of Goldsmith's works which it was to preface was approaching publication.

Actually, Percy had resigned the task to Johnson sometime before February, 1777, but Johnson failed to write the biography because the publisher Carnan had refused to release the rights to *She Stoops to Conquer* which he held under the terms of a law passed shortly after Goldsmith's death. Johnson postponed writing the biography until the play would be available for inclusion in the proposed edition of Goldsmith's works.[28] But before that time arrived, he himself died.

Scholars have told and retold the story of the accidents and disputes which combined to delay publication of Percy's Memoir of Goldsmith until 1801.[29] Meanwhile Goldsmith had been the subject of more anecdotes and, even worse, had been forced to play his old role of Dr. Minor in three books about Johnson.

Biographers of Goldsmith have inveighed often enough against Hester Thrale Piozzi, Sir John Hawkins, and James Boswell for their interpretations of Goldsmith. To be sure, there was probably, as Sir Walter Scott believed, rivalry among Johnson's satellites during his lifetime, and some of it may have colored their treatment of Goldsmith. Yet they were not deliberately malicious people; or even if they had been, they had little to gain by maligning Goldsmith ten years or more after his death. Mrs. Piozzi was discerning enough to respect his talents, but his character baffled her: it was anomalous. Hawkins, less perceptive, believed implicitly that Goldsmith was "an idiot in the affairs of

288

the world" and did not scruple to say so. Boswell knew him better and undoubtedly understood him better than either of the others; his Journal and letters show that he had been touched by Goldsmith's contagious good nature and had learned eventually that the man deserved more sympathy than censure. Yet by the time he wrote his *Life of Johnson* he had read or heard countless tales of Goldsmith's absurdity—his envy of the Horneck girls and of the fantoccini, for example—and when it came time to introduce him to the scene, he presented a sketch of his character which repeated the charges generally raised against him. Yet the careful reader of the *Life* will discover, as he proceeds, that Boswell's attitude becomes less disapproving. He records many of Goldsmith's "good things"; he even defends him at times—by saying, for example, that he was not more envious than other men, but only talked about it more—or that reports of his foolishness had been greatly exaggerated. Yet his primary purpose of displaying the character of Johnson meant inevitably that Goldsmith would often appear merely as a foil.

The result was that, long before 1801, Goldsmith's character had been fixed in the minds of the reading public: he was an inspired idiot, the great enigma of contemporary literature. Percy did his solemn best in his Memoir to reinstate Goldsmith's character, but it was too late. Besides, Samuel Rose, the "interpolator" employed by the publishers after the manuscript left Percy's hands, worked into the text some material which confirmed the popular estimate of Goldsmith's character.

But of course he was no idiot. Neither was he the martyred saint that apologetic biographers have sometimes tried to make him. The true interpretation of his character lies somewhere between the two extremes—just where, it is difficult to decide after the passage of nearly two centuries. From the dozens of anecdotes that survive, one could prove almost anything about Goldsmith. But many of those anecdotes are of dubious authenticity. Take, for example, the "turn 'em green" story. According to it, Goldsmith heard someone say of some yellow peas served at Reynolds' house that they ought to be sent out to Hammersmith. When he asked why, the reply came: "Because that's the way to Turnham

Green." Soon afterward Goldsmith found an opportunity to use the story; but when time came for the punch line, he said, "Because that's the way to make 'em green." Then, correcting himself: "I mean that's the road to Turnham Green."[30]

Surely this story is questionable. Goldsmith was never slow-witted! Besides, its pattern is too familiar; accounts of the man who attempts to tell a tale and misses its point have been told and retold, before Goldsmith's time and since. When applied to a well-known figure—a "notable man"—they are likely to seem more credible and more interesting. Goldsmith had gradually become so legendary a figure that anyone could heighten the effectiveness of a tall story by telling it of him. He was credited with many books which he did not write, and he doubtless had attributed to him many remarks which he never made.

Even more incredible is a story told by Laetitia Hawkins, daughter of Sir John. She said that Goldsmith saw a portrait at a country inn, suspected that it was an Old Master, told the owner that he would like to have it because it resembled his aunt Salisbury, bought it for a pittance—and found that it was an original Vandyke worth many times what he had paid for it.[31] This tale is unacceptable on any ground. Not only is it inconsistent with what is known of Goldsmith's character, but it is not borne out by any record of discoveries or sales of Vandykes. To give Miss Hawkins the benefit of the doubt, one may assume that she merely repeated what she had been told. She was one of several late eighteenth century purveyors of anecdotes or reminiscences—Samuel Glover, Richard Cumberland, Frances Reynolds, Samuel Foote, "Conversation" Cooke, and perhaps even Laetitia's father and Hester Thrale Piozzi were others—who were more interested in telling an effective story (and perhaps incidentally suggesting their intimacy with the great) than in checking the accuracy of their information.

Thus in any final estimate of Goldsmith's character one must depend largely on what Johnson, Reynolds, Boswell, Tom Davies, and James Northcote said about him and what can be inferred from his letters and his published writings. From such testimony one can learn that he was no saint—that, in fac., his character had serious flaws. He was wanting in certain elementary scruples: he gambled recklessly, borrowed more than he could ever repay, envied other successful writers, perhaps drank more than was good for him, and probably was no chaster than most gentlemen of his era. Moreover, he was in some ways dishonest: he lied to his relatives in order to achieve his ends when he was a young man, and he stole countless words, sentences, even paragraphs, from other writers later in life.

Furthermore, there is no gainsaying the charge of absurdity brought against him. He lent himself easily to such interpretation: in fact he reveled in absurdity and was perfectly willing to play the fool as long as he felt that his companions would be amused. But all his absurdity was not deliberate. Again and again his nonsense missed fire. He was sensitive enough to perceive the failure and proud enough to try to conceal his embarrassment— usually by a fumbling attempt which ended in even greater absurdity.

It was, indeed, a vicious circle. The more ineffectual he felt, the harder he tried to conceal his mortification—to compensate for the sense of inadequacy which had haunted him through most of his life. His ugliness as a child, his humiliation at Trinity College, his inability to settle himself in a profession, his estrangement from his mother—all bred in him a basic insecurity, for which he tried to compensate by acts of ridiculous brashness. His years of footloose wandering brought a respite from these pressures; but once he settled in London, his clownish appearance, his brogue, his failure as a physician, his years as a poor hack, and his association with more distinguished men only intensified his insecurity—and his brashness. Eventually he emerged as a "man of genius," but the emergence was too sudden to enable him to take it gracefully. And even at the height of his success he enjoyed only a fleeting satisfaction. "Scurvy circumstances" forced him to make "compilations" which he inwardly disdained; he published his one novel only with apologies; his two plays brought weeks of painful anxiety before they reached the stage. Only his two major poems, composed with effort, brought him any lasting sense of accomplishment; and in the second he wistfully bade farewell to poetry, the source of all his bliss and all his woe.

He could feel no enduring satisfaction with his essays, his novel, his plays, or his humorous verse because they were "light reading"; and regardless of how much they fulfilled his desire to make men laugh, he knew that his contemporaries looked on them as trifles. Had he been born fifty years later, he would have felt no such compulsion to be a "serious" writer, no such envy as he felt for Johnson's success in an area which was alien to his own powers. It was only later that a man of quite different standards from those of Goldsmith's time perceived that he was not inferior to Johnson, but only different from him. "Goldsmith was a fool to Dr. Johnson in argument; that is, in assigning the specific grounds of his opinions," wrote William Hazlitt in his essay "On Genius and Common Sense"; "Dr. Johnson was a fool to Goldsmith in the fine tact, the airy, intuitive faculty with which he skimmed the surfaces of things, and unconsciously formed his opinions."

Unfortunately there was no one in Goldsmith's lifetime to provide this sort of reassurance. When he attempted to supply it himself, he only seemed more absurd. He was, indeed, a pathetically lonely man. Although he constantly sought company and distraction, he lived his adult life by and within himself. Samuel Glover said that he used to leave the gay meetings of the Wednesday Club and return to his rooms to brood alone. He never found a wife who would supply the sort of consolation and reassurance which he so sorely needed; for there too his lack of self-confidence stood in his way. Again the vicious circle: he lacked the assurance to ask a woman whom he respected to share the fortunes of one whom he inwardly condemned.

It was all a part of the pattern. He was keenly aware of his faults, yet constitutionally unable to correct them. He wrote essays about the folly of gambling and improvidence, yet he continued to gamble, to spend, and to give beyond all reason. He knew that his allegedly absurd behavior brought public mockery from his foes, and he was sensitive enough to discern that it met with derision from his friends. Yet his reaction was to behave more absurdly.

At last his follies overwhelmed him. He was frightened by his mounting debts, mortified by the humiliation which he suffered before and after the production of *She Stoops to Conquer,* harried by years of exhausting work as a writer, hounded by a sense of failure and a corroding envy of others' success. Inevitably his constitution broke down, and he lacked the will to fight his way back to good health. The cause of his death was not so much Dr. James's Fever Powders or William Hawes' negligence as his own mental distress—"uneasiness of mind," as Johnson phrased it. When Dr. Turton asked him if his mind was at ease, he replied, understandably: "No, it is not."

"Death, I really believe," wrote Tom Davies afterward, "was welcome to a man of his great sensibility."[32]

Yet he triumphed at last. He triumphed as a human being because eventually his closest friends came to realize that, with all his faults and his absurdity, he was "a very great man." Though he envied those more successful than himself, he was inordinately generous to those less fortunate. Though he might lie and flatter on occasion to gain his ends, he had a certain fundamental integrity which made him refuse to write for any party or to dedicate a poem or play to anyone whom he did not love and respect. And through all his absurdity shone a warm and abiding friendliness for others, a longing to please them. He was indeed a good-natured man.

He triumphed even more as a writer. Reynolds believed that "Dr. Goldsmith was, in the truest as the most common sense of the word, a man of genius. But if we take the popular opinion of genius—that it is a gift, or supernatural power, entirely distinct from wisdom, knowledge, learning, and judgment, and that all these acquisitions contribute to destroy, rather than increase, the operations of genius—the Doctor must be acknowledged to have in this sense greater claim to the name of genius than any other man whatever."[33] But this is misleading; for surely Goldsmith's work reveals wisdom and judgment, if not knowledge and learning.

293

To be sure, he was not a profound thinker; he did not change men's minds. Indeed his friends insisted that he knew nothing. Even Reynolds declared that "Goldsmith's mind was entirely unfurnished. When he was engaged in a work, he had all his knowledge to find, which when he found, he knew how to use, but forgot it immediately after he had used it."[34] In other words, he lacked the sort of retentive memory which made Johnson's conversation so rich and varied. Yet anyone who considers the range of Goldsmith's subject matter must realize that he knew where to find information when he wanted it. Often he had to go no farther than the extensive library that he had gathered in his rooms in the Temple and that contained not only the sort of books he needed for his compilations but a remarkable selection of the works of standard authors, ancient and modern. If he had read only one-tenth of the volumes in the library, he must have absorbed a respectable knowledge of the best that had been known and thought in the world. Granted, he did not always have his information at his fingertips; or if he did, his lack of self-assurance prevented his making the most of it. But in sober truth he could have retorted to his critics that he had forgotten more than most men ever learn; or that, though he lacked facts, he had gained from his studies and observation what was far more important: an understanding of mankind.

When Johnson remarked at Boswell's dinner in 1769 that Dryden's poetry displayed a profundity lacking in Pope's, Goldsmith observed that Pope's character of Addison in "The Epistle to Dr. Arbuthnot" showed a deep knowledge of the human heart. Johnson might well have countered, "But, Sir, that is not profundity"; and of course he would have been right. But Goldsmith would have been equally right if he had replied that, whatever it was, it was just as admirable a quality as profundity. And certainly his own writing reveals it in a high degree: the knowledge of humanity disclosed in *The Citizen of the World, The Vicar of Wakefield,* and *Retaliation* proves beyond question that he had keen powers of penetration, if not profundity.

For what his mind wanted in depth, it made up in sharpness and breadth. "He felt with great exactness, far above what words can teach," Reynolds said, "the propriety in composition, how one sentiment breeds another in the mind, preferring this as naturally to grow out of the preceding and rejecting another, though more brilliant, as breaking the chain of ideas. In short, he felt by a kind of instinct or intuition all those nice discriminations which to grosser minds appear to have no difference."[35] Consider the neat coherence of his prose works, the smooth progression of his two major poems. Consider too the "nice discriminations" displayed in his choice of metaphors to express his thoughts in both verse and prose—particularly noticeable in the homely descriptions of *The Deserted Village* or the shrewd characterization of *Retaliation*. He had, indeed, that faculty for detecting relationships which William James claimed was the distinguishing characteristic of genius.

The clarity and ease of his style are further evidence of his sharpness of mind. "No man took less pains," said Tom Davies, "and yet produced so powerful an effect."[36] And his surviving manuscripts suggest that he must have had an extraordinary ability to say at once what he wanted to say and to say it well. So too do his translations, his compilations, and his abridgments, written at top speed, but always clear and finished. To his brother Henry he wrote: "Just sit down as I do, and write forward 'till you have filld all your paper, it requires no thought, at least if I may judge from the ease with which my own sentiments rise when they are addressed to you."[37] In the Preface to *Animated Nature* he remarked that "the art of writing . . . is but another name for good sense." But to write like Goldsmith, a man must have more than just good sense; he must have, as Goldsmith did, a remarkably quick, sharp mind.

Even the geniality of his style, his ability to impart to his writing the friendliness and charm which characterize it, reveals a certain sharpness. There have been multitudes of men of good will who have lacked the peculiar powers of intelligence to enable them to convey their good will as Goldsmith did. The principle which he formulated in *Polite Learning*—to please all men— is implicit in all his work, even his compilations. His success in achieving his goal is reflected in Thackeray's tribute to him as "the most beloved of English writers—what a title that is for a man!" But that success depended not merely on an accidental knack for expressing himself; it demanded an alert and sensitive intelligence. He had to understand men's minds, to know what would delight them, and to discern how to impart that delight. One of his favorite instruments was irony, and that, too, demands a subtle, flexible mind.

As for the breadth of his intelligence, that is reflected in the independence of his thinking. For while he was no iconoclast, his attitudes were his own, and his achievements were not the conventional achievements of his period. His mind was eclectic, choosing an idea or a principle because it somehow seemed right to him. And although he never broke entirely with the standards of his time, he was in many respects original. His criticism, his novel, and his plays were not at all in the main stream of eighteenth century literature. He believed that writing should be an end in itself rather than a means to political preferment. He rejected the notion that his contemporaries should imitate the ancients or be judged by their standards. He insisted that writers should strive for simplicity, should speak to all men. He was interested in the affairs of simple, unsophisticated people, interested in them as individuals, not as a species, interested in their emotions, interested even in his own emotions and not afraid to reveal them. He wanted to improve the minds and morals of men, but he wanted more to touch their hearts, to gladden them, to make them laugh. And though never wholly Romantic in theory, he was often so in practice. If he had had full confidence in his convictions and had had the leisure to develop them, he might well have been a leader in the Romantic Revival in English literature.

The breadth of his mind is reflected again in the scope of his achievements. It took a broad as well as a penetrating mind to encompass, in a fifteen-year period, so many kinds of writing and to turn out so many volumes on so high a level. He had an extraordinary ability to approach a new area of subject matter or a new genre of writing and to master its essentials at once. Granted that he had his faults: he was often careless, inconsistent, and unprincipled in his writing as in his life. Granted, too, that he wrote no one book which belongs in the very first rank of literature. But though not one of the finest of poets or essayists, of novelists or dramatists, he is one of the ablest of writers; and his cumulative achievement in criticism, the essay, biography, history, the novel, poetry, and drama entitles him to be honored as the most versatile genius of all English literature.

Notes

CHAPTER I: ANOMALY

1. Davies, II, 111. J. W. M. Gibbs points out (*Works,* I, 63) that the phrase appears in none of Walpole's published work. In his Portrait of Goldsmith written in 1776 Reynolds implies that the phrase "idiot inspired" was then commonly applied to Goldsmith. (See *Portraits,* p. 45.)

2. The story is reprinted in Prior, II, 484-5, and Dobson, pp. 194-5, from Boswell's *Life of Johnson,* ed. J. W. Croker, London, 1860, p. 141.

3. Donald C. Bryant, *Edmund Burke and His Literary Friends,* Washington University Studies, St. Louis, 1939, p. 92.

4. See Prior, II, 290-1 and 379. Cf. Stephen Gwynn, *Memorials of an Eighteenth Century Painter*, London, 1898, p. 91, for the sentence which Northcote omitted from his published account of the incident.

5. *Thraliana*, I, 83.

6. *Life of Johnson*, III, 311. Mrs. Thrale (*Thraliana*, I, 84) tells the same story, but applies it to Archbishop Cornwallis rather than Lord Camden.

7. *Harper's Magazine*, CXLIV (1921-2), 121-2.

8. *Memoirs of Lady Morgan*, ed. W. H. Dixon, London, 1862, quoted in Constantia Maxwell, *Dublin under the Georges*, London, 1936, pp. 94-5.

9. Forster, II, 364 n.

10. *European Magazine*, XXIV (1793), 261-2.

11. *New Essays*, p. 51.

12. All quotations from Reynolds in this chapter are drawn from his Portrait of Goldsmith, *Portraits*, pp. 44-59. This volume, copyrighted in 1952 by Yale University, is quoted by special arrangement with the publisher, McGraw-Hill Book Company, Inc.

13. *Thraliana*, I, 81, and *Life of Johnson*, IV, 174-5.

14. Forster (II, 348 n.) assembles the best-known versions of the fantoccini story. There are certain inconsistencies in the accounts: Boswell says that Goldsmith went with Burke to see the performance, and Arthur Murphy, that Johnson told it to him and that Reynolds and Johnson were with Goldsmith. I have, however, traced the story to the letter by "Pasquin" in the *London Packet* of March 29, 1773. Since this letter antedates any of the other versions of the story, and since it appears in a scurrilous attack on Goldsmith probably written by his bitterest enemy, William Kenrick, I am inclined to question its validity.

15. Davies, II, 121 n.

16. Hawkins, p. 418.

17. *European Magazine*, XXIV, 261.

18. *Portraits*, pp. 51-2.

19. *Thraliana*, I, 83.

20. Prior, II, 127-8.

21. *Works*, II, 51.

22. Hester Thrale claimed that Goldsmith was also jealous of Arthur Murphy, but the evidence which she presents hardly proves her point: "Murphy was too fond of telling Stories of Foote, & Dr. Goldsmith who was no match at all for him in general Conversation could only watch that Propensity, & mark [mock?] it. he stood behind my Chair one Afternoon, and as fast as Atty came out with his Stories, he kept whispering me— Story the first, and by & by Story the 2d he went on to the 4th I remember, & then I said, now have done—Doctor, or I swear I'll tell: he had done in a Moment, for he both fear'd Mr. Murphy's Powers, & envy'd his elegance of Dress & Behaviour:—What now you like Mr. Murphy says he to me, because he has that *Hat* I suppose." (*Thraliana*, I, 153.)

23. *Manuscripts and Correspondence of James, First Earl of Charlemont*, Historical MSS. Commission, London, 1891-4, I, 317.

24. *Life of Johnson*, II, 260. Cf. Davies, II, 121: "Goldsmith was so sincere a man, that he could not conceal what was uppermost in his mind: so far from desiring to appear in the eye of the world to the best advantage, he took more pains to be esteemed worse than he was, than others do to appear better than they are. His envy was so childish, and so absurd, that it was easily pardoned, for every body laughed at it; and no man was ever very mischievous whose errours excited mirth."

25. *Thraliana*, I, 174.

26. See *Horace Walpole's Correspondence with William Mason*, ed. W. S. Lewis, Grover Cronin, Jr., and Charles H. Bennett, New Haven, 1955, I, 277.

27. *Life of Johnson*, III, 252-3.

28. *Ibid.*, V (Hebrides), 97.

29. See discussion below, pp. 228.

30. *Life of Johnson*, I, 412.

31. *Whitefoord Papers*, ed. W. A. S. Hewins, Oxford, 1898, p. 223.

32. Hawkins, p. 418.

33. In the proof-sheets of his *Life of Johnson* Boswell inserted the words, "His dress [was] unsuitably gawdy and without taste," but later struck them out. (See Chauncey B. Tinker, *Young Boswell*, Boston, 1922, p. 232.)

34. *Letters*, p. 86.

35. Cradock, IV, 283.

36. "Recollections of Dr. Johnson by Miss Reynolds," *Johnsonian Miscellanies*, ed. G. B. Hill, Oxford, 1897, II, 268.

37. *Ibid.*, p. 269.

38. *Memoirs of Percival Stockdale*, London, 1809, II, 136-7.

39. Prior, II, 359-60.

40. See below, pp. 241-2.

CHAPTER II: YOUNG MAN IN A MAZE

1. Prior, I, 101. Except when otherwise specified, all biographical information in this chapter is derived from Prior, I, 1-103; from Goldsmith's own account of his life as dictated to Thomas Percy and reprinted in Balderston, pp. 12-6; and from Mrs. Hodson's Narrative of Goldsmith's Early Life reprinted in *Letters*, pp. 162-77. In this chapter and elsewhere I have consulted Percy's Memoir of Goldsmith and considered the sources of his information as recorded in Balderston; however, Prior corrected and amplified so much of the material in the Memoir that I have not attempted to point out where they differ.

2. According to a note furnished to the late R. W. Seitz by T. U. Sadleir, Ulster King of Arms, and preserved among Seitz's papers in the Yale University Library, Catherine Crofton Goldsmith was a second cousin of Sir Edward Crofton of Mote, who was created a baronet at the Restoration, and her father was the fifth surviving son of John Crofton of Lisdorne, County Roscommon, Member of Parliament for Sligo in 1632, who was buried in Elphin Cathedral in 1639. John Crofton's wife was Sarah, eldest daughter of Richard Maypowder of Killinboy, County Roscommon.

3. According to Prior, Charles Goldsmith's great-grandfather, John Goldsmith, Rector of Borrishoule (or Brashowle), County Mayo, barely escaped with his life in the Rebellion of 1641, thanks to his friendship with the Roman Catholic Viscount Bourke, who had him called away from a group of Protestants about to be slain. His son, who also bore the name John, apparently served as Fellow of Trinity College, Dublin, and Rector of Newtown, County Meath. In an unpublished article written by R. W. Seitz and preserved among his papers in the Yale University Library, Seitz identifies the elder John Goldsmith with Juan Romeiro (or Romero), the Spaniard who emigrated to England, married a Miss Goldsmith, and adopted her surname and religion. (See Balderston, p. 13.) Seitz's article has corrected or clarified for me a few minor details about the life of Charles Goldsmith left undetermined in earlier biographies.

4. In the note referred to above, note 2, T. U. Sadleir reports that the Reverend Oliver Jones was a grandson of Oliver Jones, Member of Parliament for Athlone and Chief Justice, who was a nephew of Brian Jones of Headford (or Lisnagan) Castle, County Leitrim, and Burnell's Court, Dublin, Auditor of War and Member of Parliament for Baltimore, 1639-49, and cousin of Lieutenant General Michael Jones, Cromwell's Governor of Dublin and second in command in Ireland during the Commonwealth. Evidently the Goldsmiths' family connections were more distinguished than has been supposed.

5. The dates, copied from a page of the Goldsmith family Bible since lost, are recorded in Prior, I, 14-5. Unfortunately the years of Henry's, Jane's, and Oliver's birth were torn away. Both Henry and Jane were listed as born on February 9 and may have been twins.

6. I have nothing to add to the vexed subject of exactly when Goldsmith was born. Miss Balderston (*TLS*, March 7, 1929, pp. 185-6) argued for 1730; Professor Crane (*PQ*, IX [1930], 190-1) for 1729 or 1730 (cf. Miss Balderston's reply in *PQ*, X [1931], 201-2); Professor Friedman (*N&Q*, CXCVI [1951], 388-9) for 1730 or 1731. All in all, 1730 seems to be the best compromise.

7. The Goldsmith family Bible records that Goldsmith was born at Pallas, but members of the Jones family and others insisted that he was born at his grandmother

Jones's house near Elphin. They claim that Ann Goldsmith either went to Elphin to be more comfortable during her confinement or was prematurely confined while visiting there. (See, for example, J. J. Kelly, *The Early Haunts of Oliver Goldsmith*, Dublin, 1905, pp. 17-24.)

8. As stated above, note 4, the name Oliver was also borne by Ann Goldsmith's great-grandfather. Goldsmith told Percy that he had been named after Oliver Cromwell and that his mother's family was "allied" to the Cromwells. (See Balderston, p. 13.) Although it is unlikely that he was named for Cromwell, he had some justification, as the information in note 4 reveals, for claiming that the Joneses were "allied" to the Cromwells. Goldsmith also told Percy that he was related to General Wolfe. As Prior (I, 6) points out, Wolfe's mother's maiden name was Goldsmith.

9. Prior (I, 19) reports that the house was a two-story building approximately sixty-eight feet by twenty-four feet in area.

10. Prior (I, 14-5) reprints from the Goldsmith family Bible the following record of the birth dates of the three younger sons of Charles and Ann Goldsmith:
"Maurice Goldsmith was born at Lissoy in the county Westmeath the seventh of July 1736
Charles Goldsmith junr born at Lishoy Augt 16th 1737
John Goldsmith born at Lishoy the 23d of [illegible] 1740."

11. See *Letters*, pp. 29-30, and *Works*, II, 334.

12. Prior, I, 23.

13. *Letters*, pp. 163-4.

14. Contarine is said to have been the grandson of an Italian monk named Contarini, who fell in love with a nun and eloped with her to France, where she died. Later he settled in England and married a Miss Chaloner, niece of the Provost of Trinity College, Dublin. Through her he was converted to Protestantism, took Orders in the Church of Ireland, and was given a living in or near Elphin.

15. Prior (I, 36-40) speculates that Goldsmith's early verse may have been influenced by the work of Turlogh O'Carolan (or Carolan), a friend of Thomas Contarine's correspondent Charles O'Conor, and that of Lawrence Whyte, both of whom lived near Edgeworthstown—or at least that his interest in verse may have been intensified by their work. But his references to Theseus and Aesop in the only surviving fragments of his early verse suggest that he was more influenced by neo-classical than by native Irish poetry.

16. See *Letters*, pp. 167-8.

17. Quoted in Constantia Maxwell's *Dublin under the Georges*, p. 17. I have drawn most of my information about eighteenth century Dublin from this volume.

18. *Works*, IV, 158.

19. Quoted in John William Stubbs' *The History of the University of Dublin*, Dublin and London, 1889, pp. 203-4.

20. John Winstanley, etc., *Poems*, Dublin, 1742, pp. 86-7. The poem is quoted in part in Constantia Maxwell's *History of Trinity College, Dublin, 1591-1892*, Dublin, 1946, p. 138. I have taken most of my information about Trinity College from this book and the volume by Stubbs referred to in note 19, above. For specific information about Goldsmith's college record I am indebted to Miss Helen Watson of the Assistant Registrar's Office of the College.

21. *Works*, III, 526. In the same passage Goldsmith remarks: "The sons of our nobility are permitted to enjoy greater liberties in our universities than those of private men. I should blush to ask the men of learning and virtue who preside in our seminaries, the reason of such a prejudicial distinction. Our youth should there be inspired with a love of philosophy; and the first maxim among philosophers is,—that Merit only makes distinction."

22. *Letters*, p. 59.

23. Burke and Goldsmith entered Trinity College in successive years—Burke in April, 1744, and Goldsmith in June, 1745. Since no correspondence between the two men is known to have survived, we cannot be sure how well acquainted they were while they were undergraduates. In later years Johnson said: "Goldsmith was a plant that flowered late. There appeared nothing remarkable about him when he was young; though when he had got high in fame, one of his friends [probably Burke] began to recollect something of his being distinguished at College. Goldsmith in the same manner

recollected more of that friend's early years, as he grew a greater man" (*Life of Johnson*, III, 167-8).

24. Alice C. C. Gaussen, *Percy: Prelate and Poet*, London, 1908, p. 212.

25. Quoted in Thomas Campbell's *A Philosophical Survey of the South of Ireland*, London, 1777, p. 11.

26. See Arthur P. I. Samuels, *The Early Life, Correspondence, and Writings of the Rt. Hon. Edmund Burke, LL.D.*, Cambridge, 1923, p. 28. Since the curriculum for the first year as outlined in Stubbs, pp. 199-200, contains several other titles, Burke's list may not have been complete.

27. Samuels, p. 29.

28. *Works*, IV, 158.

29. Stubbs (p. 201 n.) says twice; Prior (I, 90) says three times.

30. See [John E. Walsh], *Sketches of Ireland Sixty Years Ago*, Dublin, 1847, p. 6.

31. In the manuscript life of Goldsmith begun by Thomas Campbell, continued by Henry Boyd, and finally used as the basis for Percy's Memoir, Campbell wrote that Goldsmith "would declare that his tutor . . . etc." Percy struck out the words "would declare" and substituted "often declared" (B.M. Add. MS. 42517, f. 13). This change, made by one who knew Goldsmith well in later years, is indicative of the lasting antipathy which Goldsmith felt toward his tutor.

32. See Walsh, pp. 7-8. A modern reader is bound to wonder why Sheridan delayed so long before calling in the law. The answer is simple: Kelly was a "gentleman," and an actor like Sheridan had little chance of winning a suit against him. In fact, when the case came up for trial, a barrister is said to have remarked sneeringly that he had never seen a "gentleman player"—to which Sheridan proudly replied: "Then, Sir, I hope you see one now." To everyone's amazement Sheridan won the case, and Kelly was fined five hundred pounds and sentenced to Newgate.

33. In the manuscript life of Goldsmith, referred to in note 31, above, Thomas Campbell wrote that Goldsmith was punished "*quod seditionem favisset & tumultuantibus opem tulisset.*" He added: "I have been assured from the report of one of his cotemporaries, that when others concerned in the fray suffered that disgrace [i.e., expulsion from the College], this mild censure was passed on him in consequence of his having candidly confessed to his share of the riot, whilst others flatly denied their being present at it" (B.M. Add. MS. 42517, ff. 16-7).

34. Prior, I, 89-90. Prior suppressed Goldsmith's reply on the ground that it was "too coarse for repetition." The Senior Lecturer's Book contains, under the date of May 9, 1748, the entry: "Goldsmith turned down."

CHAPTER III: PHILOSOPHIC VAGABOND

1. Except when otherwise specified, all biographical information in this chapter is derived from Prior, I, 103-99.

2. See *Letters*, p. 170.

3. Before Goldsmith left Edinburgh he wrote to Contarine: "They speak French [at the University of Paris], and consequently I shall have much the advantage of most of my countrymen, as I am perfectly acquainted with that language, and few who leave Ireland are so" (*Letters*, p. 15). J. J. Kelly (*Early Haunts of Oliver Goldsmith*, Dublin, 1904, pp. 79-81) speculates that, since modern languages were not then taught in the universities, Goldsmith may have learned French from an Irish Catholic priest educated in France.

4. See William Shaw Mason, *Statistical Account or Parochial Survey of Ireland*, quoted in Forster, I, 39.

5. See Prior, I, 130-2. As Miss Balderston points out (*Letters*, p. xii n.), Mrs. Lawder was married when Goldsmith was only four or five years old, and biographers' assumption of a romantic attachment between the two is ungrounded.

6. *Letters*, p. 10.

7. I have followed the version of the story given in Mrs. Hodson's Narrative (*Letters*, pp. 170-6) and have occasionally quoted her words. As for the "improved" version of the story given in Prior, I, 119-25, and reprinted by Miss Balderston among "Forged Letters" (*Letters*, pp. 148-54), the manuscript life of Goldsmith now in the

British Museum provides the explanation: Thomas Campbell, first author of the Memoir, apparently composed it from Mrs. Hodson's Narrative and inserted it in his text, presumably thinking that the story would be more vivid if told in the first person. For some reason, though, he placed the first three words, "My Dear Mother," on a separate line as if they were the salutation of a letter. Someone, perhaps Prior himself, assumed that the story was actually a letter, copied it off, and added Goldsmith's signature; and it so appeared in Prior's *Life*.

8. See *Letters*, pp. 9 and 55.

9. See Northcote, I, 211-2.

10. See *Letters*, pp. 31 and 62.

11. *Ibid.*, pp. 24-5. Except when otherwise specified, all subsequent quotations from Goldsmith's letters in this chapter are copied from *Letters*, pp. 3-25.

12. Goldsmith gave as his address "Surgeon Sinclair's, Trunk Close," but he may have only received his mail there.

13. As Miss Balderston (*Letters*, p. 3 n.) remarks, Goldsmith was paying "a large amount," since Johnson stated in his *Journey to the Western Islands* that board and room at St. Andrews cost between ten and fifteen pounds for seven months. As late as 1827 Principal Lee of the University of Edinburgh reported that students were living in Edinburgh on six shillings, ninepence (or in extreme cases, five shillings) per week. (See Alexander Grant, *The Story of the University of Edinburgh*, London, 1884, II, 488.) And G. B. Hill (*Life of Johnson*, I, 103 n.) quotes the Autobiography of Dr. A. Carlyle, who recalled that in Edinburgh in 1742 one could get "at fourpence a-head a very good dinner of broth and beef, and a roast and potatoes every day, with fish three or four times a-week, and all the small beer that was called for till the cloth was removed."

14. Grant, II, 193-4. Most of my information about the University of Edinburgh is derived from this book.

15. See Forster, I, 54 n. William Freeman (*Oliver Goldsmith*, London, 1951, p. 61 n.) points out that the tailor erred in his addition and overcharged Goldsmith a penny.

16. *Works*, III, 519.

17. Percy Memoir, p. 31.

18. See Forster, I, 54 n.

19. According to Prior (I, 137), Mrs. Hodson implied that, because Goldsmith failed to report to his relatives as agreed, he did not receive all the money promised to him. Presumably she was referring to the fifteen pounds which she, her husband, and her brother Henry had pledged for his support.

20. In his *Life of Dr Goldsmith* (London, 1774) Samuel Glover said J. F. Sleigh had told him that Goldsmith was arrested in Sunderland on this charge. If so, Goldsmith's account of his arrest at Newcastle (see below, pp. 57-8) may have been composed to conceal the truth from his uncle.

21. Mr. J. B. McKeeman, of the National Library of Scotland, tells me that, according to the newspaper *The Caledonian Mercury*, there was a ship named the *St. Andrew* sailing out of Leith in 1754, but that it was reported as sailing as late as August 6 (and therefore could not have been "wreckd at the mouth of the Graronne [*sic*]" earlier in the year). Moreover, the *Calendar of State Papers* for 1754 mentions no such arrest as Goldsmith describes, although it lists several arrests of men charged with enlisting soldiers for the French forces. (See also above, note 20.)

22. See A. E. H. Swaen, "Fielding and Goldsmith in Leiden," *MLR*, I (1905-6), 328.

23. Prior (I, 168) states, without giving a source for his information, that Goldsmith "is said to have been less attentive to the acquisition of professional than miscellaneous knowledge, particularly a more familiar acquaintance with the language and literature of France, preparatory to an intended tour through that country."

24. Miss Balderston (*Letters*, p. 21 n.) points out that, although Goldsmith began his account of Holland by complaining that too often young men depend on books of travel when describing their own travels, his letter "has many striking similarities to the description of Holland given in Thomas Nugent's *The Grand Tour*, published in 1749."

25. In *The Vicar of Wakefield* George Primrose said that he went to Holland to teach English, only to realize that he could not do so until he learned to speak Dutch. By the same token, since in his published works Goldsmith never alluded to or made use of an ability to read Dutch, one may question whether he was qualified to teach English in Holland.

26. In the manuscript life of Goldsmith in the British Museum Campbell or Boyd wrote: "At Leyden, where he studied chemistry under Gawbius and anatomy under Albinus, for about a year, he felt all the vicissitudes of fortune at play, to which he was most passionately addicted." Percy crossed out the word *most* and substituted "still so"; then he crossed out the word *so* (B.M. Add. MS. 42517, f. 40). In the Memoir as finally published, the phrase reads: "to which he was now unhappily addicted." (See Percy Memoir, p. 41.)

27. *Works*, III, 489. Professor O. J. Campbell (*The Comedies of Holberg*, Cambridge, Mass., 1914, pp. 17-8) points out that Holberg did not "sing for his supper" while he was touring the Continent, and that the information about him in *Polite Learning* is "just the sort that [Goldsmith] would have obtained in chance conversations."

28. The theory that Goldsmith received his medical degree from the University of Louvain has been discredited. (See Sir Ernest Clarke, "The Medical Education and Qualifications of Oliver Goldsmith," *Proceedings of the Royal Society of Medicine*, VII [1914], 88-97, and cf. discussion below, Chapter IV, note 5.)

29. See *Works*, II, 338, and 310-11. In his *Memoir of M. de Voltaire* Goldsmith said he had spent an evening in the company of Voltaire, Fontenelle, and Diderot while he was in Paris; but it has long since been pointed out that Voltaire was not in Paris when Goldsmith was. There have been various attempts to reconcile Goldsmith's statement with the truth (see *Works*, IV, 25 n.), but they have proved very little. Goldsmith may well have been translating here from an undiscovered source; or he may simply have been claiming to have known Voltaire (as he later claimed to have known Richard Nash) in order to make his biography seem more authentic. As for the account of a visit to Voltaire in Switzerland in the letter "On the Abuse of Our Enemies," hitherto attributed to Goldsmith, Professor Arthur Friedman informs me that he has found no conclusive evidence that the letter is Goldsmith's and that he is excluding it from his forthcoming edition of the essays of Goldsmith.

30. *Letters*, p. 32.

31. Samuel Glover declared, in his *Life of Goldsmith*, that at Geneva Goldsmith took a position as "governor" to a parsimonious young Englishman on the Grand Tour and went with him as far as Marseilles, where the young man decided suddenly to save money by sailing for England immediately. Percy questioned Glover's story, regarding it merely as a retelling of the adventure of George Primrose, who had a similar experience with a young man traveling from Paris to Leghorn. Later biographers have left the matter undecided, and so it must remain. It is possible, of course, that Goldsmith served as "governor" to the Englishman whom he is said to have accompanied on the trip from Paris to Switzerland.

32. The theory that Goldsmith received his medical degree from the University of Padua has been discredited. (See note 28, above.)

33. See *Letters*, pp. xiv and 26.

34. *Works*, III, 522.

35. *Ibid*. In the second edition of *Polite Learning* Goldsmith omitted the Latin words, probably because he felt they did not befit his growing dignity as an author.

CHAPTER IV: TINKER? TAILOR?

1. Except when otherwise specified, all biographical information in this chapter is derived from Prior, I, 200-338. Prior's assumption that Goldsmith may have joined a company of strolling players need no longer be taken seriously. It was inferred from Goldsmith's "Adventures of a Strolling Player," which has been proved to be an adaptation (and sometimes a literal translation) of the second and third papers of Marivaux' *Indigent Philosophe*. (See Sells, pp. 76-9.)

2. Radcliff obligingly ignored the request, and Goldsmith presently wrote him the letter describing his travels in Europe which was lost when Radcliff's house burned. (See p. 67, above.)

3. Note also Goldsmith's complaints to Percy about having to sleep with the French teacher (Percy Memoir, p. 45); George Primrose's complaints in *The Vicar of Wakefield* about the arduousness of life as an usher; and the burlesque advertisement in

Citizen of the World, No. V: "Wanted an usher to an academy.—N.B.—He must be able to read, dress hair, and must have had the small-pox."

4. Except when otherwise specified, all quotations from Goldsmith's letters in this chapter are copied from *Letters*, pp. 26-68.

5. Although Goldsmith never received the M.D. degree, he was generally known as Dr. Goldsmith for the last fifteen years of his life. Sir Ernest Clarke (*Proc. Roy. Soc. Med.*, VII, 88-97) thinks that he might have received the Bachelor of Medicine degree from Trinity College sometime between 1756 and 1763, but Dr. Raymond Crawfurd (*ibid.*, VIII, Part II, pp. 7-25) observes that Percy sounds dubious when he reports the degree *ad eundem gradum* which Goldsmith claimed to have received from Oxford in 1767. The manuscript life of Goldsmith in the British Museum tends to confirm his suspicions: on the title-page of the manuscript Percy struck out the "M.B." following Goldsmith's name and later (f. 29v.) wrote in a margin: "I am of opinion that he never took the Degree of M.B. if he did it may be seen in the College Registers." Later he added: "The Register of the University for that Period is imperfect." (See also Chapter VII, note 42, below.)

6. Boswell (*Life of Johnson*, I, 411) states that Goldsmith was "a corrector of the press" for Richardson. Others report only that he met Richardson and had some association with him.

7. *Works*, III, 503.

8. The reviewer of Prior's *Life* in the *Gentleman's Magazine* for 1837 recalled meeting an elderly lady who said that an acquaintance of hers had been flogged by Goldsmith at the Peckham school.

9. The anecdotes about William are taken from a letter by John Evans in the *European Magazine*, LIII (1808), 373-5.

10. This review was long considered to be Goldsmith's original work. But as Miss Caroline Tupper has pointed out ("Oliver Goldsmith and 'The Gentleman Who Signs D,' " *MLN*, XLV [1930], 71-7), it was actually an abridged translation of a review in the *Bibliothèque des Sciences et des Beaux Arts* for 1756. It should not, however, be regarded as a piece of plagiarism, since, as Miss Tupper shows, Goldsmith borrowed from Dr. Grainger the signature "D" which Grainger had used regularly for translations from the *Bibliothèque*.

11. Goldsmith's contributions to the *Monthly Review* (and the authorship of most of the reviews of his books) are listed in B. C. Nangle's *The Monthly Review, First Series, 1749-1789: Indexes of Contributors and Articles*, Oxford, 1934.

12. That Burke took Goldsmith's criticism seriously and attempted to answer it in the second edition of *The Sublime and the Beautiful* is revealed in Professor Herbert A. Wichelns' article "Burke's Essay on the Sublime and Its Reviewers," *JEGP*, XXI (1922), 645-61.

13. Goldsmith sold a third interest in the translation to Dilly for £6/3/4. (See Elizabeth Eaton Kent, *Goldsmith and His Booksellers*, Ithaca, N.Y., 1933, p. 25.) Austin Dobson, in his edition of the translation (London, 1895, I, xv), assumes that there must have been a third publisher; but Griffiths might well have retained a two-thirds interest in the book.

14. For evidence that Goldsmith did not, as was formerly believed, contribute to the *Literary Magazine* at this period, see R. W. Seitz, "Goldsmith and the *Literary Magazine*," *RES*, V (1929), 410-30.

15. Goldsmith admitted in his Preface that the translation was being published under an assumed name.

16. *Letters*, p. 9.

17. Earlier biographers have assumed that Mrs. Martin was Goldsmith's landlady when he lent her the money. But she could not have become so until sometime after January 13. On that date he wrote to his brother Henry that he was living at the Temple.

18. In my discussion of Goldsmith's work for the *Critical Review* I have been guided by the investigations of Professor Friedman ("Goldsmith's Contributions to the *Critical Review*," *MP*, XLIV [1946-7], 23-52) and Professor Morris Golden ("Internal Evidence and Goldsmith's Periodical Writings," Unpublished Doctoral Dissertation, New York University, 1953, pp. 223-63).

19. Goldsmith's biography of Voltaire was withheld from publication until 1761, when it appeared in the *Lady's Magazine*. (See discussion below, p. 126.) Purdon's

translation of the *Henriade*, which was to have been published with it, appeared in the *Grand Magazine* for 1759.

20. See "The Club of Queer Fellows," in Irving's *Tales of a Traveller*.

21. B.M. Add. MS. 32336, ff. 19v.-21v.

22. See R. S. Crane and Arthur Friedman, "Goldsmith and the *Encyclopédie*," *TLS*, May 11, 1933, p. 331.

23. Since this review is no longer accepted as Goldsmith's (see Professor Friedman's *MP* article referred to in note 18, above), he can no longer be blamed for the disparaging remarks about Mrs. Griffiths that have been generally attributed to him. He may, however, have furnished the reviewer with information about her interference in the affairs of the *Monthly*.

24. A footnote reference at the word "immoralities" in the last sentence alludes to remarks about the Marquis D'Argens in *Polite Learning*.

25. *Works*, III, 466 n. The passage was omitted from the second edition of *Polite Learning*.

26. *Ibid.*, p. 474.

27. *Ibid.*, p. 512 n. The passage was omitted from the second edition of the book. Robert W. Kenny ("Ralph's *Case of Authors:* Its Influence on Goldsmith and Isaac D'Israeli," *PMLA*, LII [1937], 104-13) suggests that Goldsmith may have derived some of his ideas about authors' hardships from James Ralph, whose short pamphlet, *A Case of Authors by Profession*, was published in 1758.

28. See *Letters*, pp. xxx-xxxiii.

29. See Joseph E. Brown, "Goldsmith's Indebtedness to Voltaire and Justus Van Effen," *MP*, XXIII (1925-6), 273-84.

30. See A. J. Barnouw, "Goldsmith's Indebtedness to Justus Van Effen," *MLR*, VIII (1913), 314-23. For Goldsmith's other borrowings in *The Bee*, see this article; Crane and Friedman, *TLS*, May 11, 1933, p. 331; Roberts, *ibid.*, November 30, 1933, p. 855; Brown, *MP*, XXIII, 273-84; Seitz, *RES*, V, 410-20; and Friedman, *MP*, LIII (1955), 47-9.

31. See R. S. Crane, "Oliver Goldsmith, M.B.," *MLN*, XLVIII (1933), 462.

32. In *New Essays*, pp. 128-33, Professor Crane points out that, although the first eleven numbers of the *Lady's Magazine* (September, 1759-July, 1760) are inaccessible, advertisements and reprints in other magazines reveal that the *Lady's* contained fifteen translations from Feyjoo (in whom Goldsmith was interested at this time) and several other articles which might have been written by Goldsmith.

33. See *New Essays*, pp. 126-7, concerning two other possible contributions to the *Busy Body* by Goldsmith.

34. See *New Essays*, p. xix.

35. See *N&Q*, CLXXXVII (1944), 276. But cf. Professor Friedman's note in *English Literature 1660-1800*, Princeton, 1952, pp. 942-3.

36. In my discussion of Goldsmith's work for the *Weekly Magazine* I have been guided by Professor Friedman's article, "Goldsmith and the *Weekly Magazine*," *MP*, XXXII (1934-5), 281-99, by Professor Golden's conclusions in his doctoral dissertation referred to in note 18, above, and by a letter from Professor Friedman listing the essays which he plans to exclude from his forthcoming edition because of want of conclusive evidence that they are Goldsmith's.

37. All quotations from the *Weekly Magazine* are copied by permission from microfilms furnished by the Henry E. Huntington Library.

Chapter V: Author by Profession

1. See R. S. Crane, "A Neglected Mid-Eighteenth-Century Plea for Originality and Its Author," *PQ*, XIII (1934), 21-9.

2. See Prior, I, 340 n.

3. See the rebus quoted in Prior, I, 338. Prior questions whether Goldsmith actually wrote it, but its similarity to the rebus for Mary Nugent, quoted below, p. 215, suggests that it was his work.

4. Goldsmith numbered this paper IV, probably considering that the first two Letters of the series, printed in one issue of the *Public Ledger*, constituted a single in-

stallment. This paper appears as No. VI in the first edition of *The Citizen of the World* and in all later reprints. Throughout this book I have used the numbering and followed the text of the Letters as reprinted in *Works*, Vol. III. For the differences between this numbering and that of the original "Chinese Letters," see Hamilton J. Smith, *Oliver Goldsmith's "Citizen of the World*," New Haven, 1926, pp. 124-32.

5. Except when otherwise specified, all biographical information in this chapter is derived from Prior, I, 338-426.

6. *Letters*, p. 5.

7. *Works*, IV, 281.

8. For a more extensive discussion of Goldsmith's debt to his predecessors, see Smith, pp. 39-85, and Levette J. Davidson, "Forerunners of Goldsmith's *Citizen of the World*," *MLN*, XXXVI (1921), 215-20.

9. Concerning Goldsmith's debt to LeComte and DuHalde, see Smith, pp. 85-109 and 148-65.

10. See his review of Arthur Murphy's *Orphan of China* in the *Critical Review* for May, 1759, reprinted in Works, IV, 350-5.

11. In "Oliver Goldsmith and His *Chinese Letters*" (*T'ien Hsia Monthly*, VIII [1939], 48) Chên Shou-yi reports that none of the passages attributed to Confucius "bears any noticeable resemblance to Confucius' *Analects*."

12. See Crane and Friedman, *TLS*, May 11, 1933, p. 331.

13. In my discussion of Goldsmith's work for the *British Magazine* I have been guided by the conclusions of Professor Golden in his doctoral dissertation referred to in Chapter IV, note 18, and by information given me by Professor Friedman in the letter referred to in Chapter IV, note 36. It is now generally agreed that Goldsmith did not write the Belles Lettres series in the *British Magazine* for 1761-3. (See Caroline Tupper, "Essays Erroneously Attributed to Goldsmith," *PMLA*, XXXIX [1924], 325-42.)

14. As editors have frequently pointed out, Goldsmith erred if he believed that this tavern was the same as that which figures in *Henry IV*.

15. In this Letter Goldsmith was indebted to Johnson's *Observations on the Present State of Affairs*. (See Seitz, *RES*, V [1929], 413.)

16. For a comparison of Goldsmith's handling of this story with that of his friend Thomas Percy, see Ada Milner-Barry, "A Note on the Early Literary Relations of Oliver Goldsmith and Thomas Percy," *RES*, II (1926), 51-61.

17. As editors have suggested, Goldsmith may have had Thomas Gray's poetry in mind when he wrote these lines.

18. See Friedman, "Goldsmith and the Marquis D'Argens," *MLN*, LIII (1938), 173-6. For Goldsmith's other borrowings in his *British Magazine* articles during the year 1760, see Crane and Friedman, *TLS*, May 11, 1933, p. 331, and Crane, *ibid.*, March 1, 1934, p. 144.

19. The house was destroyed during the bombings of World War II and has been replaced by a building called "House of Goldsmith" and occupied in 1953 by Messrs. Amphlett and Company, Solicitors.

20. Davies, II, 122.

21. See *ibid.*, pp. 108-9. Prior (I, 379) and Crane (*New Essays*, p. 87 n.) point out, however, that Goldsmith's name does not appear among the applicants for the secretaryship. He may, of course, have decided not to make formal application when Garrick denied his support.

22. Davies claims that the offensive passage was in *Polite Learning*, which contains, in Chapter XII of the first edition, some reflections on theatrical managers in general. A much likelier cause of Garrick's annoyance, however, is the following, from *The Bee*, No. I: "We shall, it is feared, be told that Garrick is a fine actor; but then as a manager, so avaricious!"

23. See Sells, pp. 82 and 114-7; Brown, *MP*, XXIII (1925-6), 273-84; Friedman, *MLN*, LV (1940), 294-6, and LXVI (1951), 553-4; and Balderston, *MLN*, XLII (1927), 165-8.

24. See *New Essays*, p. xxxii n.

25. Concerning Goldsmith's work for the *Lady's Magazine*, see Prior, I, 337-8 and 365; *Works*, I, 270-4, 299-301; *New Essays*, pp. 85-8 and 128-33; and Friedman, *MP*, XXX (1932-3), 320-2. For Goldsmith's borrowing in one of his essays, see Friedman, *PQ*, XIX (1940), 409-11.

26. See discussion below, pp. 128-30.

27. Concerning Goldsmith's claim to have met Voltaire in Paris, see Chapter III, note 29.

28. Three of these translations had already been published in the *Public Ledger*. (See *Works*, IV, 28 n., and *New Essays*, p. 136.) Two of them are not included in the text of the "Memoirs" as first reprinted by Prior and copied by later editors. Concerning the differences between the original text of the "Memoirs" in the *Lady's Magazine* and Prior's "improved" version, see R. S. Crane, "The Text of Goldsmith's *Memoirs of M. de Voltaire*," *MP*, XXVIII (1930-1), 212-9.

29. No copy of *Memoirs of Milady B.* seems to have survived. As for "A Political View of the Result of the Present War," which survives in a manuscript preserved in the Huntington Library, it was compiled from several articles (two of them by Samuel Johnson) which appeared in the *Lady's Magazine* in 1756-8. (See J. W. Oliver, *TLS*, May 18, 1922, p. 324, and R. W. Seitz, *RES*, V [1929], 410-20.) However, since it was never published, it does not merit fuller discussion here.

30. From a note by Professor Crane included in *Life of Johnson*, III, 502.

31. B.M. Add. MS. 32336, f. 25v.

32. *Life of Johnson*, IV, 2.

33. Professor Crane, who reprinted three of the series for the first time in *New Essays*, speculates (p. 98 n.) that it may have been written originally for the *Public Ledger*.

34. Although Goldsmith is often credited with revising this book, no one seems to have offered any convincing proof that he did. Walter M. Crittenden, author of *The Life and Writings of Mrs. Sarah Scott* (Philadelphia, 1932) does not mention Goldsmith's supposed share in the book.

35. Evidences of style suggest that Newbery wrote the more technical sections of the book and that Goldsmith furnished the following: Chapters V, VI, XIV (to p. 196 of Vol. I), XVII, XVIII (to p. 67 of Vol. II), XIX (*passim*), and XX-XXIII.

36. Because the numbers XXV, XLIX, LVII, and CXVI were used twice, the last Letter of the first edition of *The Citizen of the World* was numbered CXIX.

37. For Goldsmith's earlier use of the phrase, see *Works*, I, 322-3; III, 74, 86, and 531; IV, 41; and *New Essays*, p. 17. For the history of the phrase, see Smith, *Oliver Goldsmith's "Citizen of the World,"* pp. 29-30.

38. The first reception of the book is discussed and longer excerpts from reviews are given in Smith, pp. 31-3. It is worth noting, in regard to Goldsmith's "borrowings," that two of the reviewers acknowledged, in effect, that the Letters were not always original, but did not damn them on that score. Literary property was not taken as seriously then as now. Also of interest is the evidence from Boswell's Journals that, when *The Citizen* appeared as a book, Goldsmith and Johnson, who had published his *Idler* in the preceding October, were given a chance to review each other's work in the *Critical*. Goldsmith was willing to act on the suggestion, but Johnson said, "No; set Reviewers at defiance." (See *Life of Johnson*, V [Hebrides], 274 and 550.)

39. See the Advertisement for the book, reprinted in Scott, p. 87.

40. *Letters*, pp. 71-2.

41. Prior (I, 401-2) identified this "conclusion" with the *History of England in Questions and Answers* that appeared in its eleventh edition on September 11, 1759, with a new section on the reign of George II. But Seitz (*MP*, XXVIII [1930-1], 335) believes that Goldsmith had no share in this work.

42. There is, however, increasing evidence that Goldsmith, here as elsewhere, took his facts where he found them. Arthur Sherbo (*MLN*, LXX [1955], 20-2) shows how he worked up an anecdote from a story in *The Bee*, and Professor Friedman (*TLS*, November 2, 1956, p. 649) offers proof that Goldsmith derived almost one-tenth of his text from John Wood's *Essay Towards a Description of Bath* (1749).

43. Donald Stauffer, *The Art of Biography in the Eighteenth Century*, Princeton, 1941, pp. 380-6. Concerning Goldsmith's debt to Johnson, see Joseph E. Brown, "Goldsmith and Johnson on Biography," *MLN*, XLII (1927), 168-71, and cf. Frances Haydon, "Oliver Goldsmith as a Biographer," *South Atlantic Quarterly*, XXXIX (1940), 50-7.

44. Newbery paid fourteen guineas for the book. As Gibbs (*Works*, IV, 48) points out, the claim that Goldsmith received an additional fifteen guineas from the Corporation of Bath (to whom the second edition of the book is dedicated) has been disproved. However, he may have received some payment from the publisher Frederick of Bath,

or, as Gibbs suggests, Newbery may have paid all or part of the expenses of his trip to Bath.

45. Even if Goldsmith was paid twenty-eight or twenty-nine guineas for his *Life of Nash*, Prior's figure is generous. He allows twenty guineas for "occasional pieces," of which Goldsmith wrote very few in 1762, and assumes that he wrote the *History of Mecklenburgh*, though actually he at most revised it.

46. Charles Welsh, *A Bookseller of the Last Century*, London and New York, 1885, p. 124.

47. I accept the version of the story given by Austin Dobson in his *Life of Goldsmith*, pp. 110-7. Incidentally, dating the sale in 1762 rather than 1764 makes more explicable Goldsmith's removal to Islington and Newbery's assumption of the role of his guardian. It explains too why Goldsmith called on Johnson rather than Newbery in his distress: Mrs. Carnan, the landlady who summoned the bailiffs, was a relative by marriage of Mrs. Newbery.

48. *Boswell's London Journal, 1762-1763,* ed. Frederick A. Pottle, New York, 1950, pp. 105-6. This volume, copyrighted by Yale University, is quoted by special arrangement with the publisher, McGraw-Hill Book Company, Inc.

Chapter VI: "One of the First Poets"

1. Whether Mrs. Fleming was the original of Hogarth's portrait entitled "Mrs. Butler, Goldsmith's Hostess" and what, if any, association Goldsmith had with the painter have been discussed by both Forster (I, 328-40) and Dobson (pp. 92-3) with no very conclusive results. As for Hogarth's supposed portrait of Goldsmith (see Dobson, *William Hogarth*, London, 1907, p. 90), Mr. David Piper of the National Portrait Gallery informs me that it "might represent any writer, and is certainly not by Hogarth." Mr. Piper's investigation of Goldsmith iconography leads him to conclude that only the two Reynolds portraits (the original now at Knole and the copy made for the Thrales' "Streatham Gallery") and the caricatures by Bunbury can be accepted as authentic.

2. Details about life at Canonbury derived from Elizabeth Smart LeNoir's *Miscellaneous Poems* and her manuscript memoir, quoted in K. A. McKenzie, *Christopher Smart, Sa Vie et Ses Œuvres*, Paris, 1925, and Edward G. Ainsworth and Charles E. Noyes, *Christopher Smart, a Biography*, University of Missouri Studies, Columbia, Mo., 1943. Forster (II, 82) claims, on the authority of a Mr. Home, whose mother-in-law's aunt lived in Canonbury Tower in the 1760's, that Goldsmith occupied "the old oak-room on the first floor," and this room is commonly shown as Goldsmith's to visitors to the Tower. However, contemporary evidence of both Elizabeth Smart LeNoir and Francis Newbery makes clear that John Newbery and his family lived in the paneled rooms on the first (in American usage, second) floor and that Goldsmith's room was higher in the building. He may, of course, have moved into the lower room after Newbery's death.

3. Except when otherwise specified, all biographical information in this chapter is derived from Prior, I, 458-500, and II, 1-106. Prior first reprinted Goldsmith's accounts with Newbery, Mrs. Fleming, and William Filby.

4. *Boswell's London Journal*, pp. 175-8.

5. *Ibid.*, pp. 282-5.

6. *Ibid.*, p. 311. Although Boswell includes this interchange in his *London Journal* in the entry for July 19, he seems not to have seen Goldsmith that day; in fact, his visit to Canonbury Tower would seem to have provided the only opportunity for him to discuss Johnson with Goldsmith.

7. *Ibid.*, pp. 286-8. In the *Life of Johnson* (I, 417) Boswell remarks at this point: "Goldsmith's respectful attachment to Johnson was then at its height; for his own literary reputation had not yet distinguished him so much as to excite a vain desire of competition with his great Master."

8. *Life of Johnson,* I, 421.

9. *Boswell's London Journal*, pp. 291-4. Cf. *Life of Johnson,* I, 423-6.

10. *Life of Johnson,* II, 118.

11. *Ibid.,* III, 252.

12. Professor Crane has discovered that Goldsmith's address as listed in the Manuscript Register of Members of the Society of Arts at this period was No. 9 Holbourn Court, Gray's Inn. (See *English Literature 1660-1800,* Princeton, 1950, p. 157.)

13. Concerning the price paid Goldsmith for his *History of England in a Series of Letters,* see Seitz, *MP,* XXVIII (1930-1), 334 n.

14. See Winifred Lynskey, "Pluche and Derham, New Sources of Goldsmith," *PMLA,* LVII (1942), 435-45, and Crane and Friedman, *TLS,* May 11, 1933, p. 31.

15. *MP,* XXVI (1928-9), 304.

16. In the second Letter of the *History of England in a Series of Letters,* published in June, Goldsmith maintained that studying the history of a single nation was more rewarding than studying universal history.

17. See Crane and Friedman, *TLS,* May 11, 1933, p. 331.

18. "Goldsmith's 'Lives of the Fathers,'" *MP,* XXVI (1928-9), 295-305. Seitz virtually disposes of Prior's claim that these two works appeared first in the *Christian's Magazine.* Prior's other claims about Goldsmith's work for the *Christian's Magazine,* discussed by Crane in *New Essays* (pp. 140-1), are pronounced "decidedly weak" by Seitz.

19. Prior (I, 477-8, 468-9) suggests three other projects which Goldsmith might have carried out for Newbery at this period: a preface for *The Martial Review; or, a General History of the Late War* (published in September, 1763) and revisions of *A Description of Millenium Hall* (March, 1763), the work of Mrs. Sarah Scott and perhaps Lady Barbara Montagu, and the four-volume *Wonders of Nature and Art* (May, 1763). The preface to the *Martial Review* is negligible—merely a paragraph maintaining that the author is impartial in his presentation. If Goldsmith wrote it, he probably was not paid for it, because Newbery had set aside the profits of the book for the benefit of his son-in-law, Christopher Smart. As for the two revisions, they can only be classed as doubtful. *Millenium Hall* shows no clear evidence of Goldsmith's hand; and Walter M. Crittenden, author of the modern biography of Mrs. Scott and editor of the recent edition of the novel, does not mention Goldsmith's supposed share in it. (Cf. Tyrus G. Harmsen, *The Book Collector,* II [1953], 155-7.) *Wonders of Nature and Art* seems to exist only in a four-volume edition published in 1758 or 1759 and a six-volume edition published in 1768. (See Williams, p. 128.)

20. *Letters,* p. 73.

21. See Forster, I, 325 n.

22. At the end of the first Letter he quotes the familiar sentence from Temple, "When all is done, human life is . . . but like a froward child . . ." (which he used also in *Polite Learning* and *The Good Natured Man*), attributing it to "your [i.e., his son's] noble ancestor."

23. In "Some of Goldsmith's Second Thoughts on English History" (*MP,* XXXV [1937-8], 279-88) R. W. Seitz pointed out that this history showed less Tory bias and more "social philosophy" than Goldsmith's later *History of England.* (See discussion below, pp. 218-20.)

24. *European Magazine,* XXIV (1793), 94.

25. See R. S. Crane and James H. Warner, "Goldsmith and Voltaire's *Essai sur les Moeurs,*" *MLN,* XXXVIII (1923), 65-76. For a curious story about the source of the Chronological Table of English Events at the end of the *History,* see R. W. Chapman, *TLS,* June 13, 1929, p. 474, or *Colophon,* III (1930).

26. See R. W. Seitz, "Goldsmith and the *Annual Register,*" *MP,* XXXI (1933-4), 183-94.

27. See Williams, pp. 131-2. Prior erroneously assumes that the book was published in 1766.

28. *Letters,* p. 73 n.

29. See "Goldsmith and the 'English Lives,'" *MP,* XXVIII (1930-1), 329-36.

30. See Welsh, *A Bookseller of the Last Century,* p. 53.

31. *Life of Johnson,* IV, 27.

32. B. M. Add. MS. 32336, f. 58v.

33. Percy Memoir, p. 106.

34. Johnson marked his nine lines in Boswell's copy of *The Traveller.* (See *Works,* II, 19.) As Professor Crane discovered (*English Literature 1660-1800,* p. 450), the lines were added to the proof-sheets of the poem. Cf. note 41.

35. Hawkins, pp. 419-20.
36. *Life of Johnson*, V (Hebrides), 344.
37. *A Prospect of Society*, the improperly printed "first" edition of the poem, has recently been edited by William B. Todd and published by the University of Virginia Press.
38. *Life of Johnson*, III, 252.
39. *Portraits*, p. 48.
40. *Life of Johnson*, III, 252-3.
41. *Portraits*, p. 86. Johnson qualified the remark with the phrase "to the best of my recollection." For a discussion of whether he wrote more than the nine lines marked in Boswell's copy, see the preface to Professor Todd's edition of *A Prospect of Society* (cited above, note 37) and cf. the review of his earlier, privately printed edition of the same in *TLS*, January 28, 1955, p. 64.
42. *Life of Johnson*, III, 252.
43. "Recollections of Dr. Johnson by Miss Reynolds," *Johnsonian Miscellanies*, II, 268.
44. *Portraits*, p. 48.
45. Prior, II, 106.
46. *European Magazine*, XXIV (1793), 170.
47. Hawkins, pp. 418-9. The story of Goldsmith's delivering his prepared address to the groom is discredited by Prior, who points out that it is probably an adaptation of an incident in *The Vicar of Wakefield*, which Goldsmith had written some time before he met Northumberland.
48. Goldsmith received from Newbery £10/10/0 for a half share in the book, but only Griffin's name appeared on the title page. Concerning a second 1765 edition of the *Essays*, probably pirated, see Friedman, *Studies in Bibliography*, V (1952-3), 190-3.
49. *European Magazine*, XXIV, 93.
50. Cradock, IV, 286.
51. William Godwin suggested to Prior that Goldsmith might have written *Goody Two Shoes*, which Newbery published early in 1765; but it was probably the work of Giles Jones, editor of the *Public Ledger*. (See *Works*, I, 19 n.) Prior himself remarked that Goldsmith might have contributed to the *Museum Rusticum et Commerciale*, which appeared in four volumes in 1764-5; but again evidence is lacking. At most Goldsmith might have revised some of the articles in the volumes, which were made up of short papers "on Agriculture, Commerce, Arts, and Manufactures Drawn from Experience, and communicated by Gentlemen engaged in these Pursuits, Revised and digested by several Members of the Society for the Encouragement of Arts, Manufactures, and Commerce." Prior also claims that Goldsmith considered translating Camoens' *Lusiads;* however, the only validation for his claim seems to be a brief memoir of William Julius Mickle, later translator of the *Lusiads*, stating that both Johnson and Goldsmith had considered undertaking the project. (See Forster, II, 294 n.) As for the manuscript translation of Vida's *Game of Chess*, written *c*. 1765 and often reprinted as Goldsmith's, Professor Crane points out in *CBEL* that it is not in Goldsmith's hand and that there is no reason for attributing it to him.

Chapter VII: Novelist, Dramatist, Historian

1. See *Boswell Papers*, VII, 82-4, and *Life of Johnson*, II, 14-5.
2. Except when otherwise specified, all biographical information in this chapter is derived from Prior, II, 106-220.
3. *Life of Johnson*, II, 17 and 478.
4. *Diary and Letters of Madame D'Arblay*, ed. Austin Dobson, London, 1904-5, I, 77.
5. Scott (p. 173) estimates that it took nine years to sell two thousand copies of the novel.
6. R. H. Murray, *Edmund Burke*, Oxford, 1931, p. 130.
7. Sir Walter Scott, *Miscellaneous Prose Works*, London, 1827, III, 283.
8. See Goethe's letter to Zelter, quoted in Dobson, p. 121.
9. See his Preface to the 1847 edition of *Pickwick Papers*.
10. *Early Diary of Frances Burney*, ed. Annie Raine Ellis, London, 1889, I, 12-3.

11. See Ernest A. Baker, *The History of the English Novel*, London, 1934, V, 78-85. For an ingenious defense of the second half of *The Vicar*, see Professor Hilles' Introduction to the American Everyman edition.

12. *Ibid.*, p. 78.

13. *Life of Johnson*, II, 17.

14. See below, p. 241.

15. See Willard H. Bonner, " 'Poems for Young Ladies,' a Bibliographical Note," *N&Q*, CLV (1928), 129-32.

16. The approximate date of this party is determined in the Hilles and Daghlian edition of Horace Walpole's *Anecdotes of Painting in England, Volume V*, New Haven, 1937, p. 46 n.

17. Except when otherwise specified, all quotations from Goldsmith's letters in this chapter are copied from *Letters*, pp. 74-83.

18. *Life of Johnson*, II, 42.

19. Forster, II, 80-1, and *European Magazine*, XXIV, 260.

20. Prior (II, 130) thinks that fifty pounds would have been a more likely figure; but William Cooke says Goldsmith himself believed that "of all his compilations . . . his 'Selections of English Poetry' shewed more 'the art of profession.' " Cooke adds: "Here he did nothing but mark the particular passages with a red lead pencil, and for this he got *two hundred pounds*—but then he used to add, 'a man shews his judgement in these selections, and he may be often twenty years of his life cultivating that judgement' " (*European Magazine*, XXIV, 94).

21. Davies, II, 112.

22. Northcote, I, 287. Northcote, who seems to be reporting the remark at second hand, dates it at the time of Goldsmith's difficulties over *She Stoops to Conquer;* but since Goldsmith seems to have had little reason to find fault with Garrick's treatment of him then, I suspect that he made the remark to Reynolds at the time *The Good Natured Man* was being considered for production.

23. *Letters*, p. 75 n.

24. In "Goldsmith and the *Present State of the British Empire*" (*MLN*, XLV [1930], 434-8), R. W. Seitz proves that a hundred pages of the book were lifted from Burke's *European Settlements in America* and speculates that the remainder of the text must have been taken bodily from other sources, since Goldsmith seems to have been paid only ten pounds for his work although the volume ran to 486 pages.

25. Davies, II, 113-4.

26. *Letters*, p. 76 n.

27. Percy confirmed Goldsmith's claim in the 1775 edition of his *Reliques* and in his Memoir. However, "The Hermit" was the subject of two later accusations: in 1797 and again in 1812 it was said to have been stolen from the French "Raimond et Angéline," which was actually a translation of Goldsmith's poem. (See Prior, II, 89-92, and Scott, p. 153.)

28. *Life of Johnson*, II, 48.

29. Donald C. Bryant, *Edmund Burke and His Literary Friends*, Washington University Studies, St. Louis, 1939, p. 68.

30. Prior, II, 159-63.

31. *Thraliana*, I, 83.

32. *Life of Johnson*, II, 48. For Goldsmith's possible debt to Marivaux, see Sells, pp. 148-55.

33. *European Magazine*, XXIV, 170.

34. *Letters*, p. 13.

35. Davies, II, 118.

36. *Journal of a Tour to the Hebrides*, ed. Frederick A. Pottle and Charles H. Bennett, New York, 1936, pp. 344-5. In *Gossip about Dr. Johnson and Others* (ed. F. H. Skrine, London, 1926, pp. 125-6) Laetitia Hawkins says that Goldsmith once asked the publisher Cadell for an advance payment for his *History of England*, on the ground that he must have the money in order to settle a debt to a tradesman who was threatening to have him jailed. Cadell supposedly gave him the money and then followed him to Hyde Park Corner, where he entered a coach with a woman of ill repute and drove off to Bath to squander the money which he had received. Miss Hawkins is hardly a reliable reporter (see below, p. 290); yet the fact that such a story should be told

about Goldsmith tends to confirm the suspicion that chastity was not one of his virtues. As Joseph Wood Krutch (*Samuel Johnson*, New York, 1944, p. 139) observes, Goldsmith's contemporaries were "little inclined to believe . . . that anyone seriously recommended chastity for men."

37. See the inventory of household furnishings auctioned after Goldsmith's death (Prior, II, 577-8).

38. Fanny Burney (*Diary and Letters of Madame D'Arblay*, ed. Dobson, II, 92) recalled hearing Burke remind Reynolds of the incident at a party at Reynolds' villa on Richmond Hill in 1782. She does not, however, report what Goldsmith said.

39. B. M. Add. MS. 32336, f. 116.

40. Charles R. Leslie and Tom Taylor, *Life and Times of Sir Joshua Reynolds*, London, 1865, I, 290.

41. B. M. Add. MS. 32336, f. 131. Percy records, in his Memorandum Book, the names of those present; but Goldsmith is not listed.

42. See Prior, II, 201, and cf. *The Correspondence of Thomas Percy and Thomas Warton*, ed. M. G. Robinson and Leah Dennis, Baton Rouge, La., 1951, p. 131 n. Although the degree is not recorded in the University records, it was reported in a contemporary journal. This, of course, only adds confusion to the vexed question as to whether Goldsmith ever was granted the M.B. by Trinity College. It is barely possible that Oxford granted him the degree because he presented proof of having a baccalaureate (of Arts, that is) from Trinity.

43. *Life of Johnson*, IV, 10.

44. Davies, II, 113.

45. See *Gentleman's Magazine*, LXXXVII (1817), 277.

46. *Life of Johnson*, II, 214-5.

47. See *Boswell Papers*, VIII, 120-1.

48. *Ibid.*, VII, 137.

49. The conversation for the entire evening is reported in *Life of Johnson*, II, 82-91.

50. Davies, II, 122.

51. Lacy Collison-Morley, *Giuseppe Baretti*, London, 1909, p. 219.

52. Forster, II, 312 n.

CHAPTER VIII: "MAN OF GENIUS"

1. Except when otherwise specified, all quotations from Goldsmith's letters in this chapter are copied from *Letters*, pp. 83-114.

2. See *Letters*, p. 85 n.

3. Maurice may have brought news of Charles' whereabouts, which Goldsmith had inquired about in his recent letter. Presently he received a letter from Charles himself. In a postscript to his letter to Dan Hodson he wrote: "I had a letter from Charles who is as he tells me possessed of a competency and settled in Jamaica."

4. Prior, II, 357-8. Except when otherwise specified, all biographical information in this chapter is derived from Prior, II, 221-376.

5. Northcote, I, 326.

6. *Ibid.*, I, 226-7, and Leslie and Taylor, *Life and Times of Reynolds*, I, 408 n.

7. The bibliographical puzzle raised by the duodecimo editions of *The Deserted Village* (some of which were once thought to have been published before the quarto edition) has at last been solved. See William B. Todd, "The 'Private Issues' of *The Deserted Village*," *Studies in Bibliography*, VI (1954), 25-44. Professor Todd finds no less than fifteen unauthorized editions of the poem published between 1770 and 1784.

8. Howard J. Bell, Jr. ("'The Deserted Village' and Goldsmith's Social Doctrines," *PMLA*, LIX [1944], 747-72) argues that Goldsmith was concerned not with the industrial or agricultural revolutions but rather with the growth of the aristocracy of wealth.

9. Nineteenth century commentators spent a good deal of time arguing the question: was Auburn Lissoy? But it is, of course, irrelevant. Goldsmith undoubtedly drew on both his recollections of his childhood and his later observations during his visits to English villages.

10. See Chauncey B. Tinker, "Figures in a Dream," *Yale Review*, N.S., XVII (1927-8), 670-89.

11. See Bell, *PMLA*, LIX, 747-72, and Franklyn C. Nelick, "Oliver Goldsmith—Traveller," Unpublished Doctoral Dissertation, University of Wisconsin, 1952. Mr. Nelick presents a challenging discussion of the development of Goldsmith's social philosophy.

12. Concerning the influence of Goldsmith's ideas on Thomas Coombe, Philip Freneau, and Timothy Dwight, see Chester E. Eisinger, "Land and Loyalty: Literary Expressions of Agrarian Nationalism in the Seventeenth and Eighteenth Centuries," *American Literature*, XXI (1949-50), 160-78.

13. See, for example, Prior, II, 282-4.

14. *Thraliana*, I, 82.

15. The amount which Griffin paid for *The Deserted Village* seems not to have been recorded. Prior's estimate of "not more than a hundred guineas" is probably, if anything, generous. Hawkins (p. 420) claimed that the poem was written to discharge a debt to Griffin, and Samuel Glover reported a rumor that Goldsmith received two hundred guineas for the poem and promptly returned them to the publisher. But there is no evidence to support either theory.

16. Prior dates William Hodson's visit in 1766, but Miss Balderston (*Letters*, p. xxii n.) has corrected his error.

17. *Life of Johnson*, II, 166.

18. "Recollections of Dr. Johnson by Miss Reynolds," *Johnsonian Miscellanies*, II, 294.

19. See above, p. 44.

20. James Clifford, *Hester Lynch Piozzi*, 2nd ed., Oxford, 1952, p. 86.

21. *Ibid.*, p. 80.

22. *Ibid.*, p. 109.

23. *Thraliana*, I, 83. Cf. Prior, II, 473, where Goldsmith is said to have asked the same question of a wealthy butcher.

24. *Thraliana*, I, 84.

25. *Ibid.*, p. 81.

26. James Granger, *Letters*, ed. J. P. Malcolm, London, 1805, p. 48.

27. "Goldsmith's *Life of Bolingbroke* and the *Biographia Britannica*," *MLN*, L (1935), 25-9.

28. *Life of Johnson*, II, 136.

29. *Horace Walpole's Correspondence with William Mason*, ed. W. S. Lewis, Grover Cronin, Jr., and Charles H. Bennett, New Haven, 1955, I, 41, and *Horace Walpole's Correspondence with the Reverend William Cole*, ed. W. S. Lewis and A. D. Wallace, New Haven, 1937, I, 310.

30. The letter is preserved in the British Museum as B. M. Add. MS. 35350, ff. 41-2.

31. Lewis Melville, *The Life and Letters of Tobias Smollett*, London, 1926, p. 256.

32. Forster, II, 363 n.

33. *Thraliana*, I, 84.

34. See R. W. Seitz, "Some of Goldsmith's Second Thoughts on English History," *MP*, XXXV (1937-8), 279-88.

35. Goldsmith's errors in calling the Reverend George Walker a Dissenting clergyman and locating the Battle of Naseby in Yorkshire have been frequently noticed. But no one seems to have remarked his discussion of the French claims of land "towards New Mexico on the East, and quite to the Apalachian Mountains on the West."

36. See Seitz, *MP*, XXXV, 279-88. For a discussion of the possible genesis of Goldsmith's opinions, see Seitz, "The Irish Background of Goldsmith's Social and Political Thought," *PMLA*, LII (1937), 405-11.

37. See Prior, II, 327. Miss Balderston (*Letters*, p. 105 n.) points out that the passage which Prior cites was taken bodily from Smollett.

38. Forster, II, 363 n.

39. *Boswell Papers*, VI, 130.

40. Northcote, I, 249.

41. Miss Balderston (*Letters*, pp. xxxiii-xxxvii) has reconstructed the details of the negotiations and reprinted Woodfall's letters.

42. *Life of Johnson*, II, 182.

43. *Letters*, p. 110 n., and B. M. Add. MS. 32336, f. 162v.

44. George Colman, Jr., *Random Records*, London, 1830, I, 110-2, 117-8.

45. *Life of Johnson*, II, 179-82. Cf. *Boswell Papers*, IX, 68-70.

46. *Life of Johnson*, II, 186. Cf. *Boswell Papers*, IX, 73.

47. Prior (II, 351-3) reprints the mocking lines, attributes them to Kenrick, describes a subsequent meeting between Goldsmith and Kenrick, and adds some anecdotes apropos of Goldsmith's fondness for masquerades.

48. Leslie and Taylor, *Life and Times of Sir Joshua Reynolds*, I, 433-5.

49. See *Boswell Papers*, IX, 262, and *Life of Johnson*, II, 182. The account in Boswell's Notes in the Journal suggests that Goldsmith returned to the farmhouse before Boswell and Mickle left, but the entry is too cryptic to be interpreted.

50. See *Boswell Papers*, IX, 263.

51. *Life of Johnson*, II, 196. Cf. *Boswell Papers*, IX, 264.

52. Davies, II, 274. Northcote told Hazlitt that both Johnson and Goldsmith "would allow no one to have any merit but themselves." (See *Complete Works of William Hazlitt*, ed. P. P. Howe, London and Toronto, 1930-4, XI, 297.)

53. *Life of Johnson*, III, 501 (note supplied by Professor Crane).

54. B. M. Add. MS 32336, ff. 169v.-70.

55. *Letters*, p. 117.

CHAPTER IX: "GOOSEBERRY FOOL"

1. Except when otherwise specified, all quotations from Goldsmith's letters in this chapter are copied from *Letters*, pp. 115-37.

2. See *Works*, II, 290-1, and *Letters*, pp. xxxviii-xl.

3. See *Letters*, pp. 115-6. The edition seems never to have been published.

4. Except when otherwise specified, all biographical information in this chapter is derived from Prior, II, 376-518.

5. In *"The History of Francis Wills*: a Literary Mystery" (*RES*, XI [1935], 1-27) A. Lytton Sells examines all available evidence, internal and external, and concludes that the novel is "more probably the work of one of the minor authors of the day, and that of these Arthur Murphy is perhaps the likeliest."

6. *Life of Johnson*, III, 321.

7. Forster, II, 390 n.

8. *Life of Johnson*, II, 208.

9. *Ibid.*, p. 258.

10. See *Letters*, pp. xlvii-xlviii; K. C. Balderston, "A Manuscript Version of *She Stoops to Conquer*," *MLN*, XLV (1930), 84-5; and Coleman Parsons, "Textual Variations in a Manuscript of *She Stoops to Conquer*," *MP*, XL (1942), 57-69.

11. The rejected epilogues are reprinted in *Works*, II, 110-5 (cf. the more complete version of the second in *Letters*, pp. xliv-xlvi), and Arthur Murphy's letter is reprinted in *PQ*, XVII (1938), 88-90. Mrs. Catley withdrew from the cast at the last minute, and her part was taken by Mrs. Kniveton.

12. *The Table Talk and Bon Mots of Samuel Foote*, ed. William Cooke, New Southgate, 1889, pp. 221-2.

13. Alice C. C. Gaussen, *Percy: Prelate and Poet*, London, 1908, p. 161, and Northcote, I, 286.

14. *Life of Johnson*, II, 500.

15. Richard Cumberland (*Memoirs*, ed. Henry Flanders, Philadelphia, 1856, pp. 186-8) gives a detailed account of the evening, but it is highly suspect. (See *Johnsonian Miscellanies*, II, 72, and Stanley T. Williams, *Richard Cumberland*, New Haven and London, 1917, p. 126.)

16. *European Magazine*, XXIV (1793), 173.

17. *Letters*, p. 120 n.

18. This Francis Newbery, who later abandoned publishing in order to manage the distribution of Dr. James's Fever Powders, is not to be confused with his cousin of the same name, who published *The Vicar of Wakefield*. Concerning Goldsmith's revisions in *She Stoops to Conquer* as published by Francis Newbery, see *Letters*, pp. xl-xlii, and the two articles cited above, note 10.

19. Johnson quoted it in a letter to Mrs. Thrale. (See *Letters of Samuel Johnson, LL.D.*, ed. G. B. Hill, Oxford, 1892, I, 214.)

20. *Life of Johnson*, II, 233.

21. *Horace Walpole's Correspondence with William Mason,* ed. W. S. Lewis, Grover Cronin, Jr., and Charles H. Bennett, New Haven, 1955, I, 79.

22. Northcote, I, 286 n.

23. B. M. Add. MS. 44515, f. 117v., includes a receipt dated March 26, 1773, for "the sum of Nine Pounds one shilling in full of all demands. per pro W. Hawes."

24. Goldsmith's letter, Chambers' reply written on or about March 19, and a second note from Goldsmith were published by R. W. Seitz in *TLS,* September 26, 1936, p. 772.

25. B. M. Add. MS. 42516, f. 68.

26. *Life of Johnson,* II, 209-10. Cf. *Boswell Papers,* VI, 77-9.

27. *Letters of James Boswell,* ed. Chauncey B. Tinker, Oxford, 1924, I, 192-3.

28. See *Boswell Papers,* IX, 107-8, and C. B. Tinker, *Young Boswell,* Boston, 1922, p. 173.

29. See *Boswell Papers,* IX, 112-3.

30. *Ibid.,* pp. 92-3.

31. *Life of Johnson,* IV, 113. Cf. *Boswell Papers,* VI, 89.

32. *Life of Johnson,* II, 214-5. Cf. *Boswell Papers,* VI, 101.

33. *Life of Johnson,* II, 216. Cf. *Boswell Papers,* VI, 104.

34. *Boswell Papers,* VI, 112.

35. See *ibid.,* p. 113. The full Journal breaks off at this point without recording the evening's conversation.

36. Conversation reconstructed from *Life of Johnson,* II, 217-9. Cf. *Boswell Papers,* VI, 118.

37. See H. N. Bell, "Goldsmith and the Pickle-Shop," *MLN,* LVII (1942), 121-2.

38. Conversation reconstructed from *Life of Johnson,* II, 220-5.

39. Hawkins, p. 418. As L. F. Powell points out (*Life of Johnson,* II, 504), Fanny Burney said that Martinelli "piqued himself upon treating the Great with rudeness."

40. Conversation reconstructed from *Life of Johnson,* II, 227-9.

41. B. M. Add. MS. 32336, f. 177v.

42. See *Boswell Papers,* VI, 121. The notes are too cryptic to be interpreted.

43. *Life of Johnson,* II, 231. Cf. *Boswell Papers,* VI, 124.

44. *Life of Johnson,* II, 231.

45. *Boswell Papers,* VI, 124.

46. Conversation reconstructed from *Life of Johnson,* II, 232-4. Cf. *Boswell Papers,* VI, 126-7.

47. *Life of Johnson,* IV, 13.

48. Conversation and events reconstructed from *Life of Johnson,* II, 235-40, and *Boswell Papers,* VI, 129-30.

49. Even this benefit caused Goldsmith trouble. Jane Green, the original Mrs. Hardcastle, wrote him a letter on April 6 claiming that Lewes had tried to appropriate the benefit which was rightfully hers. See B. M. Add. MS. 42515, f. 124.

50. Conversation and events reconstructed from *Life of Johnson,* II, 250-7, and *Boswell Papers,* VI, 133-9.

51. Conversation reconstructed from *Life of Johnson,* II, 260-1, and *Boswell Papers,* VI, 140, and IX, 109-10. Boswell preserved the song for posterity by publishing it in the *London Magazine* for June, 1774. On April 25, 1781, he sang it to "beauteous Sally," in Richmond, and "she was delighted." (See *Boswell Papers,* XIV, 205.)

52. The letter is listed in Boswell's manuscript register of letters among the unpublished Boswell Papers in the Yale University Library.

53. The only complete text of the play is that edited by Alice I. P. Wood and published by the Harvard University Press in 1931.

54. Burney's essay was probably the article "Musician" which he later contributed to *Rees's Cyclopoedia.* (See Percy Scholes, *The Great Doctor Burney,* London, New York, and Toronto, 1948, I, 364.)

55. Cradock, I, 235.

56. B. M. Add. MS. 32336, f. 179.

57. All my information about Beattie's stay in London is derived from *James Beattie's London Diary, 1773,* ed. Ralph S. Walker, Aberdeen, 1946, pp. 52-81.

58. Davies, II, 120-1.

59. Prior, II, 472.

60. Hester Lynch Piozzi, *Letters to and from the late Samuel Johnson, LL.D.*, London, 1788, I, 186.

61. *Thraliana*, I, 82 and 174.

62. Northcote, I, 300.

63. *Private Letters of Edward Gibbon*, ed. R. E. Prothero, London, 1896, I, 191.

64. Percy Memoir, pp. 102-3. Percy says that the dinner took place on August 7, but G. B. Hill (*Life of Johnson*, II, 265 n.) points out that Johnson was en route to Scotland on that day.

65. *Boswell Papers*, VI, 176, and *Life of Johnson*, V (Hebrides), 255.

66. *Life of Johnson*, V (Hebrides), 277, and *Journal of a Tour to the Hebrides*, ed. Frederick A. Pottle and Charles H. Bennett, New York, 1936, pp. 344-5.

67. *Life of Johnson*, V (Hebrides), 108-9, 274, and 137.

68. *Letters of Horace Walpole*, ed. Mrs. Paget Toynbee, London, 1903-5, VIII, 381. Mrs. Gwatkin, Sir Joshua Reynolds' niece, told of another occasion when Goldsmith and Garrick, in reversed positions, delivered Hamlet's speech to his father's ghost. (See Forster, II, 443 n.)

69. *Manuscripts and Correspondence of James, First Earl of Charlemont*, Historical Manuscripts Series, London, 1891-4, II, 359-60. The "Poetical Exordium" seems not to have survived.

70. *Ibid.*, I, 317, and II, 366.

71. Reprinted in *Letters*, p. 129 n.

72. This story has obvious resemblances to the story of Goldsmith's betting that he could leap over a fountain at Versailles. (See above, p. 209.) Either may be an adaptation of the other.

73. *Portraits*, p. 54.

74. Cradock, I, 232.

75. *Ibid.*, IV, 285-6.

76. *Ibid.*, I, 234-5, and IV, 286.

77. *Correspondence of Charlemont*, I, 318.

78. B. M. Add. MS. 32336, f. 175v.

79. Cradock, I, 235-6.

80. *Life of Johnson*, II, 275 n.

81. I follow the account of the incident given in Garrick's manuscript note reprinted in *Works*, II, 51-2. For other accounts see Northcote, I, 215-6, and Richard Cumberland, *Memoirs*, ed. Flanders, pp. 188-9.

82. *European Magazine*, XXIV (1793), 174. Concerning the report that Goldsmith was persuaded to modify his first epitaphs of the Burkes, see Dixon Wecter, *Edmund Burke and His Kinsmen*, University of Colorado Studies, Boulder, 1939, p. 10 n.

83. Hawes recorded Goldsmith's symptoms during his last illness in *An Account of the Late Dr. Goldsmith's Illness*, London, 1774. My account is drawn from it and from the supplementary details given by Prior (II, 514-8) from Francis Newbery's newspaper reply to Hawes' pamphlet. Professor Pottle (*N&Q*, CXLIX [1925], 12) presents medical evidence that Goldsmith's ailment (which would today be called Bright's disease) would hardly have been aggravated by James's Fever Powders. (Cf. *Life of Johnson*, III, 501.)

84. Cradock, IV, 287.

85. Gaussen, *Percy: Prelate and Poet*, p. 168.

86. *Life of Johnson*, III, 164.

CHAPTER X: "A VERY GREAT MAN"

1. *Portraits*, p. 50.

2. *Letters of James Boswell*, ed. Tinker, I, 201. See also Boswell's letter to Langton of April 10 and to Thrale of May 13 (*ibid.*, pp. 197-8 and 203).

3. *Boswell Papers*, X, 203.

4. *Letters of Boswell*, I, 204.

5. *Life of Johnson*, II, 280.

6. *Ibid.*, pp. 281-2.

7. *Horace Walpole's Correspondence with William Mason*, ed. Lewis, Cronin, and Bennett, New Haven, 1955, I, 144.

8. Prior, II, 532 n.

9. Cradock, IV, 287.

10. In "Goldsmith's 'Essay on Friendship': Its First Publication and the Problem of Authorship" (*PQ*, XXXV [1956], 346-52) Professor Friedman points out that there is no proof that Goldsmith wrote the essay. It appeared as No. LXXXI of Hugh Kelly's *The Babler*, "where it was no doubt reprinted from the original series in *Owen's Weekly Chronicle*" (*c.* 1763-7). Since Goldsmith and Kelly were friendly when the later numbers of *The Babler* were originally published, Goldsmith might well have contributed an essay to Kelly's series.

11. Mr. H. A. C. Sturgess, Librarian and Keeper of the Records for the Honourable Society of the Middle Temple, writes me as follows in a letter dated December 12, 1955: "There is no statue or tablet of Goldsmith [in the Temple]. For years it has been assumed by many people that the half-reclining figure against the wall of the Master's House represented Goldsmith, but it is in memory of one John Hiccocks, and the tablet next to it with bust above, is in memory of Samuel Mead. The tomb of Goldsmith is marked by a coffin-like stone about two yards west of the wall of the Master's House. This stone was protected by a wall of brick built round and over it at the beginning of the war and has not yet been removed."

12. Members of the Club, objecting to some details in the inscription and thinking that a Latin epitaph was inappropriate for an English poet, petitioned Johnson by means of a Round Robin (since no one cared to appear as the originator of the suggestion) to change it. But the Great Cham refused to be influenced; in fact he declared that he "would never consent to disgrace the walls of Westminster Abbey with an English inscription." (See *Life of Johnson*, III, 83-5.)

13. The Catalogue is reprinted as Appendix to both Prior's and Forster's biographies of Goldsmith. Hawes was apparently given Goldsmith's writing desk, a chair, and a gold-headed malacca cane—all of which are now in the Victoria and Albert Museum.

14. All in all, Hawes' case seems not as strong as he hoped to make it. As Dr. Raymond Crawfurd remarked, the affidavits which he presented read like "fair specimens of hard lying" (*Proc. Roy. Soc. Med.*, VIII [1915], Pt. II, p. 25 n.). Moreover, although Hawes claimed that Reynolds, Burke, Bott, and others of Goldsmith's friends approved his conduct of the case, he offered no statement from either Dr. Fordyce or Dr. Turton, who attended Goldsmith in the last few days of his life. Most damaging, however, is the fact that in 1776, after the death of Dr. James, Hawes attempted to set himself up in business as a rival to the Newbery company, claiming that he had formerly been employed under James in preparing the powders and that the preparation being marketed by Newbery did not follow the formula developed by Dr. James. On this occasion Johnson prepared a forcible denial of Hawes' claims (see Charles Welsh, *A Bookseller of the Last Century*, pp. 138-40) and one Francis Spilsbury wrote *Free Thoughts on Quacks and Their Medicines, Occasioned by the Death of Dr. Goldsmith and Mr. Scawen*, also in defense of the Fever Powders. I may add, however, that Hawes later took his degree in medicine and was one of the founders of the Royal Humane Society. An amusing sidelight on the controversy is offered in an unpublished letter, dated January 29, 1791, from Francis Newbery to Bishop Percy: "James's Powder rose in Estimation; for the Sale encreased considerably from the time of the Attack [i.e., Hawes' pamphlet], as my Books can incontestably show" (B. M. Add. MS. 42516, ff. 109-10).

15. Garrick's replies are reprinted in *Works*, II, 57 n.; Cumberland's and Dean Barnard's in *The New Foundling Hospital for Wit*, London, 1786, II, 254-7; Whitefoord's epitaph in *Works*, II, 59-60; the anonymous epitaph for Johnson in Prior, II, 499 n.; and Mrs. Thrale's imitations in *Thraliana*, I, 471-7. Concerning some fragments discovered later and at first supposed to be Goldsmith's work, see *TLS*, December 11, 1937, p. 947, and February 12, 1938, p. 108.

16. See Winifred Lynskey, "The Scientific Sources of Goldsmith's *Animated Nature*," *SP*, XL (1943), 33-57, and "Pluche and Derham, New Sources of Goldsmith," *PMLA*, LVII (1942), 435-45.

17. Forster, II, 295 n.

18. *Life of Johnson*, III, 84 n.

19. Boswell (*Life of Johnson*, III, 85 n.) remarks that Goldsmith followed Buffon in saying that cows shed their horns every two years, and his error has been often re-

peated. Mr. L. F. Powell (*ibid.*, p. 484) points out that both Goldsmith and Buffon said that cows lose their horns at the end of three years and then grow new and permanent ones. Thus Goldsmith was guilty of repeating Buffon's mistake, but not of making so egregious a blunder as Boswell claimed.

20. In *Goldsmith's "Animated Nature"* (New Haven, 1924, p. 37) James H. Pitman cautions that much of what Goldsmith seems to present as personal opinion on scientific matters is actually derived. Professor Pitman offers a much fuller consideration of *Animated Nature* than I can attempt here, but his conclusions should be checked against the articles by Miss Lynskey cited above (note 16), since she presents evidence of which he was unaware.

21. See Winifred Lynskey, "Goldsmith and the Warfare in Nature," *PQ*, XXIII (1944), 333-42.

22. Pitman (pp. 129-31) remarks that there is a marked strain of deism in *Animated Nature*, "though Goldsmith would strongly have objected to such a term." But Miss Lynskey reveals that, although Goldsmith's work frequently echoes the "arguments from design" used by the deists, his sources do so more often. Goldsmith has, in fact, frequently modified his borrowings in the direction of more conventional Christianity. (See *PMLA*, LVII, 435-45.)

23. Pitman (p. 134 n.) remarks that Goldsmith's ideas in the second half of *Animated Nature* "seem less and less his own, and more and more the unthinking reflection of popular taste." That is true because the ideas are following more closely the popularizers of science whom he used as sources.

24. Cradock, IV, 286.

25. See Harold Stein, "Goldsmith's Translation of the *Roman Comique*," *MLN*, XLIX (1934), 171-8.

26. Professors Crane and Friedman (*TLS*, May 11, 1933, p. 331) point out that Goldsmith borrowed again from the *Encyclopédie* in the Introduction to *Experimental Philosophy*.

27. See *Boswell Papers*, X, 157-8.

28. Because of Carnan's refusal to release the rights to *The Traveller*, Goldsmith was excluded from the anthology for which Johnson wrote his *Lives of the Poets*. Johnson seems to have tried to compensate, in some measure, by abridging Goldsmith's "Life of Parnell" for use in the book and appending to it a note of praise for the author's critical powers.

29. See Balderston, *passim*; Thomas Shearer and Arthur Tillotson, "Percy's Relations with Cadell and Davies," *The Library*, XV (1934-5), 224-36; and Theodore Besterman, *The Publishing Firm of Cadell and Davies*, Oxford and London, 1938, pp. xxii-xxvii.

30. Prior (II, 483-4) tells the story and attributes it to Topham Beauclerk.

31. *Gossip about Dr. Johnson and Others*, ed. F. H. Skrine, London, 1926, pp. 125-6.

32. Davies, II, 121.

33. *Portraits*, p. 45.

34. *Ibid.*, p. 55.

35. *Ibid.*, p. 57.

36. Davies, II, 117.

37. *Letters*, p. 62.

Index

3, 7; OG's affection for, 172-3; to France with OG, 207-10; mentioned in attack on OG, 242; keeps lock of OG's hair, 279; on OG's love of gaiety, 269-70; on OG's gambling, 270; mentioned, 174, 227, 262, 263

Hughes, the Rev. Patrick, 22-3, 32

Hume, David, 76, 145, 152, 217, 255

Humourist, The, 105

Hunter, Dr. William, 206

Irving, Washington, 93, 172, 185

James, Dr. Robert: his Fever Powders marketed by Newberys, 109; OG takes his Fever Powders, 229, 274-5, 277-8; controversy over OG's death, 280, 317n83, 318n14; mentioned, 293

James, William, 295

James I, King of England, 153

Jeffs, Mr., Butler in the Temple, 155, 163

Jessop, William, 29

Jesus Christ, 150, 192, 193

John of Leyden (Jan Beuckelszoon), 59

Johnson, Jane (Goldsmith), 15, 21, 44, 79, 198, 199

Johnson, Samuel
Life: anecdotes of OG and, 5, 205; meets OG, 100; relations with Newbery, 109; entertained by OG, 128; given chance to review *Citizen of World,* 308 n38; buys *Life of Nash,* 138; sells MS. of *Vicar of Wakefield,* 138-9; meets Boswell, 144; visited by OG, 147; forms Club with Reynolds, 147-8; his share in *Traveller,* 156, 161; receives pension, 168; interview with George III, 174-5; OG's borrowing from, 183, 307n15, 308n29, 311n41; named Professor in Royal Academy, 196; writes Latin epitaph on Parnell, 207; interest in *She Stoops to Conquer,* 234-5, 236; *She Stoops to Conquer* dedicated to, 239-40; denies writing letter for OG, 243; accused of affair with Mrs. Thrale, 245; welcomes Boswell to Club, 256; offends OG, 258-9; to contribute to Dictionary of Arts and Sciences, 262; leaves for Hebrides, 265; accords OG chair in imaginary university, 266; refuses food at OG's party, 267; reaction to OG's death, 277; epitaph for OG, 279; to write biography of OG, 288
Opinions: on biography, 126-7, 136; on dog-eating in Orient, 253; on dueling, 225; on frankness in historical writing, 248-9; on infallibility of King, 146; on literary inactivity, 166-7; on living with those of differing opinions, 225-6; on

luxury, 247; on David Mallet, 254; on martyrdom,, 256-7; on Rowley poems, 213; on royal patronage, 249; on Scotland, 146-7; on suicide, 251
Opinion of OG: defends OG, 3, 7, 144, 265, 266; on OG's envy, 8, 9, 264; on OG's proposed trip to Orient, 129; on OG's rooms at Temple, 155; on *Traveller,* 156, 160, 255; on OG's clothing, 195; on *Life of Parnell,* 206-7; envy of OG, 228; analyzes OG's character, 226-7, 227-8, 265-6; on *She Stoops to Conquer,* 240, 254; sympathizes with OG, 246-7, 252-3; on OG's compilations, 253-4, 255-6, 285; on OG's ignorance, 254-5; on *Deserted Village,* 255
Mentioned: *passim*

Jones, Giles, 311n51

Jones, the Rev. Oliver, 15, 21, 45, 300n4

Jones, Mrs. Oliver, 15, 20, 45

Jones, William, 251

Jones, Mr., Director of East India Co., 74

Junius, 180, 194

Kames, Henry Home, Lord, 195

Kauffmann, Angelica, 174

Kearney, Michael, 29, 31

Kearsley, George, 237, 280, 286, 287

Kedington, Roger, 108

Kelly, Cornelius, 23

Kelly, Hugh: OG's envy of, 8, 9, 10, 184-5, 268; his plays rival OG's, 180, 184-5, 241, 267-8; sends "Friendship" to *Universal Magazine,* 278; at OG's funeral, 279; mentioned, 161, 175, 197

Kennett, White, 152

Kenrick, William: reviews OG's works, 94-5, 99, 105, 153, 163; accusations against OG, 179, 241-2, 278; mentioned, 97, 121

King, Tom, 175

Kippis, the Rev. Andrew, 86, 138, 267

Kniveton, Mrs., actress, 315n11

Knowles, Sir Charles, 100

Lady's Magazine: OG's work for, 104, 105, 106, 124, 126, 127, 306n32, 307n25

Lamb, Charles, 98

Langhorne, John, 94, 160, 176

Langton, Bennet: charter member of Club, 147; letter from OG, 219, 220-1; mentioned, 129, 148, 189, 213, 253, 258, 266, 277

Lawder, James, 21, 67, 87, 90, 198, 199, 200

Lawder, Jane (Contarine), OG's alleged affection for, 302n5; letter from OG, 83-4; mentioned, 20-1, 40, 44, 67, 87, 90, 198, 199

LeComte, Louis, 111, 117, 120

Lennox, Charlotte, 189
LeNoir, Elizabeth (Smart). *See* Elizabeth Smart
Levett, Robert, 145
Lewes, Lee, 258
Lisburn, Earl of, 213
Literary Magazine, 105
Livy, 191
Lloyd's Evening Post, 130-1, 163
London Chronicle, 160, 184, 243
London Packet, 241-2, 242-3
Louis XIV, King of France, 60, 96
Lucius Florus, 255
Lucretius, 101
Lye, Edward, 168
Lynskey, Winifred, 284
Lyttelton, George Lyttelton, 1st Baron, 111, 151, 255

McDonnell, McVeagh, 230, 264
Mackenzie, Dr., friend of OG, 221
Macleane, Lauchlan, 29, 50, 57
McVeagh, Mr., friend of OG. *See* McVeagh McDonnell
Maffei, Marchese Francesco Scipione di, 98
Mallet, David, 254
Mallet, Paul Henri, 76
Malone, Edmond, 31, 288
Marana, Giovanni Paolo, 111
Marivaux, Pierre Carlet de Chamblain de, 122, 123
Marriott, George, 256
Marteilhe, Jean, 78, 80-2
Martin, Mrs., OG's landlady, 88, 93, 101, 102, 120, 224
Martinelli, Vincenzio, 248, 249, 250
Mary, Queen of Scots, 218
Mason, the Rev. William, 119
Massinger, Philip, 100
Mattei, Signora Columba, 18
Maupertuis, Pierre Louis Moreau de, 102
Maxwell, Dr. William, 147
Maxwell, Mr., apothecary, 275
Mayo, the Rev. Henry, 257-8
Metastasio, Pietro, 98
Mickle, William Julius, 227
Mills, Edward, 34, 82, 90
Milner, the Rev. John, 74, 75, 80, 89, 108
Milner, Mrs. John, 74
Milner, Miss, daughter of above, 192
Milton, John, 181, 285
Moffat, Mr., actor, 4-5, 215
Monro, Dr. Alexander, 48-9, 52, 53
Montagu, Basil, 180
Montagu, Mrs. Elizabeth, 131
Montaigne, Michel de, 285
Montesquieu, Charles de Secondat, Baron de, 111

Monthly Review: OG's work for, 75-8, 88, 148-9, 305n11; reviews of OG's works, 94-5, 105, 132, 136, 153, 160, 163, 169, 174, 176, 184, 192, 204-5, 212, 218, 223, 241; mentioned, 92, 111
Morgan, Sydney (Owenson), Lady, 4
Murphy, Arthur: OG reviews his *Orphan of China,* 100, 307n10; sketches Epilogue for *She Stoops to Conquer,* 236; OG's alleged envy of, 299n22; mentioned, 7, 194, 210, 222, 315n5

Nash, Richard, 134-6
Newbery, Francis, nephew of John, 168, 173, 315n18
Newbery, Francis, son of John: at Merchant Taylors' School, 138; advances money to OG, 234, 237; publishes *She Stoops to Conquer,* 238, 241; defends Dr. James's Fever Powders, 280, 318n14; mentioned, 155, 269, 275, 309n2, 315n18
Newbery, John: life and character, 109; publishes OG's works, 127, 131, 133, 134, 139, 156, 162, 173; directs OG's finances, 139, 141, 143, 148-50, 157, 165, 222; death, 180; mentioned, 122, 132, 137, 138, 142, 154, 155, 177, 229, 238, 275, 287
Newbery, Mrs. John, 109, 120
Newton, Sir Isaac, 84
Nichol, W., publisher, 154
Nollekens, Joseph, 279
North, Frederick Lord, 2nd Earl of Guilford, 180
Northcote, James: on OG's envy, 2; calls OG "a notable man," 221; enjoys *She Stoops to Conquer,* 240; mentioned, 265, 290, 299n4
Northumberland, Elizabeth Smithson, Countess (later Duchess) of, 164-5, 215-6
Northumberland, Hugh Smithson, Earl (later 1st Duke) of, 162, 164, 165, 215-6, 262
Nourse, John, 271, 283, 286
Nugent, Dr. Christopher, 147, 161, 189
Nugent, Mary, 215, 219-20, 306n3
Nugent, Robert (later Viscount Clare): discusses Moffat with OG, 4-5; friendship with OG, 161-2, 215-6; OG visits, 212, 213, 214; "Haunch of Venison" addressed to, 216, 287; mentioned, 165
Nugent, Colonel, son of above, 214, 215

O'Carolan, Turlogh, 301n15
O'Conor, Charles of Belenagare, 21
O'Moore, Colonel, friend of Edmund Burke, 1-2